MASTERING EXCEL

A PROBLEM-SOLVING APPROACH

MASTERING EXCEL
A PROBLEM-SOLVING APPROACH

James Gips
Boston College

John Wiley & Sons, Inc.
New York • Chichester • Brisbane • Toronto • Singapore

110401

Gift

Cover: *Hans Holbein the Younger, Portrait of Erasmus of Rotterdam. Louvre, Paris. Scala/Art Resource, New York.*

ACQUISITIONS EDITOR	Beth Lang Golub
ASSOCIATE MARKETING MANAGER	Leslie Hines
SENIOR PRODUCTION MANAGER	Linda Muriello
PRODUCTION EDITOR	Melanie Henick
MANUFACTURING MANAGER	Mark Cirillo

This book was set in Times New Roman by James Gips.
The cover was printed by Phoenix Color.
The book was printed and bound by Donnelley/Crawfordsville.

Recognizing the importance of preserving what has been written, it is a policy of John Wiley & Sons, Inc. to have books of enduring value published in the United States printed on acid-free paper, and we exert our best efforts to that end.

Library of Congress Cataloging-in-Publication Data

Gips, James, 1946-
    Mastering Excel: a problem-solving approach / by James Gips.
            p.   cm.
    Includes index.
    ISBN 0-471-16372-4 (pbk. : alk. paper)
    1. Microsoft Excel for Windows.   2. Business - - Computer programs.
    3. Electronic spreadsheets.   I. Title.
HF5548.4.M523G57   1997
005.369 - - DC20
                                                    96-23076
                                                    CIP

Printed in the United States of America

10 9 8 7 6 5 4 3 2 1

To Pat, Amy, and Jonathan

PREFACE

Excel is both useful and fun. Millions of people have purchased Excel to run on their personal computers, and many of them use the program every day to solve all kinds of problems. Excel is fun to learn and fun to use. The program is rich and well-designed and has many capabilities. There is a real sense of satisfaction in mastering the fundamentals of the program and then in mastering more and more of its features. As you become increasingly capable with Excel, you can use the program to solve a wider variety of problems and increasingly difficult problems.

The purpose of this book is to help you master Excel.

The book has grown out of my teaching thousands of people to use the computer over the past twenty years, both in universities and in industry. I love teaching. I love seeing people walk in knowing little or nothing about the subject and perhaps being a bit fearful, then watching the lights turn on in their minds as they become increasingly capable, and then seeing them leave brimming with confidence in their newly gained abilities.

Over the years I have been fortunate to teach people to use Excel and similar programs many times. I believe I have learned from this process and have been able to refine my presentations—to see what works and what doesn't, to see where people have problems and where people gain valuable insights and skills. I hope this is reflected in this book.

My general approach to teaching Excel is to explain and demonstrate the program at the mouse click and keystroke level, but also at the conceptual level. I like to show how a capability of Excel can be used to solve a problem, and along the way make sure that people understand the basic concept involved. But then, after an hour of listening and watching and asking, it is important for people to try to use that aspect of the program on their own to solve increasingly challenging problems.

This book is structured the same way. In the body of each chapter, we discuss new capabilities of Excel and use them to solve problems. We cover the mouse clicks and keystrokes involved and the concepts that underlie them. We look at the pitfalls and some of the unexpected applications, and I try to answer the questions that I think might arise. At the end of each chapter is a set of exercises. Some of the exercises take you step-by-step through the mechanics of using Excel. Some of the exercises are paper and pencil exercises that help you ensure that you understand the ideas in the chapter. Some of the exercises simply present you with a problem that can be solved using the capabilities and features just covered. This is where the real learning and integration takes place. It is in the exercises, in the problem solving, that the real mastery of Excel develops. An old proverb says, "I hear and I forget, I see and I remember, I do and I understand."

Overall, the book is divided into two parts: In Part I, we proceed through the *fundamentals* of Excel. Here the material is presented sequentially and the instructor or reader is encouraged to go through the material in the order presented. In Part II, we cover various *features* of Excel. Here the instructor or reader can select the chapters of interest.

There are versions of Excel for all popular machines and operating systems, including Windows 95, Windows 3.1, and Macintosh. Students and executives use a variety of machines, operating systems, and versions of Excel. This book is directed to people using Excel 7 for Windows 95, Excel 5 for Windows 3.1, and Excel 5 for Macintosh. These versions of Excel are all quite similar. I hope this book will serve you well whichever computer and operating system you are using.

This book is the successor to *Mastering Lotus 1-2-3: A Problem-Solving Approach*. The books have benefited from the suggestions of several reviewers. I would like to thank Gary Armstrong of Shippensburg University, Jim Davies of DeAnza College, Robert P. DeSieno of Skidmore College, Wallace J. Growney of Susquehanna University, Priscilla McGill of Rogue Community College, Marilyn Meyer of Fresno City College, John W. Miller of Pennsylvania College of Technology, Jack H. Ryder of Kean College of New Jersey, Pandu Tadikamalla of University of Pittsburgh, and James Teng of University of Pittsburgh for their helpful and insightful reviews of one or both of the manuscripts. (The affiliations are those at the time of review.)

Thanks to Michael McFarland, S.J., Howard Straubing, and Peter Kugel for allowing me to use exercises they developed and to other colleagues, students, and seminar participants at Boston College, Harvard University, Arthur D. Little, McGraw-Hill, Chase Manhattan Bank, and Standard & Poor's where I have taught various parts of this material in courses and seminars, who certainly have influenced material in this book.

Any book is a team project. I would like to thank Beth Lang Golub, the editor for the book, Leslie Hines, Maddy Lesure, Lisa Perrone, Amy Hegarty, Ann Renzi, Linda Muriello, Melanie Henick, Pam Landau, Mark Cirillo, Andy Bausili, Rob Mantilla, David Mlotok, Michelle Popp, Naomi Kaplan, and all of the other fine people at John Wiley & Sons, Inc. for their efforts.

Thanks to Kathy Gips for her suggestions for exercises and to Jonathan Gips for helping with the proofreading.

I welcome your comments, ideas, and suggestions. The easiest way to reach me is by email at james.gips@bc.edu. Please do feel free to write.

A brief note about the cover. The cover shows a portrait of Erasmus that was painted by Hans Holbein the Younger in 1523 and is on display in the Louvre Museum in Paris. Erasmus (1466?-1536) was a Dutch priest and scholar. He is said to have been the last person to have mastered all of human knowledge, to know all that was known at his time. All of human knowledge! If Erasmus could master all of human knowledge, surely we can master Excel.

Learning to use Excel is both useful and fun. Let's get started!

James Gips

CONTENTS

PART I FUNDAMENTALS

PART II FEATURES

PART I

FUNDAMENTALS

CHAPTER 1

INTRODUCTION

OBJECTIVES

In this chapter you will learn:

- The major uses of Excel
- The origin of electronic spreadsheets

WHAT IS EXCEL ?

Excel is a best-selling computer program published by Microsoft Corporation of Redmond, Washington. The program has been put to a wide variety of uses.

The most important and most common use of the program is as an **electronic spreadsheet**. In an electronic spreadsheet program, the main memory of the computer is divided into rows and columns. The computer is used to perform mainly numeric computations. An example of the use of Excel as an electronic spreadsheet is shown in Figure 1-1. Here, one enters in the Net Sales and different Operating Expenses for each of the quarters. The computer calculates the Year To Date totals in column F, the Total Operating Expenses figures in row 16 and the Operating Income figures in row 18.

Another important use of Excel is for creating **business graphics**. In business graphics the computer draws bar charts, line charts, pie charts, and other types of charts used in business. Excel draws these charts based on numbers in the spreadsheet. For example, the chart in Figure 1-2 was drawn by Excel from the numbers shown in the worksheet in Figure 1-1.

A third use of Excel is for **data management**. In data management the computer is used to deal with large amounts of information. An example is the worksheet in Figure 1-3, which shows the homes for sale in a town.

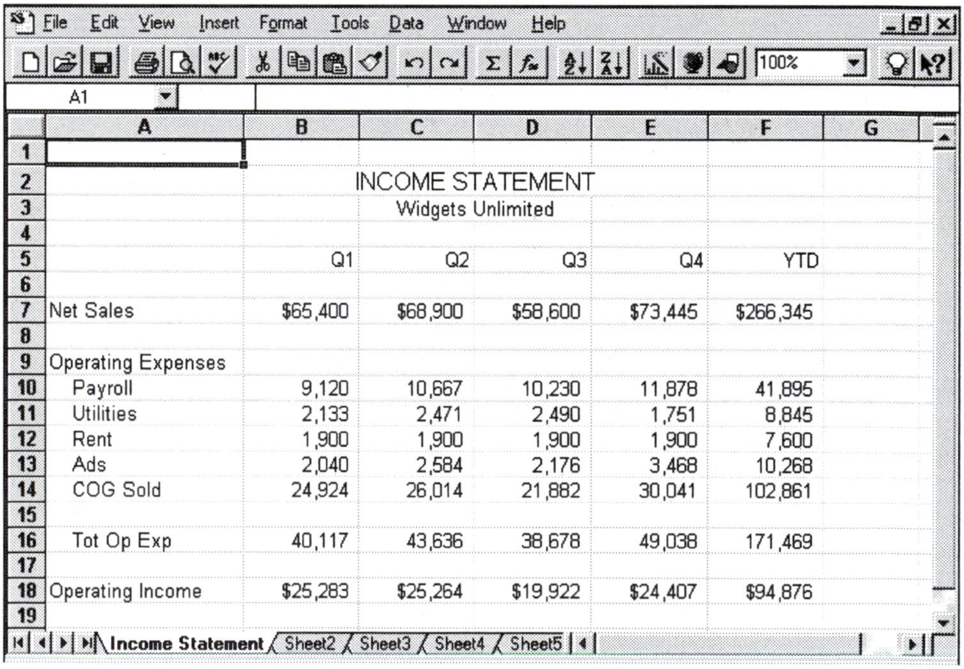

	A	B	C	D	E	F	G
1							
2			INCOME STATEMENT				
3			Widgets Unlimited				
4							
5		Q1	Q2	Q3	Q4	YTD	
6							
7	Net Sales	$65,400	$68,900	$58,600	$73,445	$266,345	
8							
9	Operating Expenses						
10	Payroll	9,120	10,667	10,230	11,878	41,895	
11	Utilities	2,133	2,471	2,490	1,751	8,845	
12	Rent	1,900	1,900	1,900	1,900	7,600	
13	Ads	2,040	2,584	2,176	3,468	10,268	
14	COG Sold	24,924	26,014	21,882	30,041	102,861	
15							
16	Tot Op Exp	40,117	43,636	38,678	49,038	171,469	
17							
18	Operating Income	$25,283	$25,264	$19,922	$24,407	$94,876	
19							

Figure 1-1. A typical Excel spreadsheet.

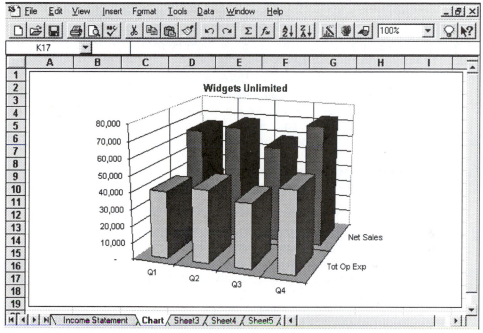

Figure 1-2. A chart drawn from the values in the worksheet in Figure 1-1.

ADDRESS	BDRMS	BATHS	LOT	HEAT	AGE	COST
		CURRENT LISTINGS				
12 Elm Street	5	3	0.4	Gas	48	$290,000
46 Hearthstone Road	5	2	1.2	Oil	3	$345,000
690 Rice Avenue	3	1	0.6	Oil	25	$109,500
90 Bay Road	2	1	0.25	Oil	33	$78,400
455 Nathan Street	2	1	0.3	Elec	16	$51,300
18 Garden Street	2	1	0.4	Elec	12	$62,700
203 Somerset Avenue	4	2	0.3	Gas	98	$159,500
34 Farley Place	7	4	2.3	Oil	52	$560,000
26 Lantern Lane	3	1	0.3	Solar	9	$104,300
11 Panama Street	3	1	0.5	Gas	38	$87,900
155 Auburn Blvd.	5	2	1.0	Oil	5	$269,600
132 Jamaica Way	4	2	0.3	Gas	67	$149,500
315 Fremont Avenue	3	1	0.4	Nuclear	8	$432,800
1322 Bellevue Road	6	3	0.3	Elec	56	$233,500
5 Pond Street	4	3	1.5	Oil	2	$275,400

Figure 1-3. Part of a real estate database in Excel.

In the real estate worksheet, each row corresponds to a different home for sale. Excel could be instructed to find all the homes with more than 3 bedrooms that have oil heat. Or, the program could be instructed to rearrange the rows so they are in order by the price.

The most common use of Excel is as an electronic spreadsheet. While we certainly cover how to use Excel to create charts and to manage data, we will spend most of our time on the many uses of Excel as an electronic spreadsheet program for solving a wide variety of problems.

A LITTLE HISTORY

In the bad, old days of computers, before the advent of personal computers and electronic spreadsheets, people who wanted to use the computer to solve some numerical or financial problem usually had to write a special-purpose computer program in a language like BASIC or Fortran. It is much easier to create a spreadsheet in Excel to solve a problem than it is to write a computer program. A problem that requires 1 hour to solve using a spreadsheet program like Excel might require 10 hours or more to solve by writing a program.

The idea of an electronic spreadsheet was invented by Dan Bricklin when he was an MBA student at the Harvard Business School.

> Sitting there in the spring of 1978, I came up with the idea of the electronic spreadsheet. With all those other classmates to contend with the professor, there's lots of time for daydreaming, especially if you sit in the front row and the professor looks out above you. I invariably made simple addition mistakes in my homework. I wanted to do what the professor did on his blackboard: he would erase one number and Louis in the back of the room would give him all the calculations that he had done all night to recalculate everything. I wanted to keep the calculations and just erase one number on my paper and have everything recalculated. (Dan Bricklin, "VisiCalc and Software Arts: Genesis to Exodus," *The Computer Museum Report*, Summer 1986, p. 8.)

Dan Bricklin and a friend, Bob Frankston, wrote the first electronic spreadsheet program, for the Apple II, and called it VisiCalc ("Visible Calculator"). VisiCalc was published by a small company, Personal Software, in 1979. VisiCalc became wildly popular, the best selling computer software of its day. Personal Software changed its name to VisiCorp and brought out related software, including VisiPlot and VisiTrend, which were written by Mitch Kapor.

Mitch Kapor became a product manager for the company, but then left to form a company called Lotus Development Corporation. Lotus brought out the program 1-2-3 for the IBM PC in 1983. The developers of VisiCalc thought that the Apple III, the ill-fated successor to the very popular Apple II, was the computer of the future and targeted their advanced version of VisiCalc for the Apple III. Bricklin and Frankston also became involved in a messy lawsuit with VisiCorp. Lotus concentrated on the IBM Personal Computer from the beginning. Lotus 1-2-3 became the best-selling applications program of its time. Later, Lotus bought out the rights to VisiCalc, which is published no more.

The arch rival of Lotus Development in the personal computer software market was Microsoft Corporation. Microsoft was best known for developing MS-DOS, the original Disk Operating System of the IBM Personal Computer and its compatibles. Lotus 1-2-3 was the most popular spreadsheet program for DOS machines. Microsoft introduced a spreadsheet program called Multiplan to compete with Lotus 1-2-3. Multiplan mutated into Excel. When Microsoft switched over from DOS to Windows, Lotus was slow to update 1-2-3. Microsoft took advantage of the situation to make Excel the most popular spreadsheet program for the Windows market. With the introduction of Windows 95, the dominance of Excel accelerated. In the Macintosh market Lotus stopped selling 1-2-3 altogether. Lotus Development Corporation was bought out by IBM in 1995. Thus, Microsoft Excel has captured the vast majority of the spreadsheet market. Its major competitors are Lotus 1-2-3 and Quattro Pro.

Excel is the third spreadsheet program to dominate the market. VisiCalc dominated the Apple II market. Lotus 1-2-3 dominated the MS-DOS market. Excel dominates the Windows and Macintosh markets.

All spreadsheet programs are reasonably similar. All are elaborations on Dan Bricklin's original idea. Once you learn Excel it is straightforward to learn to use any other spreadsheet program.

WHAT IS MICROSOFT OFFICE?

Microsoft Office is a **suite** of programs brought out by Microsoft and sold together as one package. The Microsoft Office package includes Excel, Microsoft Word (a wordprocessing program), Microsoft Access (a database program), PowerPoint (a presentation program), and perhaps Microsoft Schedule+ (a scheduling program), Microsoft Project (a project management program), Microsoft Mail (an electronic mail program), and others. The exact combination in the package varies over time. The idea is that the programs work together as a coordinated unit so that it is easy to create a spreadsheet in Excel, use it in a report created in Word and in a presentation created in PowerPoint.

WHY LEARN TO USE EXCEL?

Excel is widely used for many problems. Many of its most devoted users work with accounting and financial problems, including budgets, cash flow projections, sales reports, balance sheets, and expense accounts.

Some of these applications tabulate past results. For example, we were budgeted to spend so much in each of these different categories. So far this year we have spent this much in each of these areas. How much is left in our budget?

Other applications look to the future. We hope to sell so many copies of this proposed product at such and such a price. Our expenses for the product are expected to be so much. How much money will we earn? What if certain expenses are 25% more than expected, how will this affect our profits? What if we sell only so many copies? What if we lower our price and increase our advertising budget? This is known as using Excel to perform "**What if**" analysis. "What if" analysis is an area where spreadsheet programs excel. Indeed, if you look back at the quote from Dan Bricklin, the inventor of electronic spreadsheets, "What if" analysis is the specific type of application for which electronic spreadsheets were developed.

As the years have gone by, computers have become more and more powerful in their hardware so they support more and more powerful software. With each new version of Excel new features are added. Excel has become a powerful tool for statistical analysis, for operations research, for management science, for engineering calculations. Excel is used for nonnumerical problems as well. It is used for alphabetizing lists, for drawing charts, for looking at databases. Excel is used in marketing research, in sales analysis, in human resource management.

A good working knowledge of Excel is a requirement for many professional positions. Many a student has obtained a good summer job just on the basis of expertise with Excel.

Learning Excel is an important skill you will be able to use for the rest of your life. I hope you soon will see why.

CHAPTER 2

CREATING SIMPLE WORKSHEETS

OBJECTIVES

In this chapter you will learn how to:

- Enter information into an Excel worksheet
- Move to different cells of the worksheet
- Correct typing errors
- Create and evaluate formulas
- Create simple worksheets
- Save your work on the disk
- Print your work

THE BASIC IDEA

A simple Excel **worksheet** is shown in Figure 2-1. This worksheet was set up to give price quotes for potential customers. There are three products: widgets, grommits, and connectors. Widgets cost $1.19 each. Grommits cost $2.49 each. Connectors cost $0.69 each. A 6% sales tax is added to each order.

In Excel, the complete document or file you are working on is called a **workbook**. Each workbook contains various worksheets. Think of the workbook as being the electronic equivalent of a three-ring binder and the worksheets as being electronic sheets of paper.

Each worksheet is divided into **columns** and **rows**. The columns have letter names (A, B, C, ...). The rows have numbers for names (1, 2, 3, ...). The intersection of each row and column is called a **cell**. Each cell has a name. Cell E7 is in column E and row 7. That is, the name of each cell is the letter name of its column followed by the number name of its row.

Each cell can be **blank** or it can contain either a **label**, a **number**, or a **formula**. "Label" is a fancy name for text. A label can be a word or phrase. Cells F4 and B7 in the worksheet in Figure 2-1 are labels, because they contain words. Cells D6 and E7 contain numbers.

The key to electronic spreadsheets is the formulas. Cells in column F in the worksheet in Figure 2-1 contain formulas.

The formula in cell F6 is

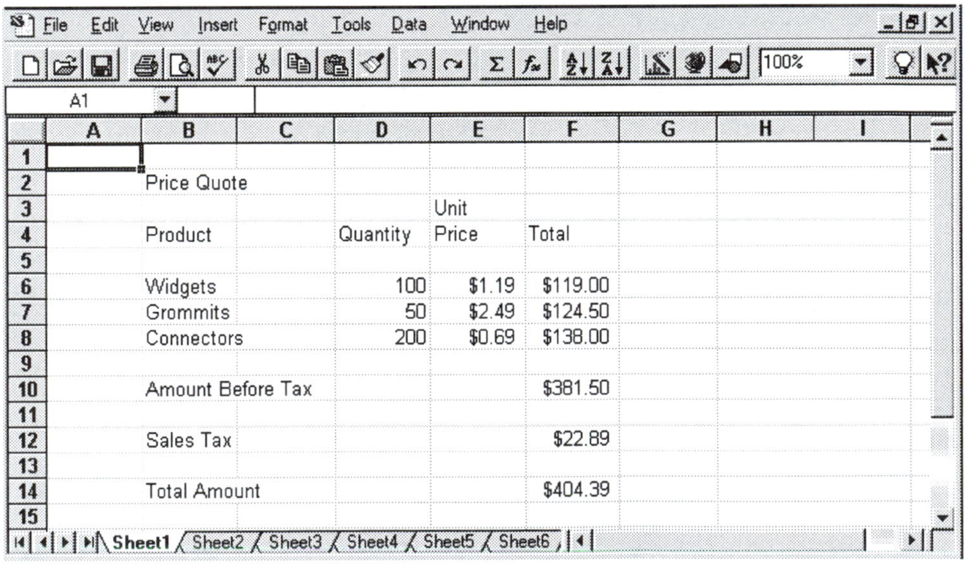

Figure 2-1. A simple worksheet for giving a price quote.

$$=D6*E6$$

The initial equal sign indicates that this is a formula. In Excel, the asterisk means multiplication. This formula tells Excel that the number displayed in cell F6 is the number in cell D6 multiplied by the number in cell E6. The formula has been typed into the cell, but the computer normally displays the result of evaluating the formula in the cell. That is, the computer displays 119.00, the result of the multiplication, in the cell.

The formulas in the worksheet are shown in Figure 2-2. Here the actual formulas are displayed in the cells, rather than the values that result from calculating the formulas. The formula in cell F7 is

$$=D7*E7$$

so the value in cell F7 is the result of multiplying the number in D7 times the number in E7. Similarly, the formula in cell F8 is

$$=D8*E8$$

Cell F10 contains the total for the order before sales tax. This value is calculated by the computer by adding the values in F6, F7, and F8. The formula is

	A	B	C	D	E	F	G
1							
2		Price Quote					
3					Unit		
4		Product		Quantity	Price	Total	
5							
6		Widgets		100	1.19	=D6*E6	
7		Grommits		50	2.49	=D7*E7	
8		Connectors		200	0.69	=D8*E8	
9							
10		Amount Before Tax				=F6+F7+F8	
11							
12		Sales Tax				=F10*6%	
13							
14		Total Amount				=F10+F12	
15							

Figure 2-2. The Price Quote worksheet with the underlying formulas displayed rather than the values that result from evaluating the formulas.

$$=F6+F7+F8$$

The sales tax is 6% of the Amount Before Tax. The formula for the sales tax in cell F12 is

$$=F10*6\%$$

Finally, the Total Amount is the sum of the Amount Before Tax and the Sales Tax. This formula, in cell F14, is

$$=F10+F12$$

SO WHAT?

Here we have spent well over $1,000 for a computer and the Excel software. Plus we have to take the time to learn to use the computer and Excel. Wouldn't it just be easier and faster to do this by hand? You could do the same "worksheet" with paper and pencil. For $10 you could buy a calculator to do the arithmetic. Why bother with a computer?

In using a computer the benefit usually is not in the first time you perform some action. The benefit is in the repetition, especially in the ability to make changes. If you have used a wordprocessing program, you know that the major benefit of wordprocessing is in the ability to make changes or revisions without retyping the entire manuscript. Similarly, the payoff of an Excel worksheet is in the third or the tenth or the hundredth time you use the worksheet.

What happens with our price quote worksheet? The potential customer says, "Oh, no. I don't want 50 grommits. I want 150 grommits." If you are using paper and pencil, you must erase the numbers in F7, F10, F12, and F14 and then recalculate the new amounts. The next person you speak with has new quantities to order. You would have to do the calculations all over again for that person's order. If you give out hundreds of price quotes each day, you would have to redo the calculations hundreds of times.

Watch what happens on the computer. We change the number in cell D7 from 50 to 150. The formulas in cells F7, F10, F12, and F14 are recalculated automatically by the computer and the results of these calculations appear automatically in the cells. (See Figure 2-3.) Similarly, we change the price for Widgets from $1.19 to $0.98 by changing the number in cell E6 from $1.19 to $0.98. As soon as we make the change, the formulas in cells F6, F10, F12, and F14 would be recalculated automatically by Excel.

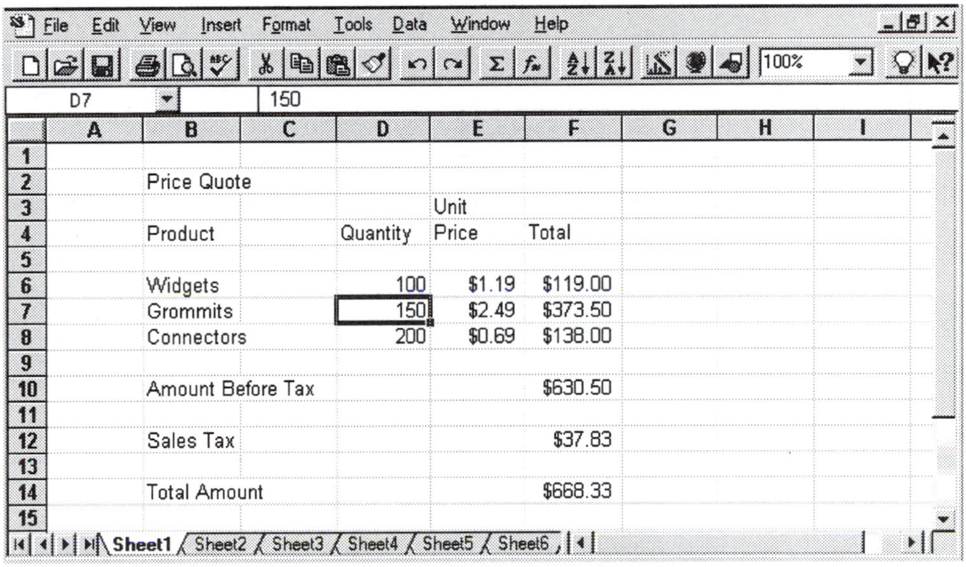

Figure 2-3. When we change the number in D7 from 50 to 150, the formulas in F7, F10, F12, and F14 automatically are recalculated.

The key to Excel is in the automatic recalculation of the formulas. Text, numbers, and formulas are entered into the worksheet. Whenever any number is changed, the relevant formulas are recalculated by the computer automatically. The lightning fast speed of the computer allows the recalculation to be done almost instantaneously.

An Excel worksheet has been described as an electronic piece of paper with a built-in pencil, eraser, and calculator. You enter the labels, numbers, and formulas into the worksheet. The computer performs all of the calculations automatically. Change one cell and the computer automatically recalculates the formulas.

As we proceed you will learn how to create larger and more complicated worksheets, involving thousands of calculations. Excel also provides us with a straightforward way of organizing and solving complicated problems.

Now we will take a look at the process of actually using Excel on the computer.

GETTING STARTED WITH EXCEL

After you start up Excel, the computer displays a blank worksheet, as in Figure 2-4. The various elements of the Excel window are indicated in the figure.

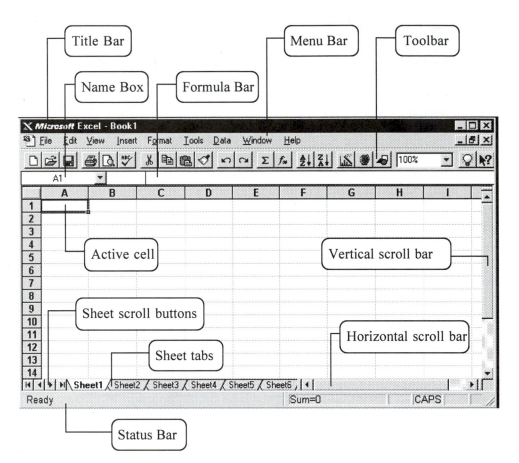

Figure 2-4. Elements of the Excel window (Windows 95).

Working our way down from the top, we see the **Title Bar**. The Title Bar tells us we are working in Excel and gives us the name of the active workbook. The current workbook we are working on is called "Book1". When we save the workbook on the disk we will give it a more descriptive name.

Below the Title Bar is the **Menu Bar**. The Menu Bar contains **pull-down menus**. The pull-down menus allow us to issue various commands to Excel to perform different functions. For example, to save the current workbook on the disk we could select the *File* pull-down menu and then select *Save* within the menu.

Below the Menu Bar is a **toolbar**. A toolbar contains various buttons that are an alternative way to issue common commands to Excel. For example, the third tool button in from the left in the toolbar in Figure 2-4 shows a picture of a disk. This is the **Save button**. Clicking on this button using the mouse is the same as selecting *Save* from the *File* pull-down menu

Excel contains several different toolbars. The toolbar that is shown in Figure 2-4 is known as the **Standard toolbar**. More than one toolbar can be visible. When you start up Excel there might be no toolbars showing. There might be one toolbar showing. There might be two or more toolbars showing. You can control which toolbars are visible on your screen by selecting *Toolbars...* in the *View* pull-down menu.

Below the toolbar is the **Name Box** and **Formula Bar**. The Name Box tells you which cell is active right now. Note that in Figure 2-4 the Name Box contains "A1" and that cell A1 has a black box around it. If you start typing, the information will go into cell A1. Cell A1 is the **active cell**. The information that you type will appear in the Formula Bar, which shows you the contents of the current active cell.

Below the Name Box and Formula Bar is the current worksheet itself. We start out with all of the cells in the worksheet being blank.

Below the worksheet are the **sheet scroll buttons** and the **sheet tabs**. The sheet tab in white is "Sheet1". This is the name of the currently active worksheet. We are working on Sheet1. A workbook contains multiple worksheets. If we want to work on Sheet2, we would click on the sheet tab that says "Sheet2". We will discuss using the Sheet scroll buttons and working on multiple sheets in Chapter 8.

At the bottom of the screen is the **Status Bar**. The Status Bar usually indicates the current status of the program. If the status bar says "Ready" or "Enter" then the program is ready for us to enter information or issue commands. The Status Bar sometimes indicates the sum of the values in the currently selected cells. The Status Bar also indicates the status of various keys on the keyboard. For example "Caps" indicates the Caps Lock is on. Many people hide the Status Bar when they are working in Excel to allow more room for the worksheet itself. To hide or show the Status Bar, select *Status Bar* in the *View* pull-down menu. The Status Bar and Name Bar are not shown in most figures in this book.

The Excel window in Figure 2-4 is from Version 7 of Excel for Windows 95. Version 5 of Excel for Windows 3.1 and Version 5 of Excel for Macintosh are just about identical. The Excel window for Version 5 for Windows 3.1 is shown in Figure 2-5. The Excel window for Version 5 for Macintosh is shown in Figure 2-6. The major differences among the three are external to Excel and have to do with the conventions of the operating systems, for example how to resize windows or where the pull-down menus appear.

Microsoft has done an excellent job in keeping the operation of Excel standard across platforms. In the book the screens are from Windows 95. However, except where noted, the techniques described should work on the versions on all three operating systems.

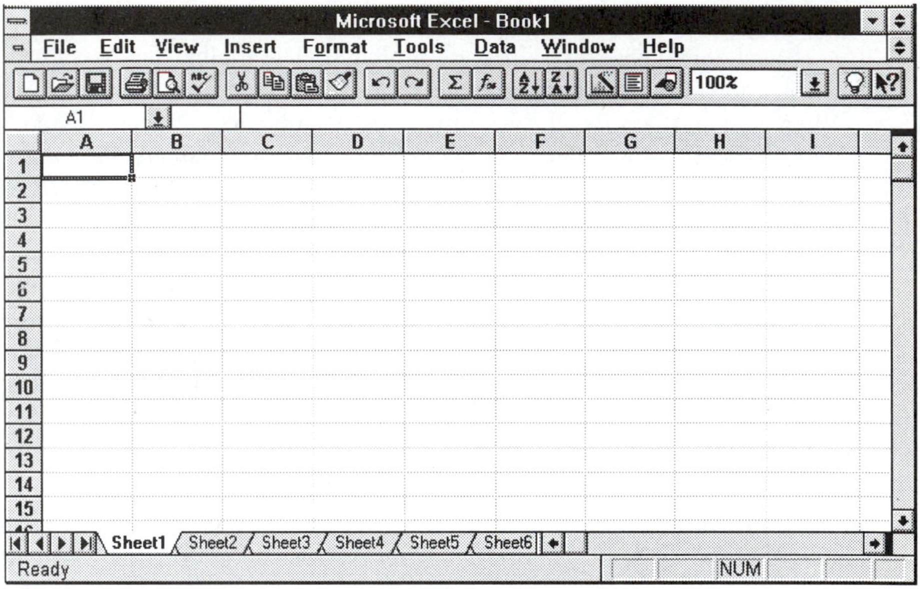

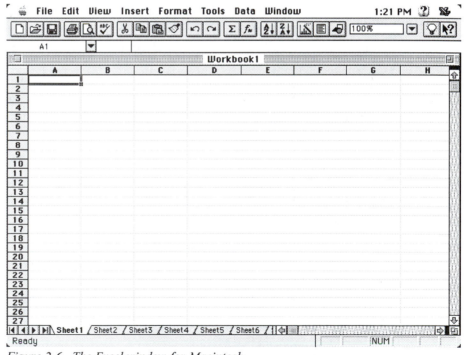

Figure 2-5. The Excel window for Windows 3.1.

Figure 2-6. The Excel window for Macintosh.

CHANGING WHICH CELL IS ACTIVE

When we start up Excel, cell A1 is the active cell. Cell A1 is the cell in the top left of the worksheet. If we want to enter information into cell A1, we simply type the information and then press the Enter key or Return key.

If we want to enter information into another cell, we need to change it to the active cell. There are two basic ways to do this. First, we can use the mouse to point to the new cell and then click the (left) button. Alternatively, we can use the **arrow keys** on the keyboard to move the active cell in any direction.

What happens if the cursor is in the bottom row on the screen, for example in row 14 in the worksheet in Figure 2-4, and you press the down arrow? The cursor moves to row 15. The screen displays rows 2 through 15. Row 1 moves off the top of the screen. This is called **scrolling**.

THE SIZE OF THE WORKSHEET

The screen actually is a window onto a much larger worksheet. When you start up Excel you typically see 9 columns (A through I) and perhaps 14 rows (1 through 14). The exact number of columns and rows will depend on the version of Excel you are using, the size of your monitor, the size of your window, what toolbars are displayed, and other factors. Each Excel worksheet contains 256 columns and 16,384 rows! The columns are named A through Z and then AA through AZ and then BA through BZ and so on until IV. The rows are named 1 through 16384. Some quick calculations show that in order to display all of the cells in the worksheet at the same size they usually appear would require a screen 20 feet wide and 720 feet high! Your computer screen would need to be as high as a 70 story building to display the entire worksheet!

CHANGING THE PORTION OF THE WORKSHEET IN THE SCREEN

The screen is best thought of as a window that displays a small portion of the entire worksheet. You can change the portion of the worksheet that is displayed in the screen in several ways. You can use the **vertical scroll bar** to the right of the worksheet and the **horizontal scroll bar** at the bottom right of the worksheet, for example by clicking on the arrows on the screen. You can use the arrow keys on the keyboard to move the cursor on the screen, thereby forcing the worksheet to scroll. To move the active cell to any cell in the worksheet, you can select *Go to...* in the *Edit* pull-down menu. It's even faster to press function key F5 on the keyboard. For example, if you want to go to cell X4000, press F5 and then type X4000 in the dialog box that appears, as in Figure 2-7.

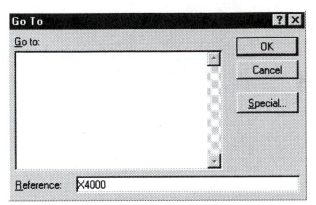

Figure 2-7. The Go To dialog box appears after selecting Go To... in the Edit pull-down menu or pressing function key F5.

When we click on *OK* after typing the cell address X4000 in the *Go To* dialog box, the computer moves the active cell to X4000, as shown in Figure 2-8. (Notice again that column AA follows column Z in the worksheet.)

How can we move the active cell back to A1? We could drag the horizontal and vertical scroll bars and then click on cell A1 with the mouse. Alternatively, we could select *Go To...* in the *Edit* pull-down menu or press function key F5 and then type A1 into the dialog box and click on *OK*.

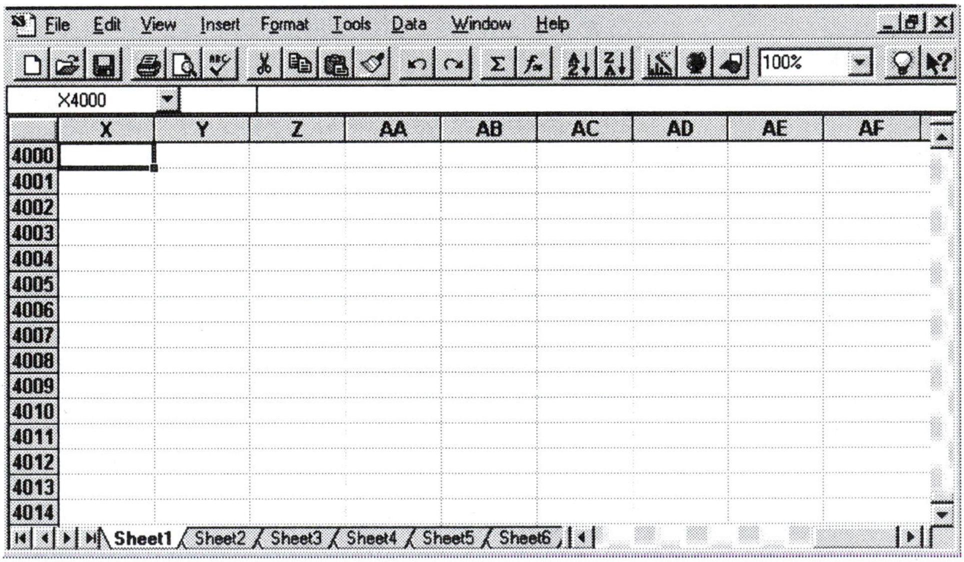

Figure 2-8. X4000 is the active cell.

ENTERING INFORMATION INTO CELLS

Suppose we want to enter the Price Quote worksheet in Figure 2-1 into the computer. We start with a blank worksheet, move the cursor to cell B2, and type the text Price Quote. Notice that the text appears both in the cell and in the formula bar at the top of the screen (Figure 2-9). Also notice that three buttons appear between the Name Box and the Formula Bar when you start typing.

Now we either press the Enter key on the keyboard or click on the **Enter button** (with a light √) that has appeared. The text is "entered" into the cell.

Move the active cell down to cell B4. Type the word Product, and so on.

How does Excel know which cells contain formulas and which contain labels or numbers? The program looks at the first keystroke, at the first character that we type into a cell. If the first character in a cell is an equal sign (=) then the cell contains a formula. If the first entry in the cell is just about any other character then the cell does not contain a formula. If the cell contains a formula, Excel displays the result of evaluating that formula in the cell.

This is an important point, a common source of error. Begin each formula with an equal sign. If you begin a cell entry with a letter or a space, rather than an equal sign, the cell actually will contain a label rather than a formula to be evaluated. If you type C7*D7 into a cell the computer will take this to be the label C7*D7 rather than a formula because it begins with a C, a letter. The computer will not evaluate the formula. Rather it simply will display C7*D7 in the cell as text.

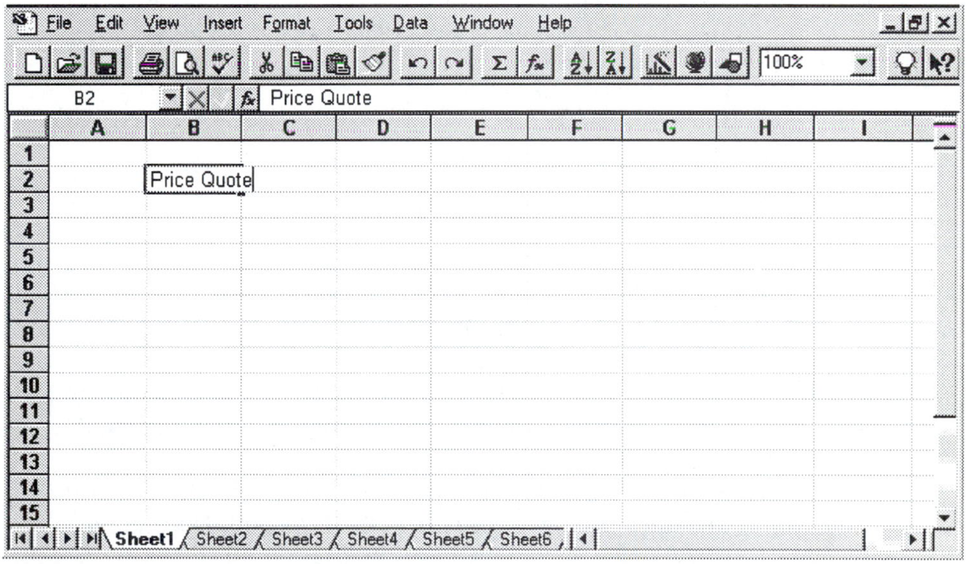

Figure 2-9. Entering text into a cell.

CORRECTING TYPING ERRORS

It is common to make typing errors. The best way to correct a typing error depends on when the error is discovered.

If you realize that you have made a mistake before what you have typed has been entered into the cell, then you can correct the error by pressing the **Backspace key** (or **delete key** on the Macintosh). The Backspace key is located on the top right of the typewriter portion of the keyboard and often is indicated with a long left arrow. The Backspace key erases the most recently typed character.

 You can instruct Excel to ignore all your current typing into the cell and return the cell to its previous contents (perhaps, blank) by clicking on the **Cancel button** that appears between the Name Box and the Formula Bar when you start typing into a cell. (See Figure 2-10.)

Again, if you click on the Enter button, to the right of the Cancel button, the text will be accepted and entered into the cell.

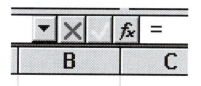

Figure 2-10. The Cancel button, Enter button, and Function Wizard button appear when you are entering information into a cell.

When typing into a cell, pressing the **Esc key** ("Escape" key) also will erase the entire entry. The Escape key usually is located on the top left of the keyboard. Here the Escape key acts as a "super-backspace" key, erasing all the characters you have just typed into the cell rather than just the most recent one. The Escape key will not erase an entry that already has been entered into a cell. In general, if you are in trouble in Excel pressing the Escape key a few times usually will get you out of trouble.

If you realize that you have made a mistake in a label or formula or number that already has been entered into a cell, simply make the cell active and retype the entry.

To erase an existing entry in a cell, make the cell active and then press the **Del key** or **Delete key** or select *Clear* in the *Edit* pull-down menu.

UNDO

Have you ever done or said something and wished immediately that you could undo it or take it back? Excel provides that opportunity.

The button with an arrow that curves counterclockwise is the **Undo button** in Excel. Clicking on this button will cause the most recent action taken to be undone. This could be a cell entry or a command issued through a pull-down menu or tool button.

An alternative to clicking on the Undo button is to select *Undo* in the *Edit* pull-down menu.

SIMPLE FORMULAS

The key part of Excel is the formulas. As discussed previously, formulas begin with an equal sign.

Examples of formulas include

$$= 3+4*5$$

$$= C4 / 5 + 7$$

$$= (D3+G5) * (H7 - (5+D6) / 8)$$

Formulas can contain numbers, cell addresses (like C4 or H7), arithmetic operators, and parentheses.

The arithmetic operators include

+	addition
-	negation or subtraction
*	multiplication
/	division
%	percent (placed after a value, as in 25%)
^	exponentiation

The minus sign can be used in two ways, as the negation of a single value (-3) and as the subtraction of one number from another (6-4).

The percent operator causes the number to the left of the percent sign to be divided by 100.

The exponentiation operator raises a number to a power. For example, 2^3 means 2 to the third power, which is 8.

EVALUATING FORMULAS

What would be the result of evaluating the formula =3+4*5? Is it 35? Is it 23? The correct answer depends on whether the computer performs the addition first or the multiplication first, on the **order of precedence** of the arithmetic operators. Generally, multiplication is done before addition. Thus, the value of the formula =3+4*5 would be 23. If we want the addition to be performed first, we would type =(3+4)*5. The parentheses tell the computer to perform the operation inside, in this case the addition, first. The value of =(3+4)*5 would be 35.

What would be the value of the formula =6-5-1? Is it 0? Is it 2? The correct answer depends on which subtraction the computer performs first. That is, it depends on whether =6-5-1 is the same as =(6-5)-1 or whether it is the same as =6-(5-1). Excel performs the left subtraction before the right subtraction so to the computer =6-5-1 is the same as =(6-5)-1, which evaluates to 0.

Now we can state the general rules that Excel follows when evaluating simple formulas:

1. Evaluate anything in parentheses first.

2. Evaluate the arithmetic operators in the following order:
   (a) negation (as in -7)
   (b) percent
   (c) exponentiation
   (d) multiplication or division
   (e) addition or subtraction

3. In case of tie, evaluate the operators from left to right.

YOU TRY EVALUATING A FORMULA

What would be the result of evaluating the formula

$$=23+((5+9)*3)/7-5$$

This problem uses each of the three general rules above. Try it before reading further. Write down your answer.

The computer first would add 5+9 to get 14. Then it would multiply the 14 times 3, which is 42. It would divide the 42 by 7 to get 6. Then it would add 23 and 6 to obtain 29. Finally it would take the 29 and subtract 5 to obtain the final answer of 24.

USING CELL ADDRESSES IN FORMULAS

Consider again the Price Quote worksheet in Figure 2-1. Suppose that in cell F6 instead of the formula =D6*E6 we put =100*1.19. (See Figure 2-11.) Would this formula work? It might first appear that this new formula works fine. After all, the result of evaluating this new formula would be the same as evaluating the original formula, namely 119. But, what would happen if we then changed the number in cell D6 from 100 to 300? The result of evaluating the original formula would change accordingly. But the result of evaluating the new formula =100*1.19 would not change at all, since the new formula does not refer to the numbers in the cells. It is very important that you use cell addresses in your formulas rather than the numbers that (now) are in the cells.

	A	B	C	D	E	F	G	H	I
F6			=100*1.19						
1									
2		Price Quote							
3					Unit				
4		Product		Quantity	Price	Total			
5									
6		Widgets		100	$1.19	$119.00			
7		Grommits		50	$2.49	$124.50			
8		Connectors		200	$0.69	$138.00			
9									
10		Amount Before Tax				$381.50			
11									
12		Sales Tax				$22.89			
13									
14		Total Amount				$404.39			
15									

Figure 2-11. A common mistake is to put the current values in formulas instead of the cell addresses. It looks like this formula works, but if the value in D6 is changed, the value in F6 will not change accordingly.

SAVING THE WORKBOOK

When you enter information into a worksheet on the screen, the information is saved in the primary memory (also called RAM or Random Access Memory) of the computer. The primary memory is temporary, working memory. If you lose electric power or if Excel quits on you unexpectedly or if you turn off the computer then the information that is in primary memory will be erased. In order for the computer to remember a workbook from one session to the next, the workbook must be saved on disk. It is your responsibility to save the workbook on disk. It is advisable to save your work on the disk early and often

The easiest way to instruct Excel to save your current workbook is to click on the Save button, the third button from the left of the standard toolbar, the button with a picture of a diskette. Alternatively, you can select *Save* in the *File* pull-down menu.

The first time you save a workbook you will be asked to fill in a file name and to select the disk and directory in which the workbook should be saved. File names are discussed in the next section.

The basic unit in Excel is the workbook. A workbook contains multiple worksheets. Thus far we have been working only with the first sheet, "Sheet1", of the workbook. When you click on the Save button or select *Save* in the *File* pull-down menu, Excel always saves the entire workbook on the disk, even though you may have used only a single sheet.

It is surprisingly easy and commonplace to lose files that are saved on disks. Removable diskettes can be misplaced or fall in a puddle. Hard disks can "crash". Files can be erased by mistake. I strongly advise you to buy an extra diskette or two and routinely keep at least two disk copies of all of your work. Diskettes are very inexpensive. The $1 for an extra diskette and the extra 20 seconds to save a second copy are an exceedingly good investment. Personally, I have been burned enough times that I will not leave the computer without having copies of my work on at least two disks. Forewarned is forearmed. To save the file a second time on a different disk or under a different file name, select *Save As...* in the *File* pull-down menu.

THE NAME OF THE WORKBOOK

In the process of saving a workbook for the first time you are asked to provide a name for the workbook. Excel provides an initial name like Book1, but it is better to change it to a name that will remind you of the contents of the workbook. If you are working on the first quarter sales report, a name like SALESQ1 is better than a name like MARY or JOHN, even if you can't get Mary or John out of your mind. The name you give when you save the workbook is used both as the name of the workbook on the screen and the name of the workbook file saved on the disk.

The allowable length of names varies from operating system to operating system. In Windows 95 you can have names of 200 characters in length. On the Macintosh you can have names of up to 31 characters. In Windows 3.1 you can have names of up to 8 characters. In Windows 3.1 the file also will have an extension, a last name, of XLS, which indicates to the computer that it is an

Excel workbook. For example, in Windows 3.1 a workbook might be named SALESQ1.XLS. There can be other restrictions on file names. In Windows 95 you are not allowed to include certain punctuation marks (* ? : [ ] + = \ / | < >) in the name. In Windows 3.1 you are not allowed to include spaces or the just-listed punctuation marks in file names.

The name of the workbook will appear at the top of the window on your display.

The easiest way to change the name of the workbook is to select *Save As...* in the *File* pull-down menu, enter in the new name, and then save the workbook on the disk using that name. The new name will be retained for the current workbook.

PRINTING THE WORKSHEET

The simplest way to print the current worksheet is to click on the **Print button**. This is the fourth button from the left in the Standard toolbar. It shows a picture of a printer.

Alternatively, you can select *Print* in the *File* pull-down menu. On occasion the computer has been known to hang up or freeze during printing, so always save your workbook on the disk before printing.

If you would like to see what will be printed before it actually is sent to the printer, click on the **Print Preview button**, which shows a picture of a magnifying glass over a sheet.

Alternatively, select *Print Preview* in the *File* pull-down menu.

Printing will be covered in greater detail in Chapter 7.

CLOSING THE WORKBOOK AND STARTING A NEW ONE

Suppose you just have completed one of the computer exercises that follow. You have constructed a worksheet, tested it, saved it, printed it. Now you would like to erase the worksheet and start over on a new exercise. To do this you can select *Close* in the *File* pull-down menu. This closes the workbook you are working on. ("Close" means the workbook is erased from the primary memory of the computer and from the screen.) If you have not yet saved the workbook before closing it, the computer will ask you if you wish to save your work on the disk before it vanishes.

To start up a new workbook select *New* from the *File* pull-down menu. Or, you can click on the **New Workbook button**. This button has a picture of a blank worksheet on it and is the leftmost button in the Standard toolbar.

If you would like, you can have two or more different workbooks open at once in different windows of your screen.

To resume work on a workbook previously saved on the disk, select *Open...* from the *File* pull-down menu. Alternatively, if you have worked on the document recently on this computer it might appear toward the bottom of the *File* pull-down menu, where you can select it directly.

EXITING FROM EXCEL

To exit from Excel, simply select *Exit* (or *Quit*) from the *File* pull-down menu. You will be asked if you would like to save any unsaved workbooks that you have been working on.

PAPER AND PENCIL EXERCISES

2-1.   Consider the following worksheet

What would be the result of evaluating each of the following formulas? Write out your answers on paper. Do not use the computer.

(a) =B7+1
(b) =B6+2*D7
(c) =C4*(D7+B4)-6*C5+A8
(d) =C4*25%-3-B4
(e) =256/C4/2/B4
(f) =B5^2+B4^3
(g) =-B6-B4*-B3*2/C4+B5^D7-1

2-2. Salespeople earn a base salary of $10,000 per year plus a commission of 4% of sales. The following worksheet has been created for our four salespeople.

	A	B	C	D	E	F	G	H	I
1									
2		SALESPEOPLE							
3							TOTAL		
4		NAME	SALES	SALARY	COMMISSION		EARNINGS		
5									
6		ADAMS	795000	10000	31800		41800		
7		BAKER	243000	10000	9720		19720		
8		CAREY	4700	10000	188		10188		
9		DUNN	2400300	10000	96012		106012		
10									
11		TOTAL	3443000	40000	137720		177720		
12									
13									

Columns E and G and row 11 contain formulas.

(a) Cell E6 gives Adams' Commission. What is the formula in E6?
(b) Cell E7 gives Baker's Commission. What is the formula in E7?
(c) Cell G7 gives Baker's Total Earnings. What is the formula in G7?
(d) Cell E11 gives the Total Commission. What is the formula in E11?
(e) Cell G11 gives the Grand Total of the Earnings. What is the formula in G11?
(f) Give an alternative formula for G11.

COMPUTER EXERCISES

2-3. Start up Excel. You should see a blank Excel worksheet.

(a) Use the arrow keys to move the active cell right and left and down and up.
Use the mouse to move the active cell.
Move the active cell to F12.
Move the active cell to K23.
In cell K23 type the word HELLO and press the Enter key or click on the Enter button.

(b) Use the arrows, scroll bars, and mouse, or the F5 key to return to A1.

(c) Enter your name in cell D4.
Type EXERCISE 2-3 in cell D5.
Type the date in cell D6.
(You should type your name, the exercise number, and the date at the top of each worksheet you do for homework.)

(d) Type the number 140 in cell B2.
Type the number 233 in cell B3.
Type the formula =B2+B3 in cell B5.
(The number 373 should appear now in B5.)

(e) Change the number in cell B2 to 56.
(The total in B5 should change automatically to 289.)

(f) Change the number in cell B3 to 375.6.
(The total in B5 should change again.)

(g) Save the workbook on your disk.

(h) Print the worksheet.

(i) Close the workbook.

2-4.   Put your name in cell F2. Put EXERCISE 2-4   in cell F3. Put the date in F4.

(a) Enter the worksheet at the top of the next page exactly as shown.

(b) Change the number in D8 to 31.
(The numbers in D11, D15, and D19 should change automatically.)

(c) Change the number in D13 to 83.
(The numbers in D15 and D19 should change.)

(d) Save the workbook.

(e) Print the workbook.

(f) Close the workbook.

	B	C	D
3		UNITED GROMMITS	
4		THIRD QUARTER	
5			
6			
7		GROMMITS	34
8		WIDGETS	27
9		CONNECTORS	63
10			
11		TOTAL SALES	=D7+D8+D9
12			
13		COST OF GOODS SOLD	55
14			
15		GROSS MARGIN	=D11-D13
16			
17		SELLING EXPENSES	42
18			
19		NET PROFIT	=D15-D17

2-5. Enter the worksheet of Exercise 2-2 into the computer. Remember that columns E and G and row 11 contain formulas. Change Carey's Sales to 615,000. Do all the other numbers change appropriately?

2-6. Create a well-labeled worksheet that allows you to enter two numbers: the number of feet and inches in a person's height. The worksheet then should calculate the person's height in centimeters. Try your worksheet on the following heights: 5 feet 2 inches, 6 feet 0 inches, 7 feet 4.5 inches.

2-7. Joggers often are curious about how fast they run. Create a worksheet like the one at the top of the next page that allows you to enter two numbers: a distance in miles and the number of minutes required to run the distance. The worksheet then should calculate two quantities: the average number of minutes per mile and the average miles per hour for the run. Try the worksheet on the following runs: 1 mile in 4 minutes, 3.5 miles in 42 minutes, 26.21875 miles in 129.7 minutes by changing the numbers in E4 and E5.

	A	B	C	D	E	F	G	H	I	
1										
2		Jogger's Calculator								
3										
4		Number of miles run:			4.5					
5		Time in minutes:			36					
6										
7		Average minutes per mile:			8					
8		Average miles per hour:			7.5					
9										
10										

Sheet1 / Sheet2 / Sheet3 / Sheet4 / Sheet5 / Sheet6

2-8. The Widget Division factory purchases 25,000 couplers per year for use in its widget manufacturing process. The Director of Purchasing has determined that it costs $20.00 (in personnel and computer time) for the company to process an order to purchase couplers. It costs the company $4.00 per year to carry a coupler in inventory (including space allocation, breakage, theft, insurance). As the new Assistant to the Director of Purchasing your job is to calculate how many couplers should be ordered at one time. If you order 100 couplers at a time, orders will be arriving almost daily so you will have low carrying costs but you will have to pay for 250 purchases per year. If you order 100,000 couplers at a time, you will have low purchase costs but very high inventory carrying costs.

The Economic Order Quantity (EOQ) is the amount that should be ordered at one time to minimize carrying and ordering costs. The EOQ is calculated by

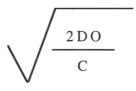

$$\sqrt{\frac{2DO}{C}}$$

where D is the annual demand, O is the cost for processing an order, and C is the annual carrying cost for a unit in inventory.

(a) Create a worksheet for determining the Economic Order Quantity. You should have an appropriate heading at the top. You should have separate well-labeled cells for the annual demand, order cost, and annual unit carrying cost.

Your worksheet should work for any quantities entered. (Note that the square root of a quantity can be calculated by raising the quantity to the 0.5 power.) How many couplers should be purchased at a time? Try your worksheet on the numbers in the first paragraph. Print the worksheet.

(b) Suppose demand for widgets increases dramatically and now we need to purchase 100,000 couplers per year. How many should be purchased at a time? Change the value in the cell that contains the annual demand. Print the worksheet.

2-9.   We would like to create a worksheet that will allow us to compare what we were supposed to sell in each region (our "goal") with what we actually sold.

(a) Enter the following worksheet with appropriate formulas in the blank cells in the bottom row and right column. Just as a check, the number calculated for AMOUNT OVER GOAL for AFRICA should be 3.3

SALES IN $ MILLIONS

REGION	GOAL	ACTUAL	AMOUNT OVER GOAL
AFRICA	24	27.3	
ANTARCTICA	3	89.4	
ASIA	20	33.5	
EUROPE	32	31.2	
LATIN AMERICA	17	11.8	
NORTH AMERICA	25	46.1	
TOTAL			

(b) Change the ASIA ACTUAL sales to 56.7 and the LATIN AMERICA ACTUAL sales to 15.1. The numbers in the TOTAL row and AMOUNT OVER GOAL column should change automatically.

(c) Add formulas in a new column that calculate PERCENT OVER GOAL for each of the regions and for the TOTAL. The PERCENT OVER GOAL calculated for AFRICA should be 13.75. For EUROPE it should be -2.5.

2-10. Create a worksheet to calculate the Break-Even Point for a product. Allow the user to enter three values: a unit Selling Price, the percentage of the selling price required for the Variable Cost of each unit, and the total Fixed Cost. The worksheet should be well-labeled and should contain formulas to calculate automatically two values: the Break-Even Point in units sold and the Break-Even Point in dollar volume sold. The worksheet also may calculate some intermediate values, if you wish. Print your worksheet with the following sets of input values: (a) Selling Price 200, Variable Cost Percent 60, Fixed Cost 40000, (b) Selling Price 250, Variable Cost Percent 50, Fixed Cost 50000. Write out by hand on your printout the formulas that appear in each cell.

2-11. The Body Mass Index (BMI) often is used by scientists and physicians to determine whether a person is underweight or overweight. The BMI is calculated as follows:

Step 1.   Multiply your body weight in pounds by 0.45.
Step 2.   Multiply your height in inches by 0.025.
Step 3.   Square the answer from Step 2.
Step 4.   Divide the answer from Step 1 by the answer from Step 3.

A healthy BMI is between 19 and 25. The BMI is said to work equally well for both men and women. Create a worksheet to calculate a person's BMI. There should be four values entered into the worksheet: the person's name, the person's weight in pounds, and the person's height in feet and inches. The worksheet should calculate the total height in inches, the values for each of the steps, and then show the resulting BMI.

(a) Try your worksheet for the following people:

Jan: 115 pounds, 5 feet 8 inches.
Fran: 325 pounds, 5 feet 1 inch.
Dana: 240 pounds, 6 feet 4 inches.
Slim: 104 pounds, 5 feet 6 inches.

(b) A person is 5 feet 8 inches. Use the worksheet to determine the lowest healthy weight for this person and the highest healthy weight. Use trial and error. That is, try different weights until the BMI comes out to just above 19 and then to just below 25. Don't worry about fractions of a pound.

CHAPTER 3

CHANGING THE APPEARANCE OF THE WORKSHEET

OBJECTIVES

In this chapter you will learn how to:

- Change the width of columns
- Select ranges of cells
- Set the font, style, and size of text
- Change the alignment of text in cells
- Format numbers
- Place borders around cells
- Change the color of text and cells
- Give your worksheet a three-dimensional shading effect
- Display the formulas in your worksheet

Excel has many ways of changing the appearance of the information in the worksheet, both on the screen and as printed on the page. The general term for changing the appearance of information is **formatting**. Here we are not concerned with the contents of the information, but rather with how it appears. Proper formatting can make a worksheet easier to understand and more visually pleasing.

COLUMN WIDTH

Consider the Price Quote worksheet again. (See Figure 3-1). Notice that cell B2 contains the text "Price Quote". But this text does not quite fit into the cell. When you start up Excel the columns are all set at the same width. Each cell holds about 9 or 10 characters, depending on the font that you use for the characters. If you type in text that is longer than what will fit in the cell, the computer will display the full text as long as the cell to the right is blank. If you look carefully you will notice that the line between cell B2 and C2 is missing, indicating that the extended B2 is being displayed on top of C2. If cell C2 contained some information, then all of B2 would not be displayed. Rather, only the information that fit within the cell boundaries would show. Similarly, you can see that the entries in B8, B10, and B14 are too long for the cells.

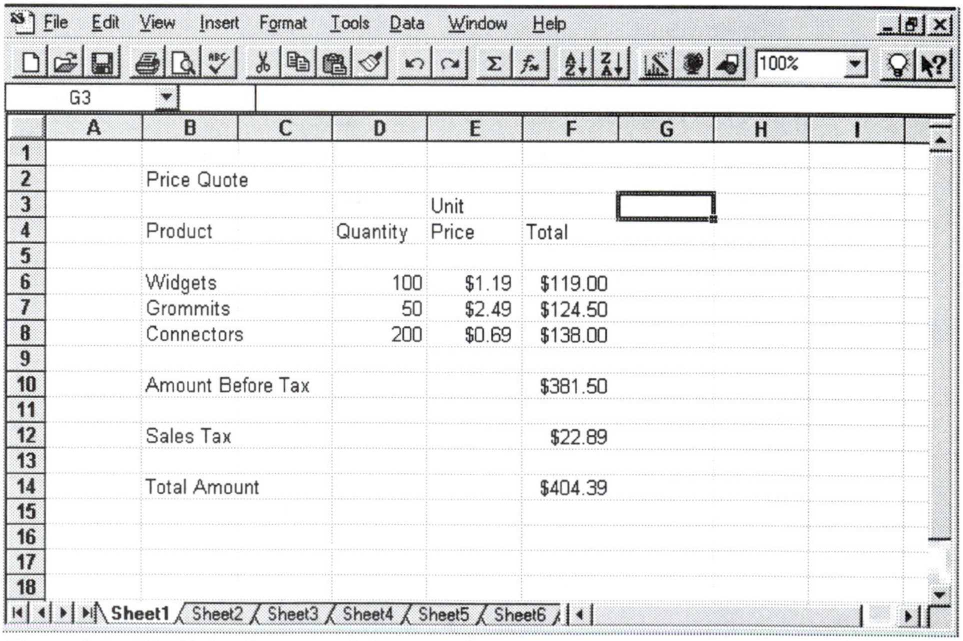

Figure 3-1. The Price Quote worksheet.

It is easy to change the width of the cells in column B so that all of the text fits. Simply move the mouse pointer up to the area right between column head B and C. The mouse pointer shape will change to a vertical line with arrows pointing left and right, as in Figure 3-2. Depress the (left) mouse button and drag the width of column B to the size you would like.

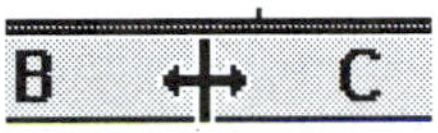

Figure 3-2. When the mouse pointer assumes this shape you can change the width of the column to the left of the pointer by depressing the mouse button and dragging.

Now we can move the cursor up to the column head between the C and the D, and drag the cursor to the left to make column C narrower. (See Figure 3-3.)

We can make the rows different heights in the same way, but this technique usually is used only with columns. We can change the row heights automatically by changing the size of the letters in the cells.

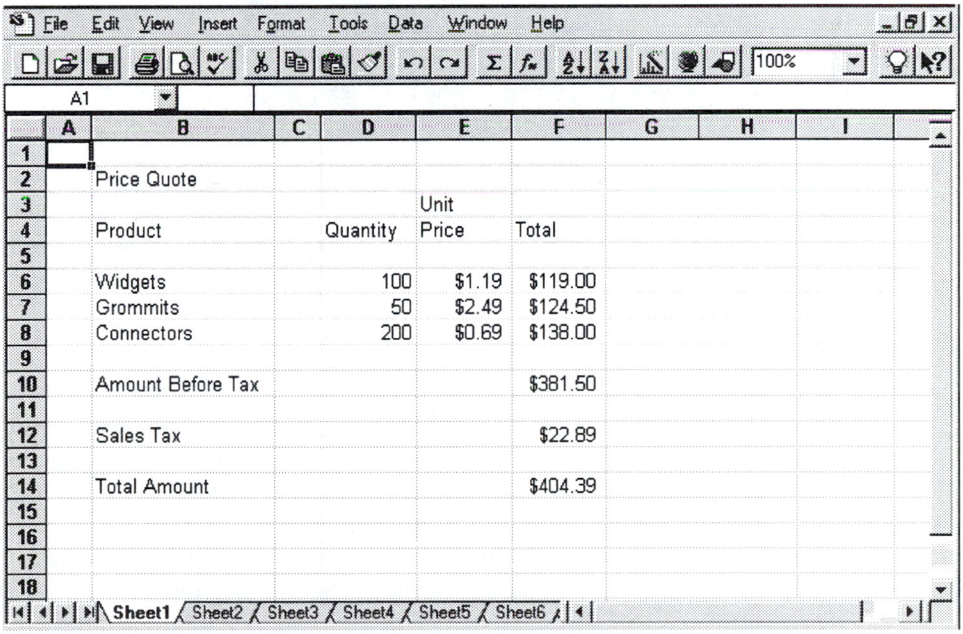

	A	B	C	D	E	F	G	H	I
1									
2		Price Quote							
3					Unit				
4		Product		Quantity	Price	Total			
5									
6		Widgets		100	$1.19	$119.00			
7		Grommits		50	$2.49	$124.50			
8		Connectors		200	$0.69	$138.00			
9									
10		Amount Before Tax				$381.50			
11									
12		Sales Tax				$22.89			
13									
14		Total Amount				$404.39			
15									
16									
17									
18									

Figure 3-3. The Price Quote worksheet with the widths of columns B and C adjusted.

SELECTING CELLS

The characters (letters, digits, punctuation) are all of the same font, size, style, and color in the worksheet. To change the appearance of cells, we first need to select the cells to be changed. Cells can be selected by dragging across them with the mouse while the (left) mouse button is pressed. For example, to select the rectangular range of cells from B2 through F14, place the mouse pointer in B2, press down on the button, and drag the mouse to F14. Selected cells are blackened except for cell in the top left corner of the selection, which is white. In Figure 3-4, the range of cells in B2 through F14 has been selected.

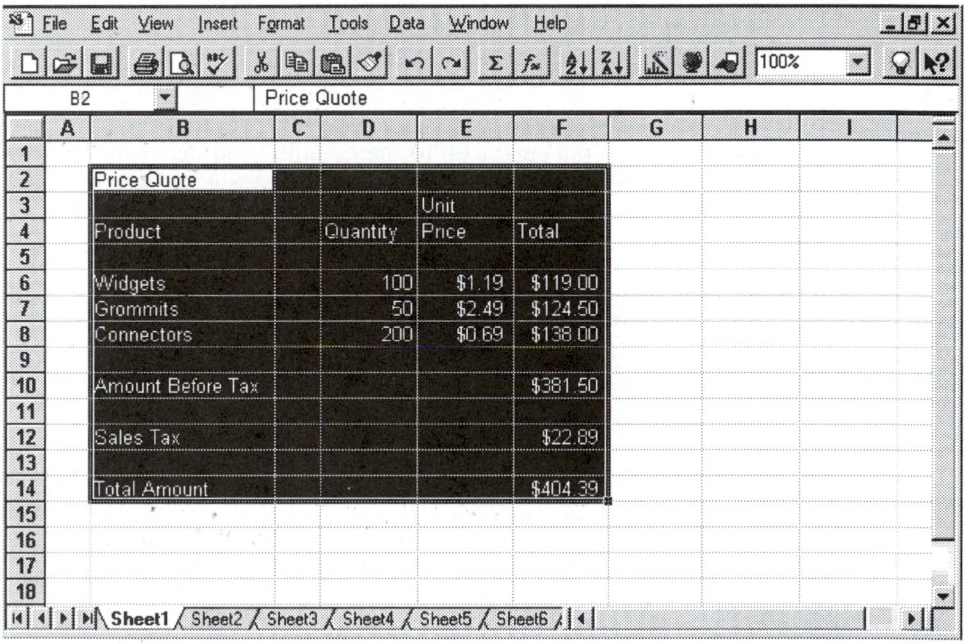

Figure 3-4. The darkened area indicates that the range from B2 through F14 is selected.

It is possible to select a **noncontiguous range** of cells by holding your finger down on the Ctrl key (or Control key) while you do the selection. For example, we could select B12 through B14 by dragging across the cells and then press down on the Ctrl key on the keyboard and with the Ctrl key pressed drag from D6 through F8. This selects two separate areas, as shown in Figure 3-5.

We can select all of the cells in the entire worksheet by clicking on the button above the 1 and to the left of the A, just to the top left of cell A1 in the worksheet.

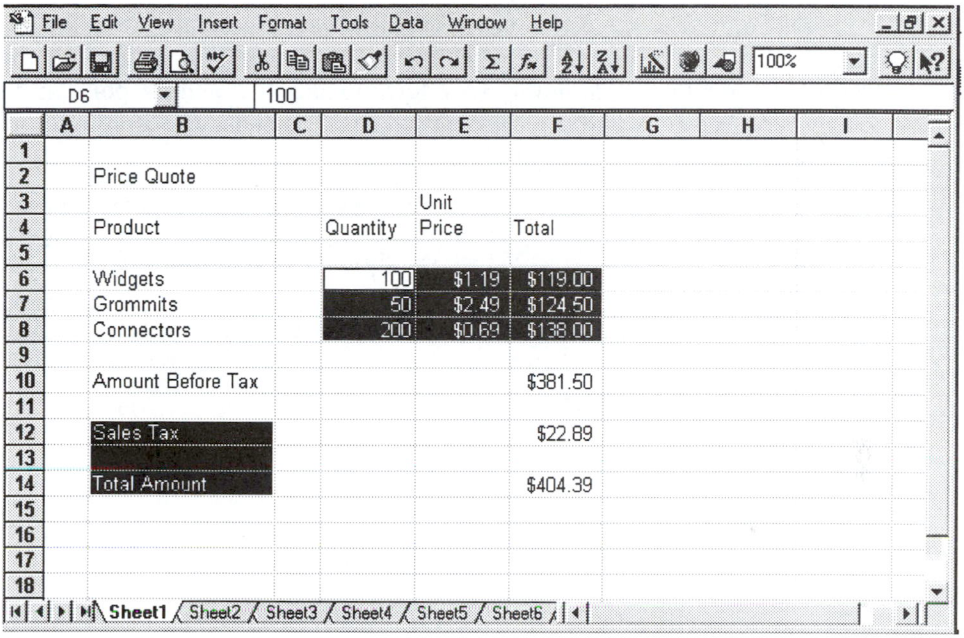

Figure 3-5. Use the Ctrl key (Control key) to select multiple areas

FORMATTING CELLS

Once cells have been selected they can be formatted by selecting *Cells...* in the *Format* pull-down menu. For example, we would like to make cell B2, which contains "Price Quote", more prominent. So we click on B2 to select it. We select *Cells...* in the *Format* pull-down menu and then click on the tab for *Font*.

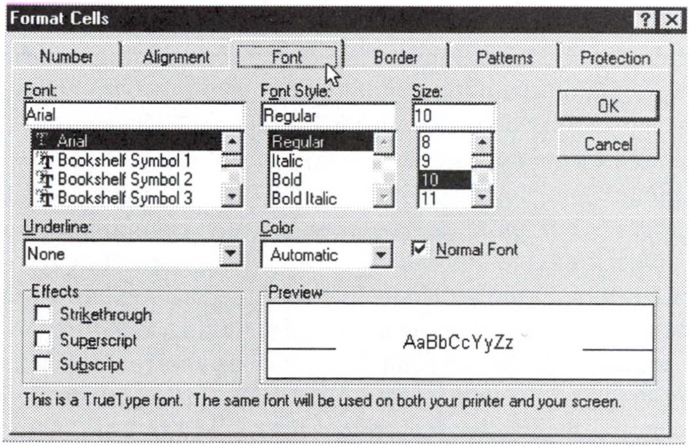

Figure 3-6. Selecting the font of the selected cells.

We see the *Font* selection sheet in Figure 3-6. Currently, cell B2 is in Arial Regular 10 point. We go through and select *Times New Roman* in the *Font:* dialog box and then *Bold* in the *Font Style:* dialog box and *24* point in the *Size:* dialog box We click on *OK*. The text in cell B2 is changed accordingly to Times New Roman Bold 24. (See Figure 3-7.)

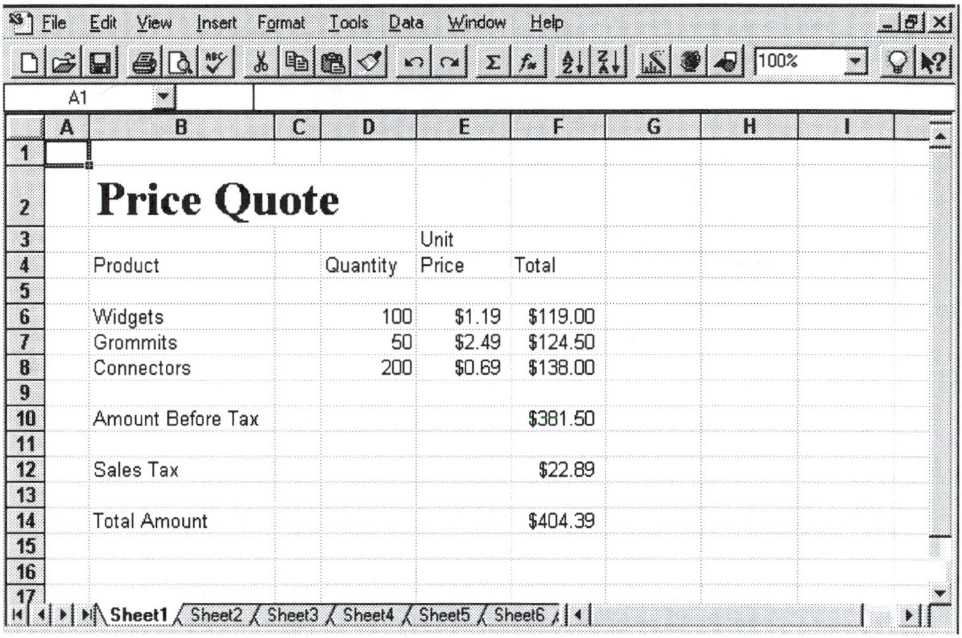

Figure 3-7. Changing the font, style, and size of cell B2.

The particular fonts available will depend on the fonts that have been loaded into your computer.

Alternatively, we can make use of the **Formatting toolbar**. The Formatting toolbar contains buttons that provide shortcuts for formatting cells. The Formatting toolbar does not appear in the Excel window in Figure 3-7. To have the Formatting toolbar appear on the screen, select *Toolbars...* in the *View* pull-down menu. A dialog box with all of the various toolbars available will appear on the screen. (For more on toolbars, see the beginning section of Chapter 7.) Click a check next to *Formatting*. Now, when you click on *OK*, the Formatting toolbar appears on the screen, below the Standard toolbar, as in Figure 3-8. With the Formatting toolbar visible, many formatting operations are available with a single mouse click. For example, to change the font of cells, select the desired cells by dragging the mouse across them (with the button depressed) so they are darkened and then select the desired font from the **Font menu** on the left of the Formatting toolbar, as in Figure 3-9.

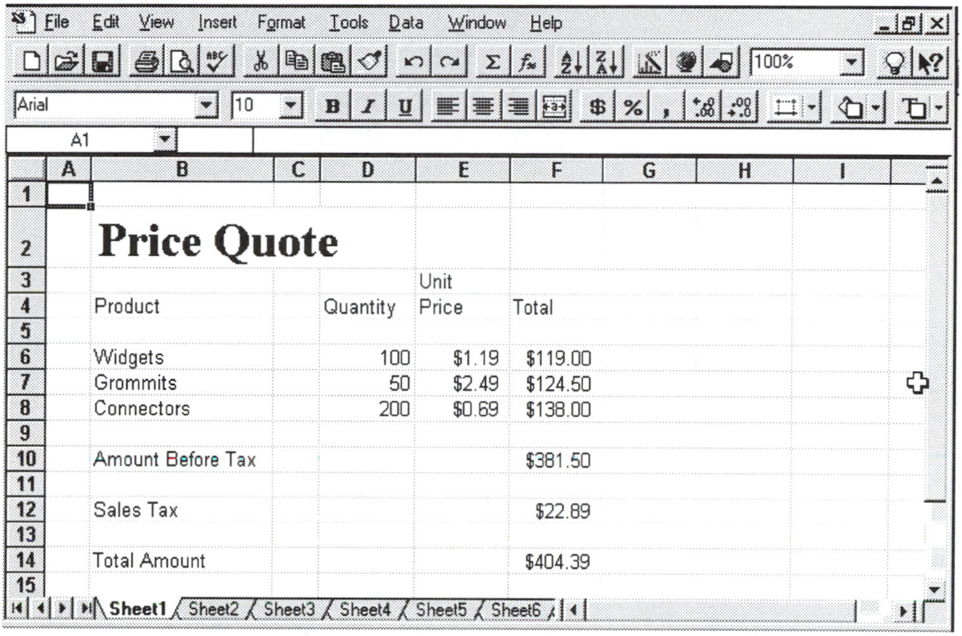

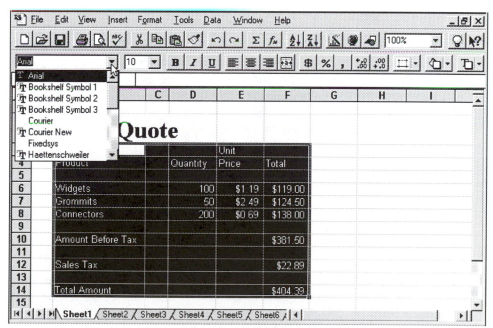

Figure 3-8. The Formatting toolbar appears below the Standard toolbar.

Figure 3-9. Changing the font of the selected area using the Font menu in the Formatting toolbar.

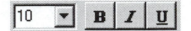

Figure 3-10. Character Size menu and
style buttons in the Formatting toolbar.

Similarly, we can change the size of the text by selecting the cells and then using the **Size menu** in the Formatting toolbar. (See Figure 3-10.) The button with a **B** is the **Bold** button. Pressing this button makes the selected cells appear bold. (Or it "unbolds" cells that already are bold.) The button with the *I* is the *Italics* button. The button with the U̲ is the U̲n̲d̲e̲r̲l̲i̲n̲e̲ button. Pressing this button causes the text in the selected cells to be underlined. (Or if the text already is underlined it removes the underline.)

ALIGNMENT

As you may have noticed, Excel automatically aligns labels to the left of each cell and numbers to the right of each cell. This allows the user to see at a glance which cells are labels and which cells are numbers. However, it also means that numbers usually do not line up under column titles. For example, in the Price Quote worksheet in Figure 3-8, the word "Quantity" in cell D4 is aligned on the left of the cell whereas the numbers below it, in cells D6, D7, and D8, are aligned on the right of the cells. Similarly, the titles "Unit Price" and "Totals" do not line up with the numbers below them. Here, we want to change the alignment of the titles in cells D4, E3, E4, and F4 so they are aligned to the right of the cells like the numbers below them.

If you wish to change the alignment of the text within cells, you can select the cells and then press one of the **Text Alignment buttons** to the right of the Underline button in the Formatting toolbar.

Figure 3-11. Text Alignment buttons

The first Alignment button, the **Align Left button**, causes information in the selected cells to be aligned to the left of the cell. The second button, the **Center button**, causes information to be centered in the cell. The third of these buttons, the **Align Right button**, not surprisingly causes information to be aligned to the right of the cell.

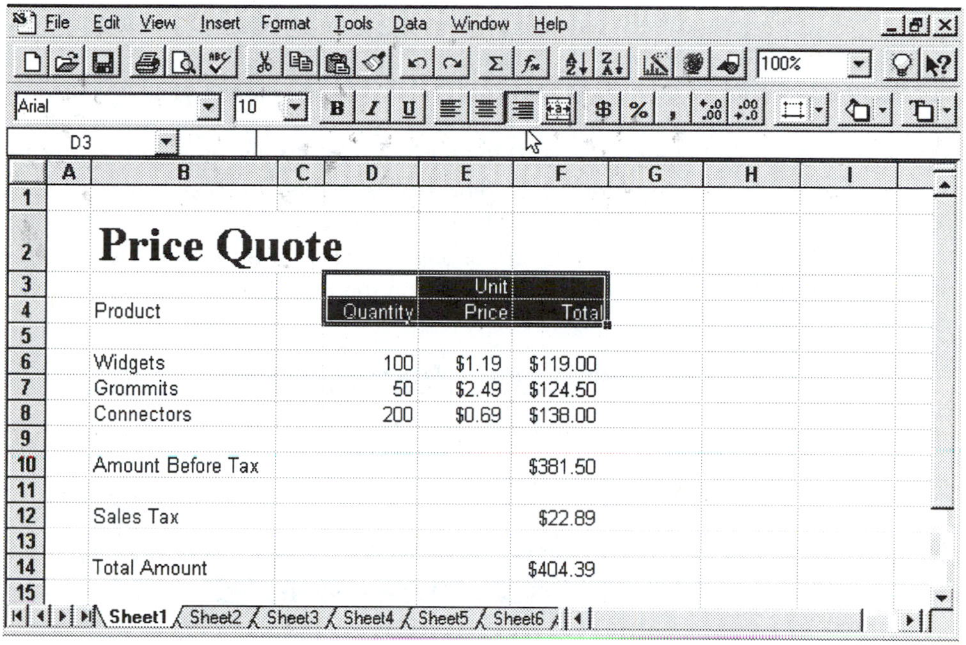

Figure 3-12. Aligning text to the right of the cells.

In the Price Quote worksheet, we can drag across D3 through F4 to select these cells. We then click on the Align Right button and the text is aligned on the right of the cells, as in Figure 3-12.

The rightmost of the Text Alignment buttons in the Formatting toolbar (see Figure 3-11) is the **Center Across Columns button**.

The Center Across Columns button allows information to be centered across multiple cells. First, enter information into a cell. Then, select that cell and several blank cells to the right of the cell and click on the Center Across Columns button. The text will appear centered across the selected cells, though it actually will remain located in the original cell.

You also can change the alignment of cells by first selecting the cells and then using the *Alignment* tab in the window displayed by selecting *Cells...* in the *Format* pull-down menu. (See Figure 3-6.)

HELP!

Excel has a myriad of commands, menus, functions, tools. No one could remember all of the features and details of operating Excel. Our brains can retain only so much.

Excel has a very extensive **Help system** to assist us. As usual with Excel, there are several ways to access the Help system. The easiest way is simply to double-click on the **Help button**, the rightmost button on the Standard toolbar, with a question mark next to an arrow.

Double-clicking on the Help button brings you into the *Index* or *Search* dialog box, as in Figure 3-13. (The Help systems vary from one version of Excel to another.) Here we type in a word, for example "align". We then click on one of the selections and click on the *Display* (or *Show Topics*) button. The Excel Help system will provide information on the topic desired.

Help Topics: Microsoft Excel

Contents | Index | Find | Answer Wizard

1 Type the first few letters of the word you're looking for.

align

2 Click the index entry you want, and then click Display.

alias recipient
aligning cell contents
aligning chart text
aligning decimal points
aligning pages
alphanumeric order (sorting)
AM/PM formats
America Online
AMORDEGRC worksheet function
AMORLINC worksheet function
amortization
ampersand
Analysis ToolPak
AND worksheet function
angles
annotating sheets using cell notes
    copying notes

Display | Print... | Cancel

Figure 3-13. Searching for help on "align".

A second approach is to click on the Help button just once with the mouse. The mouse pointer now turns into the arrow with question mark that is pictured on the Help button. If you now click the mouse somewhere in the Excel workspace, Excel will give you the Help screen for that feature in Excel. For example, click once on the Help button and then click on the button with a **B** and Excel will display the Help screen for the Bold button.

You also might have noticed that if you hold the mouse pointer over a button for a while without pressing the button, Excel will give you a little clue in yellow about what the button does.

The Help system is enormously useful.

FORMATTING NUMBERS

You may have noticed that some numbers in the Price Quote worksheet have dollar signs in front of them and some do not. These numbers have different formats. The cells with dollar signs are said to be in **Currency format**. The important point to be remembered here is that the format of a cell only affects how the cell is displayed. The format of a cell does not affect the actual contents of the cell. For example, a cell might contain the number 347.4725. If it is formatted as Currency to two decimal places, it will appear as $347.47. But the contents of the cell will remain unchanged. If the cell is used in calculations, the number used will be 347.4725 even though the number that appears in the cell is 347.47.

There are several ways to set the **Number format** of a cell. If the cell contains a number that you typed, the cell naturally will pick up any format you used in typing in the number. For example, if you enter $425.24 then the cell will be formatted automatically as currency. Five of the tool buttons on the Format toolbar affect the Number format of a cell.

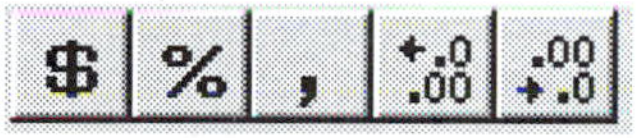

Figure 3-14. Buttons on the Formatting toolbar for changing the format of numbers.

The **Currency format button**, with a picture of a dollar sign, changes the selected cells to Currency format. That is, all selected cells will be displayed with a dollar sign in front and with commas marking off every three places to the left of the decimal point. Negative numbers will be displayed in parentheses.

The **Percent format button** changes the selected cells to Percent format. The contents of the cells will be displayed as multiplied by 100 and will be followed with a percent sign %. For example, if a cell contains 0.0789, it will be displayed as 7.89%.

The **Comma format button** changes the selected cells to Comma format. Here, the numbers will be displayed with commas marking off every three places to the left of the decimal places. No dollar signs are displayed. Negative numbers are not displayed with parentheses around them, but rather with minus signs in front. This could be considered a "normal" format for numbers.

The **Increase Decimal Places button** increases the number of decimal places displayed in the selected cells by one for each time the button is pressed. For example if a selected cell displays 304 and this button is pressed twice, the number will be displayed as 304.00.

The **Decrease Decimal Places button** decreases the number of decimal places displayed in the selected cells by one for each time the button is pressed. For example, if a selected cell displays 304.872 and this button is pressed twice, the number will be displayed as 304.9. The computer rounds off the number displayed but it leaves the actual number stored in the cell unchanged.

If a formatted number is too long to be displayed, then ######### will be displayed in the cell. This is a signal to you that you should widen the column of the cell or decrease the number of decimal places or change the format or the font size.

The five number format buttons displayed in the Format toolbar are only the tip of the iceberg of the number formats available. To reach the full range of choices for number formats, first select the cells in the worksheet to be formatted. Then select *Cells...* in the *Format* pull-down menu and click on the *Number* tab. (See Figure 3-15.)

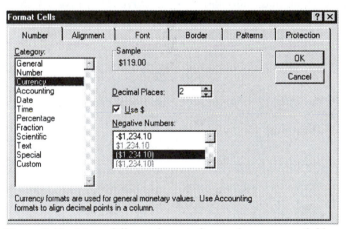

Figure 3-15. Many different formats for numbers are available.

There are hundreds of choices for formats of numbers. If you are not satisfied with the choices Excel provides, you can create your own **Custom format** by clicking on *Custom* at the bottom of the list in the *Category* box in Figure 3-15. The *Custom format* dialog box for Windows 95 is shown in Figure 3-16. Here we can create our own format by typing in a **format code** in the box in the middle. In the example in Figure 3-16, we are displaying the number in rupees. The first part of the code gives the format for a positive number; the second part gives the format for a negative number. The two parts of the format code are separated by a colon. The rupees currency symbol (Rs) is entered in quotes. The appearance of the number in the cell is shown in the *Sample* area.

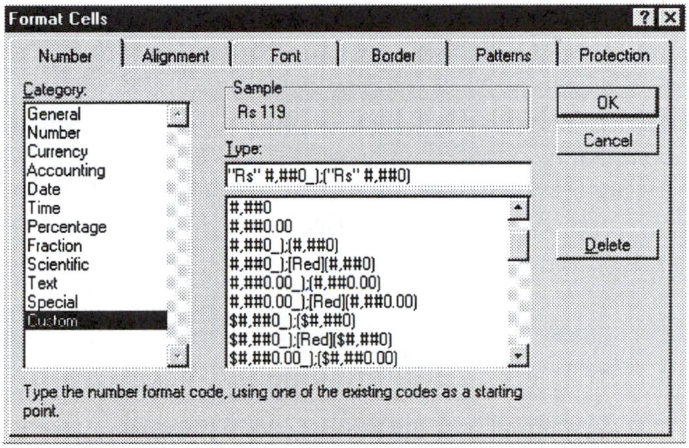

Figure 3-16. Entering a Custom format for displaying a number in rupees.

Incidentally, in Windows 95 or Windows 3.1 to enter a pound currency symbol (£) press the **Alt key** on the keyboard and while pressing the Alt key type the code 0163 on the keys of the numeric keypad. (Believe it or not, you must use the digit keys in the numeric keypad, not the digit keys above the letters on the keyboard.) To enter a yen currency symbol (¥) press the Alt key and while pressing the Alt key type the code 0165 on the keys of the numeric keypad.

BORDERS

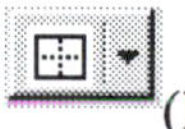

The **Borders button** in the Formatting toolbar allows you to put a border (lines) around selected cells.

First select the cells in the worksheet around which you wish to place a border by dragging across them with the mouse. Click on the small downward pointing triangle on the right of the Borders button in the Formatting toolbar. The **Borders palette** pops down. (See Figure 3-17.)

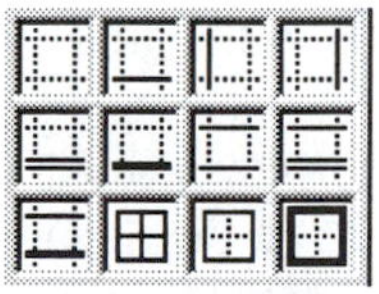

Figure 3-17. Different types of borders are available in the Borders palette.

Each of these buttons causes a different type of border to be placed around the selected cells. The type is indicated in the picture on the button. For example, pressing the bottom right button in the Borders palette will put a thick box completely around the selected cells, with no lines between cells.

To undo borders that were previously set, select the bordered cells and then press the top left button in the Border palette, the button with no borders around the cells.

COLORS

The rightmost two buttons on the Formatting toolbar let you change the colors of cells.

The **Color button** has a paint can behind a rectangle. This button allows you to change the color of the selected cells.

Clicking on the small downward pointing triangle on the right of the Color button causes the **Color palette** to drop down.

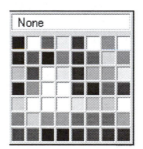

Figure 3-18. The Color palette
(printed in shades of gray, obviously).

To cause a group of cells in the worksheet to be displayed in yellow, select the cells by dragging across them, click on the right part of the Color button, and then click on the desired shade of yellow in the color palette. Note that the gridlines between the cells in the group no longer show if any color except *None* is selected.

As mentioned earlier, we can select all of the cells in the entire worksheet by clicking on the button above the 1 and to the left of the A just beyond the top left corner of the worksheet. Once all of the cells in the worksheet have been selected we can color all of them by selecting a color in the Color palette. Now the background of the entire worksheet will be a certain color. Coloring all the cells in white is one way of erasing the gridlines from the display.

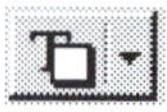

The **Font Color button** has a colored rectangle in front of the letter T. This is the rightmost button in the Formatting toolbar.

The Font Color button allows you to change the color of the text that appears in the cell. With this tool you can cause the characters in a cell to be blue or yellow or whatever rather than the normal black. The button works essentially the same as the Color button. Select the cells containing the text you wish to make a different color. Click on the triangle on the right part of the Font Color button. A color palette drops down. Select the desired color for the text from the palette.

Warning: If you make the font color the same as the background color, the text will seem to disappear.

EXAMPLE

We take the Price Quote worksheet. We make the background gray, change the font and size of cell B2, draw some borders, make some cells bold, make the font size of cells B14 and F14 larger. The result is shown in Figure 3-19.

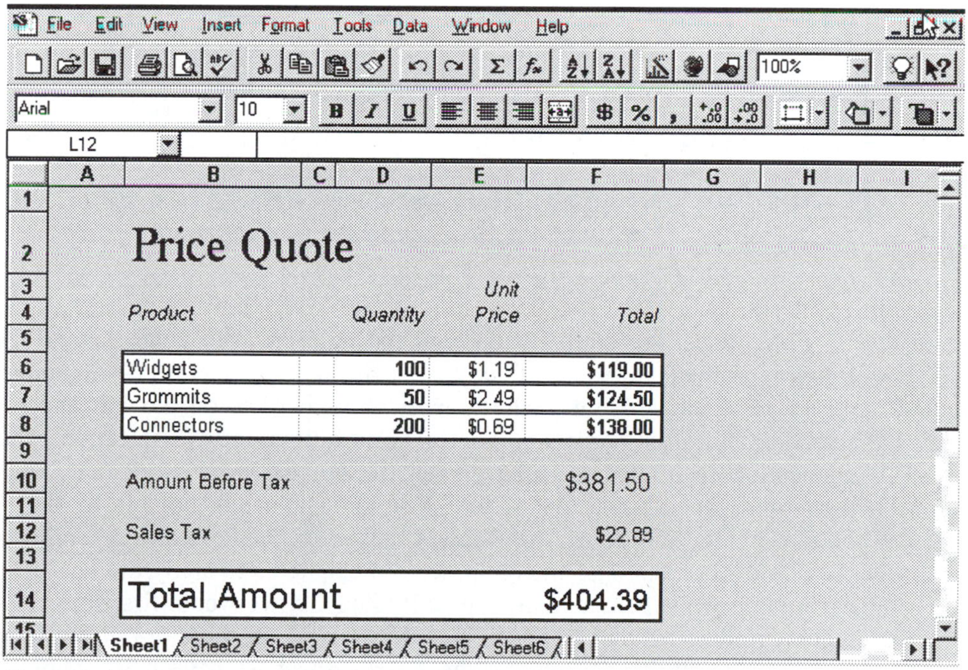

Figure 3-19. One approach to formatting the Price Quote worksheet.

3-D SHADING

It is possible to give your worksheets a three-dimensional effect by the judicious use of colors and borders. An example with the Price Quote worksheet is shown in Figure 3-20.

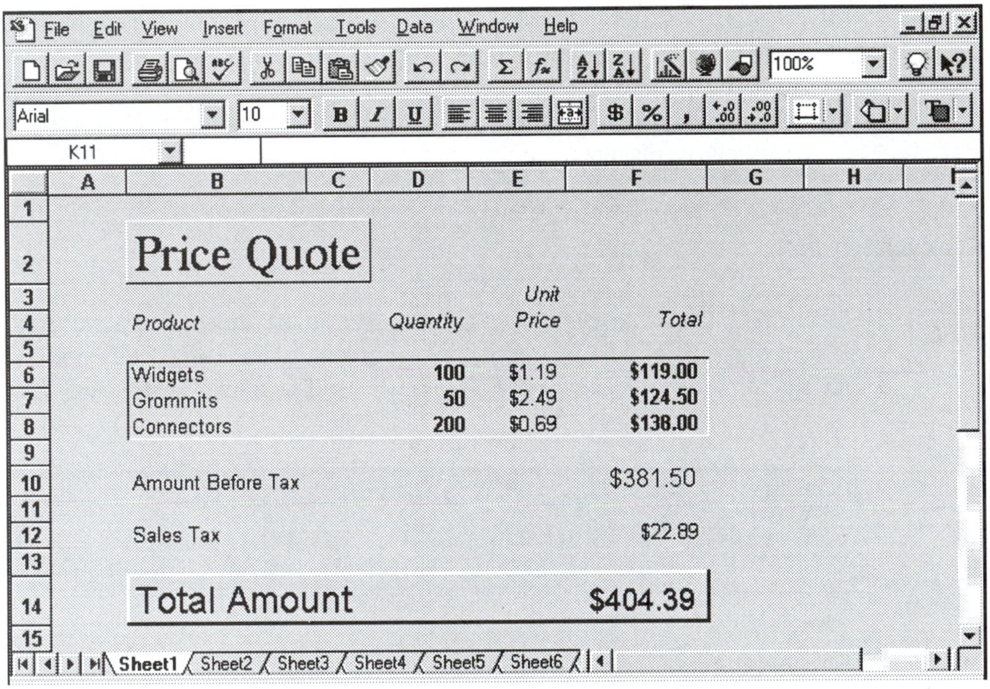

Figure 3-20. Three-dimensional shading of the Price Quote worksheet.

First, select the entire worksheet and color it with some neutral color, for example a medium shade of gray. To format a selection so it appears to be raised, to be above the worksheet, apply white borders on the left and top of the selection and black borders on the right and bottom of the selection. To format a selection so it appears to be sunken, to be below the worksheet, apply black borders to the left and top of the selection and white borders to the right and bottom of the selection. The Borders button in the Formatting toolbar does not provide enough options, enough power, to enable us to apply the borders we need. To apply a white border to the top of B2 and C2, we would first select B2 and C2 by dragging across them. Then we select *Cells...* in the *Format* pull-down menu and click on the *Border* tab. In the *Border* sheet we have many choices for the borders. (See Figure 3-21.)

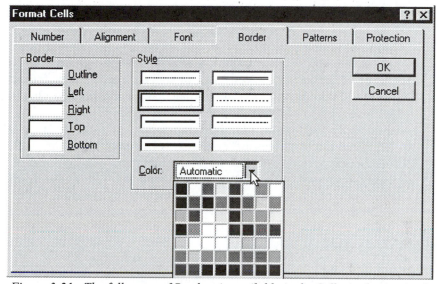

Figure 3-21. The full range of Borders is available in the Cells... selection in the Format pull-down menu.

We first select the thickness of the line of the border in the *Style* section of the *Border* sheet. The thicker the line, the more pronounced the three-dimensional effect will be. We next click on the white square in the *Color* pull-down menu. We click on *Top* and then click on *OK*. We will see a white border applied above B2 and C2. The order of selections here matters. In particular, it is important that we select the thickness and the color before selecting *Top*.

We would use the same technique for each of the other borders. We select B2 and apply a white border to its left. We select B2 and C2 and apply a black border to the bottom of the cells. We select C2 and apply a black border to the right of the cell. This process is somewhat tedious, but the resulting worksheet in Figure 3-20 sure looks snazzy.

THE FORMAT PAINTER BUTTON

If you already have a cell that is formatted in a way that you like, you can capture that format and "paint" it on to other cells using the **Format Painter button**.

The Format Painter button is located on the Standard toolbar to the left of the Undo button. To use the Format Painter button: (1) select a cell or range of cells whose format you wish to duplicate, (2) click on the Format Painter button, and (3) click on the cell to which you wish to apply the format or drag across a range of cells to which you wish to apply the format. The format that is captured and then applied includes font, size, style (bold, italics), alignment, borders, and colors.

You can apply one format to multiple ranges of cells by following this sequence of actions: (1) select a cell or range of cells whose format you wish to duplicate, (2) double-click on the Format Painter button, (3) click on the cell to which you wish to apply the format or drag across a range of cells to which you wish to apply the format, (4) apply the format to other cells by selecting them or dragging across ranges of cells, (5) when you have finished applying the format, click once on the Format Painter button. The Format Painter button will stay depressed during this operation and the cell whose format you have captured will be identified with a dashed line moving around it.

DISPLAYING THE FORMULAS

We can instruct Excel to display the formulas in the cells by selecting *Options...* in the *Tools* pull-down menu and then clicking on the *View* tab. Clicking on *Formulas*, as in Figure 3-22, instructs Excel to display the formulas in the cells rather than the results of evaluating the formulas. The result of displaying the formulas is shown in Figure 3-23.

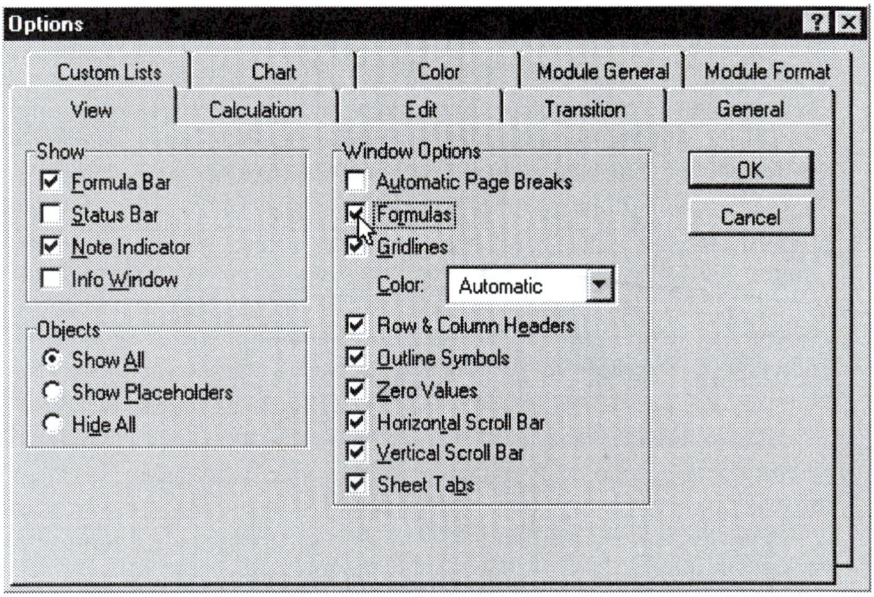

Figure 3-22. Specifying that formulas be displayed in the worksheet.

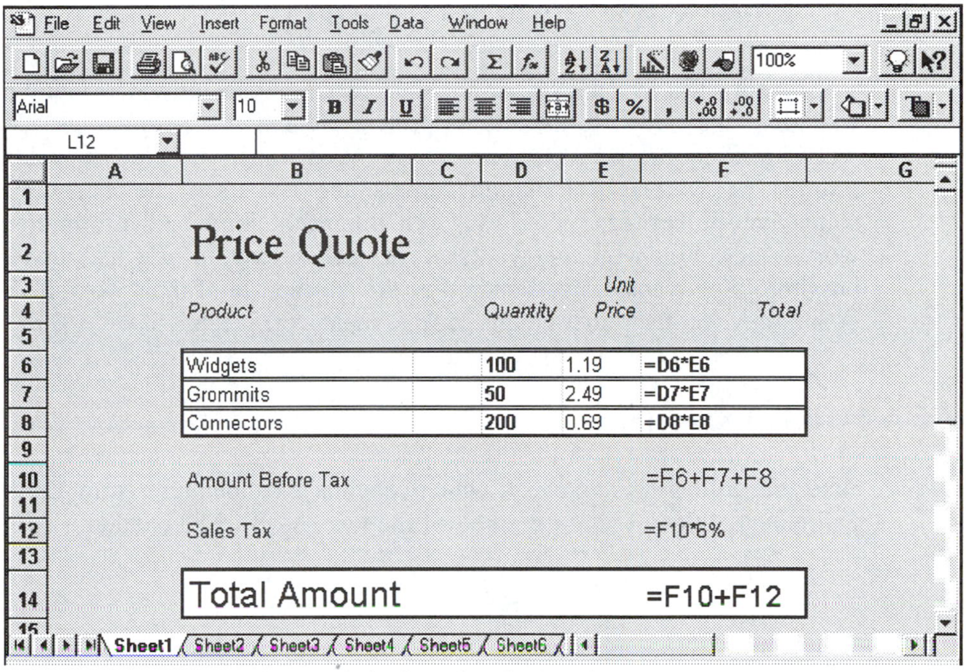

Figure 3-23. The worksheet with the formulas displayed.

This is very useful way of seeing the formulas that underlie your worksheet. In the worksheet shown in Figure 3-23, we manually changed the widths of the columns so all of the information fits on the screen. Instructing Excel to display the formulas causes the program to change the column widths and cell alignments, not always optimally.

If you print the worksheet in Figure 3-23, the formulas will be printed in the cells. If you hand in your homework on paper, your instructor might ask you to print out copies of the worksheet with both the values showing and the formulas showing. Incidentally, if you are going to print the worksheet with the formulas displayed, you'll probably want to instruct Excel to print the Column Headings (A, B, C, ...) and Row Headings (1, 2, 3, ...) as well. You do this by selecting *Page Setup...* in the *File* pull-down menu and then selecting the *Sheet* tab and clicking on *Row and Column Headings*. We will discuss the options in *Page Setup* in more detail in Chapter 7.

As you can see from Figure 3-22, there are a wealth of possibilities for changing the appearance of the worksheet in the *Options...* selection in the *Tools* pull-down menu. For example, you can instruct Excel not to display the gridlines in the worksheet by clicking on the box to the left of the word *Gridlines* so the check mark there vanishes.

FINDING A LOOK FOR YOUR WORKSHEETS

"Beauty lies in the eyes of the beholder." Excel provides many tools for changing the way worksheets appear. Sometimes people just leave the worksheets in the dry, standard style. Sometimes people go wild with an astonishing variety of fonts and colors and borders. The best approach is somewhere in between. You want to highlight the important information in your worksheet. You want the worksheet to be as easy to use and understand as possible. Some companies standardize the appearance of their worksheets. Some people develop their own unique look to their worksheets.

COMPUTER EXERCISES

3-1. Enter the following worksheet, which converts a temperature from Centigrade to Fahrenheit. Widen column B so all of the text shows. Make column A narrow.

CELL	CONTENTS
B1:	*Your Name*
B2:	*Today's date*
B3:	EXERCISE 3-1.
B5:	WORKSHEET TO CONVERT TEMPERATURES
B7:	HELLO
B8:	ENTER THE TEMPERATURE IN CENTIGRADE:
C8:	10
B10:	EQUIVALENT TEMPERATURE IN FAHRENHEIT:
C10:	=(1.8*C8)+32

Cell C10 should show 50, the Fahrenheit equivalent of 10 degrees Centigrade.

(a) Change the format of cell C10 so it shows one decimal place to the right of the decimal point (for example, 50.0).

(b) Move to C8. Enter the number 20. The number in C10 should change to 68.

(c) Select cell B7. Press the Del (or Delete) key. The word HELLO should be erased.

(d) Save the workbook on your disk. Give it a name you will remember, like EXER3_1.

(e) Print the worksheet.

(f) Display the formulas in the worksheet rather than the values. Print the worksheet again. Change the view back to the original, so the result of evaluating the formulas is displayed in the cells.

(g) Format the worksheet to make it as attractive as possible. Change the fonts and sizes. Draw borders. Color in the cells. Save the workbook as EXER3_1G. Print the worksheet again.

(h) Now take the original worksheet and format it with a completely different look. Perhaps you might use three-dimensional shading if you didn't in the previous part. Save the workbook as EXER3_1H. Print the worksheet again.

3-2.   Here is a strange one.

Cell D8 really does contain the formula =D5+D6. Explain exactly how this is possible since 2 + 2 is not equal to 5.

3-3.   Take a worksheet from the exercises at the end of Chapter 2.

(a) Format the worksheet to make it attractive and easy to understand.

(b) Format the worksheet in a second style.

(c) Which do you prefer. Why?

CHAPTER 4

SIMPLE FUNCTIONS AND THE FILL OPERATION

OBJECTIVES

In this chapter you will learn how to:

- Use the SUM, AVERAGE, COUNT, MAX, and MIN functions
- Enter ranges for arguments of functions
- Point to cells in formulas
- Identify and avoid the error of circular reference
- Enter SUM functions automatically with the AutoSum tool
- Use the Function Wizard
- Fill formulas down columns or across rows
- Enter series of numbers using AutoFill

In the first three chapters we have seen how to create, use, and format simple worksheets. The basic idea is that each worksheet is organized as a two-dimensional grid made up of rows and columns. The intersection of each row and column is called a cell. Initially all the cells are blank. We can fill each of the cells with labels (text), numbers, or formulas. The key to Excel is in the formulas. Whenever any cell is changed, all of the relevant formulas are recalculated.

In this chapter we begin to explore how to construct larger, more realistic worksheets. There are two important tools for doing this: built-in functions and the Fill operation. In many ways this is the key chapter of the book. Once you understand how to use built-in functions and the Fill operation you are well on your way to knowing Excel.

BUILT-IN FUNCTIONS SAVE YOU TYPING

Figure 4-1 is a worksheet that shows the monthly sales by region for the first half of the year. The total sales for Africa is in cell H7. What would be the formula in this cell? Clearly, it could be

=B7+C7+D7+E7+F7+G7

Suppose we would like to analyze sales for 60 months. Our formula would have 60 terms. Or, suppose we had 400 regions and would like to find the total

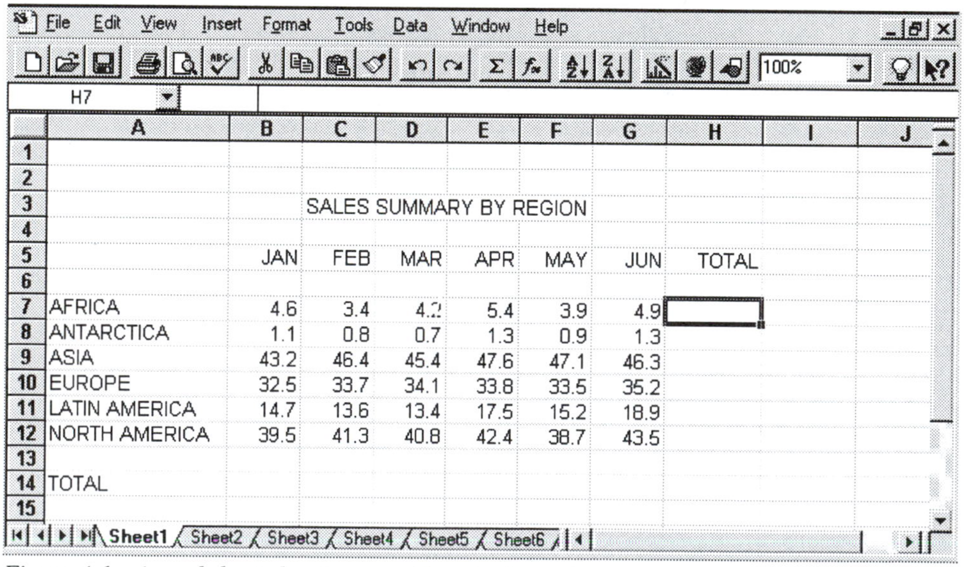

	A	B	C	D	E	F	G	H
1								
2								
3			SALES SUMMARY BY REGION					
4								
5		JAN	FEB	MAR	APR	MAY	JUN	TOTAL
6								
7	AFRICA	4.6	3.4	4.2	5.4	3.9	4.9	
8	ANTARCTICA	1.1	0.8	0.7	1.3	0.9	1.3	
9	ASIA	43.2	46.4	45.4	47.6	47.1	46.3	
10	EUROPE	32.5	33.7	34.1	33.8	33.5	35.2	
11	LATIN AMERICA	14.7	13.6	13.4	17.5	15.2	18.9	
12	NORTH AMERICA	39.5	41.3	40.8	42.4	38.7	43.5	
13								
14	TOTAL							
15								

Figure 4-1. A worksheet showing monthly sales by region.

sales for January. The formula would have 400 cell addresses and 399 plus signs.
We need an easier and shorter way of specifying formulas like this.

The best way to add up a list of numbers is to use **SUM**, which is a **built-in
function**. The formula in H7 could be

$$=SUM(B7:G7)$$

This formula tells Excel that the number which should appear in H7 is the result
of adding all the numbers from B7 through G7. Similarly, the formula in cell B14
could be

$$=SUM(B7:B12)$$

If we had 400 regions, we could add up all of the sales for January with the
formula

$$=SUM(B7:B406)$$

Typing this formula clearly is easier than typing out 400 cell addresses and all the
plus signs.

Built-in functions can save lots of typing. They help make large worksheets
easy to construct.

THE VARIETY OF FUNCTIONS

There are hundreds of built-in functions in Excel. We will discuss five of the
more common functions here. Other functions will be discussed in Chapters 11
through 15 and elsewhere in the book.

The most frequently used function by far is SUM. Other common functions
include:

AVERAGE	Calculates the average or arithmetic mean of a list of values
COUNT	Counts how many numbers are in a list
MAX	Finds the largest value in a list
MIN	Finds the smallest value in a list

Thus, for the worksheet in Figure 4-1, =AVERAGE(B7:G7) would find the
average monthly sales for Africa. The result of evaluating the formula would be
4.4. The formula =MAX(B7:G7) would find the highest monthly sales for Africa,
namely 5.4. The formula =COUNT(B7:G7) would count the number of sales
figures for Africa, namely 6.

The AVERAGE function is simply the SUM function divided by the COUNT function. The formula =AVERAGE(B7:G7) is exactly the same as the formula =SUM(B7:G7)/COUNT(B7:G7). This is important for understanding how missing values are treated in the AVERAGE function. If the number in F7, the May sales for Africa, were missing and the cell were blank, the average would be computed by adding the remaining numbers and dividing by 5, rather than 6. If one of the cells in the range of an AVERAGE function is a label, it will be ignored (treated as if it is blank) because it does not contain a number. Similarly, if there is a cell in the range of an argument of the SUM function (or MAX or MIN) that contains a label, the label is ignored in the calculations.

Built-in functions not only save typing. They also provide a wide variety of calculations. Some of these calculations are impossible to specify using the normal arithmetic operators. For example, there is no formula using the normal arithmetic operators (+ - * / % ^) for calculating the largest number in a list. SUM saves typing. MAX provides a completely new capability.

ARGUMENTS AND RANGES

The inputs to a function are placed inside the parentheses and are called **arguments**. Multiple arguments in a function are separated by commas. For example, the formula =SUM(C6,3,4*B2) instructs Excel to add up the number in cell C6, the number 3, and the result of multiplying 4 times the number in B2. The SUM function here has three arguments: C6, 3, and 4*B2. The functions SUM, AVERAGE, COUNT, MAX, and MIN can have up to 30 arguments.

The most useful type of argument for these functions is a **range**. The argument in =SUM(B7:G7) is B7:G7, which is a range.

Ranges are very important in Excel. A range normally specifies a rectangular portion of a worksheet. The range B7:G7 consists of a cell address followed by a colon followed by another cell address. The first cell address gives one corner of the range. The second address indicates the diagonally opposite corner of the range. Usually, the first address is the top left corner of the range; the second address is the bottom right corner of the range.

The range B7:G7 is a one cell by six cell horizontal rectangle. The range B7:B12 is a six by one vertical rectangle. The range B7:G12 would contain 36 cells in a rectangle six cells across from column B through G and six cells down from row 7 through row 12.

What should be the formula in cell H14 in the worksheet in Figure 4-1? This is the grand total of the sales for the six months. There are three choices. The formula could be

=SUM(H7:H12)

This formula would calculate the grand total by adding up the product totals. The formula in H14 could be

$$=SUM(B14:G14)$$

This formula would calculate the grand total by adding up the monthly totals. The third possibility is for the formula in H14 to be

$$=SUM(B7:G12)$$

This formula would calculate the grand total by adding up the original 36 monthly sales numbers. All three formulas would give the same answer.

How many numbers would be added up in the formula

$$=SUM(23,C12,B4:B7,47,C2:E5)$$

There are five arguments:

1. the number 23   --   1 number
2. the cell C12   --   1 number
3. the range B4:B7 --   4 numbers
4. the number 47   --   1 number
5. the range C2:E5 --   12 numbers

Thus this formula instructs the computer to add 19 numbers.

Be careful with the commas and the colons. The formula =SUM(B7,G12) instructs the computer to add up 2 numbers, the values in B7 and G12. The formula =SUM(B7:G12) instructs the computer to add up 36 numbers, the values in the rectangular range of cells from B7 through G12.

POINTING

A convenient way to specify cell addresses in a range is to **point** to them instead of typing them. The idea of pointing is to use the mouse to point to the address that you would like to include in a formula. Pointing is especially useful when specifying a range, because when you point to a range Excel highlights the range on the screen.

To illustrate, consider the worksheet in Figure 4-2. We are in the process of entering the formula for cell H7. We have typed =SUM(and now are entering the range. Instead of typing the addresses of the range we simply drag across the desired range with the mouse (with the button pressed down). The computer

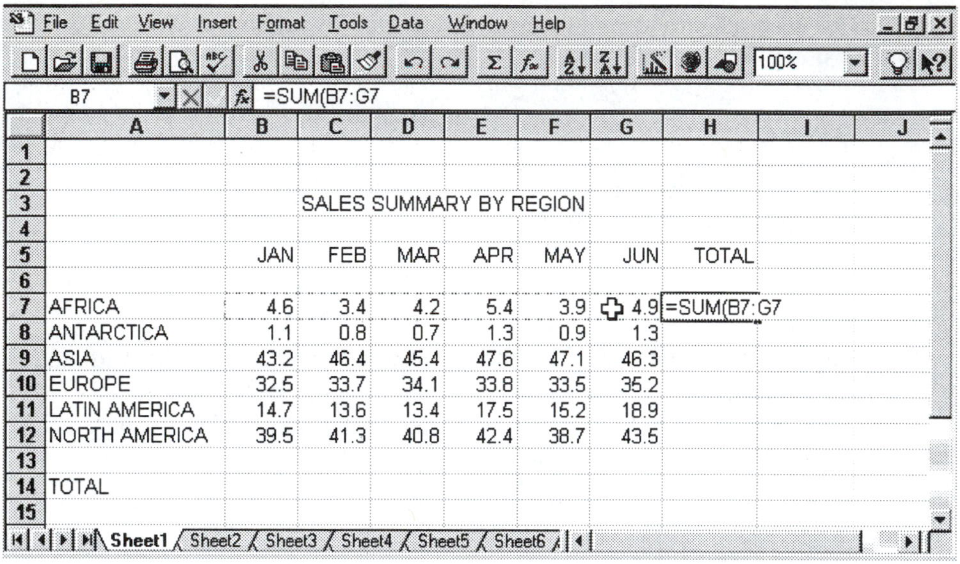

Figure 4-2. Enter a range of addresses by dragging across the range with the mouse.

automatically fills in the range pointed to in the formula, and, if you look carefully, you can see that as an added aid to the user the computer has placed dashed lines around the range selected.

Pointing is not restricted to ranges. If you want to enter the formula =3*B2+C4, you can type =3*, then point and click on B2, type the +, point and click on C4, and then type the Enter key or click on the Enter button.

A COMMON ERROR: CIRCULAR REFERENCE

A common error made when entering a formula is to include the address of the cell in the formula itself. An example is shown in Figure 4-3. The formula in H7 should be =SUM(B7:G7). By mistake in H7 we have entered the formula =SUM(B7:H7). This typically occurs when we are pointing to the range and mistakenly extend the range over H7. The formula =SUM(B7:H7) instructs the computer that the value to be shown in H7 is the sum of the numbers from B7 through H7. That is, the computer needs to know the value in H7 in order to calculate the value in H7.

A formula that depends on its own value has a **circular reference**. As you can see, Excel warns you when it encounters a circular reference. There are a few cases where you want a circular reference, but normally it is a mistake that needs to be corrected.

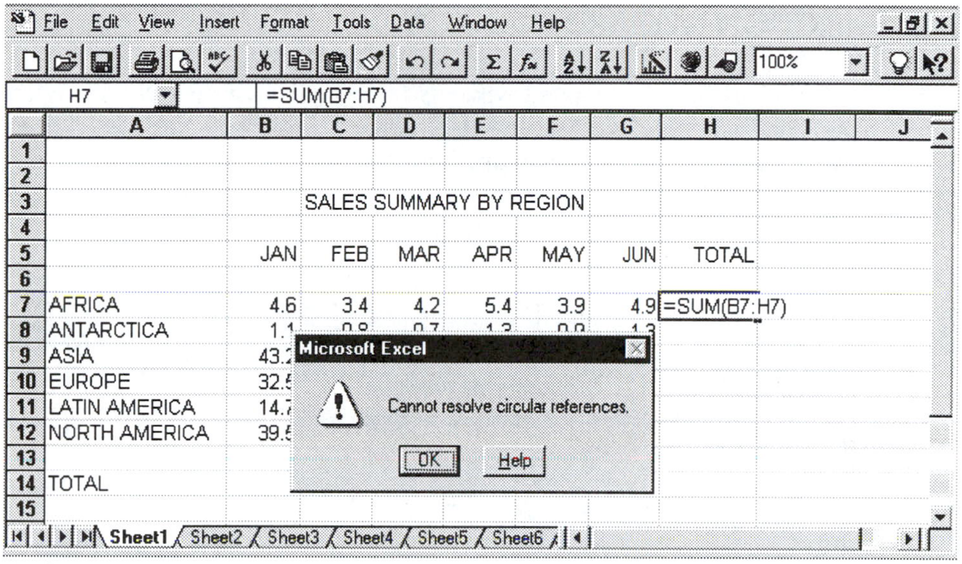

Figure 4-3. A mistake has been made. A circular reference occurs because the cell H7 contains a formula that refers to itself.

OVERUSE OF THE SUM FUNCTION

Sometimes people become so enamored with the SUM function that they use it in every formula. If we want a formula that adds C4 and D6, we can simply use the formula =C4+D6. We could use =SUM(C4,D6) but it is a bit of overkill. Similarly, if we want to multiply the number in F5 by 3, we would write =F5*3. The formula =SUM(F5*3) would work, but the use of the SUM function here is wholly superfluous.

THE AUTOSUM TOOL

The SUM function legitimately is used so often that Excel provides a special tool button, the **AutoSum button**, for automatically entering the SUM function. Simply select the cell in which you want a SUM function (as in Figure 4-1) and then click on the AutoSum button in the Standard toolbar. Excel will look at the worksheet and guess what row or column of numbers you want to add up. In this case if you select H7 and then click on the AutoSum button, Excel will guess that you want the formula =SUM(B7:G7) and this formula automatically will be entered in H7 for your approval.

THE FUNCTION WIZARD

Excel includes automated **wizards** for complicated operations. Wizards hold your hand and take you step by step through important tasks. The **Function Wizard** helps you enter functions into formulas.

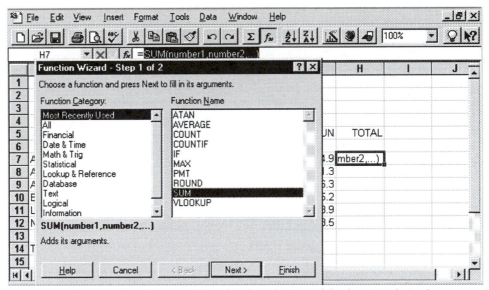

Selecting H7 and clicking on the Function Wizard button yields the *Function Wizard* dialog box, as shown in Figure 4-4.

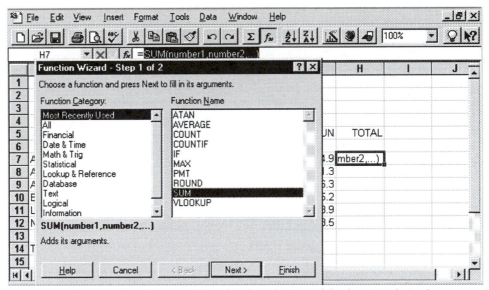

Figure 4-4. Step 1 of the Function Wizard is the selection of the function desired.

The Function Wizard works in two steps. In the first step we select the function we wish to use. Along the way it's easy to get information on a particular function by selecting the function and then by pressing *Help* at the bottom of the dialog box. After the proper function has been selected, press *Next* to proceed to the second step of the Function Wizard. In the second step we enter in the argument(s) of the function selected.

NESTED FUNCTIONS

The arguments of a function can include other functions. A function inside another function results in a **nested function**. An example of a nested function is

=MAX(SUM(C7:C10),SUM(D7:D10),SUM(E7:E10))

Here the MAX function has three arguments. Each of the arguments is a SUM function. The computer would add up C7 through C10. Then it would add up D7 through D10. Then it would add up E7 through E10. The value calculated by the whole formula would be the largest of these three totals. This is the number that would appear in the cell.

THE FILL OPERATION

Built-in functions with ranges provide an important tool for constructing large worksheets. They allow us to enter a formula that adds up 400 numbers by entering SUM and two addresses. The **Fill operation** allows us to make multiple copies of the formula so we do not have to type it over and over again into a column of cells or row of cells.

Return to our example of tabulating the monthly sales by region. In the worksheet in Figure 4-5 the final formula =SUM(B7:G7) in cell H7 is shown.

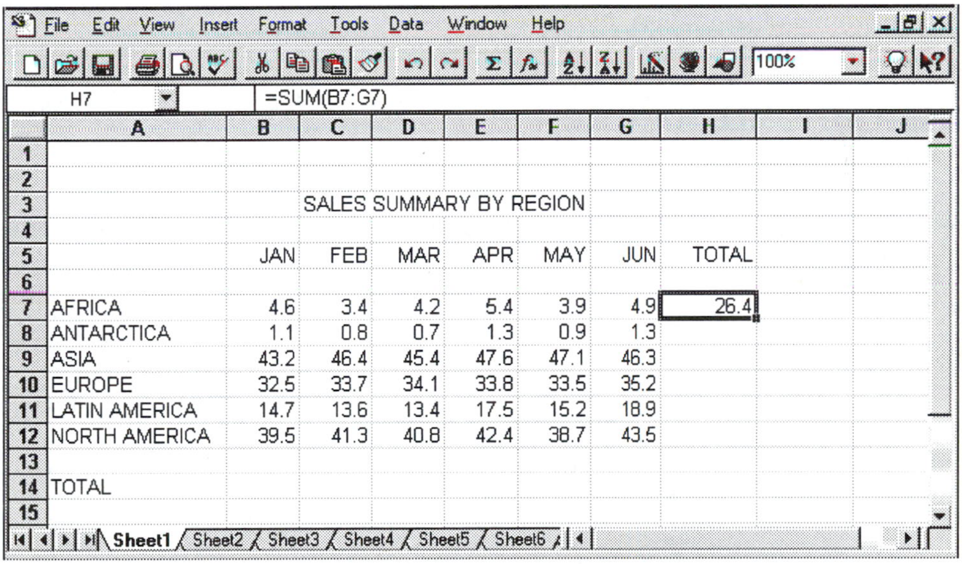

	A	B	C	D	E	F	G	H	I	J
1										
2										
3			SALES SUMMARY BY REGION							
4										
5		JAN	FEB	MAR	APR	MAY	JUN	TOTAL		
6										
7	AFRICA	4.6	3.4	4.2	5.4	3.9	4.9	26.4		
8	ANTARCTICA	1.1	0.8	0.7	1.3	0.9	1.3			
9	ASIA	43.2	46.4	45.4	47.6	47.1	46.3			
10	EUROPE	32.5	33.7	34.1	33.8	33.5	35.2			
11	LATIN AMERICA	14.7	13.6	13.4	17.5	15.2	18.9			
12	NORTH AMERICA	39.5	41.3	40.8	42.4	38.7	43.5			
13										
14	TOTAL									
15										

Figure 4-5. We are ready to fill the formula in H7 down the column.

We now would like to enter the formulas to total each of the other regions. The formulas for these cells would be as follows:

H8:	=SUM(B8:G8)
H9:	=SUM(B9:G9)
H10:	=SUM(B10:G10)
H11:	=SUM(B11:G11)
H12:	=SUM(B12:G12)

We could type each of these formulas, although it would be tedious. But suppose we had 400 regions. We would have to type the =SUM formula 400 times. A better solution than typing all of the formulas is to type the first formula and then use the Fill operation.

Once we have entered the formula in cell H7, we can use the Fill operation to tell Excel to fill the formula down the column into the other cells. But notice that we do not want Excel to fill an exact copy of the formula in cell H7 into the other cells. If it did fill an exact copy, then each of the cells from H8 through H12 would contain the formula =SUM(B7:G7) and the number that appeared in each of the cells would be the total for Africa. Rather, Excel has an "intelligent" Fill operation. As Excel fills the formula down the column it automatically adjusts the row numbers in the formula. So =SUM(B7:G7) in H7 becomes =SUM(B8:G8) in cell H8 and =SUM(B9:G9) in cell H9, and so on for each formula that is filled into the cells.

USING THE FILL HANDLE

The simplest way to fill a formula down a column or across a row is to use the **Fill Handle**. The Fill Handle is the small square at the bottom right of the active cell.

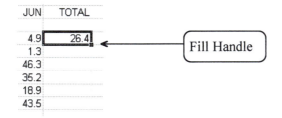

If we move the mouse pointer right on top of the Fill Handle, the mouse pointer becomes a thin cross.

JUN	TOTAL
4.9	26.4
1.3	
46.3	
35.2	
18.9	
43.5	

We press down on the mouse button and drag down over the cells we would like to fill.

JUN	TOTAL
4.9	26.4
1.3	
46.3	
35.2	
18.9	
43.5	

We lift our finger off the mouse button and the formulas are filled down automatically.

JUN	TOTAL
4.9	26.4
1.3	6.1
46.3	276
35.2	202.8
18.9	93.3
43.5	246.2

We click somewhere else and we are finished. Sure enough, the formula =SUM(B7:G7) was changed as it was filled down the column. (See Figure 4-6.)

Now we would like to enter the row of monthly totals in row 14. First we click on cell B14. Click on the AutoSum button. The AutoSum button guesses that we want the formula =SUM(B7:B13) to appear in cell B14. We click on the Enter button to accept the formula and enter it into the cell. To fill the formula across the row, we move the mouse pointer on top of the Fill Handle in the bottom right corner of cell B14 until the mouse pointer becomes a thin cross. We press the mouse button and drag the Fill Handle to the right all the way over to H14. We lift our finger off the mouse button and click somewhere else. We are finished. Row 14 now contains appropriate formulas for calculating the column totals. (See Figure 4-7.)

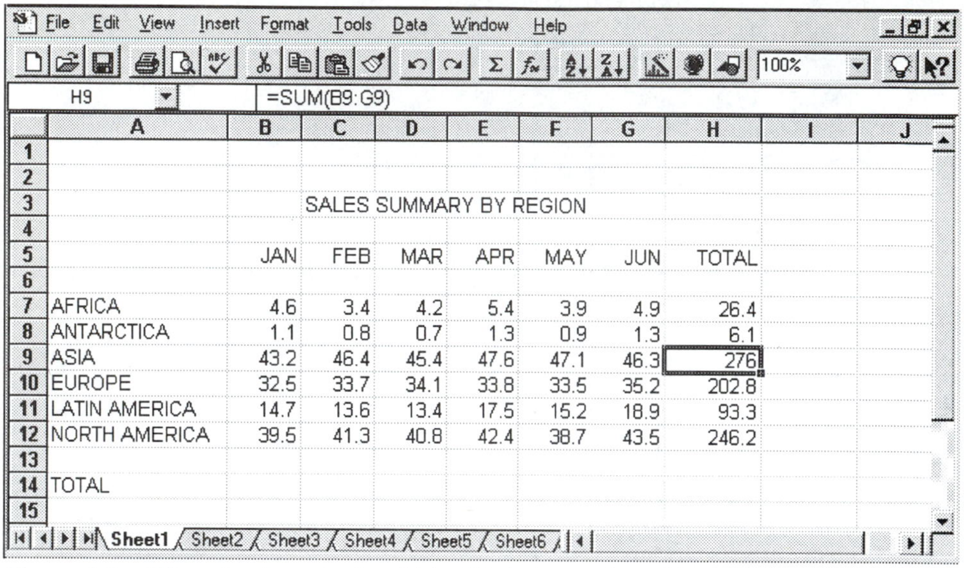

Figure 4-6. When the formula in H7 is filled down, the addresses in the formula are adjusted automatically.

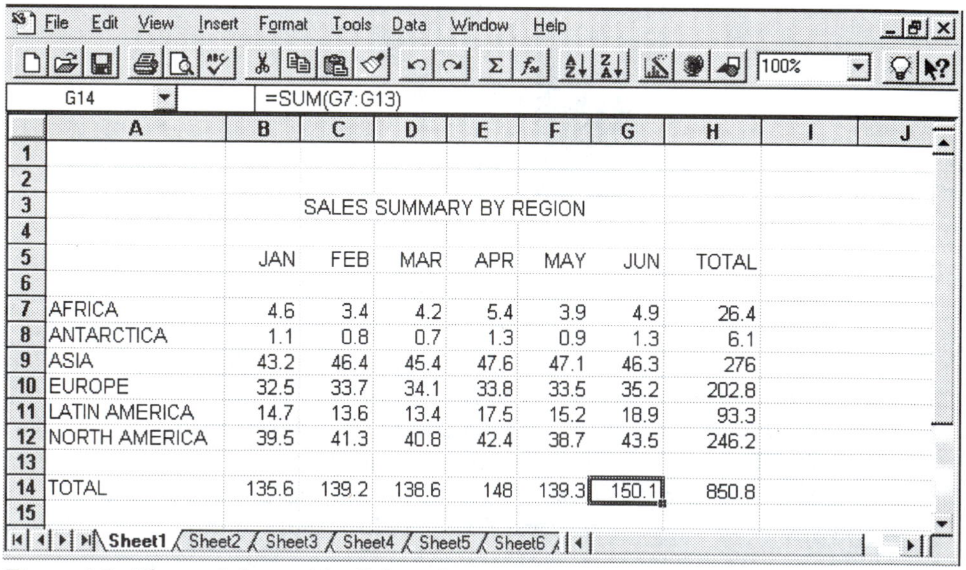

Figure 4-7. The worksheet with all formulas entered.

FILLING BY DOUBLE-CLICKING

There is an even faster way to fill these formulas down or across. In Figure 4-8, simply point to the Fill Handle in H7 and double-click the mouse button. The formulas automatically are filled down. This trick works only if the cells to the immediate left or directly above are not empty.

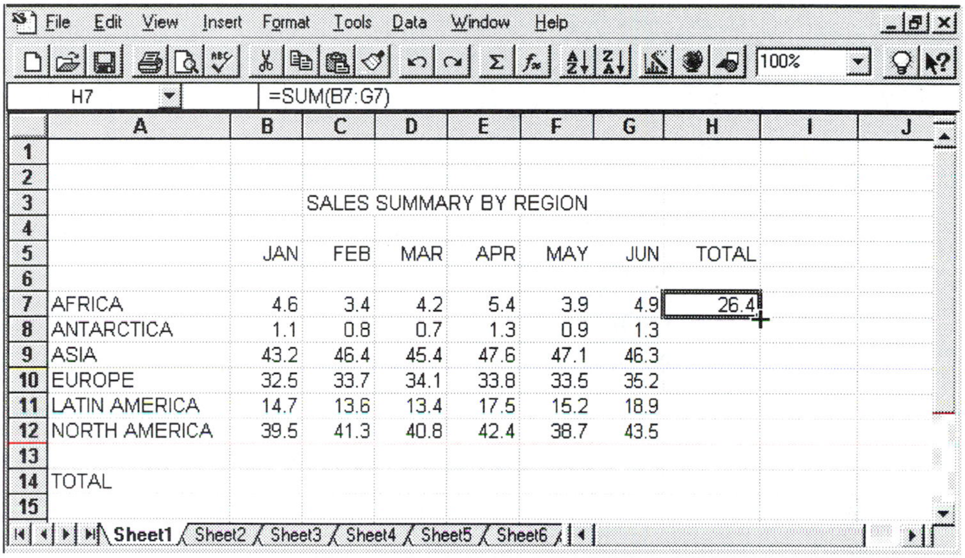

	A	B	C	D	E	F	G	H	I	J
1										
2										
3				SALES SUMMARY BY REGION						
4										
5		JAN	FEB	MAR	APR	MAY	JUN	TOTAL		
6										
7	AFRICA	4.6	3.4	4.2	5.4	3.9	4.9	26.4		
8	ANTARCTICA	1.1	0.8	0.7	1.3	0.9	1.3			
9	ASIA	43.2	46.4	45.4	47.6	47.1	46.3			
10	EUROPE	32.5	33.7	34.1	33.8	33.5	35.2			
11	LATIN AMERICA	14.7	13.6	13.4	17.5	15.2	18.9			
12	NORTH AMERICA	39.5	41.3	40.8	42.4	38.7	43.5			
13										
14	TOTAL									
15										

Figure 4-8. A shortcut to filling down the formula is to double-click on the Fill Handle.

AUTOFILL

An interesting feature of Fill allows us to automatically create a series of values. For example, we might want to create a worksheet that has the weeks from 1 through 6 in a column. We could enter a 1 and 2 in successive cells. Then we select the cells by dragging across them.

We grab the Fill Handle in the bottom right corner of the selection and drag down four cells.

When we let up on the mouse button, Excel automatically fills in the values from 3 through 6.

We click somewhere else in the worksheet and the process is complete.

The AutoFill technique is remarkably flexible. If we had entered 2 and 5 instead of 1 and 2, Excel would have filled in the series 2, 5, 8, 11, 14, 17. If we had entered Jan, Feb, Excel would have filled in the month names Jan, Feb, Mar, Apr, May, Jun. If we had entered in Q1, Q2, Excel would have filled in Q1, Q2, Q3, Q4, Q1, Q2, because it would interpret Q1 as standing for Quarter 1.

Even more remarkably, AutoFill automatically will fit a straight line to a series of 3 or more values. For example, if we enter 3, 9, 6, 7 into successive cells, select those cells, and then drag the Fill Handle down four more cells, we will get the sequence 3, 9, 6, 7, 8.5, 9.4, 10.3, 11.2. Excel uses the values entered as the basis for its prediction of the new values.

SUMMARY

Two critical tools for creating larger worksheets are built-in functions and the Fill operation.

Excel provides built-in functions for many types of calculations. The inputs to a function are called arguments. The use of a range as the argument to a built-in function allows calculations to be performed on a large rectangular portion of the worksheet by specifying only the addresses of two of the diagonally opposite corners of the rectangle. For example, the formula =SUM(C101:AA1100) instructs the computer to add up the values of the 25,000 cells in a range 25 columns wide and 1,000 rows down. Ranges can be specified either by typing or by pointing.

The Fill operation allows a given formula to be filled down a column or across a row. For example, to find the sum of each of 1,000 rows of numbers we could enter the formula to sum the top row and then command the computer to fill the formula down through the remaining 999 rows. The Fill operation automatically adjusts the addresses in the new formulas created.

The AutoFill feature allows us to easily create a series of values by entering just the first few values in the series, selecting those values, and then dragging the Fill Handle.

PAPER AND PENCIL EXERCISE

4-1. Consider the following worksheet.

What would be the result of evaluating each of the following formulas? Write out your answer on paper. Do not use the computer. The point of this exercise is to ensure that you understand what functions do.

(a) =SUM(A5:D5)
(b) =COUNT(A5:D5)
(c) =AVERAGE(A5:D5)
(d) =MAX(A5:D5)
(e) =MIN(A5:D5)
(f) =AVERAGE(A3:A7)
(g) =COUNT(A3:A7)
(h) =SUM(AVERAGE(B4:B7),MAX(B4:B7),MIN(B4:B8))
(i) =SUM(3*B4,B4:C7,MAX(A5:C7),2*MIN(A4:B6))

COMPUTER EXERCISES

4-2. Enter the following worksheet, adding the appropriate formulas. Use the built-in functions and the Fill operation. Test the worksheet by changing some of the numbers and checking the bottom two rows and the right two columns. Format the worksheet appropriately. Save and print the worksheet.

Sales Analysis

Product	Winter	Spring	Summer	Fall	Total	Max
Golf	32000	62000	57000	39000		
Tennis	47000	52000	71000	29000		
Skiing	37000	21000	11000	52000		
Surfing	12000	21000	29000	13000		
Total						
Average						

4-3. Set up a worksheet to help you track the amount of time you spend on computers this semester. Use the built-in functions and Fill. Enter appropriate values to test the worksheet. Save and print the worksheet.

Hours Spent On Computers

Week	Mon	Tues	Wed	Thur	Fri	Sat	Sun	Total
1								
2								
3								
...								
14								
15								

Total:
Average:
Max:

Maximum No. Hours Spent In Any One Day During The Semester:

4-4. The following table shows the U.S. government receipts and outlays for 1980, 1985, 1990, and 1995.

U.S. Government Receipts And Outlays In Billions Of Dollars

	1980	1985	1990	1995
Receipts				
Individual Income Taxes	244	335	467	588
Corporate Income Taxes	65	61	94	151
Social Insurance Taxes	158	265	380	484
Excise Taxes	24	36	35	58
Other	26	37	56	65
Total Receipts				
Outlays				
National Defense	134	253	299	272
Social Security	119	189	249	336
Income Security	87	128	147	223
Medicare	32	66	98	157
All Other Government	166	181	275	317
Interest	53	129	184	234
Total Outlays				
Surplus (Deficit)				

(a) Enter the worksheet into the computer. Add formulas for the Total Receipts, Total Outlays, and Surplus. Use the SUM function for the Totals and Fill. Format the worksheet appropriately.

(b) Use AutoFill to show the predicted values of the individual items for 2000 and 2005 if they continue in a linear trend. Fill the formulas for Total Receipts, Total Outlays, and Surplus (Deficit) across. What would be the deficit in 2000 and 2005 if the past trends continue?

4-5. Create a worksheet to calculate the wages for hourly employees.

(a) Start off with a heading, the names of the employees, and the hours worked each day. Try using AutoFill for the days of the weeks. Type in the numbers of hours worked each day. Use a variety of numbers.

Payroll

Week of

Name	Mon	Tue	Wed	Thu	Fri	Sat	Sun
Abel, Ann							
Jones, John							
Smith, Sam							
Wall. Joan							

(b) Add a column at the end to calculate total hours worked for each employee. Use the SUM function.
(c) Add a column with the hourly wage for each employee. Use a different wage for each employee. Be generous.
(d) Add a column to automatically calculate the gross wages earned for the week.
(e) Add a column for federal tax withholdings of 20%.
(f) Add a column for state tax withholdings of 5%.
(g) Add a column for medical deduction of $12 per week.
(h) Add a column for take-home pay (gross wages minus withholding and deductions).
(i) Add rows at the bottom for the total and the average of each of the columns. Use the SUM and AVERAGE functions and Fill.
(j) Format appropriate cells with $ signs and to two decimal places to the right of the decimal point.
(k) Format the worksheet so it appears as attractive and readable as possible.

CHAPTER 5

OPERATIONS ON CELLS

OBJECTIVES

In this chapter you will learn how to:

- Move cells in a worksheet
- Erase a range of cells
- Delete rows and columns
- Insert new rows and columns
- Attach a note to a cell
- Use Copy and Paste to move information

In this chapter we will discuss some of the more commonly used operations on cells in Excel.

MOVING CELLS

Excel provides an easy way to move a group of cells to another location in the worksheet. First select the range of the worksheet you would like to move by dragging across it with the (left) mouse button down. Release the button and move the mouse so the mouse pointer is pointing to the very top of the selection. The pointer should change to a white arrow, as in Figure 5-1.

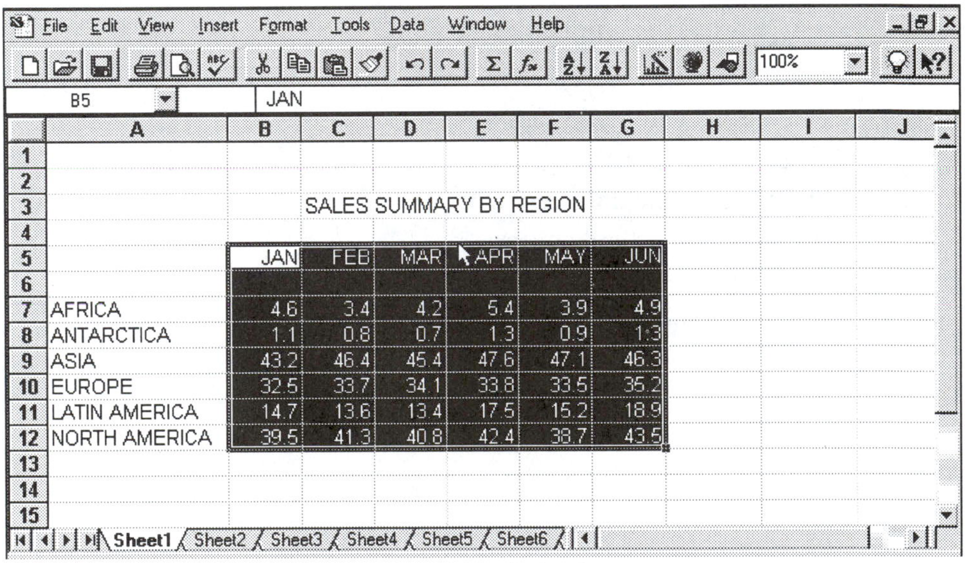

Figure 5-1. Getting ready to move a range of cells by dragging.

Now depress the mouse button and drag the selected range to wherever you would like to place it. As you drag, you will see an outline of the range move along with the mouse pointer. Release the mouse button and the selected portion of the worksheet will move. This operation is a form of **drag and drop**.

After you move a range of cells within a complex workbook, you should look to make sure that all the formulas still work correctly. Excel does its best to adjust all relevant formulas, both the formulas that are moved and the formulas in other cells that refer to the cells that are moved.

If by mistake you move the range on top of cells containing information, you can press the Undo button or select *Undo* in the *Edit* pull-down menu.

ERASING A RANGE OF CELLS

The easiest way to erase a range is to select the range by dragging across it and then with the button up move the mouse pointer down to the bottom right hand corner of the range. The pointer will change into a thin cross. Depress the mouse button and drag the mouse back through the range to the top left corner of the range. The range will turn gray as you drag. When you release the mouse button, the contents of the cells will be erased.

If you erase a range by mistake, you can press Undo.

DELETING ROWS AND COLUMNS

To delete a row, first select the row by clicking on the row number to the left of the worksheet. (See Figure 5-2.) Now select *Delete...* in the *Edit* pull-down menu. The entire row will be deleted. All cells below the row will move up.

Excel adjusts references in formulas as best it can. If you have referred to one of the deleted cells in a formula, the formula might evaluate to #REF!, meaning there is an unresolvable reference in the formula.

To delete multiple rows at once, drag across the row numbers to select the multiple rows and then select *Delete...* in the *Edit* pull-down menu.

Columns are deleted in the same way.

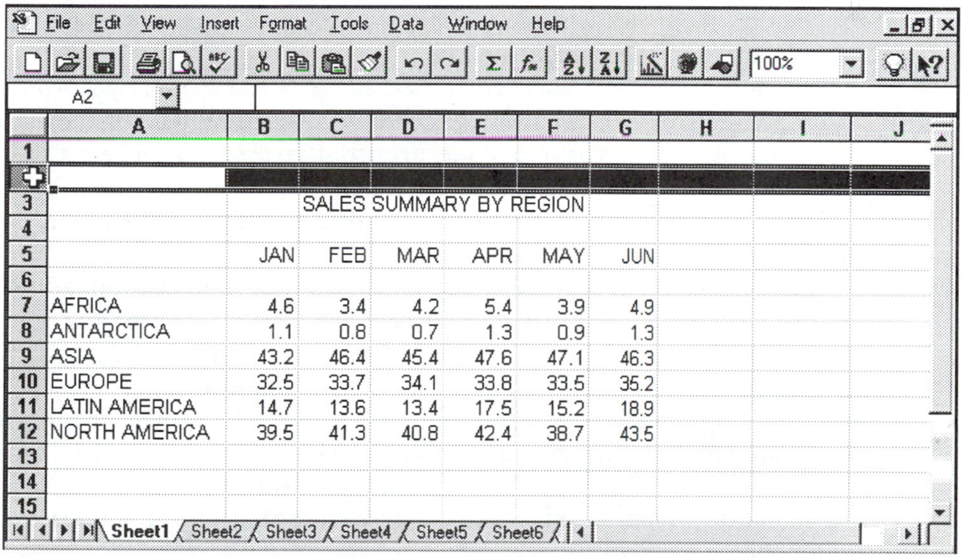

Figure 5-2. Click on the row number to select the entire row.

INSERTING ROWS AND COLUMNS

To insert a new row in a worksheet, select the row where you want a new row inserted. For example, if you would like a new row 6 inserted, select the current row 6 by clicking on the row number 6 on the left of the worksheet. Now select *Rows* in the *Insert* pull-down menu. A new blank row 6 will be inserted. Everything from row 6 down will be moved down one row. References in formulas will be adjusted accordingly.

If you would like to insert three rows beginning at row 6, simply drag across the row numbers 6, 7, and 8 so that these three rows are selected. Now select *Rows* in the *Insert* pull-down menu. Three new rows (6, 7, and 8) will be inserted. All information previously in row 6 and below will be moved down three rows. Formulas will be adjusted accordingly.

Alternatively, you simply can click on any cell in row 6 to make it the active cell and then select *Rows* in the *Insert* pull-down menu to insert a new row at the location of the active cell.

Ditto for columns.

ANNOTATING A CELL

You can attach a **note** to a cell, either a written message or, if your computer allows it, a spoken message. For example, if a formula in a cell is particularly complex, you can explain the formula in a note. If you are making an important assumption about the inflation rate in a worksheet, you can add a note to the cell with a statement about the assumption.

To attach a note to a cell, click on the cell and then select *Note...* in the *Insert* pull-down menu. You will see the *Cell Note* dialog box, as shown in Figure 5-3. You can either type your note or record your spoken note. Click on *Add* and then *OK* and your note is attached to the cell.

Cells that have notes attached are marked in the worksheet with a tiny red dot in the top right corner of the cell.

To see a note in Excel for Windows 95, just let the mouse pointer rest on the cell for a short period of time and the note will appear. To see the note attached to a cell in Excel for Windows 3.1 or in Excel for the Macintosh, you must click on the cell and then select *Note...* in the *Insert* pull-down menu.

Attaching notes is an excellent way to provide documentation for your workbook both for yourself and for other people who will be using it. For people who work jointly on Excel workbooks it also provides an easy way to communicate with each other about the specific contents of various cells in the workbook.

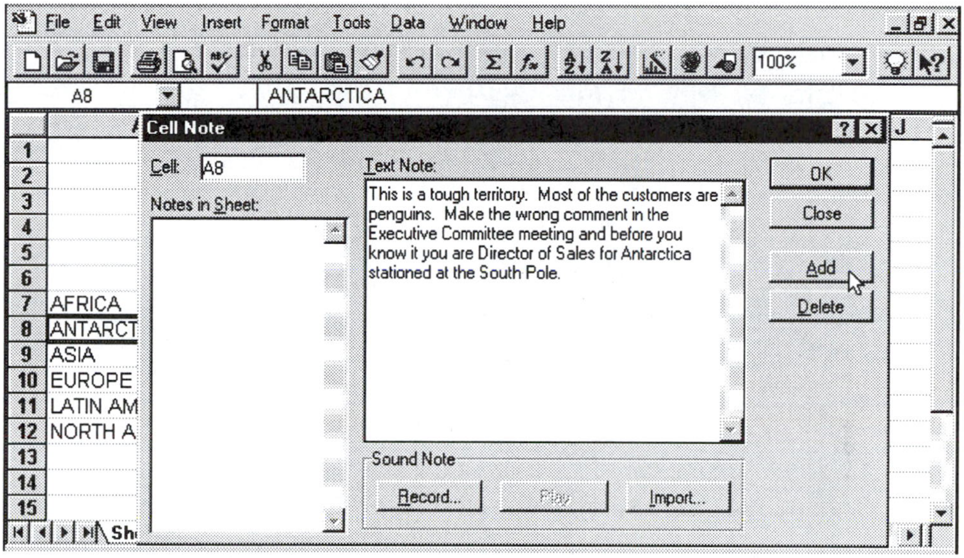

Figure 5-3. Attaching a text note to cell A8.

COPY AND PASTE

You may be familiar with the operations of Copy and Paste from other applications, for example wordprocessing. Copy and Paste is a common method for moving information from one place to another.

The basic idea is that there is a usually hidden part of the computer's memory called the **Clipboard**. The Clipboard holds the most recent information that was Copied (or Cut).

To Copy information into the Clipboard, first select the information by clicking on it or dragging across it and then select *Copy* in the *Edit* pull-down menu or click on the **Copy button** on the Standard toolbar.

The copied information is held temporarily in the Clipboard.

To Paste the information from the Clipboard into the worksheet, select the destination cell or range in the worksheet. Then select *Paste* in the *Edit* pull-down menu or click on the **Paste button** in the Standard toolbar.

The information will be pasted from the Clipboard into the worksheet.

Copy and Paste can be used to fill a formula down a column. In Figure 5-4, we click on the Copy button to copy the contents of cell H7 into the Clipboard. We select cells H8:H12 by dragging down them and clicking on the Paste button. The result is shown in Figure 5-5. The formula from cell H7 has been copied and then pasted down column H. Note that this is an "intelligent" Copy and Paste, so the addresses in the formula have been adjusted.

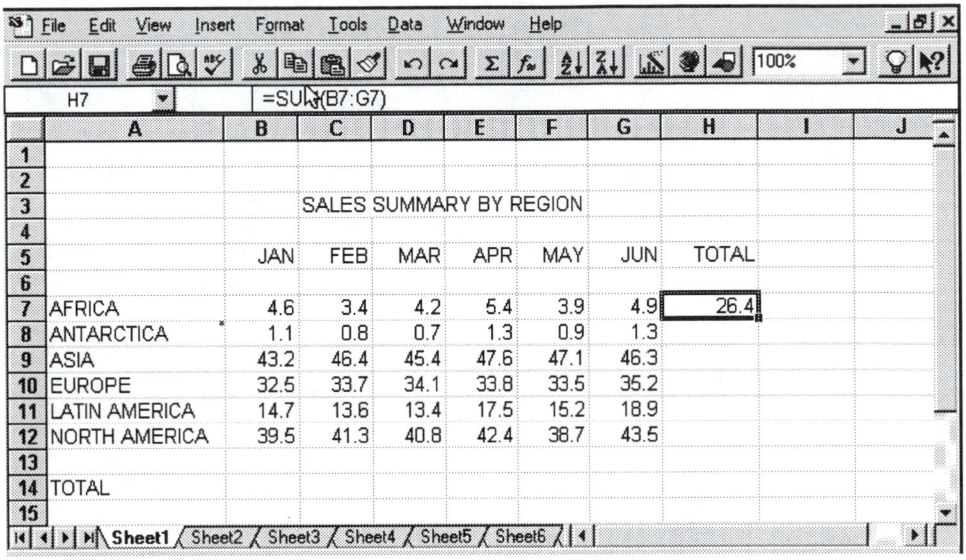

Figure 5-4. Click on cell H7 to select it. Then click on the Copy button to copy the formula in H7 into the Clipboard.

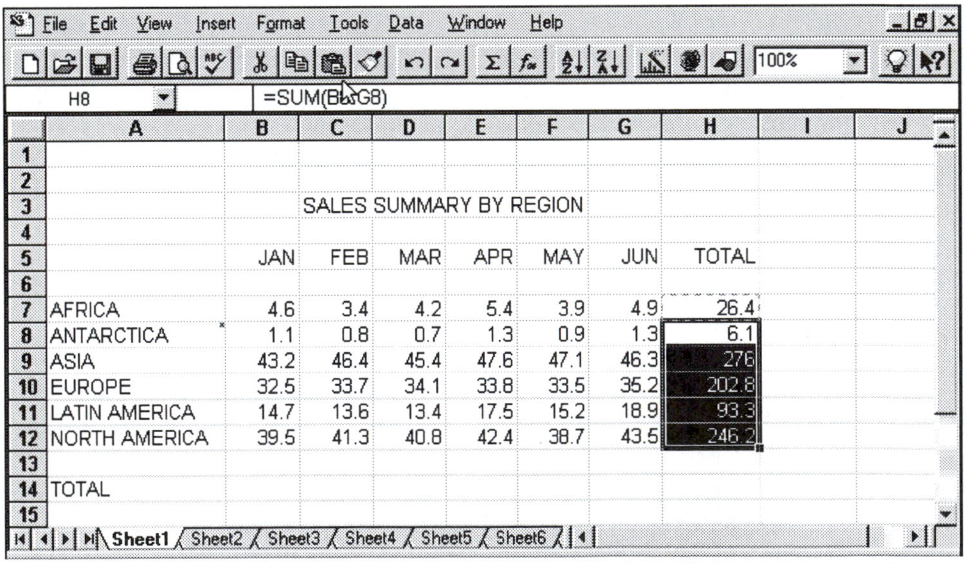

Figure 5-5. Drag down across H8:H12 to select these cells. Click on the Paste button. The formula will be pasted from the Clipboard into the cells with the addresses adjusted.

In this instance we are using Copy and Paste as a substitute for dragging the Fill Handle, as a substitute for the Fill operation. Copy and Paste is more general than Fill because you can paste copied information anywhere in your workbook, or into any other workbook, or into any other program for that matter.

For example, we could copy the names of the regions in column A into the Clipboard by selecting A7:A12, by dragging across those cells, and then by clicking on the Copy button. Next we could scroll over to column T and click on cell T7. Now if we click on the Paste button, the names will be pasted from the Clipboard into cells T7:T12.

PASTE SPECIAL

When we use the normal Paste operation, as in Figure 5-5, formulas are pasted into the cells. The *Paste Special* selection in the *Edit* pull-down menu gives us several other options, as shown in Figure 5-6.

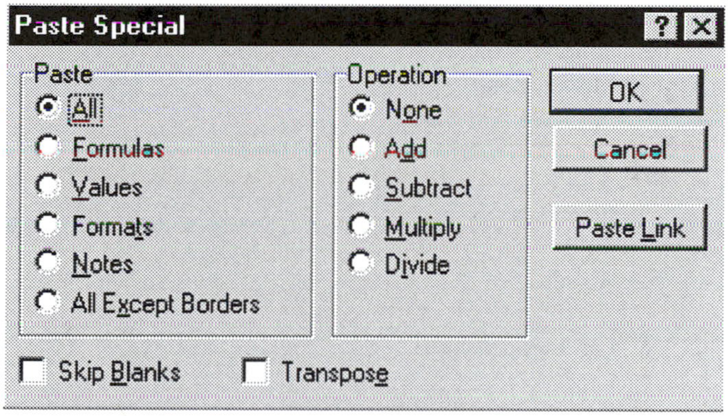

Figure 5-6. The Paste Special dialog box.

For example, we might want to paste the current values in the copied cells, rather than the formulas. And, we might want to add those values into the current values in the cells to which we are pasting.

COMPUTER EXERCISE

5-1. We Love Plants, Inc. is a small company in the houseplant care business. People can arrange for the company to come into their apartment or house to care for their plants when they are away on business or on vacation or all-year around. The company has begun offering the same service to businesses and offices.

The most recent Income Statement for the company looks as follows.

WE LOVE PLANTS, INC.
Income Statement
For the Year Ended December 31

Revenues:		
Home plant care revenue	$197,329	
Office plant care revenue	65,545	
Total Revenues		$262,874
Expenses:		
Salaries expense	72,488	
Payroll tax expense	9,803	
Rent expense for office	7,800	
Utilities expense	1,377	
Advertising expense	23,103	
Automobile expense	35,292	
Supplies expense	24,550	
Misc. expense	8,500	
Total Expenses		$182,913
Pretax Income		$79,961
Income tax expense		15,992
Net income		$63,969
Earnings per share		$1.60

The company pays 20% in income taxes. There are 40,000 shares of stock.

(a) Create a "template" worksheet for the Income Statement where each of the numbers in the middle column is 0. All of the numbers in the right column should be the results of formulas and should appear as 0 also. The numbers should be formatted as they appear above. Save the worksheet on the disk.

(b) Now fill in the numbers in the middle column. The numbers in the right column should match. Save the worksheet. Print the worksheet.

(c) Move the entire range of cells with entries over two columns to the right and one column down by selecting the range and dragging it.

(d) Erase the first four of the expenses categories and values by selecting the range containing the cells and dragging the Fill Handle back over the range.

(e) Undo the erase.

(f) Delete columns A and B. (They should be empty as the result of the move in part (c).)

(g) Insert a new row in the middle of the expenses. Enter in Insurance Expense 7,300.

(h) Attach the annotation "We need to get better control of these" to the cell for Misc. Expense.

(i) Select the information in the rightmost two columns by dragging across it. Then click on the Copy button or select *Copy* in the *Edit* pull-down menu. Click on the cell two columns to the right of the top right cell of the copied range. Now click on the Paste button or select *Paste* in the *Edit* pull-down menu to paste a new copy of the information two columns over. This could be used as the basis for entering in next year's income statement to compare it with this year's.

(j) Erase the information just pasted either by selecting Undo or by erasing the range of cells.

(k) Save the worksheet on the disk.

(l) Format the worksheet so that it looks as attractive as possible. Save the worksheet again.

(m) Print the worksheet.

CHAPTER 6

RELATIVE VS. ABSOLUTE ADDRESSING

OBJECTIVES

In this chapter you will learn how to:

- Use absolute addressing in formulas
- Create worksheets for "What if" analysis
- Use the split bars to split the window
- Name cells and ranges of cells
- Use mixed addressing in formulas

What makes the Fill (or Copy and Paste) operation so powerful in making multiple copies of formulas is that Excel adjusts the addresses in the formulas as it makes the copies. For example, if the formula in H7 is =SUM(C7:G7) and we fill the formula down the column, then the formula in H8 will be =SUM(C8:G8), the formula in H9 will be =SUM(C9:G9), and so on. In Chapter 4, we referred to this as an "intelligent" Fill operation. The Fill operation as described usually works well. However, there are some cases where we do not want the address in the formula to be adjusted as the formula is filled, where changing the address causes an error in the formula. In this important chapter we will examine how to instruct Excel not to change an address in a formula when filling the formula down a column or across a row.

AN EXAMPLE WHERE THE FILL OPERATION SEEMS TO FAIL

We would like to know the proportion of the world's population in each continent. Some research yields the population for each continent shown in the worksheet in Figure 6-1.

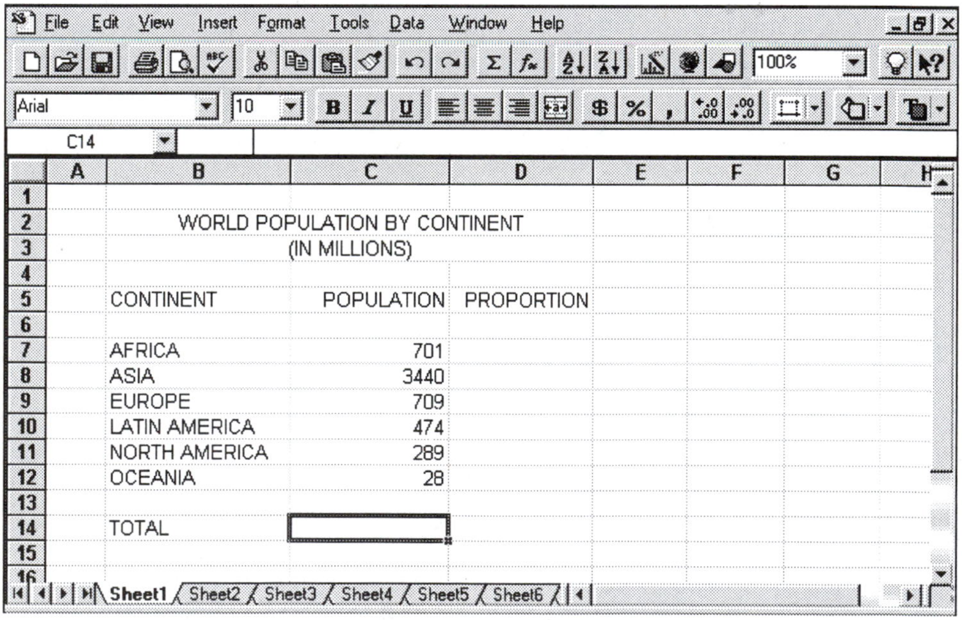

Figure 6-1. A worksheet for determining the proportion of the world population in each continent. Mexico is included as part of Latin America in these figures.

To find the total population on the planet we put the formula

$$=SUM(C7:C12)$$

into cell C14. There are approximately 5,641 million people on the planet, of whom 701 million live in Africa. To calculate the proportion of people in Africa, we divide the population of Africa by the total population for the planet. The formula in D7 can be

$$=C7/C14$$

as in Figure 6-2. Thus, 0.1242, or approximately one-eighth, of the world's population lives in Africa.

Now we would like to Fill the formula down the column to calculate the proportion of the world's population living in each of the other continents. We click on D7 to select the cell. We move the mouse pointer over the Fill Handle in the bottom right of the cell and drag the Fill Handle down the column to D12. When we release the mouse button, the formula is filled down into D8:D12. Here is the key point. Filling the formula in D7 down the column yields the worksheet in Figure 6-3.

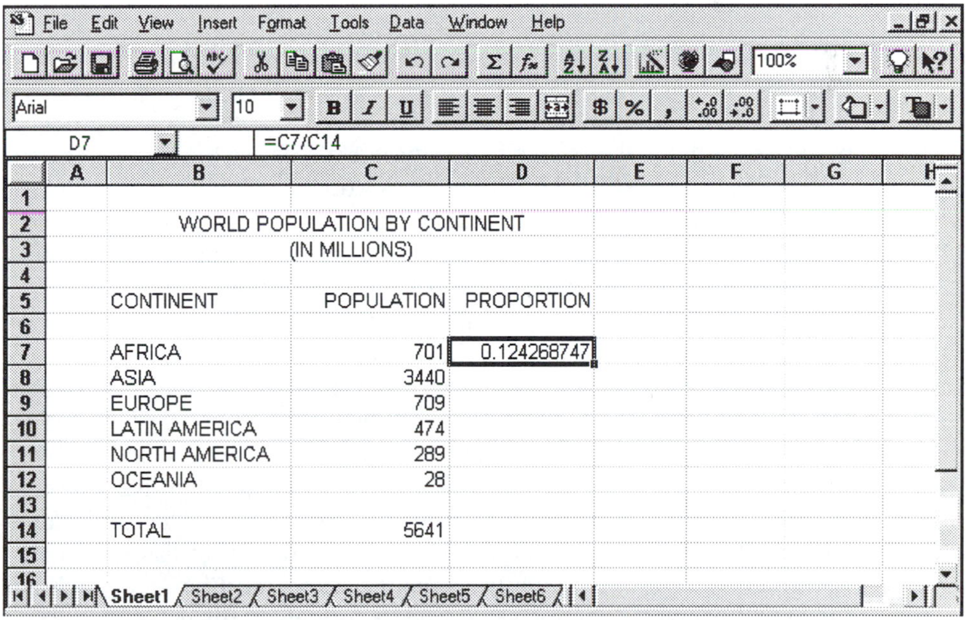

Figure 6-2. To find the proportion of the population in Africa, divide the Africa Population by the Total Population.

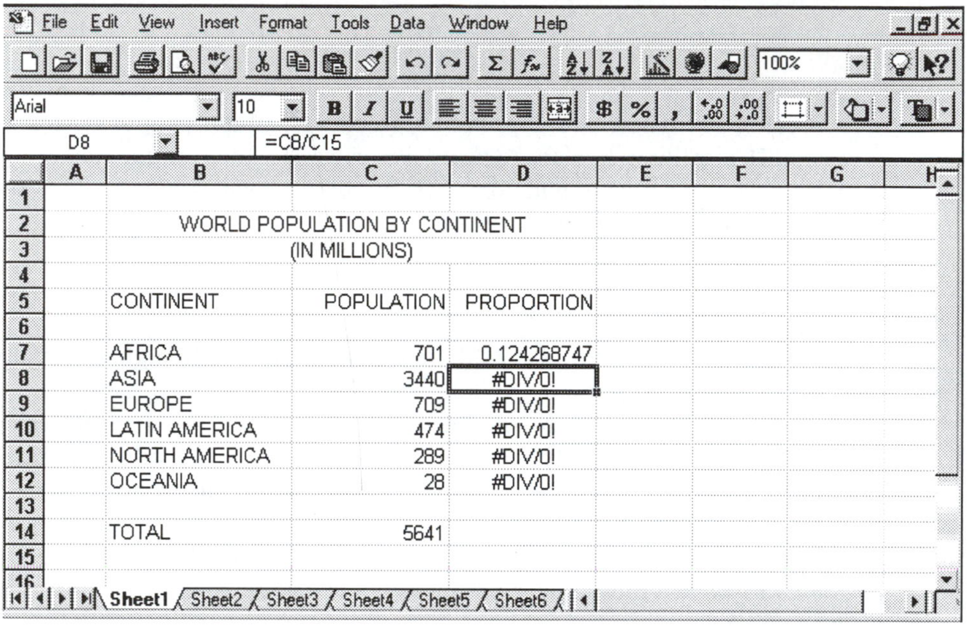

Figure 6-3. Filling down the formula just entered in D7 produces a very instructive error.

What has happened? The cells into which we filled the formula are full of #DIV/0! messages. These are error messages that indicate that we instructed Excel to divide a value by 0. Division by 0 is undefined and, so, produces an error message. What is the source of the problem? If we look at the formula in D8, we see that it is =C8/C15. The C8 is correct. But C15 is a blank cell. In evaluating the formula =C8/C15 the computer divides 3440, the number in C8, by 0, the "number" in C15. Dividing any number by 0 yields the error message.

What should the formula in D8 be? We would like it to be the population of Asia divided by the total population, =C8/C14, rather than =C8/C15. What happened in Figure 6-3? When the formula =C7/C14 in cell D7 was filled down the column, both of the addresses were adjusted by the Fill operation. So =C7/C14 in D7 became =C8/C15 in D8 became =C9/C16 in D9, and so on. We wanted =C7/C14 in D7 to become =C8/C14 in D8 to become =C9/C14 in D9, and so on. That is, we want the Fill operation to adjust the first address C7 in the formula in =C7/C14 but not the second address, C14. The cell address for the total population, C14, should remain unchanged. Excel has an "intelligent" Fill operation but not a brilliant Fill operation. Excel must be told which addresses to adjust and which to keep the same when a formula is filled.

ABSOLUTE ADDRESSING

An address written in the normal way (for example, C14) automatically is adjusted by Excel and is called a **relative address** or **relative reference**. To instruct Excel that an address in a formula is not to be changed when copied, the address is written with dollar signs before the column name and row name, for example, as $C$14. An address that is not to be adjusted when copied is called an **absolute address** or **absolute reference**. The dollar signs have nothing to do with money or currency here. For reasons not apparent, the dollar signs were selected to denote an absolute address.

Returning to our example, now we see that the formula in cell D7 should be written

$$=C7/\$C\$14$$

When filled down the column, this formula becomes =C8/$C$14 in D8, which becomes =C9/$C$14 in D9, and so on, as in Figure 6-4. The $C$14 is evaluated in the formula just the same as is C14, as the value in cell C14. The only difference in using an absolute address rather than a relative address occurs when the formula is filled or copied and pasted.

	A	B	C	D	E	F	G	H
1								
2		WORLD POPULATION BY CONTINENT						
3		(IN MILLIONS)						
4								
5		CONTINENT	POPULATION	PROPORTION				
6								
7		AFRICA	701	0.124268747				
8		ASIA	3440	0.609820954				
9		EUROPE	709	0.125686935				
10		LATIN AMERICA	474	0.084027655				
11		NORTH AMERICA	289	0.051232051				
12		OCEANIA	28	0.004963659				
13								
14		TOTAL	5641					
15								
16								

Figure 6-4. We do not want the reference to cell C14 to be adjusted when the formula in D7 is filled down so we use absolute addressing.

Why are the terms "relative address" and "absolute address" used? Consider, again, the original formula in cell D7 in Figure 6-2. The formula =C7/C14 in D7 can be interpreted as "Take the number one column to the left and divide it by the number in the cell one columns to the left and seven rows down" because the addresses are adjusted when the formula is filled or copied. Hence, the addresses C7 and C14 are "relative addresses". In contrast, the formula =C7/$C$14 in D7 can be interpreted as "Take the number one column to the left and divide it by the number in cell C14" because the address C7 is adjusted as the formula is copied but the address $C$14 remains the same. Hence, the address C7 is relative, but the address $C$14 is absolute.

To complete the example, we format the cells in column D as Percent with one decimal place and add up the percentages in D14. We change the size and style of some of the text. We add some borders and coloring. The final worksheet is shown in Figure 6-5. Well over half the world's population lives in Asia.

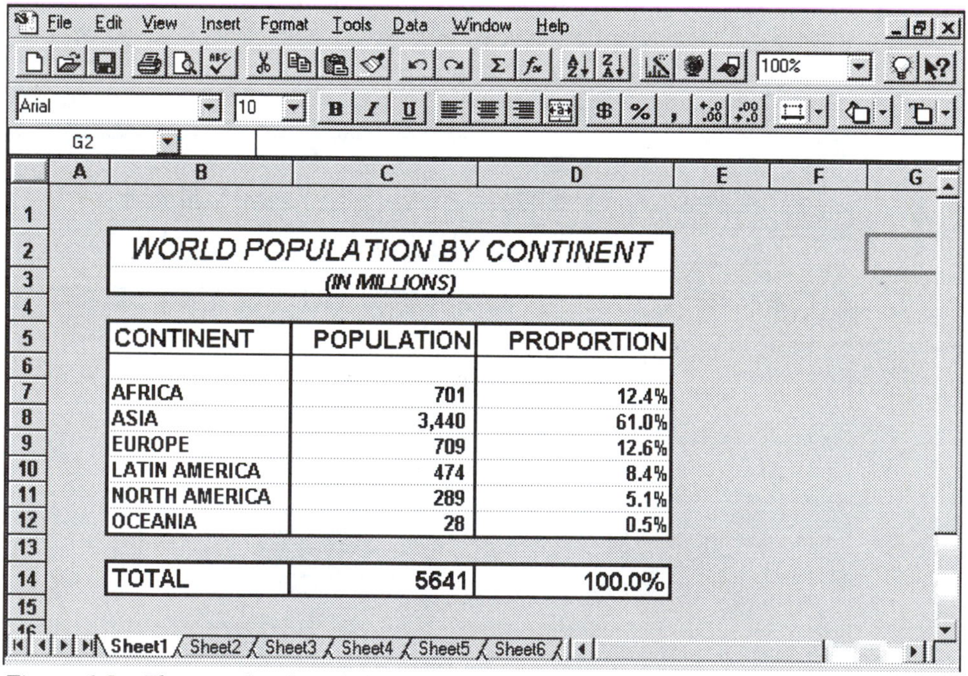
File Edit View Insert Format Tools Data Window Help
Arial
10
100%
G2
WORLD POPULATION BY CONTINENT
(IN MILLIONS)
CONTINENT POPULATION PROPORTION
AFRICA 701 12.4%
ASIA 3,440 61.0%
EUROPE 709 12.6%
LATIN AMERICA 474 8.4%
NORTH AMERICA 289 5.1%
OCEANIA 28 0.5%
TOTAL 5641 100.0%
Sheet1 Sheet2 Sheet3 Sheet4 Sheet5 Sheet6

Figure 6-5. The completed worksheet for calculating the percentage of the population on each continent.

PETER MINUIT

Absolute addressing is especially important in worksheets where key numbers are put into separate cells. To illustrate this, let's do another example.

Peter Minuit was the director-general of the Dutch West Indies Company's settlements in North America. In 1626 he negotiated a deal with local tribal chiefs and purchased the island of Manhattan from them for pieces of bright cloth, beads, and other trinkets valued at 60 guilders, or about $24. Today the island of Manhattan forms the core of New York City and is worth a fortune. But did Peter make such a great deal? Suppose Peter had taken the money and put it into a Money Market Account at the Dutch National Bank. How much would it be worth today? What would be the value of the investment each year from 1626 to 2000?

We need one more piece of information. What interest rate would Peter have received on his money over 365 years? For now, let us assume a constant 3% per year. We will change this assumption later.

Figure 6-6 is a start toward a worksheet that calculates what Peter's investment would be worth.

In the worksheet, the years from 1626 through 2000 will be in column B.

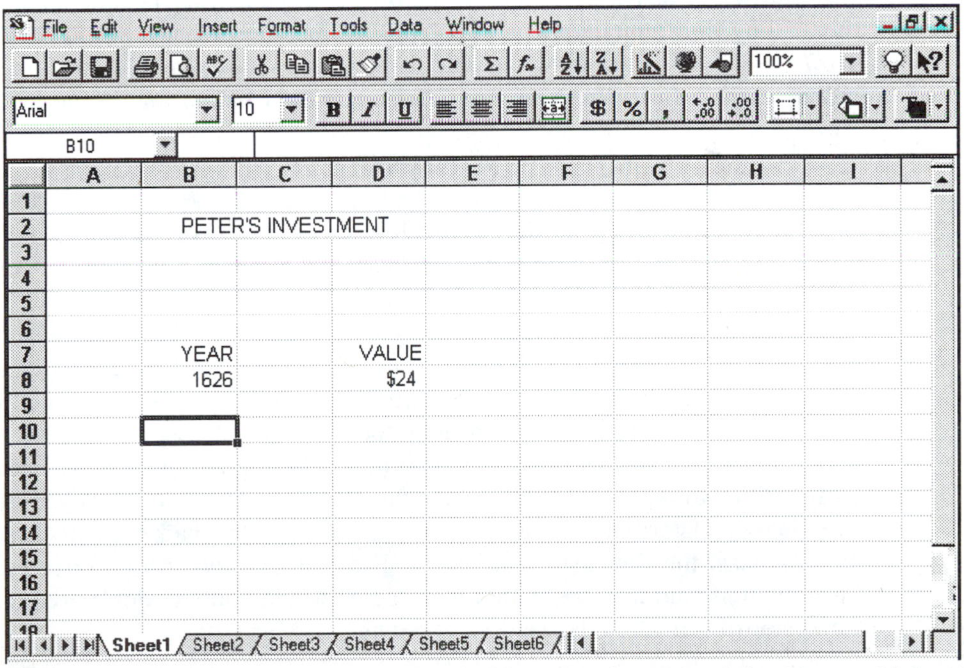

Figure 6-6. Beginning the worksheet to calculate what the value of the $24 would be if Peter Minuit had deposited it in a bank instead of purchasing Manhattan island.

The corresponding value of the investment each year will be in column D.

How can we obtain the years in column B? We could type each one of them, but who wants to type 375 numbers? We could enter 1627 in cell B9 and then use AutoFill as discussed at the end of Chapter 4. Another solution is to put a formula into B9 and then fill the formula down the column. Each number in column B is to be one greater than the number in the cell above. So in cell B9 we will put the formula

$$=B8+1$$

We then fill the formula down the column through B382. To do this, we click on B9, grab the Fill Handle in the bottom right of the cell by pressing down on the mouse button, and with the button held down we move the mouse pointer down column B below the bottom of the worksheet, forcing the worksheet to scroll down to B382. We then release the mouse button. Formulas will fill from B9 through B382. The formula in B10 will be =B9+1, the formula in B11 will be =B10+1, and so on. There will be a chain of formulas down the column, each adding one to the value of the cell above. The years from 1626 through 2000 will appear in column B.

How can we obtain the value of the investment each year in column D? We will follow the same technique of entering a formula for the cell in row 9 and then filling the formula down the column. How much money would Peter have in 1627? Peter would have the amount from the previous year plus the interest the money earned during the year. At 3% interest the formula for D9 would be

$$=D8+D8*3\%$$

We fill the formula from D9 down through D382. We format the values in column D as Currency with 0 decimal places, and widen the cells in column D. The resulting worksheet is shown in Figure 6-7.

Scrolling down to row 382, we can see the bottom of the worksheet in Figure 6-8. What would Peter's $24 investment in 1626 be worth today if he received 3% interest per year? A little over a million dollars. What does a little more than a million dollars buy in Manhattan today? A condo, an apartment in a nice building. It appears that Peter was wise in purchasing Manhattan. (Of course, the British fleet took over the city from the Dutch in 1664 and changed the name from New Amsterdam to New York. If the 60 guilders had been invested in the bank, at least the Dutch still would have had their money. And, in true New York fashion, it is said that the chiefs who "sold" Manhattan to Peter were from the Canarsie tribe in Brooklyn and had no claim to Manhattan.)

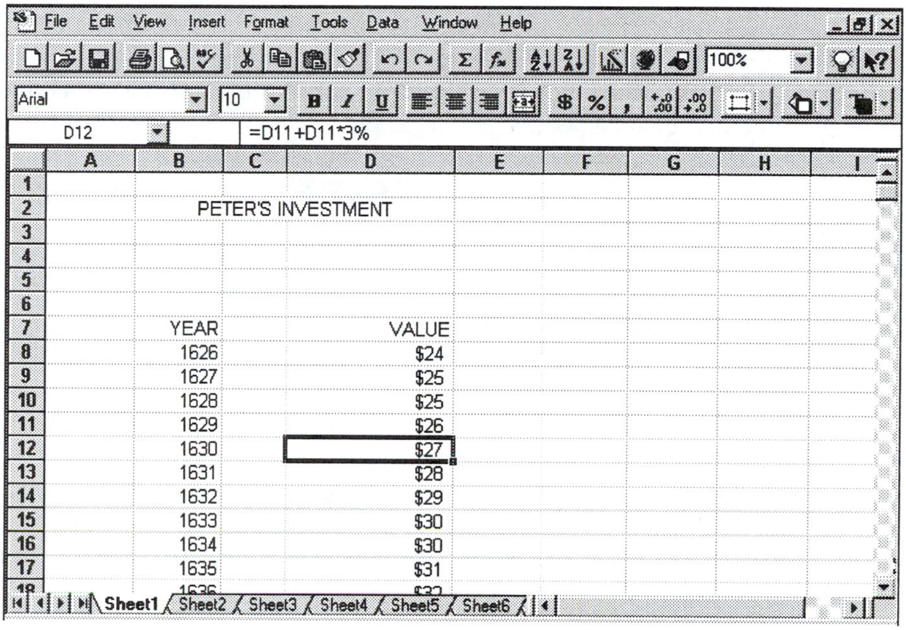

Figure 6-7. Calculating the value of the investment assuming a 3% interest rate.

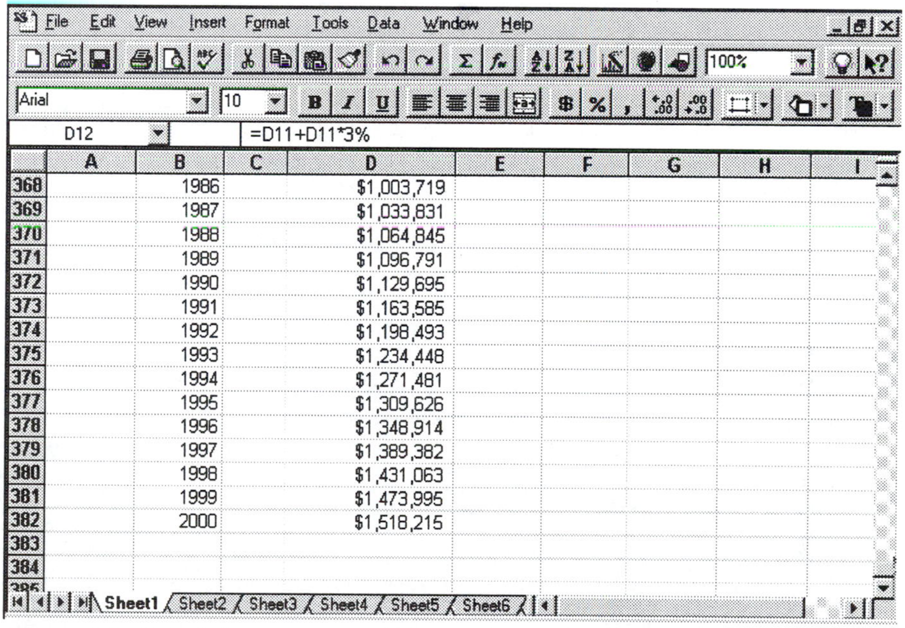

Figure 6-8. Peter's investment would be worth over $1,000,000 today at 3% interest. Not much.

But what if Peter had received 5% annual interest rate instead of 3%? What would Peter's account be worth now? To answer this question we need to change the worksheet. In particular, we need to change the formulas in column D. The formula in D9 could be changed to

$$=D8+D8*5\%$$

Then the formula would be filled down to D382. But suppose we then wanted to see what the value of the investment would be if the annual interest rate were 7% or 9% or 11%. In order to change the interest rate we would have to change the formula in D9 and then fill the new formula down the column each time.

A better approach is to put the interest rate in a separate cell and refer to that cell in the formulas in column D. Now if we want to see what would happen with a different interest rate, we would just need to change the number in the cell rather than changing all 375 formulas. This approach is shown in Figure 6-9.

This worksheet illustrates a good general rule: Any value that you might want to change should be placed in a separate cell, rather than being built explicitly into formulas.

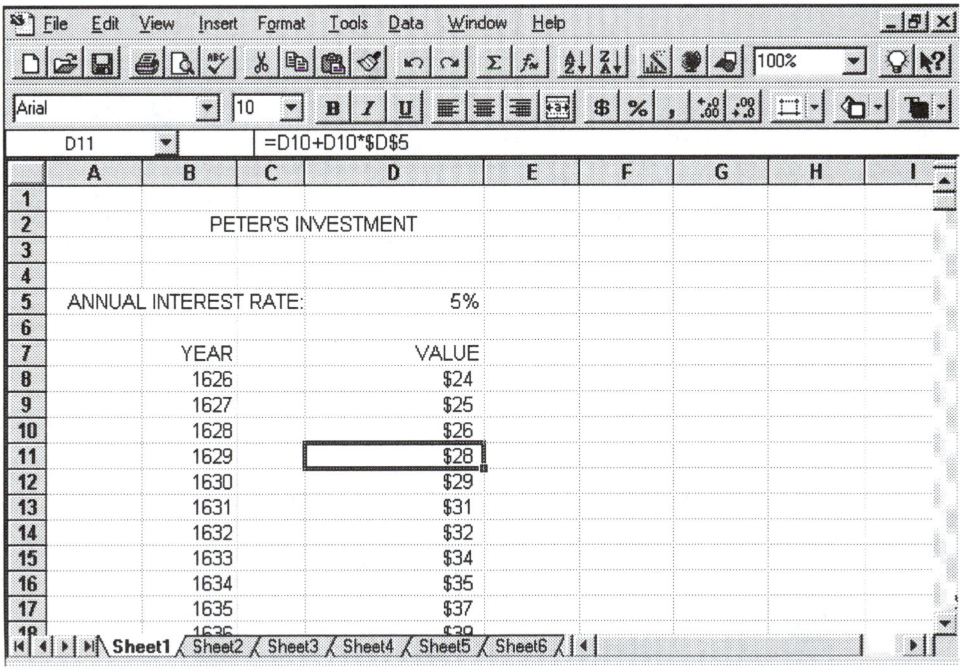

Figure 6-9. A better approach is to place the annual interest rate in a separate cell and refer to the cell in the formulas using absolute addressing.

The Annual Interest Rate is in cell D5, which has been formatted to percentage with 2 decimal places. The formula in D9 is

$$=D8+D8*\$D\$5$$

This formula has been filled from D9 down through D382. We refer to the interest rate as an absolute address ($D$5) so that the address is not adjusted as the formula is filled down the column. In Figure 6-9 the cursor is on D11 and indeed we can see that the formula in D11 is

$$=D10+D10*\$D\$5$$

SPLITTING THE WINDOW

Wouldn't it be nice to be able to change the interest rate and be able to see immediately the resulting value of the investment today? Excel has a **Horizontal Split Bar** and a **Vertical Split Bar**. The Horizontal Split Bar is the small horizontal black rectangle right above the up scroll arrow. The Vertical Split Bar is the small vertical black rectangle to the right of the right scroll arrow.

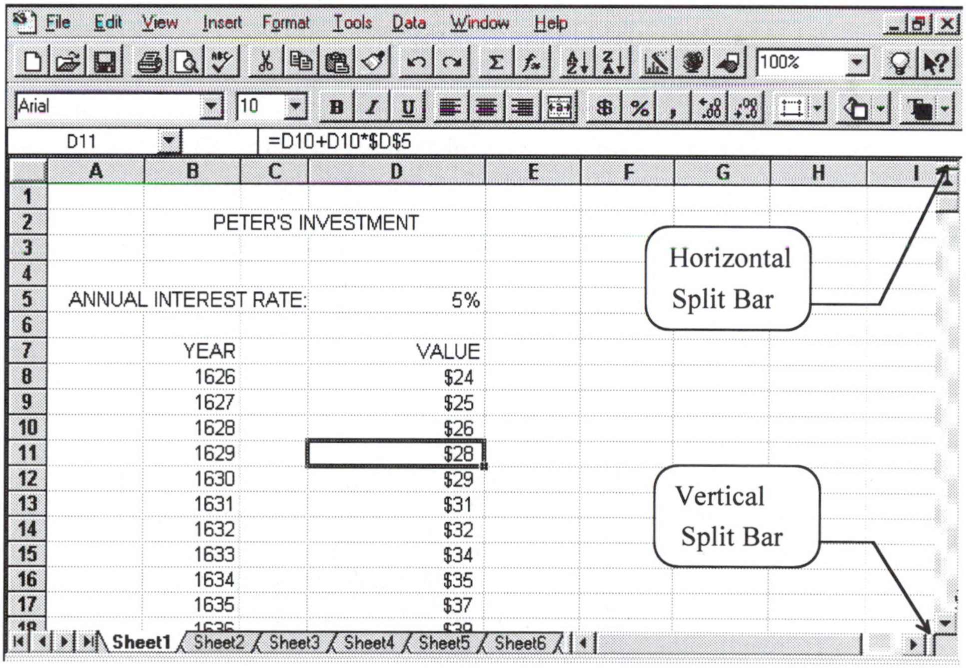

Figure 6-10. The locations of the Horizontal and Vertical Split Bars.

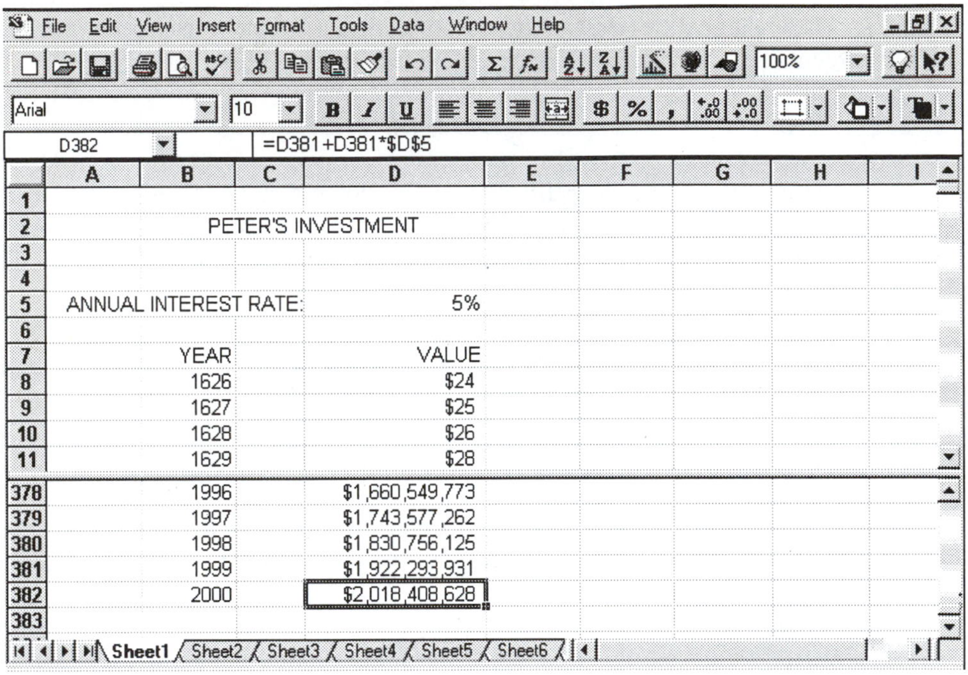

Figure 6-11. The Horizontal Split Bar allows the display of two parts of the worksheet at once.

Dragging the Horizontal Split Bar down allows us to split the window in half. Each portion can be vertically scrolled independently. By scrolling the bottom portion down to row 378 we can see the two portions of the screen shown in Figure 6-11. At 5% interest Peter's $24 investment in 1626 would be worth almost $2 billion today. With almost $2 billion you could buy some major office buildings in Manhattan and a nice hotel or two.

In Chapter 1 we discussed how electronic spreadsheets were developed to facilitate "What if" analysis. Here is an example. We can easily determine "What if" Peter received some annual interest rate on his investment. To see "What if" we change the number in D5 to the annual interest rate we wish to try. As soon as we enter the new rate, the new values for the investment go rippling down the screen. With the worksheet designed so that the annual interest rate is in a separate cell and with the window divided into two portions, we can change the interest rate to 7% and see almost instantaneously that if Peter had invested $24 in 1626 at 7% annual interest, it would be worth about $2 trillion today. (See Figure 6-12.) Now we're talking about some money!

To remove the split in the window, we simply drag the Horizontal Split Bar back up to the top of the worksheet.

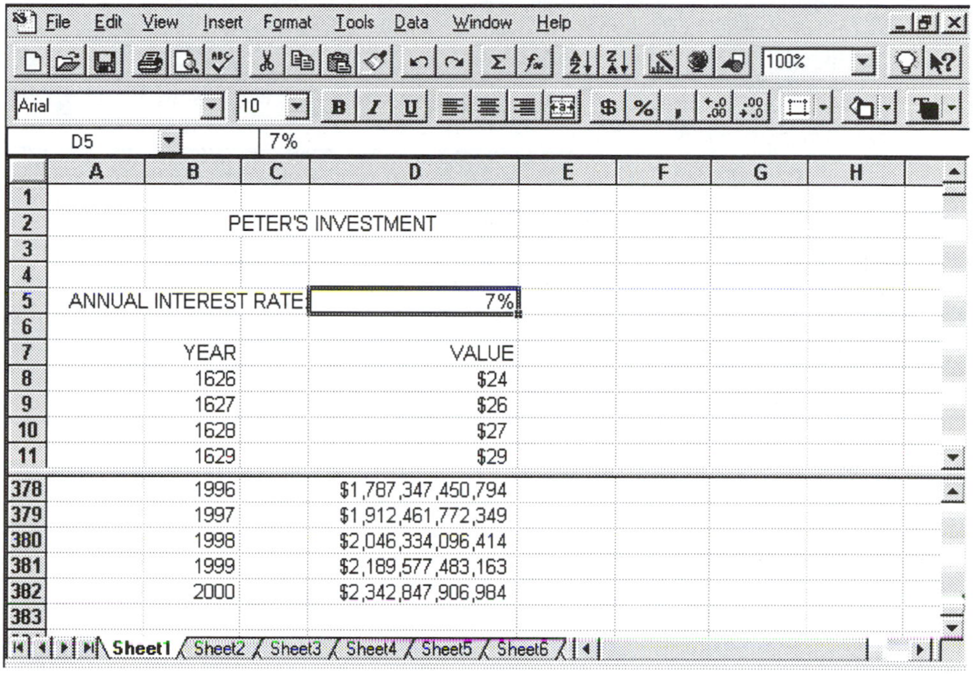

Figure 6-12. At 7% interest you might prefer the bank account over Manhattan island. What would 9% produce? 11%?

NAMING CELLS

In larger worksheets it is easy to forget which cells contain which quantities. When reading the formulas in a larger worksheet it can be cumbersome to determine which quantities are referred to by cell addresses in the formulas. Excel provides the capability of giving names to cells and ranges of cells and using these names in formulas instead of the cell addresses. It is good practice to name key cells in larger worksheets.

For example, in this worksheet we could give cell D5 the name INTEREST_RATE. Then the formula in cell D9 would be

$$=D8+D8*INTEREST\_RATE$$

rather than

$$=D8+D8*\$D\$5$$

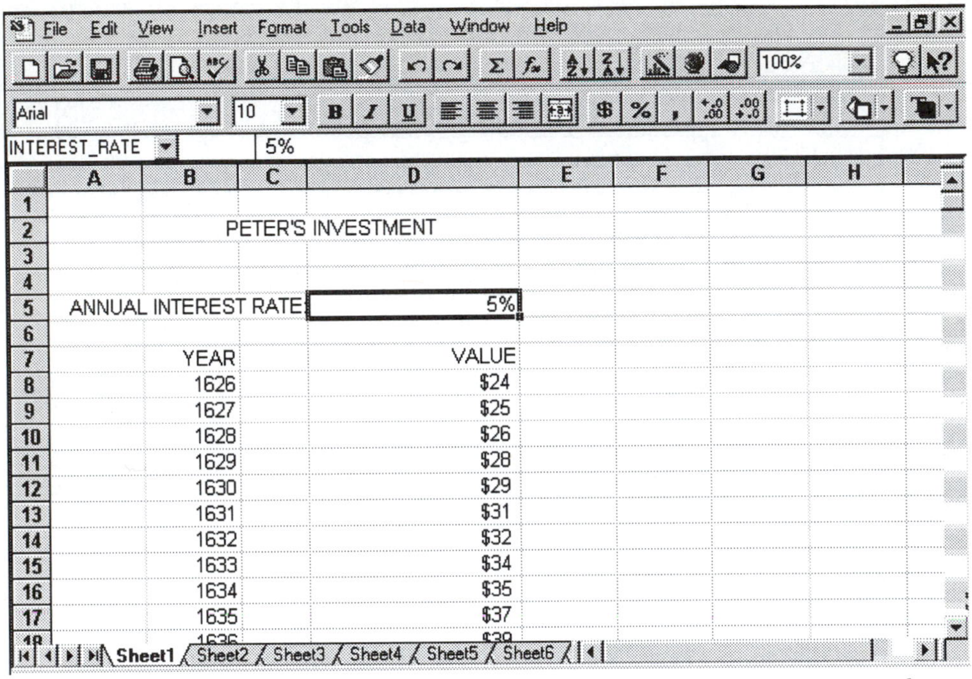

Figure 6-13. To give a name to cell D5, select D5 and then click in the Name Bar at the top left of the worksheet and type in the desired name, in this case INTEREST_RATE.

To give cell D5 a name, we first select D5 by clicking on it. Then we click in the **Name Bar**. The Name Bar is the box right above the A column heading. In the Name Bar we type the new name of the cell, as in Figure 16-13.

The name can contain up to 255 characters. It should begin with a letter. The name can contain letters, digits, and underscores (_) but not spaces or arithmetic operators or most punctuation characters. Do be careful in naming ranges. Select a name that makes sense, that you will remember.

To use a name in a formula we can simply type the name instead of the cell address. Alternatively we can select from the list of drop-down names in the **Name Menu** by clicking on the down arrow on the right of the Name Bar and then selecting from the list of names we have defined that appears there. In Figure 6-14 we have begun entering the formula in D9. Instead of typing the address of the interest rate or the name INTEREST_RATE, we select the name INTEREST_RATE from the drop-down Name Menu.

Excel assumes that a name refers to an absolute address. In this case, Excel assumes that the name INTEREST_RATE refers to the absolute address $D$5. So if we use the name in a formula and then fill the formula, the name will continue to refer to the same cell in the filled copies of the formula. (See Figure 6-15.)

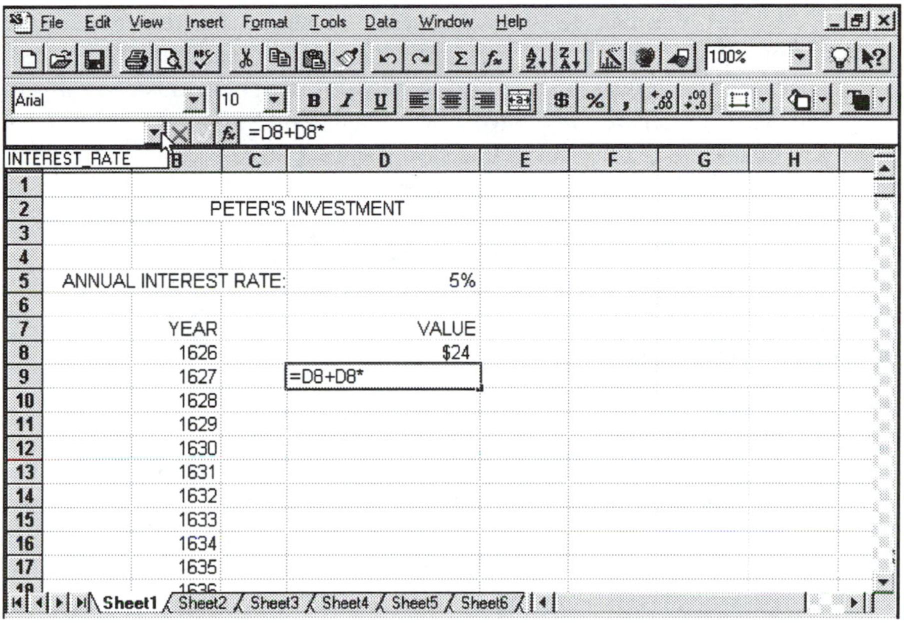

Figure 6-14. The names of cells appear in the drop-down menu below the Name Box. We can enter a name into a formula from the menu instead of typing the name.

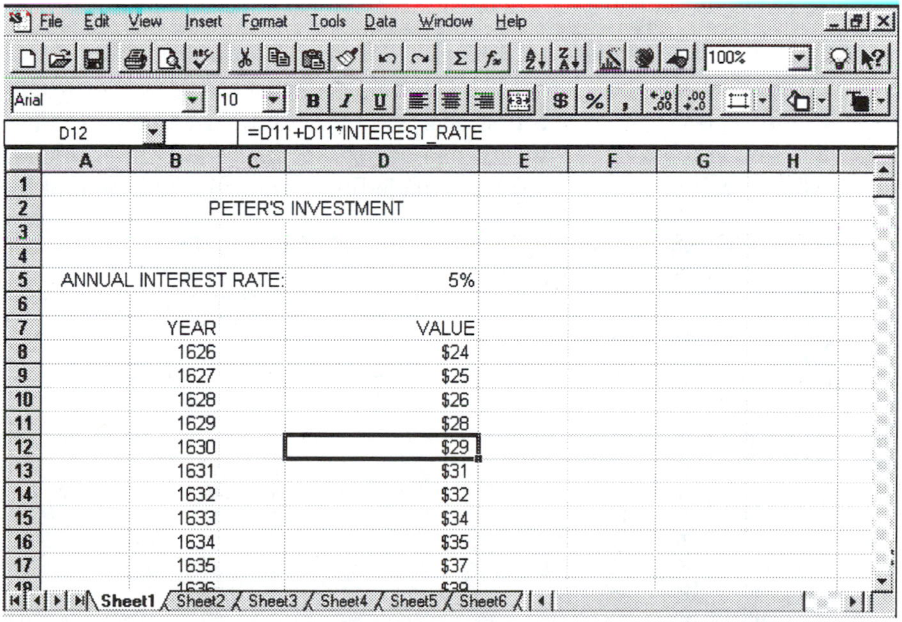

Figure 6-15. The name INTEREST_RATE is treated as an absolute reference to the cell D5. The reference is unchanged after the formula is filled down.

Names also can be given to ranges of cells. For example, in the sales by region worksheet in the previous chapter we could have selected the range B7:G12 and given it the name SALES. Then instead of the formula =SUM(B7:G12) we could have written =SUM(SALES).

It also is possible to define new names in Excel using *Define* in the *Name* selection of the *Insert* pull-down menu.

Incidentally, names in Excel are "case insensitive". This means that the name SALES is the same as Sales which is the same as sales.

MIXED ADDRESSING

On occasion we might want the column part of the address of a cell in a formula to remain absolute and the row part of the address to be relative. Or we might want the column part of the address of a cell in a formula to be relative and the row part of the address to be absolute. An address in a formula that is to be absolute in one part and relative in the other dimension is called a **mixed address** or **mixed reference**.

The worksheet in Figure 6-16 illustrates a double use of mixed addressing. Each cell in the range B3:M12 is the product of the number in column A for the row and the number in row 2 for the column. Thus the formula in B3 is =$A3*B$2. The body of the table is produced by filling that formula across from B3 through M3 and then filling all of those formulas down from B3:M3 to B3:M12. As a check on your understanding, what would be the resulting formula in, say, cell G11? In the first address in the formula column A is absolute while the row is relative. In the second address in the formula the column is relative while row 2 is absolute. So the formula filled into cell G11 would be =$A11*G$2.

	A	B	C	D	E	F	G	H	I	J	K	L	M
1		Multiplication Table											
2		1	2	3	4	5	6	7	8	9	10	11	12
3	1	1	2	3	4	5	6	7	8	9	10	11	12
4	2	2	4	6	8	10	12	14	16	18	20	22	24
5	3	3	6	9	12	15	18	21	24	27	30	33	36
6	4	4	8	12	16	20	24	28	32	36	40	44	48
7	5	5	10	15	20	25	30	35	40	45	50	55	60
8	6	6	12	18	24	30	36	42	48	54	60	66	72
9	7	7	14	21	28	35	42	49	56	63	70	77	84
10	8	8	16	24	32	40	48	56	64	72	80	88	96
11	9	9	18	27	36	45	54	63	72	81	90	99	108
12	10	10	20	30	40	50	60	70	80	90	100	110	120

*Cell B3 = =$A3*B$2*

Figure 6-16. A simple worksheet that uses mixed addressing.

PENCIL AND PAPER EXERCISE

6-1. The widget industry is dominated by two companies. United Widget (UW) has total sales of $87.2 million this year. However, their sales are decreasing by 0.8% per year. Widgets International (WI) has sales of $53.4 million this year. Their sales are increasing by 3.2% each year. We have developed a worksheet (using Fill) that shows their future performance if this trend continues. The growth rates are in separate cells. Changing one of the growth rates in C4 or D4 causes the predictions to change appropriately.

	A	B	C	D	E	F	G	H	I
1									
2			Widget Industry Forecast						
3									
4		Growth Rate:	-0.8%	3.2%					
5									
6			Year	UW	WI	Total			
7			this year	87.2	53.4	140.6			
8			1	86.5	55.1	141.6			
9			2	85.8	56.9	142.7			
10			3	85.1	58.7	143.8			
11			4	84.4	60.6	145.0			
12			5	83.8	62.5	146.3			
13			6	83.1	64.5	147.6			
14			7	82.4	66.6	149.0			
15			8	81.8	68.7	150.5			
16			9	81.1	70.9	152.0			
17									
18			Total	841.3	617.8	1,459.1			
19									

What is the formula in each of the following cells:
(a) B12
(b) C12
(c) D12
(d) E12
(e) C18
(f) E18

COMPUTER EXERCISES

6-2. There are eight students in your math class. They all took a quiz. Enter the eight names in one column and eight (different) scores in an adjoining column. At the bottom of the column calculate the class average. Now add a new column that calculates the points above or below the class average for each student. Use the Fill operation. Change one of the scores. Do the class average and all of the points above or below change accordingly?

6-3. In the example in the text on the value of Peter Minuit's investment if he had placed the money in a bank account, we assumed that there would be one interest rate for all 375 years. Set up a worksheet that is similar to the one in the chapter except that it has an extra column for the interest rate. For each year the corresponding cell in the column would give the interest rate for the year. What would be the value of Peter's investment if from 1626 through 1970 he received 3% and from 1971 through now he received 7%?

6-4. The major regions of the earth and their areas in millions of square miles are shown below.

	Area in 1,000,000's of square. miles
Pacific Ocean	64
Atlantic Ocean	33
Indian Ocean	28
Arctic Ocean	5
other oceans	9
Asia	17
Africa	12
North America	9
South America	7
Antarctica	5
Europe	4
Australia	3
other land	1

(a) Enter this data into a worksheet.

(b) Add well-labeled cells for the total area covered by the oceans, the total area covered by land, and the total area of the earth. Name these cells.

(c) Add a column that shows the percentage of the earth covered by each of the 13 regions listed. Use the Fill operation.

(d) Add a column that shows the percentage of the total area covered by ocean that each of the ocean regions occupies. Use the Fill operation.

(e) Add a column that shows the percentage of the total area covered by land that each of the continents occupies. Use the Fill operation.

6-5. You are planning to deposit a fixed amount at the beginning of each year in a bank account for 20 years. Assume that you will earn a constant interest rate on your money. Design and implement a worksheet that will show you how much you will have accumulated at the end of each of the 20 years. You should have separate, well-labeled cells for the amount of your annual deposit and for the interest rate. If you change either of these cells, all the accumulations should change automatically.

Try you worksheet on

(a) a deposit of $5,000 per year and an interest rate of 5% per year,

(b) a deposit of $5,000 per year and an interest rate of 10% per year,

(c) a deposit of $10,000 per year and an interest rate of 5% per year, and

(d) a deposit of $10,000 per year and an interest rate of 10% per year.

(e) How much do you need to deposit each year to have exactly $1,000,000 in 20 years assuming that you earn 8% interest per year? Use trial and error.

(f) What annual interest rate would you need to obtain in order to accumulate $1,000,000 at the end of 20 years if you deposit $10,000 per year? Use trial and error.

6-6. The cost of a college education has been rising rapidly, as I am sure you are aware. You would like to estimate what it will cost you to put your children through college. First we will need to gather some data and make some assumptions. Find out the current cost of attending your favorite college or university in terms of (1) tuition and (2) all other expenses. If you do not have any children now, assume that your first child will be born five years from now and your second child will be born three years later. Assume that your children will enter college at age 18 and that they will attend for four years each and then graduate with high honors. (Of course they will be model students.) Further we will assume that there will be a single annual rate of increase over the years for tuition and other expenses.

Your worksheet will have a separate section at the top for parameters and data that might be changed. In particular, there should be well-labeled cells for current tuition, current other expenses, and rate of increase. The body of the worksheet should have four columns: year, tuition, other expenses, total expenses. The values that appear in these columns will depend in part on the values in the input section of the worksheet. At the bottom (or top) of the worksheet there should be a well-labeled output cell that gives the total projected cost of sending your two children to college.

Try your worksheet with an annual rate of increase of 6%. Now change the annual rate of increase to 9%. Do all of the appropriate numbers change? Don't worry. You will have a terrific job. The money you spend on college expenses for your children will be small change.

6-7. The population of the developed countries of the world was 1,245,000,000 at the end of 1995 and is growing at the rate of 0.4% per year. The population of the developing countries of the world was 4,486,000,000 and is growing at the rate of 1.9% per year.

(a) Create a worksheet to predict the future population if the current trends continue. You should have four input cells at the top of your worksheet: for the two population figures and the two growth rates. You should have four well-labeled columns: for year, population in the developed countries, population in the developing countries, total world population, and percentage of the world population that lives in developing countries. You should have rows for 30 years of projections. Changes in any of the four input cells should ripple through your worksheet. What is the projected world population in the year 2025? What is the percentage of people who will live in the developing countries?

(b) Suppose the population growth rate of the developed countries is 0% for the following 30 years and the growth rate of the developing countries is 2.1%. What would be the world population in the year 2025?

6-8. Paul and Maria are married. Together they earn a salary of $85,000 per year Their plan is to save enough money to retire to Bali for the rest of their lives. They believe that if they could save $500,000 they should be set for life. Their expenses this year totaled $78,000, including taxes, living expenses, and everything else. They have decided to put the rest in a tax-free mutual fund to save up for their retirement.

Now Paul and Maria would like to do some projections to see when they can retire. They estimate that their salaries should go up by 8% per year. They hope to hold their expenses to an increase of 3% per year. Whatever is left at the end of each year, they will put into the account. They figure they should be able to earn interest of 4% per year on the money in the account, which will be accumulated in the mutual fund.

Your job is to set up a financial planning worksheet for Paul and Maria. You should have a separate input area with well-labeled cells for: current salary, current expenses, annual percentage increase for salary, annual percentage increase for expenses, and annual percentage interest rate earned in the mutual fund. Changing any of these numbers should result in changes throughout the worksheet.

The body of the worksheet should be the forecast for the next 25 years. Each row would represent a separate year. There should be separate columns for: Year, Salary, Expenses, Mutual Fund Interest Earned, Deposit in Mutual Fund, Mutual Fund End-of-Year Balance.

Please try your worksheet three times: (1) assume the above numbers, (2) assume salary increases by 5% each year while expenses increase at 5% each year and they earn 5% in their mutual fund, and (3) one showing the percentage increase (or decrease) for expenses required if Paul and Maria wish to retire in only 8 years given that their salaries increase by 10% per year and they earn 6% per year in their mutual fund. This latter case can be solved by trial and error. For each of these last two cases you should need to change only cells in the input area.

6-9. Compsys is a start-up computer company. This quarter they expect Sales of $550,000. They expect their Sales to grow at a rate of 9% per quarter. Their Cost of Goods Sold is running at 34% of Sales and is expected to stay at that rate. Their Selling Costs are 12% of Sales and are expected to stay at that rate. Their General and Administrative Costs (including Research and Development) are $420,000 this quarter and are scheduled to rise at 2% per quarter.

(a) Design and implement a worksheet to make a 20 quarter income statement projection for Compsys. You should have a separate input area with well-labeled separate cells for each of the numbers above. You should have a separate row for each item in the income statement and a separate column for each quarter. The final row should be for Earnings Before Taxes. Use the Fill operation wherever possible.

In the initial quarters, Compsys should show operating losses (negative Earnings Before Taxes). Under the assumptions stated above, what is the first quarter in which Compsys shows an operating profit (positive Earnings Before Taxes)?

(b) Suppose Sales grow at 12% per quarter. Now in what quarter would Compsys first show an operating profit?

(c) Suppose Sales grow at 9% per quarter and General and Administrative Costs grow at 6% per quarter and Selling Costs are 15% of sales. Now in what quarter will Compsys first show an operating profit?

6-10. The Fibonacci series is named after Leonardo Fibonacci, an Italian mathematician of the thirteenth century. The Fibonacci series is an infinite series of numbers 0, 1, 1, 2, 3, 5, 8, 13, ... The first two numbers in the series are 0 and 1. Subsequent numbers are formed by adding the two previous numbers in the series. The Fibonacci series appears in many unexpected places. Indeed, there is a regularly published journal that is devoted to applications of the Fibonacci series.

What proportioned rectangle is the most aesthetically pleasing? What is the ratio of height to width that people most prefer in a rectangle? Since the Renaissance it has been claimed that The Golden Ratio is the most aesthetically pleasing ratio for a rectangle. The Golden Ratio has been shown to appear often in Western art. The Golden Ratio usually is defined as the proportion that results from dividing a line in two sections such that the ratio of the length of the smaller section to the larger section is the same as the ratio of the length of the larger section to the length of the line as a whole. Another way of computing the Golden Ratio is to take the ratio of successive terms of the Fibonacci series. Thus 0/1, 1/1, 1/2, 2/3, 3/5, 5/8, ... form closer and closer approximations of the Golden Ratio. (So, a 3 x 5 card or a 5 x 8 piece of paper should seem to be aesthetically pleasing rectangles.)

Create a worksheet with three well-labeled columns. In the first column should be the numbers 0, 1, 2, 3, 4, through 20. In the second column should be the successive terms of the Fibonacci series. In the third column should be the successive approximations to the Golden Ratio, printed as a decimal between 0 and 1. Use the Fill operation for all three columns.

6-11. Averosas are a new breed of small, furry animal that resemble guinea pigs. They are becoming all the rage as pets. You have decided to earn some extra money by raising averosas in your room. For Christmas you ask Santa Claus to help you out. You must have been good this year because sure enough on Christmas morning under the Christmas tree there is a one-month-old male averosa and a one-month-old female averosa in a cage.

Averosas are quite prolific, and predictably so. They have their first litter at six months of age. Every three months from then on, each female has a litter of on average four baby averosas (assume two males and two females). Of course, these babies will go through the same breeding cycle. At the end of each quarter (three months) you plan to sell all the averosas that have reached two years of age to the local pet stores. This is how you will make your fortune. You won't have any expenses because your roommate works in a restaurant and you figure your roommate can bring home the leftovers from the salad bar to feed the animals.

This sounds like a great scheme but your roommate would like to know (1) how many averosas will be born in your room each quarter and, more important, (2) how many averosas will be living in the room each quarter! You would like to know (3) how many averosas you'll be able to sell at the end of each quarter so you can plan what to do with all the money you'll earn. Incidentally, your roommate will be (somewhat) relieved to learn that averosas don't smell too bad if their cages are cleaned often.

Set up an Excel worksheet to answer these three questions. Assume you will have the averosa colony for the next five years. Of course you will use the Fill operation wherever possible. Use several columns. Label all columns clearly. Assume the quarter ends at January 1, April 1, July 1, and October 1.

Assuming everything goes as planned, what is the total number of averosas you will have owned during the five years? What is the maximum number of averosas that will be in your room at any one time? How long will it be before your roommate leaves?

6-12. The worksheet below gives the interest for different principal amounts and interest rates. The amounts of the interest rates at the tops of the columns in row 6 are determined by the entries in F2 and H2. For example, if the number in H2 is changed to 1.5%, the values in row 6 would change to 5.0%, 6.5%, 8.0%, 9.5%, 11.0%, 12.5%, 14.0%, and 15.5%, and the values in B8:I16 would change accordingly. Similarly, the values in A8:A16 are determined by the entries in F3 and H3. Thus B6:I6 and A8:A16 contain formulas as do B8:I16. The formulas in B8:I16 were created by filling an original formula in B8 and contain formulas with mixed addressing. Your task is to reconstruct the worksheet below accordingly. Use the Fill operation. The only inputs to your worksheet should be the four cells in white: F2, H2, F3, and H3. All other numbers are calculated by formulas.

Change the Principal Start (F3) to $900 and the Principal Increment (H3) to $150. Do all of the numbers in the table change appropriately? Change the Interest Rate Start to 8% and the Interest Rate Increment to 2%. Do all of the numbers in the table change appropriately?

	A	B	C	D	E	F	G	H	I
1						Start		Increment	
2	INTEREST TABLE			Interest Rate:		5.0%		1.0%	
3				Principal:		$10,000		$2,000	
4									
5			Interest Rate						
6		5.0%	6.0%	7.0%	8.0%	9.0%	10.0%	11.0%	12.0%
7	Principal								
8	$10,000	500	600	700	800	900	1000	1100	1200
9	$12,000	600	720	840	960	1080	1200	1320	1440
10	$14,000	700	840	980	1120	1260	1400	1540	1680
11	$16,000	800	960	1120	1280	1440	1600	1760	1920
12	$18,000	900	1080	1260	1440	1620	1800	1980	2160
13	$20,000	1000	1200	1400	1600	1800	2000	2200	2400
14	$22,000	1100	1320	1540	1760	1980	2200	2420	2640
15	$24,000	1200	1440	1680	1920	2160	2400	2640	2880
16	$26,000	1300	1560	1820	2080	2340	2600	2860	3120
17									

CHAPTER 7

COMMON OPERATIONS

OBJECTIVES

In this chapter you will learn how to:

- Work with toolbars
- Add drawings to your worksheet
- Create textboxes on your worksheet
- Import pictures
- Make your printouts more readable
- Protect cells in your worksheet from being changed

In this chapter we look at some common operations in Excel.

TOOLBARS

Toolbars provide buttons for performing different tasks. We can specify which toolbars we want displayed by selecting *Toolbars...* in the *View* pull-down menu. The *Toolbars* dialog box appears, as in shown Figure 7-1.

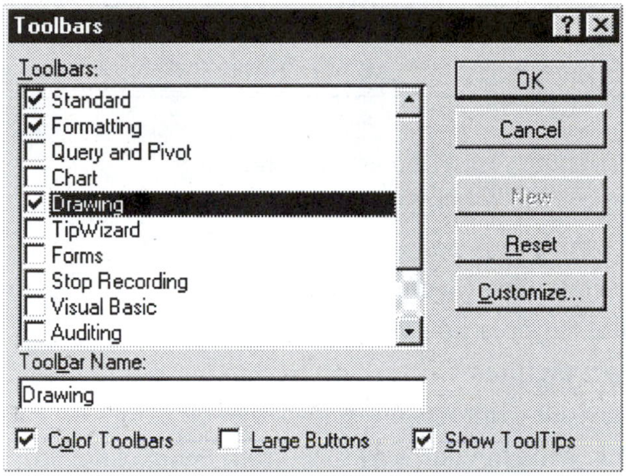

Figure 7-1. The Toolbars dialog box.

Whichever toolbars we click a check next to will appear on the screen. Clicking on multiple toolbars can provide multiple buttons, but little space for your worksheet. (See Figure 7-2.) There obviously is a trade-off between the convenience of toolbars and the space they occupy in the window. Real estate on your computer display is a valuable and limited commodity.

Toolbars can be dragged to wherever you like in the window. They can appear horizontal on the upper part of the window or they can be dragged into a rectangle that floats above a convenient location of your worksheet.

By selecting a toolbar in the *Toolbars* dialog box and pressing *Customize* (see Figure 7-1) you can customize your toolbar by adding new buttons, for example, from other toolbars, or by eliminating seldom-used buttons. Clicking on *Reset* will restore the toolbar to its original configuration of buttons.

Using the check marks at the bottom of the *Toolbars* dialog box you can cause a toolbar to appear in color (or black and white) or with extra large buttons. The check box at the bottom right (*Show ToolTips*) enables the useful feature of showing a brief description of the button in the toolbar when the mouse pointer pauses on top of the button.

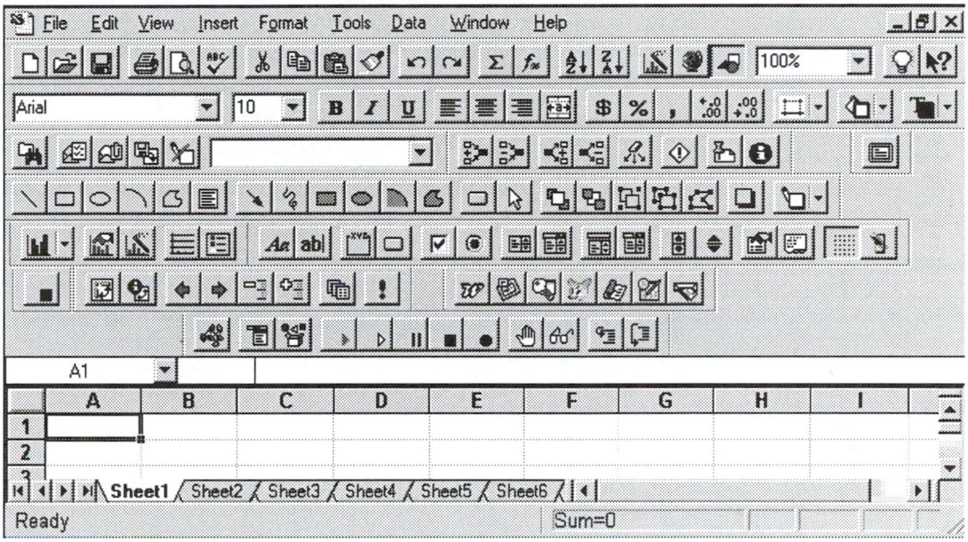

Figure 7-2. Lots of toolbars. Not much worksheet space.

DRAWING

The Drawing toolbar provides a standard palette of drawing tools so you can add drawings to your worksheet (or chart). Select *Toolbars...* in the *View* pull-down menu and select *Drawing*.

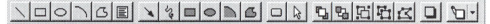

Alternatively, you can Click on the **Drawing button** on the Standard toolbar. Clicking on this button causes the Drawing toolbar to appear.

The Drawing toolbar is shown in Figure 7-3.

Figure 7-3. The Drawing toolbar.

The five buttons on the left of the Drawing toolbar allow you to draw lines, unfilled rectangles, unfilled circles, arcs of circles, and unfilled freeform shapes. Once the shape is drawn you can double-click on the shape to see a dialog box that allows you to specify the thickness and color of the lines and other properties of the shape.

People sometimes confuse **drawings**, especially drawings of rectangles, with borders. Drawings generally float on top of the worksheet. Drawings can be dragged around the worksheet. The size and location of a drawing can be changed by selecting the drawing and dragging on the handles. On the other hand, borders always are formed around the outside of selected cells.

The **Text Box button** allows you to add text boxes to your worksheet. Text boxes are boxes that contain text that float on top of your worksheet.

To create a text box, press the Text Box button. The mouse pointer becomes a crosshairs. The text box appears wherever you drag the pointer. You can type text into the text box. You can format the text the way you would like it to appear just as you can format any text that appears within a normal cell. You can color the text using the Text Color button on the Formatting toolbar.

You can select a text box by clicking on the edge. The box should appear in outline with various handle points on it.

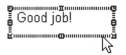

Once the box is selected you can move it around or change its size by dragging on the handles. You also can change the background color within the box by using the Color button on the Formatting toolbar. Thus you could have a yellow text box or a red text box.

The **Arrow button** allows you to create different types of arrows to place on your worksheet or chart. First click on the Arrow button. Then drag the mouse where you would like the arrow to appear. Be sure to drag in the direction of the arrow. (Start at the thin end and finish at the arrowhead.)

Double-clicking on the arrow allows you to change its thickness, color, and other properties. Arrows can be dragged into the exact shape and location you like.

The **Drop Shadow button** draws a box around the selected range or object and adds a dark border to the right side and bottom. This provides a nice way of highlighting certain cells. The drop shadow box combines characteristics of borders and drawings.

The rightmost button in the Drawing toolbar is the **Pattern and Color button**. This button allows us to change the pattern and color of a selected cell, graphic object, or chart item.

To delete any drawn object, select it and then press the del key or select *Cut* from the *Edit* pull-down menu or click on the **Cut button** on the Standard toolbar. (The Cut button has a picture of a scissors on it.)

In Figure 7-4 we have added a drop shadow box around C3:F3. We have added a text box and an arrow to the worksheet. These drawn objects float above the cells in the worksheet but are part of the worksheet and will be saved and printed with the rest of the worksheet.

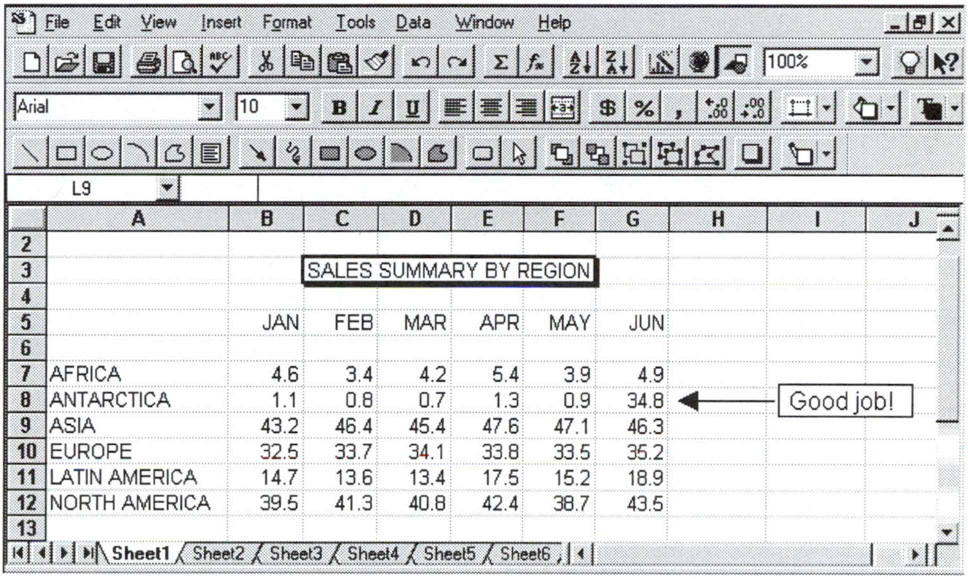

Figure 7-4. A worksheet with drop shadow box, arrow, and text box.

IMPORTING PICTURES

Maybe you are as unskillful at drawing as I am. You can import pictures into your worksheet from anywhere on your disk using the *Picture...* command in the *Insert* pull-down menu. The picture can be from any source: a scanner, a digital camera, the net, a clip-art collection, a paint or draw or modeling program. The picture is another graphic object that floats on your worksheet. It can be selected by clicking on it, moved, resized, copied and pasted, just like any other graphic object.

PRINTING: PAGE SETUP

Many options for printing the worksheet are found in the *Page Setup* command in the *File* pull-down menu.

In the *Page* sheet of the *Page Setup* dialog box (see Figure 7-5) you can specify that the worksheet be printed in **Landscape** mode (sideways) rather than in the traditional **Portrait** mode. Since many worksheets are wider than they are long, this often makes sense. You also can inform Excel to shrink the printout by some fixed percentage or, more usefully, so it fits exactly on some number of pages. Usually it's a good idea to preview the printout first by clicking on the Print Preview button so you know that what will be printed is what you want.

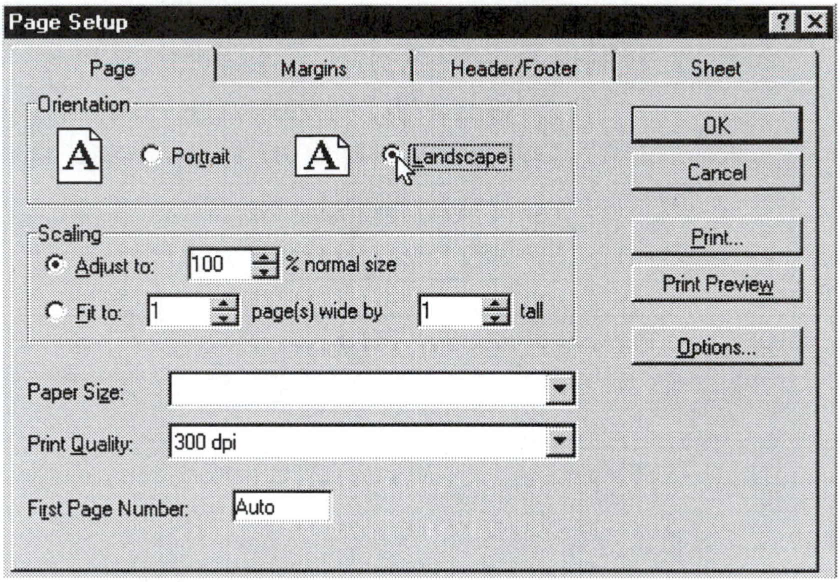

Figure 7-5. Determining how your worksheet will be printed.

In the *Margins* sheet of the *Page Setup* dialog box (see Figure 7-6) you can specify the exact margins on the page and whether the worksheet should be centered on the page when printed.

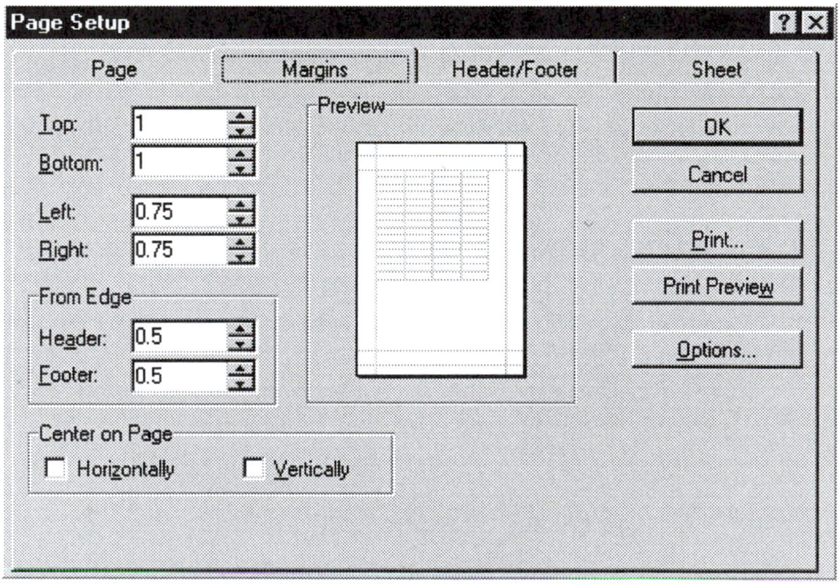

Figure 7-6. Specifying margins and centering for your printout.

In the *Header/Footer* sheet of the *Page Setup* dialog box (Figure 7-7) you can select the **Header** and **Footer** for the printout. A Header is text that appears at the top of every page. A Footer is text that appears at the bottom of every page. By pressing *Custom Header...* or *Custom Footer...* you can specify the exact Header or Footer you would like on your printouts. The Header or Footer can contain information, such as the page number, the date, the time, the file name, your name, the exercise number, or any other text you would like to include with each page of the printout.

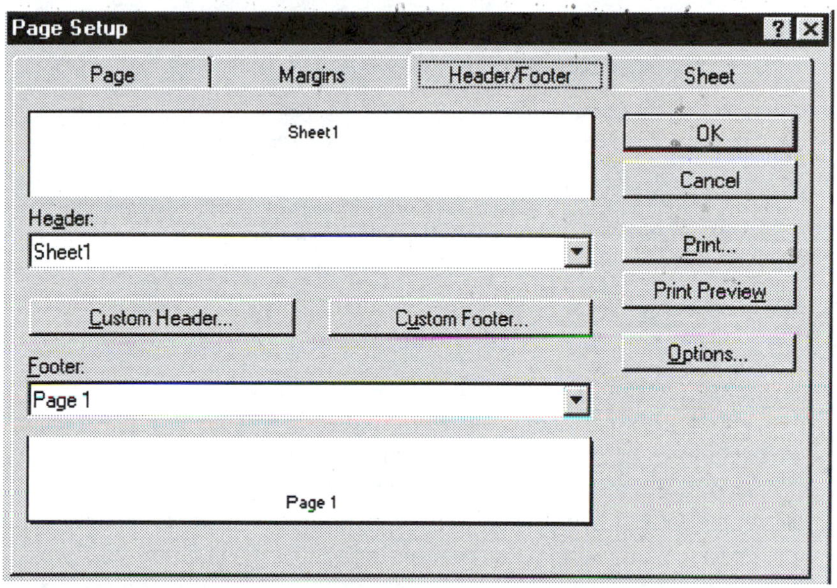

Figure 7-7. Specifying the header and footer for the printout.

In the *Sheet* sheet (sorry about that) of the *Page Setup* dialog box (see Figure 7-8), you can specify which area of the worksheet is to be printed. You can specify whether certain rows or columns are to be printed at the top or left of each page. (This is useful if the rows or columns contain titles for a very large range of numbers.) You can specify whether the gridlines (the dotted lines between cells) are printed. You can specify whether the notes attached to cells are printed. You can specify whether the row numbers and column letters are printed. Printing the row numbers and column letters is especially useful if you are printing out a worksheet with the formulas displayed in the cells so you can easily determine which cells are referred to in the formulas. You also can specify the order of printing for a large worksheet that requires multiple sheets of paper to print. Do you want Excel to print out the worksheet "Down, then Across" or "Across, then Down"? (See the illustration at the bottom of Figure 7-8.)

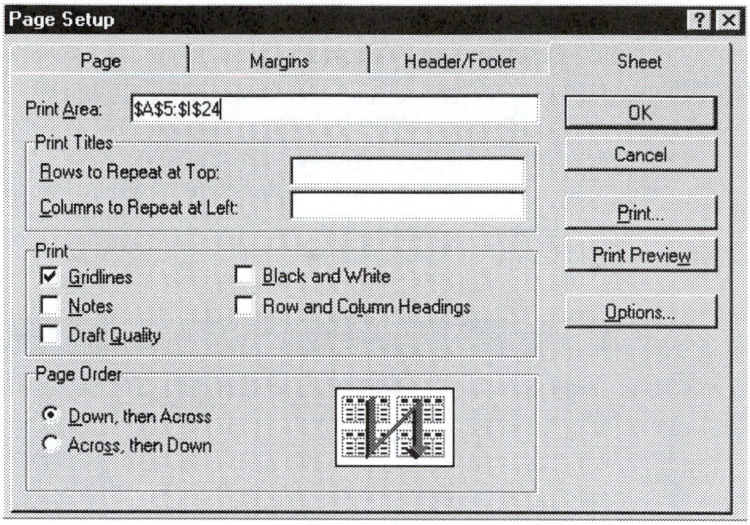

Figure 7-8. Even more choices for printing.

MANUAL RECALCULATION

Excel normally recalculates formulas whenever a cell is changed. In a large workbook this can mean an annoying wait whenever a piece of data is entered. Excel allows us to suppress **Automatic Calculation**. Select *Options...* in the *Tools* pull-down menu. Click on the *Calculation* tab. (See Figure 7-9). Click on *Manual* under *Calculation* and the formulas will be recalculated only when you press function key F9, the **recalculation key**, or when you press the Calc Now button or, if you so specify, whenever you save the workbook on the disk.

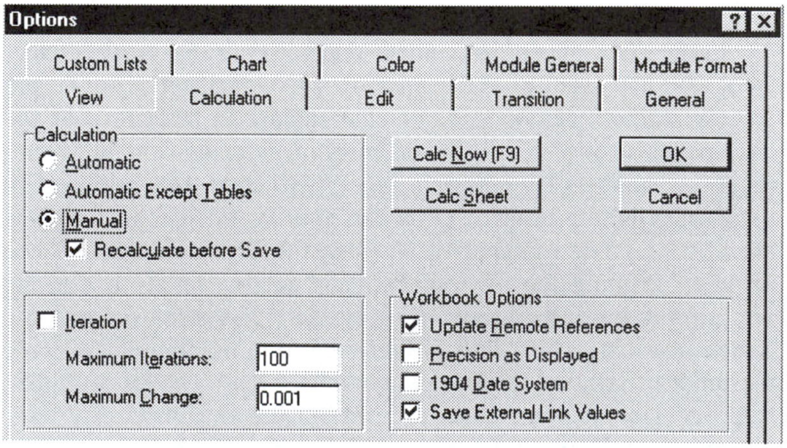

Figure 7-9. Specifying manual calculation.

CELL PROTECTION

Cell protection is an important capability of Excel that should be used with almost all worksheets. Cell protection prevents the user from inadvertently changing or erasing cells in a worksheet. There are two steps to protecting cells in a worksheet. First we specify which cells should *not* be protected. Then we turn on the protection for the worksheet.

The first step is to inform Excel which cells we wish to be able to change, which cells should be **unlocked**. For example, in the Price Quote worksheet shown again in Figure 7-10 only cells D6:D8 should be left unlocked because these are the only cells we wish the user to be able to change.

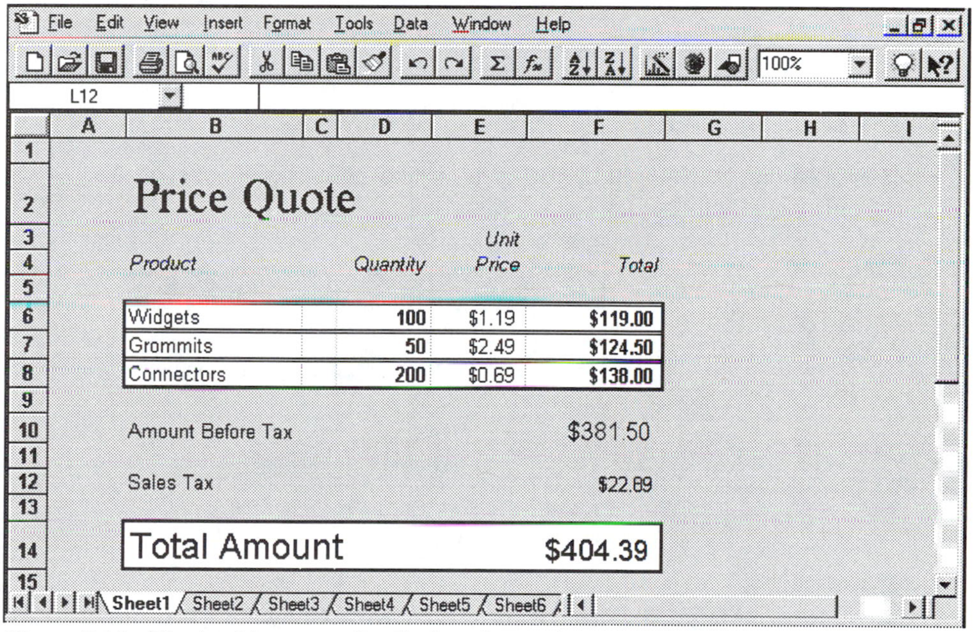

Figure 7-10. We should protect all cells from being changed except cells D6:D8.

To cause the cells D6:D8 to be unlocked, we select D6:D8 by dragging across them and then select *Cells...* in the *Format* pull-down menu. We click on the *Protection* tab and then click to clear the *Locked* box in the dialog box, as in Figure 7-11, for the selected cells. Thus, cells D6:D8 will be the only cells in the worksheet that are *not* locked.

The second step in the process is to enable (turn on) the cell protection for the worksheet. This is accomplished in the *Protection* selection in the *Tools* pull-down menu. Once the protection is enabled then only the cells that are not

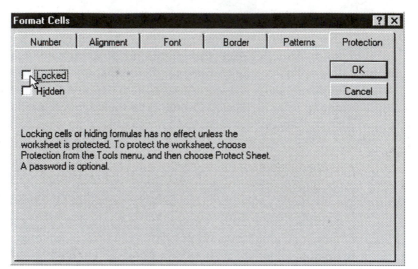

Figure 7-11. Unlocking the cells we wish the user to be able to change.

locked can be changed by the user. If the user tries to change one of the locked cells Excel will display the warning box in Figure 7-12.

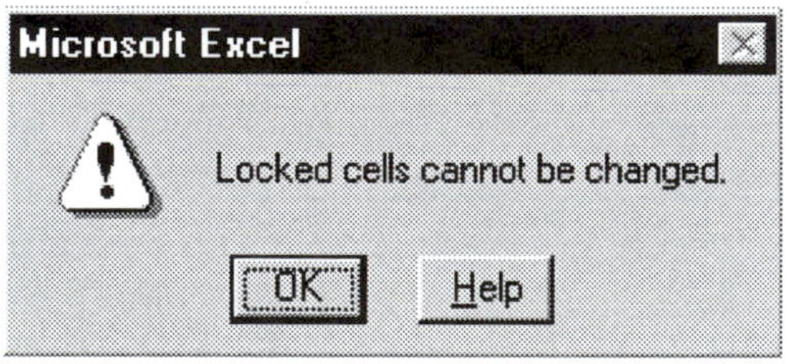

Figure 7-12. Trying to change a locked cell results in this warning.

It even is possible to put **password protection** on the worksheet, so that the user must know the password in order to turn off protection of the worksheet. Password protection can be specified in the *Protection* selection in the *Tools* pull-down menu when the protection is turned on.

The method for cell protection can take time to get used to. Basically, you first unlock the cells you want to be able to change. Then you enable (turn on) the cell protection. You can think of the first step as building an electric fence around the cells that can be changed. The second step is turning on the electric power in the fence. If you simply enable protection without first unlocking specific cells, then all the cells will be locked and protected. In this case, nothing in the worksheet could be changed.

Cell protection is especially useful when a worksheet you create is going to be used by naive users. Only certain cells are meant to be input cells. These cells are unlocked. The other cells contain formulas that you have worked hard on, and you don't want the users mangling them with inputs. These cells are all locked and protected.

COMPUTER EXERCISE

7-1.   Enter the following worksheet.

	A	B	C	D
1				
2		STOCK PORTFOLIO		
3				
4	STOCK	SHARES	PRICE	TOTAL
5				
6	IBM	500	106.75	
7	MICROSOFT	2759	118.25	
8	NETSCAPE	837	68.50	
9				
10	TOTAL			
11				

Align the column headings (SHARES, PRICE, TOTAL) on the right sides of the cells.

Enter the formulas for column D for the TOTALS for D6, D7, D8, and D10.

We just have purchased 1250 shares of INTEL at $75.50 per share. Insert a new row between IBM and MICROSOFT. Fill in the new row 7 with appropriate entries, including a formula in cell D7. Inspect the formula in cell D11. Does the formula need to be adjusted? What happened to the formula when you inserted the row?

Format the PRICE cells in column C and the TOTAL cells in column D so they are displayed with dollar signs and two places to the right of the decimal point. Widen the columns if necessary to accommodate the formatted numbers.

Save the worksheet on the disk. Print the worksheet.

Next day, the stock prices are as follows: IBM 108, INTEL 76.25, MICROSOFT 118.825, NETSCAPE 79.875. Change the worksheet appropriately. Do the numbers in D6:D9 add up to the number in D11?

Print the worksheet.

The stocks were purchased for the following amounts: IBM 81.5, MICROSOFT 48.625, NETSCAPE 68.75. Add a new column that lists the purchase price for each. Add another column that indicates the amount of money we have gained (or lost) on each stock since we purchased it. Finally, add another column that indicates the percentage gain or loss from the purchase price. Format the numbers in this column as percentages with two decimal places.

Spend some time formatting the worksheet so it looks nice. Include different colors or shades for different cells. Include different fonts of different sizes and styles. Add a textbox or two with arrows to point out highlights. You might want to use three-dimensional shading. Add a drawing. Import an appropriate clip-art picture if you can find one. Add a header and footer.

Protect the cells in the worksheet so that only the cells containing the current stock prices can be changed by the user. Try changing one of the other cells. Do you get the nasty message box?

Save your worksheet. Print your worksheet.

CHAPTER 8

WORKBOOKS WITH MULTIPLE WORKSHEETS

OBJECTIVES

In this chapter you will learn how to:

- Move between worksheets
- Insert new worksheets
- Make a duplicate copy of a worksheet
- Modify multiple worksheets at the same time
- Use cells from other worksheets in formulas
- View multiple worksheets and workbooks
- Link to data in other workbooks

So far, we have been doing all of our work on a single worksheet. An Excel workbook holds multiple worksheets, just as a printed book has multiple pages. Using multiple sheets can make many problems easier to solve in Excel.

MOVING BETWEEN WORKSHEETS

An Excel workbook usually starts out with 16 worksheets and can contain up to 255 sheets. Initially, the worksheets are named Sheet1, Sheet2, Sheet3, ... Sheet16. To move to another worksheet within a workbook simply click on the appropriate **sheet tab** at the bottom of the window. In Figure 8-1, we have clicked on the tab for Sheet3. You can tell we are working in Sheet3 because the tab for Sheet3 is white. Usually we can see six sheet tabs at a time. We can scroll so that other sheet tabs are visible using the four buttons to the left of the sheet tabs at the very bottom left of the window.

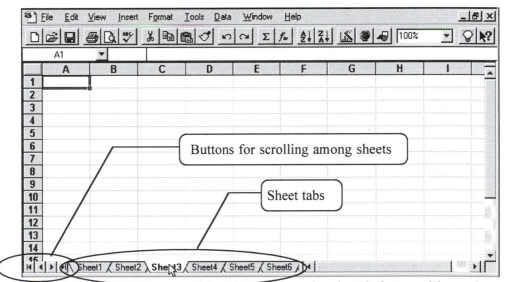

Figure 8-1. Select a different worksheet by clicking on the tab at the bottom of the window.

 instructs Excel to scroll left all the way to the first sheet tab

instructs Excel to scroll left one sheet tab

instructs Excel to scroll right one sheet tab

instructs Excel to scroll right all the way to the last sheet tab

USING MULTIPLE WORKSHEETS

Audio International is a small but exclusive chain of stores that sells and installs top-of-the-line audio equipment. AI carries four types of products: home audio, automobile audio, personal audio, and commercial audio equipment. AI has stores in Beverly Hills, Geneva, Riyadh, and Tokyo. Each quarter the stores send their sales data to world headquarters for compilation. For convenience, all stores report their sales in millions of U.S. dollars. We would like to create a workbook for keeping track of AI's sales for the year. A simple worksheet for keeping track of the sales in the quarter is shown in Figure 8-2.

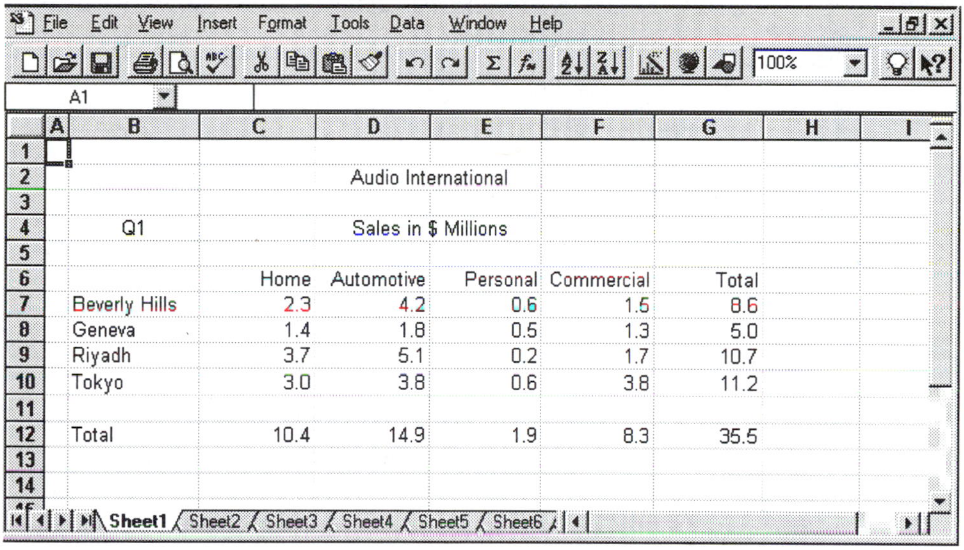

		Audio International				
	Q1	Sales in $ Millions				
		Home	Automotive	Personal	Commercial	Total
	Beverly Hills	2.3	4.2	0.6	1.5	8.6
	Geneva	1.4	1.8	0.5	1.3	5.0
	Riyadh	3.7	5.1	0.2	1.7	10.7
	Tokyo	3.0	3.8	0.6	3.8	11.2
	Total	10.4	14.9	1.9	8.3	35.5

Figure 8-2. Audio International's sales for the first quarter.

Now the second quarter's sales are in and we would like to enter them. The best place to do this is on the next worksheet. First let's name the current worksheet. To change the name of the current worksheet just double-click on the sheet tab, where it says Sheet1. The *Rename Sheet* dialog box appears.

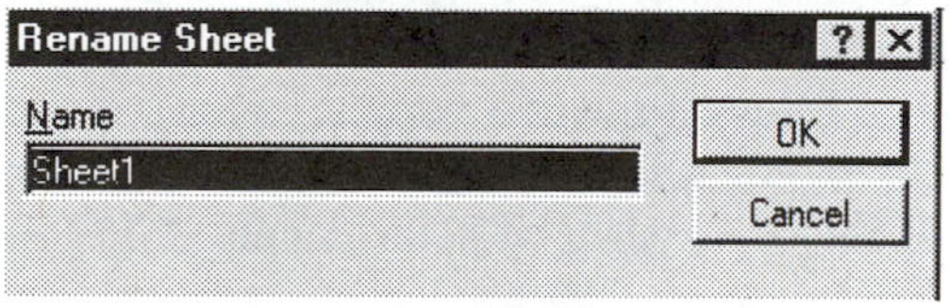

Figure 8-3. Renaming Sheet1.

We type in Q1 and the sheet is renamed Q1. The next step is to copy the information from the first sheet to the second sheet. One approach is to use Copy and Paste. We select the range A1:G11 by dragging across it. Now we select *Copy* from the *Edit* pull-down menu or simply click on the Copy button. This copies the range into the Clipboard. Now click on the tab for Sheet2 at the bottom of the window. Click on cell A1 of Sheet2 to select the cell. Now select *Paste* from the *Edit* pull-down menu or simply click on the Paste button. The range will be copied into Sheet2 beginning at A1, as in Figure 8-4.

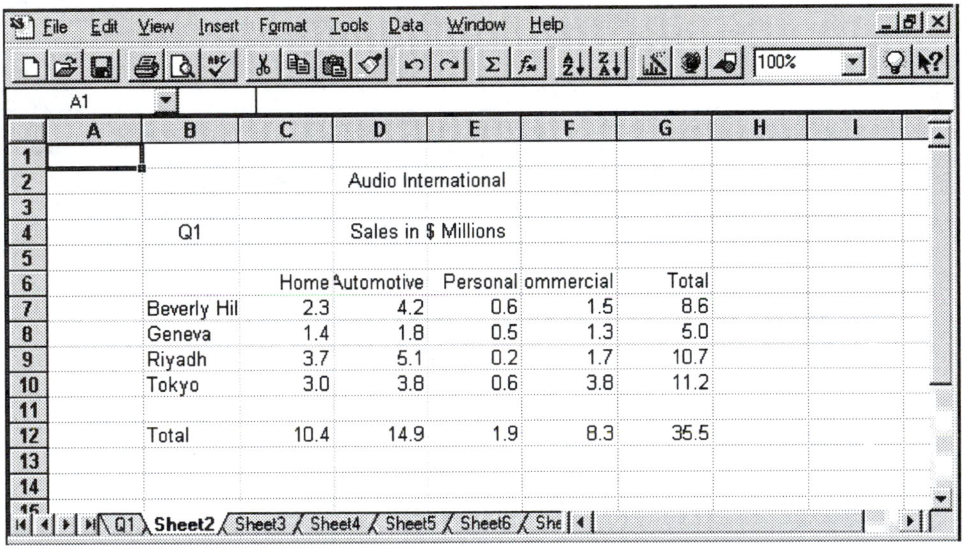

Figure 8-4. The result of copying and pasting from sheet Q1 to sheet Sheet2.

The Copy and Paste operation sort of worked, but notice that the column-width information was not transferred. Let's take another approach. We delete this entire worksheet by selecting *Delete Sheet* in the *Edit* pull-down menu. This command doesn't just erase the worksheet. It tears the entire worksheet out of the workbook.

A better approach to duplicating a worksheet is to use the *Move or Copy Sheet...* command in the *Edit* pull-down menu. This yields the dialog box in Figure 8-5. The name of the workbook we are working on is AISALES.XLS. We click on the *Create a Copy* box at the bottom of the dialog box because we want to make a second copy of the worksheet rather than just moving it. We click on *Sheet3* because we want the new copy to appear just before Sheet3. (Notice that there is no Sheet2 because we just deleted it.) Click on *OK* and an exact duplicate of the worksheet Q1 appears with the name Q1[2], meaning the second copy of worksheet Q1.

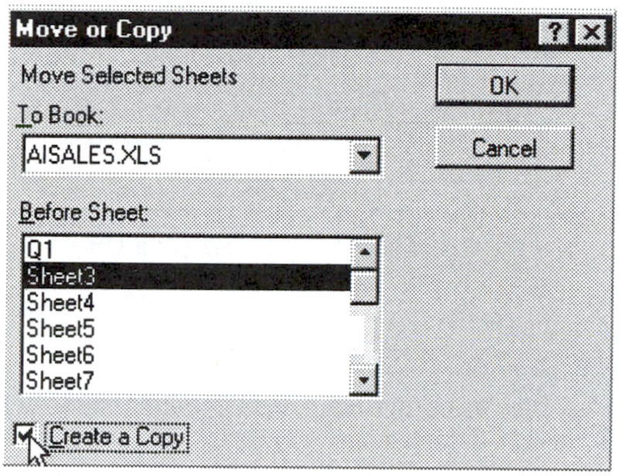

Figure 8-5. Making a copy of a worksheet.

We double-click on the sheet tab and name the new worksheet Q2. Now we go in and change cell B4 to Q2 and enter in the sales figures for the second quarter. An even better approach might have been to create a copy of the sheet with no sales figures filled in and then used that to make the new quarterly sales worksheets.

As the third and fourth quarter sales figures come in, we copy the prior quarter's worksheets into new worksheets called Q3 and Q4 and fill in the appropriate sales figures. We now have a workbook with four worksheets.

We decide that we would like to insert a first sheet and make it a cover sheet for the workbook. We move to worksheet Q1 by clicking on the tab that says Q1 at the bottom of the window. To insert a new worksheet in front of Q1 we select *Worksheet* in the *Insert* pull-down menu. We name this worksheet Cover by double-clicking on the new tab. We enter information into the worksheet and format it.

WORKING WITH MULTIPLE SHEETS AT THE SAME TIME

We decide to jazz up the worksheets themselves. We'd like to place boxes, adjust the fonts, and so on. We would like the changes to take place on all four quarterly worksheets at once. We want to avoid formatting the worksheet for Q1 and then repeating the formatting for worksheet Q2 and so on. The secret is to select multiple sheets before doing the formatting.

There are two ways to select multiple sheets at once. If you hold your finger down on the Ctrl or Control key while you click on the sheet tabs, you can select Q1, and then Q2, and then Q3, and finally Q4. Using **Ctrl-clicking** you can select whichever sheets you would like one at a time. Alternatively, if you would like to select a sequence of sheets, you can click on the first sheet tab Q1 and then hold your finger down on the Shift key and click on sheet tab Q4. All of the sheets from Q1 through Q4 will be selected, as in Figure 8-6. This is **Shift-clicking**.

Figure 8-6. Changes are made simultaneously to all four selected worksheets.

Now whatever actions we perform on worksheet Q1 will be performed simultaneously on worksheets Q2, Q3, and Q4. After we are finished we click once on an unselected sheet tab (Sheet3) to undo the group selection and then click back on worksheet Q3 to see the result in Figure 8-7.

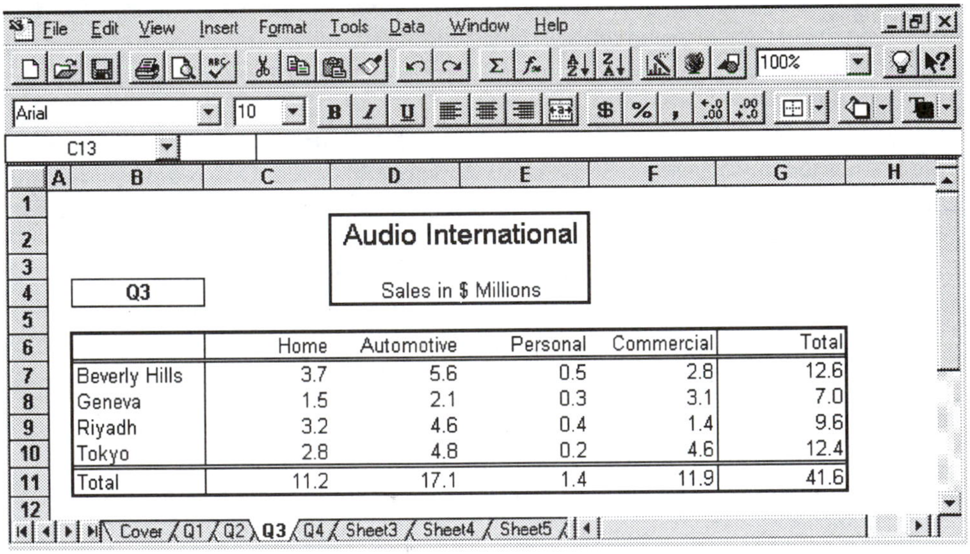

Figure 8-7. The result of formatting all four worksheets at once.

CALCULATIONS ACROSS WORKSHEETS

We would like a Totals worksheet that adds up the quarterly figures. We make a copy of worksheet Q4 and place it before the next sheet. We name the new sheet Totals. We enter Total for the Year in B4. We clear the data values in C7:F10 from the worksheet by selecting them and then dragging the Fill Handle back and up across them.

We are ready to enter the formulas into the body of the worksheet, into cells C7:F10. We want cell C7 in the Totals sheet to be the sum of C7 in the Q1, Q2, Q3, and Q4 worksheets. So we click on C7 in the Totals worksheet to activate it. We type in =SUM(and then we click on sheet tab Q1, hold our finger down on the Shift key, and click on sheet tab Q4. Thus far we have selected the four sheets Q1:Q4 in the formula. Now we click on cell C7 in sheet Q1 and then type the closing parenthesis and the Enter key. The formula in C7 in sheet Totals is

$$=SUM('Q1:Q4'!C7)$$

This formula instructs Excel to add four numbers together, the numbers in C7 in sheet Q1, C7 in sheet Q2, C7 in sheet Q3, and C7 in sheet Q4. The worksheet names usually are included within apostrophes (') in a formula. A range of worksheets is indicated by the colon (:). The names of the worksheets are separated from the addresses of the cells within the worksheets by the exclamation mark (!).

We now can fill this formula across row 7 in sheet Totals by dragging the Fill Handle at the bottom right of C7 across to F7. Without clicking anywhere, with C7:F7 still selected, we drag the resulting Fill Handle at the bottom right of F7 down to F10 and click on D9 to unselect the range. The resulting worksheet is shown in Figure 8-8. You can see that the formula in cell D9 of the Totals worksheet adds up the four corresponding cells in worksheets Q1, Q2, Q3, and Q4.

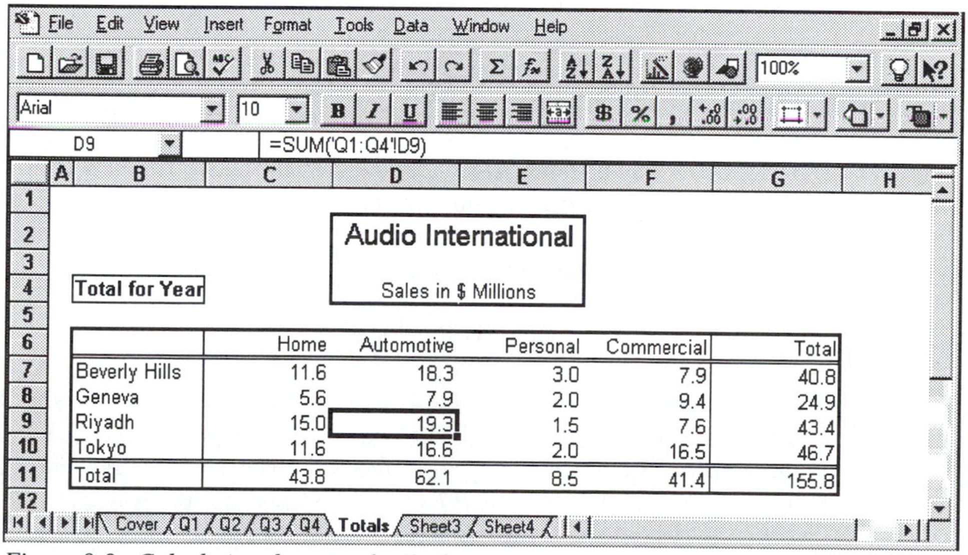

Figure 8-8. Calculating the sum of cells through four worksheets.

There are several possible formulas for cell G11 in the Totals worksheet. One possible formula is

$$=SUM('Q1:Q4'!C7:F10)$$

This formula would instruct Excel to add up a 4 x 4 x 4 cube of cells, 64 cells, the cells in the range C7:F10 on sheets Q1, Q2, Q3, Q4.

VIEWING MULTIPLE SHEETS AND WORKBOOKS

It is possible to view as many worksheets as you would like at once. Simply select *New Window* in the *Window* pull-down menu. Each time you select *New Window* a new window will invade your workspace. The window will be named something like SALES:2, meaning it's the second view of the SALES workbook.

You also can view multiple workbooks at once. Simply start a new workbook with an old one open or open a second workbook. Each workbook will appear in a different window. This is convenient for copying information from one workbook into another or for linking multiple workbooks.

All open windows are listed at the bottom of the *Window* pull-down menu and can be selected there. The windows can be manipulated just like any other window on your computer. You can move each window around by dragging the top of the window. You can shrink it by dragging the bottom right corner of the window up and to the left. If you want Excel to make your windows appear nice and neat, you can select *Arrange...* in the *Window* pull-down menu.

LINKING WORKBOOKS

In addition to viewing multiple workbooks at the same time, it is possible to link workbooks. That is, it is possible to instruct Excel to obtain a value from a cell in some other workbook saved on the disk (or on the network). For example, in a cell we could enter the formula

$$='[SALES]Sheet1'!\$H\$7$$

This formula tells Excel that the value that is to appear in the cell is the value in H7 in the worksheet called Sheet1 of the Excel workbook called SALES. This is a **dynamic link**. The value displayed in the cell always will be the current value in H7 in SALES. If the value in H7 in SALES changes, the value in the cell in this workbook will reflect the change. Thus, to refer to a cell in another workbook, put the name of the workbook file in square brackets [ ].

In addition to typing in the link in the formula, it is possible simply to point to the cell to which we wish to link. For example, if we are working in a workbook called US_SALES and in cell D8 we would like to refer to a cell in a workbook called ATLANTA, we can open up the ATLANTA workbook, click on D8 in US_SALES, type the = sign to begin a formula, and click on the cell in ATLANTA whose value we want to appear in D8 in US_SALES. The link will be entered in the formula in cell D8. We press the Enter key to enter the formula. We then can close the ATLANTA workbook. The value that appears in D8 in US_SALES will be the current value in the linked cell in ATLANTA.

COMPUTER EXERCISES

8-1. As a professional at a consulting firm, you would like to set up a workbook to keep track of your hours. You have three current clients (Acme, Beta, and Carlysle) that you bill by the hour. In addition you spend nonbillable time cultivating new clients and nonbillable time at work on other tasks, such as attending internal meetings and staring out the window (though you usually like to be thinking about a client's problem when you're staring out the window, so the time is billable).

Set up a workbook to help you keep track of your time and billing. Each worksheet should represent a different week. There should be five rows: one for each different client, one for time cultivating new clients, one for "nonproductive" time spent at work. You should have columns for each of the seven days of the week. Entries will be filled in for the number of hours spent each day in each of the categories. There should be row totals for the number of hours spent in each category and column totals for the number of billable hours, the number of nonbillable hours, and the total number of hours you worked each day.

You bill your clients at $175 per hour. This value should be entered into a separate cell in the worksheet, because it is subject to change (upwards). You should have cells for the dollar amounts to be billed each client each day and for the week. The final cell should give the total amount to be billed for the week.

Your firm bills its clients every four weeks. You should have a worksheet in your workbook for each week in the cycle. Each of these worksheets should have the week number. After these weekly worksheets you should have a Totals worksheet that lists all useful totals, including the total accumulated hours for the cycle for each category, the total amount to be billed each client for the cycle, and the total amount billed for the cycle.

8-2. Design a workbook to keep track of a stock portfolio. You own shares in five different companies:

Shares	Company	Purchase Price	Current Price
1000	Allied Networks	34.5	38.75
3500	Bionic Controls	8.25	56.50
9000	Cortical Connections	2.75	1.75
2000	Dilapidated Housing	15.75	18.50
500	Energy Management	78.25	83.00

Create a workbook with multiple worksheets that allows you to keep track of your portfolio over the next 10 business days. During those 10 days the price of the shares will change, but you can assume that you will neither purchase nor sell any shares. Once the workbook is set up, you will enter in only 50 values, the closing price of each of the stocks on each of the days. All other cells should be protected and calculated automatically.

The workbook will tell you for each day the total value of each stock holding, the change from the previous day in both dollar amount and percent, and the change from original purchase price in both dollar amount and percent. There also will be cells that tell you the highest price of each stock over the 10 days and the highest value of your portfolio over the 10 day period.

There are several ways to organize the workbook in terms of what appears on each worksheet. The exact organization is up to you.

CHAPTER 9

THE PROBLEM-SOLVING PROCESS

OBJECTIVES

In this chapter you will learn:

- The process of developing workbooks
- Common forms of documentation for workbooks

In the first eight chapters we have looked at the basics of creating Excel workbooks. Now it is time to step back and look at the process of using Excel to help solve problems. This process usually involves five phases.

1. PROBLEM DEFINITION

What is the problem to be solved? What are we trying to accomplish? What information would we like to have? It is very important that you understand the problem before trying to solve it. You do not want to spend hours developing and perfecting a workbook that solves the wrong problem; that is of little use.

2. DESIGN

Is Excel the right tool to use to solve the problem? Sometimes people become so enamored with Excel that they try to use the program to solve problems that would be better solved by other means. There is an old saying "To a person with a hammer, everything looks like a nail." Excel is a powerful and useful tool, but it is not the solution to every problem. If a calculation is to be performed only once, sometimes it is easier just to do the calculation by hand, to use paper and pencil and a calculator. For problems that are better solved using the computer, several different types of computer software are available. Many problems are better solved using, say, a database program rather than Excel or by using some specialized software. For example, if you would like the computer to help you keep the books of a small business, you could create custom Excel workbooks, but you might save a lot of time and trouble by just buying one of the several small business accounting programs available.

Once you decide that Excel is the right tool to use, it is best to design the workbook on paper first. What are the inputs? What information needs to be provided? What are the outputs? What are we trying to learn? What should be the format of the outputs? Are there any special printed reports that need to be produced? What should they look like? How do you get from the inputs to the outputs? Are there any key formulas to be developed? Could you perform the calculations by hand given enough time and a calculator? You want to be sure that there is nothing mystical in your workbook design, no key steps that need to be calculated but that you do not know how to specify.

As we saw in the Peter Minuit example in Chapter 6, an important principle for designing effective workbooks is that any number that might be changed should be placed into a separate cell. Do not put numbers that might be changed, like interest rates, directly into formulas. Rather put them into separate cells and always refer to these cells in the formulas. All of the numbers that might be varied should be placed together in a separate, well-labeled input area of the workbook.

In designing a workbook you might have four separate areas: introduction, input, calculations, and output. The introduction contains a description of the workbook, the name of the developer, the date, instructions to the user, and documentation. The introduction might encompass the entire first sheet of the workbook. The input area contains all of the cells that will be entered by the user. In a worksheet for "What if" analysis, the input area would contain all of the assumptions, all of the numbers that might be varied. The calculations area contains the formulas. The output area pulls the results of special interest out of the calculations area. The output area might be located next to the input area for easy viewing.

3. IMPLEMENTATION

Normally it is best to have the worksheets designed on paper before proceeding to the computer. Implementation should be straightforward. It is useful to name the important cells and ranges and to use these names in the formulas. Names should remind you of the contents of the cell or range. If a formula is going to be filled, be careful about using relative, mixed, or absolute addressing. Think about whether the address is relative, whether it is to be adjusted as it is replicated, or whether the address is absolute, always referring to the same cell or range of cells. Use the cell protection capability of Excel to protect all of the cells except the input cells from being changed by mistake.

It is customary to store a frequently used workbook as a template. A template is a workbook where all of the input values are set to zero. The user would retrieve the template workbook from the disk, enter in the input values, and save the filled-in workbook on the disk under a new name. The template would remain on the disk unchanged.

4. TESTING

Beginners often expect their Excel workbooks to work correctly the first time. Sometimes they do, but even the best planned and designed workbooks often contain errors. It is best to assume that a new workbook is full of errors and then test it extensively to make sure it is correct. Testing a workbook involves working out the numbers ahead of time with pencil, paper, and calculator before trying them on the computer. It is important that the workbooks be tested on a wide variety of inputs, on typical inputs and on extreme inputs.

There are several types of errors in Excel workbooks that can be uncovered. There can be errors in your understanding of the problem. Sometimes you create a workbook and then realize that you did not quite understand the problem. The workbook might "work" but it does not produce the answers you need. In this case, you would need to go back to step 1 to reanalyze the problem. There can be errors in your design of the workbook. You might have used an erroneous formula. You might have built a number that needs to be changed into a formula in a worksheet. You might not have foreseen some condition that might occur. In this case, you would need to go back to step 2 to modify your design for the workbook. There can be errors in your implementation of the workbook. You might have a number that is too large for the width of the column. You might forget to use absolute addressing where it is required. You might have made an error in typing a formula or pointing to an address. These errors in step 3 can be corrected right on the computer.

5. DOCUMENTATION

Documentation is the part of the problem-solving process that involves making the workbook understandable by people, rather than just by the computer. Documentation includes external paper documentation as well as instructions within the workbook itself. In a sense, documentation includes everything in a workbook except for the numbers and the formulas themselves. Documentation should not be an afterthought but rather an integral part of the entire development process.

The extent of the documentation required depends on the uses to which your workbook will be put.

If you are the only person who will ever use your work, then you should provide yourself with sufficient labels and instructions so that the workbook will be understandable to you six months in the future.

If the workbook is being handed in as an assignment, your instructor will determine the level of documentation required. Certainly you should include your name, the date, and the assignment number. You should indicate any extra assumptions you have made and explain any tricky aspects of your work. Your instructor might ask you to hand in printed documentation, including printouts of the worksheets and their formulas, or you might submit disks, or you might submit the work over the network.

A workbook produced for class generally is seen by just two people—yourself and the person who grades the assignment. In industry there often are several people who use and modify the workbooks you will create.

In industry, workbooks often are used by people other than the creator of the workbooks. These people may have only a superficial understanding of Excel and its operation. Therefore it is important to include explicit instructions with your workbooks in these situations. The instructions should include where the data should be entered, how and where to save the work, and how to print out reports. Important instructions are best included as text in the worksheets themselves as well as on a separate piece of paper. Paper instructions can easily be separated from the workbooks or lost altogether. The cell protection capabilities should be used so that only input cells can be modified easily.

In industry, workbooks often are modified by people other than the person who creates them. You create an Excel workbook as part of your job and then you are rapidly promoted twice. Someone else is hired for your old position. This person inherits your work. Can this person make sense of your workbooks? Where did these data come from? What is this formula? What are the assumptions underlying this worksheet? What happens at the end of the year? Here you would like the work to be transparent, self-explanatory. List assumptions for the workbooks. List sources for data. Explain unusual formulas. Give explicit instructions. Put yourself in the place of the person who will succeed you. Could you understand this workbook the way it is written if you hadn't developed it yourself?

With important workbooks in industry it is customary to create a full documentation binder. The documentation binder could include:

- a description of the problem the workbook is designed to solve
- a general discussion of the workbook, its design and operation
- full, detailed instructions for a novice user
- full documentation for someone who will modify the workbook, including any assumptions, a discussion of formulas, any pitfalls or possible errors in the workbook, features that might be added
- a full printout of the worksheets with values displayed
- a full printout of the worksheets with formulas displayed
- two semi-sealed, write-protected disks or other removable storage media containing the workbook and documentation to be used for emergency backup.

Many people tend to provide too little documentation for their workbooks. The reason is simple. It takes a long time and a lot of effort to produce good documentation. It can take as long to document a workbook as it does to identify the problem, design the workbook, implement the workbook, and test the workbook all combined. A little extra effort with documentation can save users of your workbook many hours of work.

COMPUTER EXERCISES

9-1. Do you live with other people and share a telephone? If so, create an Excel workbook to determine how much each person owes. Follow the rules you use to divide up the bill. Perhaps you split the cost of the basic service charge and pay for your own long distance calls. Perhaps unclaimed long distance calls are split evenly. You should have an entry in your workbook for each separate entry that appears on your phone bill. Don't forget the tax. The design is up to you. You might place all of the data and calculations for each month on a single worksheet. Or you might use a separate worksheet for breaking out the expenses of each person. In the workbook all cells should be protected except for the input cells. Try to make the workbook as useful as possible. Data should need to be entered only once. Save a template on the disk that you can then open and use each month. Go through the process of problem definition, design, implementation, testing, and documentation.

9-2. Your courses each have different requirements—different types of assignments, quizzes, exams, etc. Create a workbook to keep track of all of the grades you receive. Every grade should appear in the workbook along with a description of what it is for, and the date received. You probably will want a different worksheet for each course. Your workbook should calculate your average in each class, if possible using the weighting system of the instructor. In the workbook all cells should be protected except for the input cells. Go through the process of problem definition, design, implementation, testing, and documentation.

9-3. Create a workbook to help keep track of a checking account. There should be separate entries for each check, deposit, ATM withdrawal, and service charge. These entries should include the date, the amount, the check number (if any), the payee (if any), and the purpose. The workbook should keep track of the balance in your account and should help you check for errors in the statement you receive from the bank each month. Go through the process of problem definition, design, implementation, testing, and documentation.

9-4. Create a workbook that helps you budget income and expenses for each month. Include separate entries for income and expense items. Allow for both budgeted and actual. You may use fictional data if you wish. Go through the process of problem definition, design, implementation, testing, and documentation.

9-5. If you have a car, how much does it cost to operate? Create a workbook that will allow you to track operating expenses for your car for a year. Your workbook should allow you to record money spent for gas, oil, repairs, insurance, registration, and any other expenses. For each expense, you should record the date, the odometer mileage, the payee, a description of the expense, and an amount. The workbook should calculate subtotals for each type of expense, the total amount of money spent, and the cost per mile and the cost per day to drive your car. Go through the process of problem definition, design, implementation, testing, and documentation.

9-6. Perhaps you belong to a group, such as a campus organization or a church group, that is considering undertaking an activity, for example, a picnic or a dance or a raffle. Create a workbook that will allow you to model the financial aspects of the activity. You might have cells for the number of tickets sold and the price of the tickets and for any other revenue variables and for each of the different expense variables. The workbook should allow you to try out different scenarios. For example, what would happen if all of the tickets are sold? What would happen if only 20 tickets are sold? What would be the financial consequences if it rains on the day of the picnic? In the workbook all cells should be protected except for the input cells. Go through the process of problem definition, design, implementation, testing, and documentation.

9-7. Read through the first six exercises for this chapter. Create a workbook that you would find useful in whatever area you would like. Go through the process of problem definition, design, implementation, testing, and documentation.

PART II

FEATURES

CHAPTER 10

CHARTS

OBJECTIVES

In this chapter you will learn how to:

- Create charts using the ChartWizard
- Modify charts
- Make and manipulate three-dimensional charts
- Chart data in noncontiguous areas of your worksheet
- Create separate chart sheets
- Use trendlines to forecast the future

Charts have visual impact. People often respond more favorably to charts than they do to tables of numbers. An important part of Excel is the ability to turn tables of numbers into bar charts and pie charts and other types of charts. Charting in Excel is easy, useful, and fun.

FUNDAMENTALS OF CHARTS

In Excel, charts are made from ranges of numbers in a workbook. Basically we need to specify (1) the cells that contain the values to be charted, (2) the location where the chart is to be placed, and (3) the type of chart we want drawn.

As an example, consider the totals worksheet for Audio International, from Chapter 8, shown in Figure 10-1.

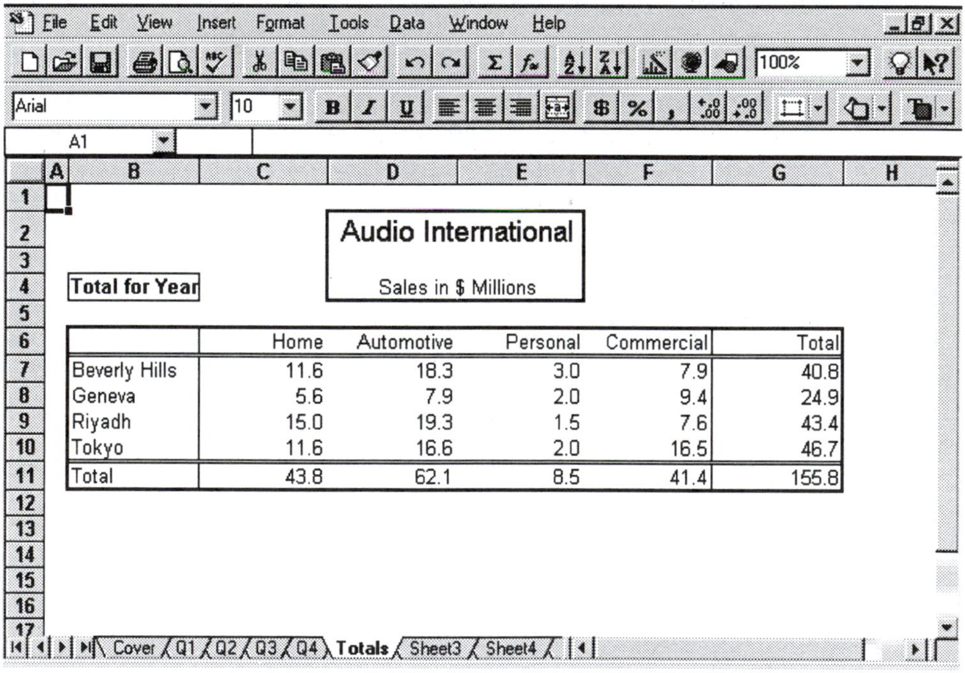

Audio International

Sales in $ Millions

Total for Year

	Home	Automotive	Personal	Commercial	Total
Beverly Hills	11.6	18.3	3.0	7.9	40.8
Geneva	5.6	7.9	2.0	9.4	24.9
Riyadh	15.0	19.3	1.5	7.6	43.4
Tokyo	11.6	16.6	2.0	16.5	46.7
Total	43.8	62.1	8.5	41.4	155.8

Figure 10-1. A worksheet to chart.

There are many different charts that could be drawn from this worksheet. Let's start simple. Suppose we want to draw a vertical bar chart that has the locations along the horizontal axis and the annual sales of home audio equipment as the height of the bars, as in Figure 10-2.

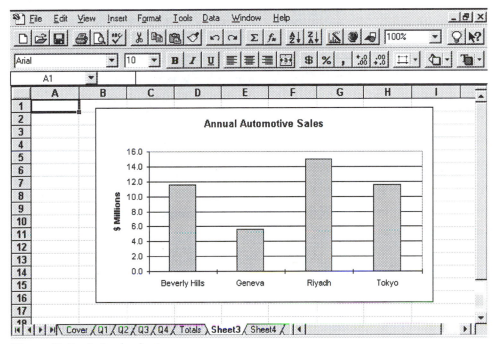

Figure 10-2. A simple chart.

Excel provides a **ChartWizard** to guide us through the process of creating a chart. The first action in creating a chart is to specify the range of cells to be charted. We start by dragging the cursor across B6:C10 to select the range of cells whose values we wish to chart.

The second action is to select the ChartWizard by clicking on the ChartWizard button on the Standard toolbar. The ChartWizard button shows a magic wand on top of a chart.

The third action is a bit confusing. Once you click on the ChartWizard the mouse pointer becomes a crosshairs with a small graph or period next to it. Excel is waiting for you to tell it where you would like it to draw the chart. You can scroll over to the right and drag across a blank area of the existing worksheet if you would like. For this example, let's click on the next worksheet, Sheet3, and then drag across an area on that worksheet. This informs the ChartWizard we would like the chart drawn on Sheet5.

Now the ChartWizard is ready to begin. The ChartWizard has five steps, five dialog boxes for us to respond to, before we are finished specifying our chart.

In Step 1 the dialog box confirms that the cells we want to chart are B6:C10 on page Totals (see Figure 10-3). If we made an initial mistake we could change this address by typing or dragging with the mouse. Be sure not to include any empty columns or rows in the range of data to be charted.

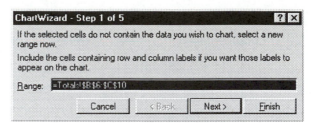

Figure 10-3. *Select the data to be charted.*

Now the fun begins. In Step 2 we are asked to select a chart type. We select *Column* chart, which is Excel's term for vertical bar chart, and click on *Next*.

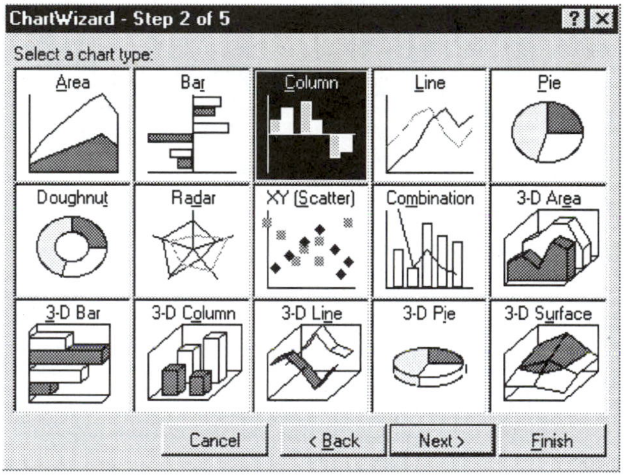

Figure 10-4. *Select the type of chart.*

In Step 3 we select which type of Column chart we want.

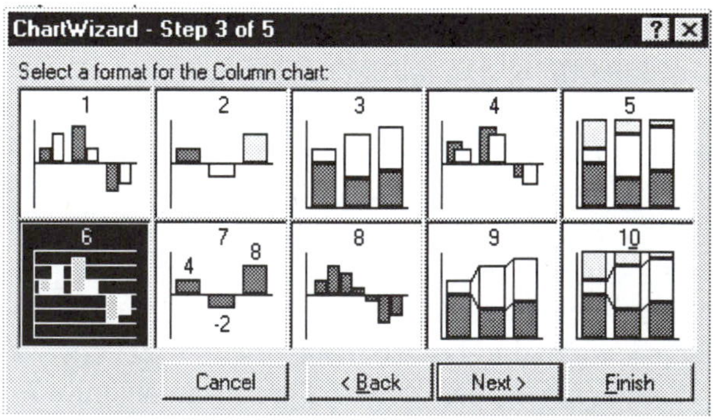

Figure 10-5. *There are 10 varieties of two-dimensional Column charts from which to choose.*

In Step 4 we confirm that the data are organized by columns and that the first column, B6:B10, in the range selected does not contain data. Rather it contains the X axis labels. That is, "Beverly Hills", "Geneva", and so on are not values to be charted; they are to be used to label the X axis. Similarly, the first row (containing "Home") is not a value to be charted, but a description of the data.

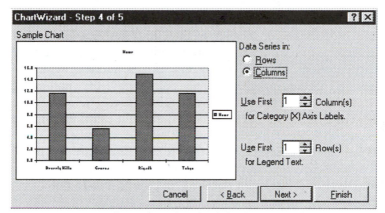

Figure 10-6. Specifying some details of the data to be charted.

In the fifth and final step we inform Excel that we do not want a **legend**. A legend is the box to the right of the chart in Figure 10-6 that identifies the different series of data charted. If we had charted all four types of audio equipment, a legend would have been very useful in identifying which color bar goes with which type of equipment. Since we are charting only home equipment sales, we don't really need a legend here. In Step 5 we also enter an overall title for the chart and a title for the Y axis. Each time we make a new entry, the change is reflected in the preview of the chart in the *Sample Chart* box.

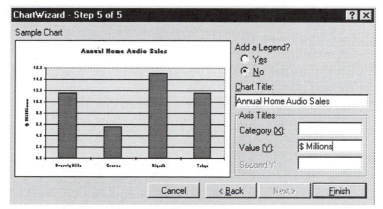

Figure 10-7. Specifying titles for the chart.

Now, at last, we click on *Finish* and our chart in Figure 10-2 is drawn for us. The ChartWizard makes drawing charts nice and easy.

MAKING CHANGES TO THE CHART

A chart in a worksheet is simply another graphical object. To change the size, proportions, or location of the chart, first select the chart by clicking once on the chart. Handles appear around the edges of the chart. To change the size or proportions, point to one of the handles and drag with the mouse. To move the chart in the worksheet, simply point within the chart and drag the chart.

To change some feature in the chart itself, we need to first double-click on the chart. After we have double-clicked on a chart, the *Insert* and *Format* menus change to refer to the chart rather than the worksheet. To change some aspect of the chart, simply point to that part of the chart and double-click again. For example, Excel usually does a very good job at automatically selecting the minimum and maximum values of the vertical axis from the data that is being charted. If we are unhappy with Excel's choices, we can double-click on the vertical axis. The *Format Axis* box appears. Select *Scale* by clicking on the tab and now we can enter new minimum and maximum values. (See Figure 10-8.) When we click on *OK*, the chart will be redrawn to the new scale. Within *Format Axis* we also can change the *Font* of the numbers written along the axis as well as the format of the numbers and the *Alignment* of the numbers. The *Patterns* tab lets us specify the appearance of the tick marks (the small horizontal lines) along the vertical axis. We have control over the smallest details of the chart.

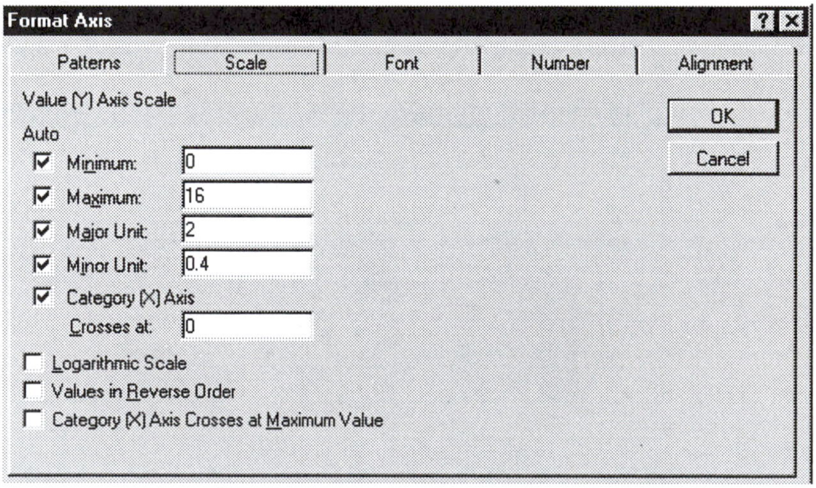

Figure 10-8. Specifying the scale of the vertical axis of the chart.

Other parts of the chart are changed in a similar manner. First double-click on the chart. Once the chart is selected by double-clicking, then double-click on the aspect of the chart you wish to modify. As another example, we can change the color or pattern of the bars in the chart by double-clicking on one of the bars. Each set of data that is charted is called a **series**. In the chart we just created there is just one series of data that is charted—the Home sales. (In the next section we will chart all four series, all sixteen data values, in one chart.) When we double-click on one of the bars in this chart, the *Format Data Series* box appears. By clicking on the *Patterns* tab (see Figure 10-9) we can change the color and pattern of the bars for the series.

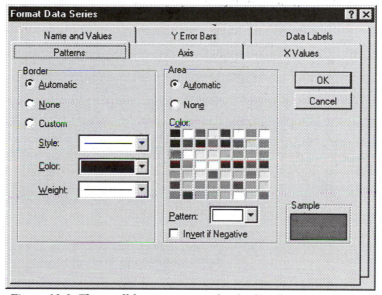

Figure 10-9. The small boxes appear to be shades of gray in the book but they actually are a rainbow of colors. We can select a cross-hatching in the Pattern pull-down menu below the color selection.

Suppose we would like to change the type of chart itself. Instead of a Column chart, we would like to display the data as a Pie chart. First we select the chart by double-clicking on it. As mentioned previously, when a chart is selected by double-clicking, the *Format* menu and *Insert* menu change to refer to charts. We can select *Chart Type* in the new *Format* pull-down menu. A display of the different types of charts available appears. We can select a Pie chart, select *Legends* from the new *Insert* pull-down menu, and have the data redrawn. The resulting Pie chart is shown in Figure 10-10.

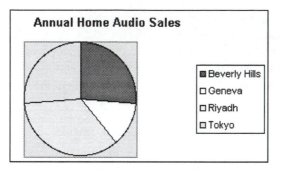

Figure 10-10. The data redrawn as a Pie chart.

MORE COMPLEX CHARTS

We charted only four values, Home sales, in the Totals worksheet. Suppose we would like to produce a chart that helps us visualize more of the data.

We begin by selecting B6:F10 in the original worksheet in Figure 10-1. We don't include the Total column and the Total row because if we include these values the computer would just consider "Total" to be the name of another city or product line, which would cause confusion in the charts. We go through the same process of clicking on the ChartWizard, clicking on Sheet4, and selecting a large area for our chart, and then answering the questions in the five steps of dialog boxes. This time we select *3-D Column* chart in Step 2 and request that the data be organized by rows in the worksheet. The ChartWizard draws a 3-Dimensional Column chart.

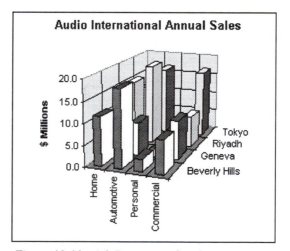

Figure 10-11. A 3-Dimensional Column chart.

We can change the three-dimensional orientation of the chart by double-clicking on the chart to select it and then by double-clicking on the bottom center corner (between "Commercial" and "Beverly Hills") and then dragging the corner. As shown in Figure 10-12, Excel displays a three-dimensional outline of the chart. The mouse pointer has become a + shape. Dragging the mouse changes the three-dimensional orientation. The new chart in Figure 10-13 is perhaps easier to read than the original chart in Figure 10-11.

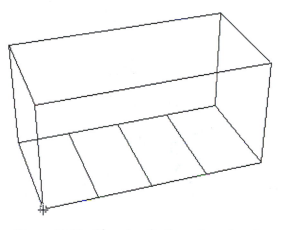

Figure 10-12. Changing the three-dimensional orientation of the chart.

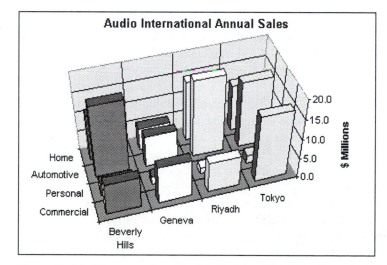

Figure 10-13. The same chart displayed with a different orientation.

We can change the organization so the data are organized by columns (product types) of the worksheet rather than by rows (cities) in the chart. This was specified initially in Step 4 of the ChartWizard. The ChartWizard can be recalled and the organization of the data revised at any time. To recall the ChartWizard, select the chart and then click on the ChartWizard button. Requesting that the data be charted by columns instead of by rows produces the chart in Figure 10-14. Can you see the difference?

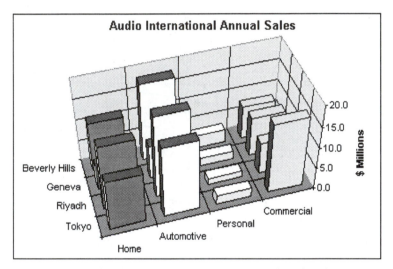

Figure 10-14. The chart organized by columns rather than by rows.

CHARTING NONCONTIGUOUS RANGES

Often we want to chart noncontiguous areas of a worksheet, areas that are not next to each other. For example, we might want to chart only Home and Commercial sales. Home sales are in column C. Commercial sales are in column F. To select noncontiguous portions of the worksheet use the Ctrl or Control key. That is, select the first portion of the worksheet by dragging across it and then hold your finger down on the Ctrl key while you drag across other portions. The result will be that multiple rectangular ranges will be selected, as discussed in Chapter 3. You then can summon the ChartWizard. The multiple ranges will appear in the Step 1 dialog box separated by a comma.

Another approach to charting different ranges of data from a workbook in a single chart is to set up a special area in a worksheet that contains just the data to be charted in just the order you want. The cells in this area can be copied and pasted from different sections of the workbook, or they can contain simple formulas that refer to the values to be charted.

The result of charting Home and Commercial sales as a **3-D Line chart** is shown in Figure 10-15. Notice the legend to the right of the chart.

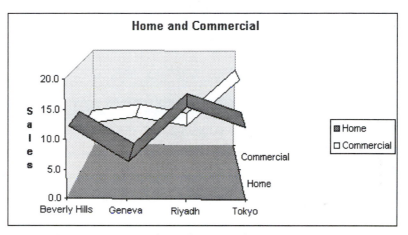

Figure 10-15. A 3-D Line chart of Home and Commercial sales.

CHART SHEETS

We have been placing the graphs on worksheets. It also is possible to have a separate sheet devoted just to a chart. A **chart sheet** does not contain rows or columns or cells. It just contains a single chart. The easiest way to set up a chart sheet is to select a range to be charted and then select *Chart* in the *Insert* pull-down menu. Within *Chart* select the sub-menu *As new sheet*. This will launch you into the ChartWizard, as before. However, the chart will appear on a separate sheet of its own.

Chart sheets are most useful if the end result is that the chart is going to be printed. Chart sheets can be difficult to read on the screen unless you have a large monitor, but chart sheets generally print in the right size and proportions.

Thus, you have three options as to where to place a chart. A chart can be placed on a worksheet next to existing data and formulas. A chart can be placed on a blank worksheet. Or, a chart can be placed on a separate chart sheet.

When printing, if a chart is placed on a worksheet and you print the worksheet, the chart will appear along side whatever else is on the worksheet. If you double-click on a chart in a worksheet and then select *Print*, only the chart will be printed on the page. If the chart is on a separate chart sheet and you print the chart sheet, then only the chart will be printed. It is a good idea to select *Print Preview* before printing so you can ascertain that the printout will be what you want.

TRENDLINES

Audio International has gone public, and we are considering purchasing some of their stock. We have obtained the closing price of the stock at the end of each of the 25 weeks since it was issued and entered the data into the worksheet in Figure 10-16.

	File	Edit	View	Insert	Format	Tools	Data	Window	Help			_ 8 x

	A	B	C	D	E	F	G	H	
1									
2		**Audio International Stock Prices**							
3									
4		**Week**	**Closing Price**						
5		1	$15.500						
6		2	$17.250						
7		3	$19.875						
8		4	$18.500						
9		5	$23.250						
10		6	$20.000						
11		7	$19.500						
12		8	$21.125						
13		9	$21.500						

Chart1 \ **AI Stock** / Sheet2 / Sheet3 / Sheet4 / Sheet5

Figure 10-16. Audio International goes public.

First, we would like to chart the stock so we can see what the change in price looks like. We select B4:C29, click on the ChartWizard button, scroll to the right, and drag out an area for the chart to the right of the data. We then go through the five screens in the ChartWizard, selecting an XY (Scatter) chart. The result is shown in Figure 10-17.

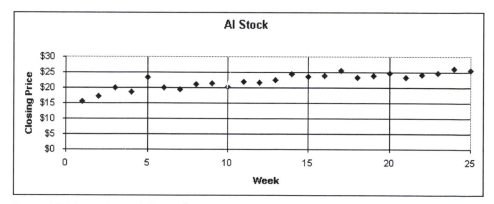

Figure 10-17. A chart of the stock prices.

That is the past. We are thinking of investing, so we are interested in forecasting the price of the stock for future weeks. One of the nicest features of Excel is that it will automatically compute and display **trendlines**. Trendlines are a way of using the past data to suggest what the future data will be.

To obtain a trendline, first we double-click on the chart to select the chart. Then we click on one of the data points in the chart to select the series of data values. The data points change to a different color to show they are selected. Now we select *Trendline* from the *Insert* pull-down menu. Excel displays the *Trendline* dialog box shown in Figure 10-18.

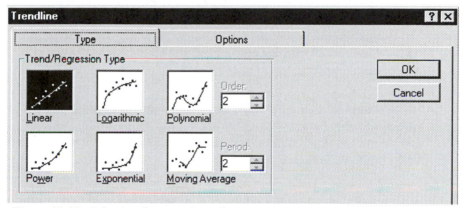

Figure 10-18. Selecting the type of trendline.

(Note that selecting the chart and then the data series within the chart can take some trial and error as exactly where to click. Once you have selected the chart then the *Insert* pull-down menu will change to be relevant to the chart rather than the worksheet. One of the new selections in the *Insert* menu will be *Trendline*, but at first it will be in gray, so it cannot be selected. As soon as you successfully click on a data point to select a data series within the chart, the *Trendline* selection in the *Insert* pull-down menu becomes enabled—turns black instead of gray. Once the *Trendline* selection in the *Insert* pull-down menu turns black, you are ready to proceed. Another indication that you have been successful is the changing of color of the data points in the series in the chart.)

In the dialog box in Figure 10-18 we are being asked to select a type of trendline. The idea is that Excel will fit a trendline of the type we select to the existing data. There are half a dozen different types of trendlines based on common forms of equations. The nicest part is that Excel will do all of the math for us automatically. We select *Linear*, which means we want Excel to fit a straight line to the data. Now we click on the *Options* tab in Figure 10-18. Excel displays the dialog box shown in Figure 10-19.

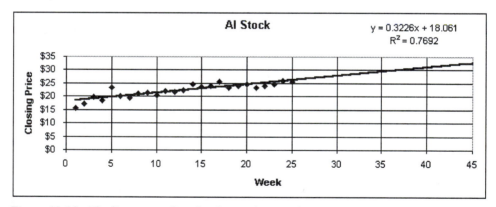

Figure 10-19. We would like Excel to extend the trendline ahead for the next 20 weeks.

We enter 20 in the *Forward* box. We want Excel to predict the prices for 20 weeks into the future. We also click on the *Display Equation on Chart* option and on the *Display R-squared Value on Chart* option. We click on *OK* and the result is shown in Figure 10-20.

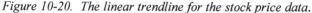

Figure 10-20. The linear trendline for the stock price data.

Excel has fitted a straight line to the data and has displayed the line for 20 weeks into the future. If the trend holds true, the price of the stock should be over $32 in 20 weeks. On the top right of the window is a text box that displays the equation and the R-squared value. The equation is

$$y = 0.3226x + 18.061$$

Here x is the week. The equation gives the formula that Excel found for predicting the price of the stock (y) given the week number (x). The R^2 value is 0.7892. R is the correlation between the values predicted by the equation and the actual values. The square of R is used as an indication of the goodness of fit of the line to the data. If all of the data points were right on the line and there was no deviance at all, the R^2 value would be 1. If the data values were randomly scattered and the line does not fit at all, the R^2 value would be 0.

If you are unhappy with the straight line trendline, you can select logarithmic, polynomial, power, exponential, or moving average. For example, fitting a polynomial of order 3 to the data gives us the trendline shown in Figure 10-21. (Order 3 means that 3 is the highest exponent of x in the polynomial equation.)

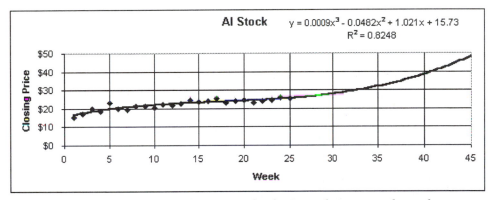

Figure 10-21. Fitting a polynomial equation of order 3 greatly improves the performance predicted for the stock price.

We have improved the R^2 value to 0.8248. The equation that Excel found is

$$y = 0.0009x^3 - 0.0482x^2 + 1.021x + 15.73$$

The nicest aspect of this equation is that according to this trendline in 20 weeks the stock price should be over $48 per share! And, it looks like the trend after 20 weeks is ever upwards! To determine what the trendline predicts for a longer period of time, we double-click on the chart and then select the trendline and double-click. In the *Trendline* dialog box we click on the *Options* tab (see Figure 10-19 again) and change the number of Forward Units requested from 20 to 40. We click on *OK*. The resulting chart is shown in Figure 10-22. According to the trendline, the stock will rise to over $130 in just 40 more weeks!

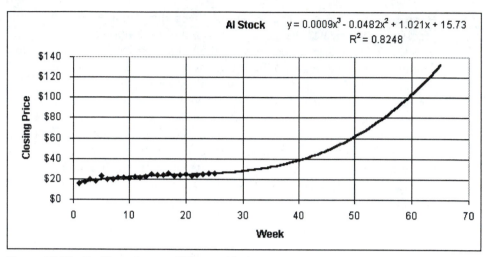

Figure 10-22. In 40 weeks we will be wealthy!

We'll make a fortune! *Caveat emptor.* Buyer beware. Trendlines based on past performance are not always good predictors of the future.

COMPUTER EXERCISES

10-1. Enter the Audio International Totals worksheet in Figure 10-1. Duplicate the charts that appear in Figures 10-2, 10-10, 10-11, 10-13, 10-14, and 10-15.

10-2. The following worksheet was used in Exercise 4-2. Either enter the worksheet with formulas or retrieve the worksheet from your disk.

Sales Analysis

Product	Winter	Spring	Summer	Fall	Total	Max
Golf	32000	62000	57000	39000		
Tennis	47000	52000	71000	29000		
Skiing	37000	21000	11000	52000		
Surfing	12000	21000	29000	13000		
Total						
Average						

All of the following charts should be as understandable as possible and should be clearly identified with titles, legends, and so on. Be careful not to include blank rows or columns in the data to be charted.

(a) Create a Column chart of total sales by season. Here, the total sales row would be plotted as columns (vertical bars) and the season names would be the X axis values. There should be four bars in the graph.

(b) Create a 3-D Column chart of sales for each of the different products by season. Do not include any totals. There should be 16 vertical bars in the chart.

(c) Display the chart in (b) as a Bar chart organized by columns.

(d) Display the chart as a Bar chart organized by rows.

(e) Display the chart in (b) as a Line chart.

(f) Which of the graphs in (b), (c), (d), or (e) is most effective? Why?

(g) Display the Tennis sales as a 3-D Pie chart with one season for each slice.

10-3. Produce a well-labeled chart that illustrates the difference in obtaining fixed annual compound interest rates of 5%, 10%, and 15% on an investment of $100,000 over the course of 10 years. Your chart should show three curves: the value of the investment growing at 5% per year, 10% per year, and 15% per year. You first should create a worksheet with all of the values to be charted.

10-4. Create a worksheet that keeps track of your major living expenses over the past five months. Include at least four different categories of expenses (for example, room and board, school, transportation, clothing, misc.). Fill in numbers. You may use fictional numbers if you wish. Calculate row and column totals. Print the worksheet. Create and print four well-labeled charts, as follows:

(a) A Pie chart of your expenses for the most recent month.

(b) A Line chart of your total expenses over the past five months.

(c) Some type of chart showing all the expenses over the past five months.

(d) A Bar chart of your choice.

10-5. The world population over the past 2000 years is estimated as follows:

Year	Population
1	200,000,000
1650	500,000,000
1850	1,000,000,000
1930	2,000,000,000
1975	4,000,000,000
1995	5,750,000,000

In the year A.D. 1, at the time of Jesus, there were fewer people in the entire world than there are in the United States today.

(a) Enter these values in a worksheet. (You may want to enter the populations in millions of people and leave off the six rightmost 0's.) Draw an X-Y (Scatter) chart of the population. The years should be the X axis values.

(b) Fit a trendline to the data. You choose the best type of trendline to use. Display the equation. Have Excel draw the trendline out past the year 2100. What will be the world population in the year 2100 according to the trendline? Does the trendline appear reasonable to you, to be a reasonable fit to the data? What do you think accounts for this?

(c) Create your own formula to fit the data. Your formula should be some function of the year and should yield the best possible approximation to the population in that year. Create a new column in your worksheet that shows the prediction made by your formula for each of the years in your worksheet. Now add the years 2000, 2010, through 2100 and your predictions for those years. Create an X-Y (Scatter) chart that has the year as the X axis values and both the actual population and your calculated population as data values. Does your formula appear to match the data? How does your trendline compare with the trendline calculated by Excel?

10-6. You have been asked to make a presentation to the United States Congress about the United States government finances and its trends. Here are data from Exercise 4-4. You can either retrieve the worksheet from your disk or enter the data and then fill in formulas for the Total receipts, Total Outlays, and Deficit.

U.S. Government Receipts And Outlays In Billions Of Dollars

	1980	1985	1990	1995
Receipts				
Individual Income Taxes	244	335	467	588
Corporate Income Taxes	65	61	94	151
Social Insurance Taxes	158	265	380	484
Excise Taxes	24	36	35	58
Other	26	37	56	65
Total Receipts				
Outlays				
National Defense	134	253	299	272
Social Security	119	189	249	336
Income Security	87	128	147	223
Medicare	32	66	98	157
All Other Government	166	181	275	317
Interest	53	129	184	234
Total Outlays				
Surplus (Deficit)				

(a) Use the worksheet to prepare four charts that best capture the most important historical points to be made about the U.S. budget. Your charts should be well thought out, well labeled, and self-explanatory.

(b) Create a chart that shows the deficit over the past four five-year time periods and then uses a trendline to forecast what the deficit would be up through 2010 if the trend continues.

(c) Prepare the text of your testimony. State in English the important points that your charts illustrate.

(d) Create a PowerPoint presentation to accompany your testimony. Include the charts in the presentation along with other appropriate screens.

10-7. The following are hourly compensation rates in U.S. dollars for production workers in selected countries. Hourly compensation includes wages, premiums, bonuses, vacation, holidays, and other leave, insurance, and benefit plans.

Country	1975	1980	1985	1990	1995
Canada	5.98	8.67	10.98	15.94	16.03
Hong Kong	0.76	1.51	1.75	3.20	5.14
Japan	3.00	5.52	6.34	12.80	23.45
Mexico	1.44	2.21	1.59	1.64	2.78
Switzerland	6.09	11.09	9.66	20.86	26.04
United States	6.36	9.87	13.01	14.91	17.45

Enter this information into a worksheet. Create a single well-labeled chart that best conveys all of this information as clearly as possible. This may take some experimentation on your part.

10-8. Obtain a recent financial statement or Annual Report for your college or university or for a company or organization with which you are familiar.

(a) Use the financial data to prepare four charts that best capture the most important points to be made about the financial situation of the organization. Your charts should be well thought out, well-labeled, and self-explanatory.

(b) Produce charts that use trendlines to show the future course of the organization if trends continue.

(c) Produce a written report on the financial health of the organization. Include your charts.

10-9. From the Internet, from a commercial on-line service, or from elsewhere obtain a series of prices for an individual stock or for the Dow Jones average. Create a chart of the data. Fit an appropriate trendline to the data. What does the trendline predict for the future?

CHAPTER 11

LOGICAL FUNCTIONS

OBJECTIVES

In this chapter you will learn how to:

- Use IF functions to select between alternatives
- Create logical tests using comparison operators
- Use nested IF functions to select among multiple alternatives
- Implement complex conditions using the AND, OR, and NOT functions

Sometimes we would like a cell to display one of two or more alternative values. If you sell over $2 million you receive a bonus of $1,000, otherwise you receive no bonus. People caught driving at a speed over 80 miles per hour (mph) on the Interstate owe a fine of $200; people caught driving between 66 and 80 mph owe $90; otherwise, no fine. In this chapter we will look at functions that are designed to solve the problem of selecting among alternatives.

THE IF FUNCTION

For orders under $100 there is a $5 Shipping and Handling charge. For orders of $100 or more there is no charge for Shipping and Handling. The total of the order is in cell D35 of a worksheet. What formula will calculate the amount of Shipping and Handling to charge?

The solution is to use an **IF** function, as follows:

$$=IF(D35<100,\ 5,\ 0)$$

The IF function always has three arguments:

$$=IF(logical\_test,\ value\_if\_true,\ value\_if\_false)$$

The first argument is a **logical test**. A logical test is an expression that evaluates to **TRUE** or **FALSE**. In this case the logical test is D35<100. If D35 is less than 100 then the logical test is TRUE otherwise the logical test is FALSE.

Logical tests usually contain one or more of the following **comparison operators**:

operator	meaning
<	less than
<=	less than or equal to
=	equal to
>=	greater than or equal to
>	greater than
<>	not equal to

Note that the operators <= >= <> are formed by two consecutive keystrokes.

The second argument in an IF function is the value of the IF function if the logical test is TRUE. The third argument is the value of the IF function if the logical test is FALSE. That is, the result of evaluating an IF function is always either the second argument or the third argument. If the first argument is TRUE then the IF function evaluates to the second argument. If the first argument is FALSE then the IF function evaluates to the third argument.

In the example, if the value in D35 is 34, then the condition (the logical test) in the IF function is TRUE and the value of the IF function is 5. If the value in cell D35 is changed to 200, then the condition becomes FALSE and the value of the IF function changes to 0.

The second and third arguments in the IF function can be any formula. For example, suppose orders under $100 are charged 5% for shipping. Then the formula would be

$$=IF(D35<100, 5\%*D35, 0)$$

A cell can contain just a logical test. That is, a cell could contain the formula =D23<>4 or a cell could contain =X17>(.08*Q55). In this case, Excel would show either TRUE or FALSE in the cell. TRUE and FALSE are called **logical values**.

ANOTHER EXAMPLE

Suppose that salespeople who sell at least $2,000,000 are entitled to a free trip to Hawaii. The names of the salespeople and their sales figures are listed in the worksheet in Figure 11-1.

	A	B	C	D	E	F	G	H
					=IF(C14>=$F$4,"FREE TRIP TO HAWAII","")			
2		**Salesperson Summary**						
3								
4			Minimum sales required for free trip to Hawaii:			$2,000,000		
5								
6								
7			Annual					
8		Name	Sales		Result			
9		Aaron	$552,030					
10		Baker	$23,400					
11		Brown	$7,358,800		FREE TRIP TO HAWAII			
12		Carey	$1,488,900					
13		Chu	$3,500,400		FREE TRIP TO HAWAII			
14		Church	$995,000					
15		Dark	$7,560					
16		Davis	$1,557,100					
17		Delaney	$5,922,000		FREE TRIP TO HAWAII			
18		Denning	$461,120					

Figure 11-1. People with sales of at least $2,000,000 are entitled to a free trip to Hawaii.

What formula should be entered into cell E9 (and filled down) so that the cell contains "FREE TRIP TO HAWAII" if the person is eligible and appears blank otherwise? The answer is

=IF(C9>=$F$4, "FREE TRIP TO HAWAII", "")

The second and third arguments are character strings that are enclosed in quotation marks. Thus if the logical test C9>=$F$4 is TRUE then the result of evaluating the function is the label "FREE TRIP TO HAWAII". If the condition C9>=$F$4 is FALSE the result of evaluating the function is the label that contains nothing, that is blank.

Text must be enclosed in quotation marks. The formula =IF(C9>=$F$4,FREE TRIP TO HAWAII,"") will not work. If the quotation marks were absent from the second argument then Excel would attempt to interpret FREE TRIP TO HAWAII as the name of a cell. Since no cell has that name (and indeed because the phrase contains a space it would be an illegal name anyway) if you try to leave the quotes off, the computer would display #NAME? in the cell, an error message meaning it does not recognize a name.

NESTED IF FUNCTIONS

Suppose that salespeople who sell under $100,000 are to be fired. Now there are three choices for the cells in column E. Cell E9 should contain FREE TRIP TO HAWAII if cell C9 contains a value of at least $2,000,000. Cell E9 should appear blank if cell C9 contains a value between $100,000 and $2,000,000. Cell E9 should contain FIRED if cell C9 is under $100,000. This is illustrated in Figure 11-2. So far, IF functions have allowed us to create formulas that select between two possibilities depending on a logical test. In this example, we need a formula that allows us to select among three possibilities. The following formula in E9 will correctly select among these three possibilities:

=IF(C9>=$F$4, "FREE TRIP TO HAWAII", IF(C9<$F$5,"FIRED",""))

This formula contains nested IF functions. This means that one IF function contains another IF function as an argument. The key to working with nested IF functions is to remember that IF functions always should have exactly three arguments.

The preceding formula can be read as follows: "If C9 is greater than or equal to F4 then this cell should show FREE TRIP TO HAWAII. Otherwise, if C9 is less than F5 then this cell should show FIRED otherwise this cell should appear blank."

| | | =IF(C14>=$F$4,"FREE TRIP TO HAWAII",IF(C14<$F$5,"FIRED","")) |

E14

	A	B	C	D	E	F	G	H
1								
2		**Salesperson Summary**						
3								
4		Minimum sales required for free trip to Hawaii:				$2,000,000		
5		People who sell under this amount are fired:				$100,000		
6								
7			*Annual*					
8		*Name*	*Sales*		*Result*			
9		Aaron	$552,030					
10		Baker	$23,400		FIRED			
11		Brown	$7,358,800		FREE TRIP TO HAWAII			
12		Carey	$1,488,900					
13		Chu	$3,500,400		FREE TRIP TO HAWAII			
14		Church	$995,000					
15		Dark	$7,560		FIRED			
16		Davis	$1,557,100					
17		Delaney	$5,922,000		FREE TRIP TO HAWAII			
18		Denning	$461,120					

Sheet1 / Sheet2 / Sheet3 / Sheet4 / Sheet5 / Sheet6 /

Figure 11-2. People with sales of under $100,000 are fired. Now there are three possibilities.

What are the arguments here? The outer IF function has three arguments:

1. The logical test: C9>$F$4
2. The value if the condition is TRUE: "FREE TRIP TO HAWAII"
3. The value if the condition is FALSE: IF(C9<$F$5,"FIRED","")

The inner IF function is the third argument. It, too, clearly has three arguments:

1. The logical test: C9<$F$5
2. The value if the condition is TRUE :   "FIRED"
3. The value if the condition is FALSE: ""

YOU TRY

A worksheet for tabulating the results of the Tiger football season is given in Figure 11-3. We would like the cells in column G to say WIN if the Tigers won, TIE if the number of points each scored was equal, and LOSE if the Tigers lost. What should be the formula in G7? Write out your answer before continuing.

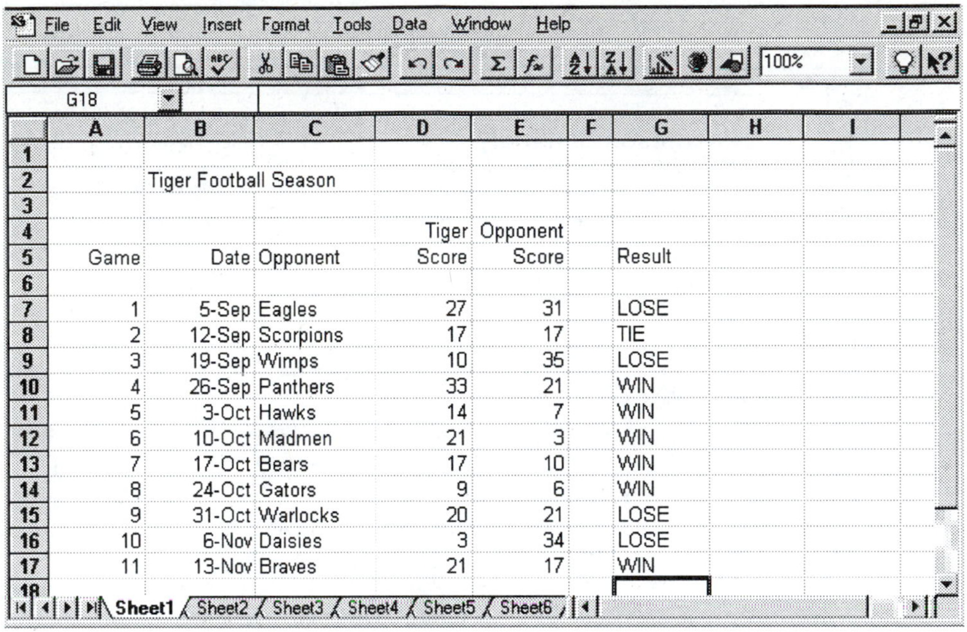

Figure 11-3. What formula has been placed in G7 and filled down?

There are several possible correct answers. A good solution would be

=IF(D7>E7, "WIN", IF(D7=E7,"TIE","LOSE"))

Here the computer first checks to see if D7 is greater than E7. If that logical test is TRUE then the answer is WIN and the evaluation is over. If D7 is not greater than E7 then the computer evaluates the third argument, the inner IF function. Now the computer checks the first argument of the inner IF function. The computer checks to see if D7 equals E7. If D7 does equal E7 then the answer is TIE. If the first condition is FALSE and then the second condition is FALSE then the answer is LOSE. With nested IF functions the computer always makes its way from the outside in.

We could rearrange the order, for example, by checking for a tie first:

=IF(D7=E7, "TIE", IF(D7>E7,"WIN","LOSE"))

There are four other similar rearrangements that would work.

Suppose we want the cells in column G to contain the name of the team that won (or the word "Tie") as in the worksheet shown Figure 11-4. What formula would you put in cell G7 and then fill down?

Here, what we would need to do is to change two of the arguments, as follows:

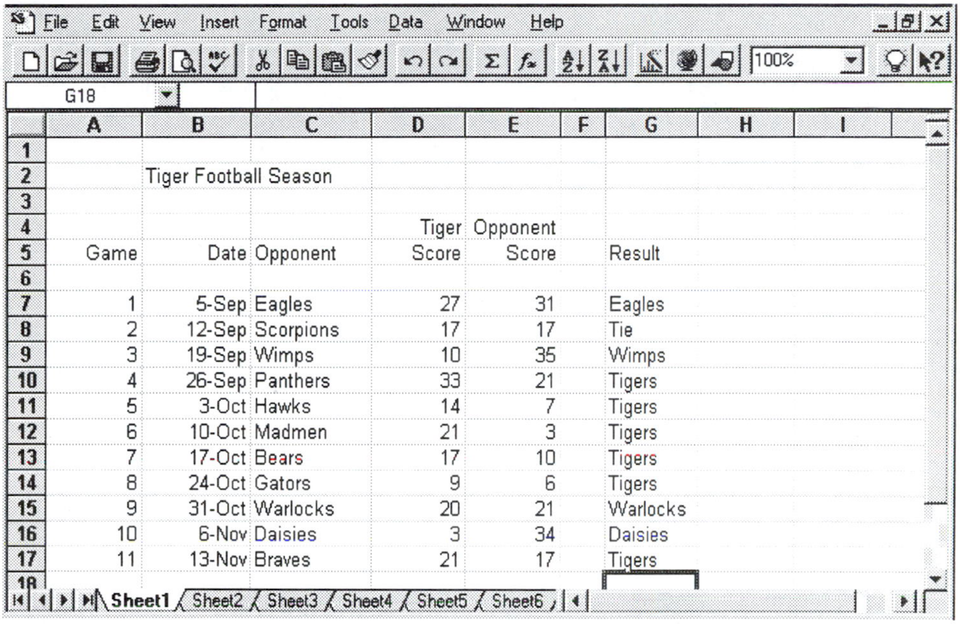

	A	B	C	D	E	F	G	H	I
1									
2		Tiger Football Season							
3									
4				Tiger	Opponent				
5	Game	Date	Opponent	Score	Score		Result		
6									
7	1	5-Sep	Eagles	27	31		Eagles		
8	2	12-Sep	Scorpions	17	17		Tie		
9	3	19-Sep	Wimps	10	35		Wimps		
10	4	26-Sep	Panthers	33	21		Tigers		
11	5	3-Oct	Hawks	14	7		Tigers		
12	6	10-Oct	Madmen	21	3		Tigers		
13	7	17-Oct	Bears	17	10		Tigers		
14	8	24-Oct	Gators	9	6		Tigers		
15	9	31-Oct	Warlocks	20	21		Warlocks		
16	10	6-Nov	Daisies	3	34		Daisies		
17	11	13-Nov	Braves	21	17		Tigers		

Figure 11-4. We would like the name of the winner to appear in column G or the word "Tie" if there is a tie. What is the formula in cell G7?

=IF(D7>E7, "Tigers", IF(D7=E7,"Tie",C7))

The cell C7 contains the name of the opponent. Of course, when this formula is filled down, the row numbers of C7, D7, and E7 will be adjusted accordingly.

If we wanted to choose among four alternatives, we would need three nested IF functions. There can be up to seven nested IF functions in a formula. Of course, all IF functions must have three arguments. Any of these arguments can be other IF functions.

LOGICAL FUNCTIONS AND, OR, NOT

At the Tropical Resort there are 600 guest rooms. The guest rooms are classified as either suites, doubles, or singles. Some face the beach; some face the pool; some face inland (the parking lot). The resort manager has decided to charge $259 per night for suites that face the beach. All other rooms will be $179 per night. The worksheet in Figure 11-5 shows a list of the guest rooms. Each cell in column E should contain the price of the room. What formula should appear in cell E6 and then be filled down?

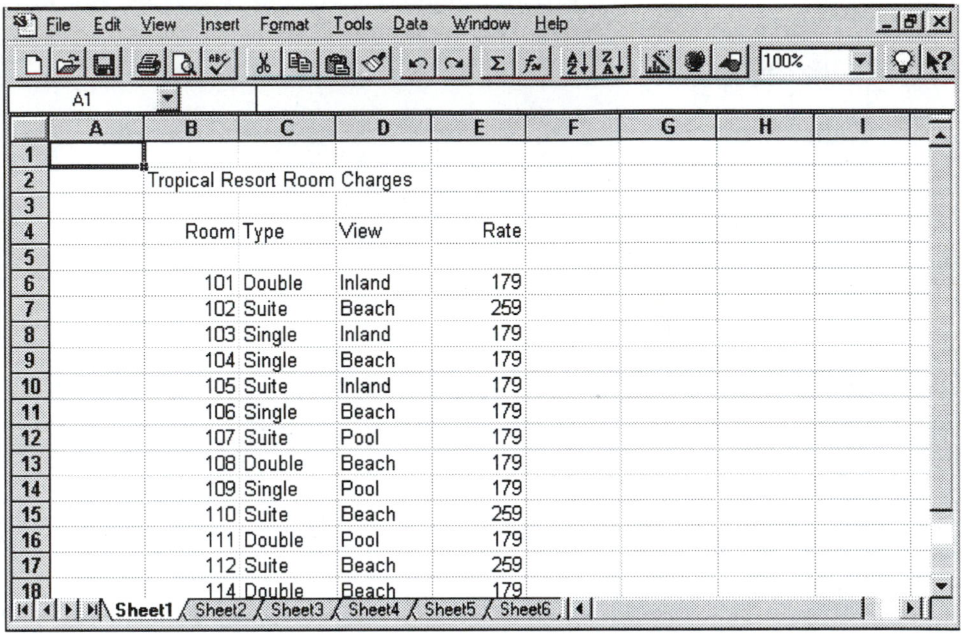

	A	B	C	D	E
1					
2		Tropical Resort Room Charges			
3					
4		Room	Type	View	Rate
5					
6		101	Double	Inland	179
7		102	Suite	Beach	259
8		103	Single	Inland	179
9		104	Single	Beach	179
10		105	Suite	Inland	179
11		106	Single	Beach	179
12		107	Suite	Pool	179
13		108	Double	Beach	179
14		109	Single	Pool	179
15		110	Suite	Beach	259
16		111	Double	Pool	179
17		112	Suite	Beach	259
18		114	Double	Beach	179

Figure 11-5. Suites that face the beach are $259 per night. All other rooms are $179 per night. What formula has been placed in E6 and filled down?

Clearly, we want to use an IF function here as there are two alternatives. The IF function would have the basic form

=IF(logical_test, 259, 179)

Now we need to fill in the logical test. There are two parts to the logical test, both of which must be TRUE for the logical test as a whole to be TRUE. That is, in order for the room to cost $259 the room both must be a suite and must face the beach.

First, we can check whether a cell contains a specific label with a logical test like C6="Suite". This logical test will be TRUE if C6 contains the word "Suite" and FALSE otherwise.

Excel provides the **AND** function for the purpose of testing whether two or more logical values all are TRUE. The completed formula would be

=IF(AND(C6="Suite",D6="Beach"), 259, 179)

The logical test is AND(C6="Suite",D6="Beach") This logical test will be TRUE only if both C6 contains the word "Suite" and D6 contains the word "Beach".

The AND function sometimes is called a **Boolean function**. (George Boole was an English mathematician who developed key ideas of symbolic logic. His best known book is *The Laws of Thought*, which was published in 1854.) Boolean functions work on arguments that are logical values, that are TRUE or FALSE, just the way that arithmetic functions like SUM and AVERAGE work on arguments that are numbers. The value produced by a Boolean function also is a logical value (just the way that the value produced by an arithmetic function is a number). An AND function always evaluates to TRUE or FALSE.

The AND function corresponds closely to the meaning of the word "and" in English. An AND function can have up to 30 arguments. Each of the arguments must evaluate to TRUE or FALSE. The value of the AND function is TRUE only if all of its operands are TRUE. The value of an AND function is FALSE if any of its arguments is FALSE. For example, if we look at an AND function with two arguments:

Function	Value
AND(TRUE,TRUE)	TRUE
AND(TRUE,FALSE)	FALSE
AND(FALSE,TRUE)	FALSE
AND(FALSE,FALSE)	FALSE

So, for example, the value of

$$=AND(2+2=4,3+3=5)$$

would be FALSE.

There are two other Boolean functions: **OR** and **NOT**.

If we wrote the formula =IF(OR(D6="Suite",E6="Beach"), 259, 179) then a room would cost $259 if it is a suite or if it faces the beach or both.

The OR function also corresponds closely to the meaning of the word "or" in English. An OR function can have up to 30 arguments. Each of the arguments must evaluate to TRUE or FALSE. The value of the OR function is TRUE only if any of its operands is TRUE. The value of an OR function is FALSE only if all of its arguments are FALSE. For example, if we look at an OR function with two arguments:

Function	Value
OR(TRUE,TRUE)	TRUE
OR(TRUE,FALSE)	TRUE
OR(FALSE,TRUE)	TRUE
OR(FALSE,FALSE)	FALSE

So, for example, the value of

$$=OR(2+2=4,3+3=5)$$

would be TRUE.

The NOT function transforms TRUE into FALSE and FALSE into TRUE.

Function	Value
NOT(TRUE)	FALSE
NOT(FALSE)	TRUE

The NOT function can have only a single argument. The NOT function also follows normal English usage. I hold a black belt in the martial arts. Not!

ANOTHER EXAMPLE

Suppose the manager decides that suites that face the beach will be $259. All other suites will be $189. Doubles that do not face inland will be $189. All other rooms will be $149. (See Figure 11-6.)

Now we have three possibilities. The formula for cell E6 could have the form

$$=IF(logical\_test1, 259, IF(logical\_test2,189,149))$$

We need to fill in the logical tests. Logical_test1 is the same as before, namely

$$AND(C6="Suite",D6="Beach")$$

The tough one is logical_test2. Logical_test2 consists of an OR of two parts. The first part of logical_test2 is

$$D6="Suite"$$

The second part of logical_test2 is

$$AND(C6="Double",NOT(D6="Inland"))$$

So the entire formula would be

$$=IF(AND(C6="Suite",D6="Beach"), 259, IF(OR(C6="Suite",$$
$$AND(C6="Double",NOT(D6="Inland"))),189,149))$$

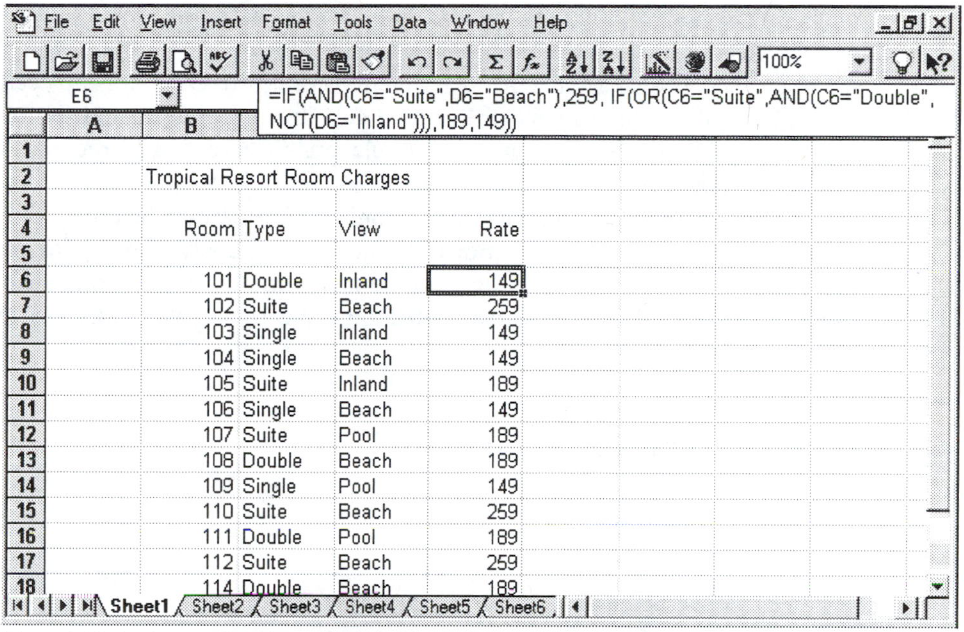

Figure 11-6. Suites that face the beach are $259 per night. All other suites are $189 per night as are doubles that do not face inland. All other rooms are $149.

Alternatively, the formula could be written

$$=IF(AND(C6="Suite",D6="Beach"), 259, IF(C6="Suite",189,$$
$$IF(AND(C6="Double",NOT(D6="Inland")),189,149)))$$

Here we have treated the two parts of logical_test2 separately. Another nested IF has been added to accommodate this extra condition. This formula resembles the original statement of the problem on the previous page. Do you see how these two formulas are equivalent? If not, you might take a few minutes to work through the two formulas by writing out the arguments for each of the IF functions and applying the formulas to the examples in Figure 11-6.

TESTING IF FUNCTIONS

Testing worksheets that contain IF functions presents a challenge. Consider the worksheet for salespeople in Figure 11-2. The worksheet basically contains one nested IF function that has been filled down column E. To test this worksheet you should try Annual Sales values of (1) a number more than $2,000,000 (for example $5,000,000), (2) the number $2,000,000 exactly, (3) a number between $2,000,000 and $100,000 (for example $995,000), (4) the number $100,000 exactly, and (5) a number below $100,000 (for example $23,400). You also should try varying the value in C9 (the top cell in the column) and the value in C89 (the bottom cell in the column) and the value in a cell between just to be sure that the formula was filled down correctly. You also should try changing the threshold values in F4 and F5.

IF functions with complicated conditions require careful testing. Worksheets with many independent IF functions require very extensive testing to make sure that they are correct. It is quite possible and common for a worksheet with IF functions to work correctly most of the time but to fail when certain relatively unlikely conditions are true.

PENCIL AND PAPER EXERCISES

11-1. Consider the following worksheet:

	A	B	C	D	E	F	G	H	I
1									
2		Exercise 11-1							
3									
4	86	-4	-8	fun					
5	-47	5	26	37					
6	2.3	7	Excel	198					
7	computer	18	4.6	3					
8	56	102		-19					
9									

What would be the result of evaluating each of the following formulas?

(a) =IF(B5>6,"YES","NO")
(b) =IF(B4<D6,C5,A6)
(c) =IF(SUM(B4:D4)>=D5,A4,"NOPE")
(d) =B5<A3
(e) =(2*B6)>(C4+10)
(f) =IF(B3=12,47,IF(C4<D5,59,B7))
(g) =IF(C4=26,IF(B5=19,2,4),IF(A7=56,6,8))
(h) =AND(A7>A5,D6<B6)
(i) =IF(AND(OR(B4=7,C5="Excel"),NOT(B6>20))),44,33)
(j) =IF(OR(NOT(B5<6),D7>3),A7,IF(AND(C4=2*B4,D8>D7),C6,D4))

11-2. We are creating a worksheet to select stocks for our clients. We have gathered some of the relevant data in the following worksheet. (The P/E Ratio is the closing price divided by this year's earnings.)

	File Edit View Insert Format Tools Data Window Help						
	F8	=E8/D8					
	A	B	C	D	E	F	G
1							
2		**Our Stock Recommendations**					
3							
4	Stock	Earnings	Earnings	Earnings	Closing	P/E	We
5		2 yrs ago	Last yr.	This yr.	Price	ratio	Recommend
6							
7	AA Electronics	$3.47	$3.59	$3.83	$48.50	12.7	
8	Ardvark Intl	$0.69	$1.24	$0.53	$15.75	29.7	
9	Abaco	$4.23	$5.89	$5.92	$33.25	5.6	
10	Abandon Mines	$0.12	$0.15	$0.23	$2.25	9.8	
11	Abernathy	$1.27	$1.31	$0.98	$21.00	21.4	

What formula would go into cell G7 and be filled down for each of the following recommendations? Each of the cells in column G should contain BUY, HOLD, SELL, or appear blank. When no recommendation is made, the cell should appear blank. I have answered part (a) just to give you the basic idea.

Each part is independent of the others.

(a) BUY if the P/E Ratio is below 10. *Answer: =IF(F7<10,"BUY","")*

(b) BUY if the earnings have increased this year.
    SELL if the earnings have decreased this year.

(c) BUY if the earnings have increased for each of the two years and the P/E
        Ratio is below 10.
    SELL if the earnings have decreased for each of the two years.

(d) BUY if this year's earnings are up over 20% from last year and this year's
        earnings are up over 30% from 2 years ago or if the P/E ratio is below 8.
    SELL if this year's earnings are down over 20% from last year or if the P/E
        ratio is above 20.
    HOLD otherwise.

COMPUTER EXERCISES

11-3. At Hill University students who register for at least 12 credits are considered Full-Time students and pay a flat $4,320 tuition. Students who register for fewer than 12 credits are considered Part-Time students and pay $360 per credit. Create a worksheet that allows you to enter a student's name and the number of credits for which he or she is registering. The worksheet should then display (1) the status of the student (Full-Time or Part-Time) and (2) the amount of tuition owed.

Try your worksheet on the following three students: Maria 15 credits, John 6 credits, Yu 12 credits.

11-4. At the county courthouse speeders pay a fine of $50 plus $5 for every mph above the speed limit. Anyone caught driving 90 mph or over pays an extra $200. Create a worksheet that will allow you to enter a driver's name, the speed limit on the road where the driver was caught, and the driver's speed. If the driver's speed did not exceed the speed limit, then the worksheet should display SORRY! NO FINE. Otherwise the worksheet should display the fine owed.

Try your worksheet on the following five tickets:

Name	Speed Limit	Driver's Speed
Alicia	40	55
Bob	55	97
Carlos	65	65
Darlene	25	28
Ernie	45	17

11-5. An employee is eligible for retirement if he or she satisfies at least one of the following three criteria:

    (i)   the employee has worked here for at least 40 years
    (ii) the employee is 65 or over
    (iii) the employee has worked here for at least 30 years and is 60 or over

(a) Create a worksheet that allows one person to enter in his or her age and the number of years worked here. A cell in the worksheet should respond either CONGRATULATIONS! YOU ARE ELIGIBLE FOR RETIREMENT or it should respond BACK TO WORK.

(b) Add a cell that will indicate how many years it will be until the employee is eligible for retirement if he or she is not now eligible.

You may use extra cells in your worksheet.

11-6. Salespeople receive $10,000 base salary plus a commission of 1.5% of sales. Anyone who sells over $3 million receives a free vacation in Tahiti for two people. Anyone who sells over $5 million receives an additional $4,000 bonus. At the end of the year salespeople are rated as follows: under $2 million DUD, $2 million through $5 million STAR, over $5 million SUPERSTAR. Create a worksheet that allows you to enter a salesperson's name and annual sales amount and then calculates the following:

SALESPERSON SUMMARY

NAME:	(input)
ANNUAL SALES:	(input)
BASE SALARY:	$10,000
COMMISSION:	(formula)
BONUS:	(formula)
TOTAL PAY:	(formula)
FREE VACATION?	(formula)
STATUS:	(formula)

11-7. The administration and faculty at New Ivy University have thought long and hard about their admission criteria. They have decided to forget about activities, athletics, parents who graduated from NIU, interviews, recommendations, etc. in deciding which high school students should be admitted. NIU is going to decide admission strictly on academics. Only standardized test scores and grades will count.

Applicants will not have to write essays. All they will have to submit are five numbers: three test scores (Math SAT score, Verbal SAT score, and one SAT II subject test score), rank in graduating class, and number of students in graduating class. SAT test scores always range from 200 to 800.

The following criteria are used in deciding admissions:

1. If an impossible number is submitted, the applicant is refused admission.
2. If any test score is 800, the applicant is accepted.
3. If any of the test scores is below 300, the applicant is refused admission.
4. If the Math and Verbal SAT scores average above 600 and the applicant is in the top quarter of the graduating class, the applicant is accepted.
5. If any two of the test scores are below 400 or the applicant is in the bottom quarter of the graduating class, the applicant is refused admission.
6. Otherwise the applicant is put on the waiting list.

These criteria are applied in order. Thus, any impossible number disqualifies an applicant. If the five numbers are valid, then any test score of 800 means acceptance, regardless of the other numbers. If the first two criteria do not hold, then check the third criterion. And so on.

For this exercise you are to create a worksheet to decide whether an applicant is admitted. Your worksheet should be designed to accept the information for a single applicant. Thus a visiting high school senior could enter the information into your worksheet and find out the admission decision. In your worksheet you should have a different cell for each criterion. Then you should combine all six criteria into a final decision of either ACCEPTED, DENIED ADMISSION, or WAITING LIST.

Try your worksheet on each of the following 11 applicants:

Student	Math SAT	Verbal SAT	SAT II Subject	Rank	Class Size
A	520	480	450	103	298
B	643	121	800	3	137
C	256	302	800	492	506
D	593	602	720	352	440
E	598	800	740	193	160
F	650	680	240	53	800
G	598	702	550	120	410
H	310	520	390	42	77
I	430	290	453	10	240
J	470	510	423	-15	137
K	602	723	934	210	982

11-8. The number 371 is a "special" number because the sum of the cubes of the digits that compose it is equal to the number itself:

$$3^3 + 7^3 + 1^3 = 3*3*3 + 7*7*7 + 1*1*1 = 27 + 343 + 1 = 371$$

This is very unusual. Most numbers are not "special". For example, 502 is not "special" because $5^3 + 0^3 + 2^3 = 125 + 0 + 8 = 133$ rather than 502.

Create a worksheet that will find the highest three-digit "special" number. (Three digit numbers are 100, 101, 102, ... 998, 999.) The answer should be calculated by the worksheet and appear automatically in an appropriately labeled cell at the top of the worksheet. This cell must have a formula in it, not just the answer typed in. Do not solve the problem by typing 900 separate entries in the worksheet. Use formulas and the Fill operation throughout.

11-9. The Game of Life was invented by the Cambridge mathematician John Conway in the 1960s. The Game of Life takes place on an infinite two-dimensional grid. Each cell in the grid is either dead or alive. Each cell has eight neighbors, the cells that touch its sides or corners.

If a cell is alive it will survive into the next time period (next generation) if it has two or three neighbors that also are alive. If a cell is alive and has four or more neighbors that are alive, it will die of overcrowding. If a cell is alive and has zero or one neighbor that is alive, it will die of exposure.

If a cell is dead it will remain dead in the next generation unless exactly three of its neighbors are alive. In this case, the cell will be "born" in the next generation.

The rules are applied simultaneously to all cells from one generation to the next. We begin the game at Generation 1 with some configuration of living cells specified by the user. Each subsequent generation is determined by the rules established by Conway. The living cells can flourish and expand or stay the same or die off.

For example, suppose we start with the following configuration:

Applying Conway's rules, cell E7 dies off because it has only one living neighbor. Cell F7 survives because it has two living neighbors. Cell G7 survives. Cell H7 dies. New cells are born at F6, G6, F8, and G8 because all were dead but have three living neighbors. No other cells are born. The result is the following configuration:

	A	B	C	D	E	F	G	H	I	J	K	L	M	N
1														
2		Generation						2						
3														
4														
5														
6						1	1							
7						1	1							
8						1	1							
9														
10														

Applying the rules to these cells we get the following configuration:

	A	B	C	D	E	F	G	H	I	J	K	L	M	N
1														
2		Generation						3						
3														
4														
5														
6						1	1							
7					1			1						
8						1	1							
9														
10														

This configuration is stable. All of the living cells have two or three neighbors so all survive. No new cells are born. So the next generation looks the same as the previous generation.

	A	B	C	D	E	F	G	H	I	J	K	L	M	N
1														
2		Generation						4						
3														
4														
5														
6						1	1							
7					1			1						
8						1	1							
9														
10														

The colony is immortal. It stays the same forever.

Implement the Game of Life in Excel. Living cells should be represented by 1's. Dead cells should appear blank. (Hint: You might want to represent dead cells by 0's but not display the 0's by clicking off the *Zero Values* box in the *View* sheet in the *Options...* selection in the *Tools* pull-down menu.) You should use at least a 20 x 20 universe and draw a box around the universe. The universe should be surrounded by a blank row or column on all four sides so nothing leaks at the edges of the universe. At the top of each universe you should display the generation number.

The top left of the first sheet in the workbook should be a special universe for the user to enter in the initial configuration of 1's into Generation 1. The rest of the workbook should be protected from being changed. Any initial configuration of 1's should be acceptable. It is up to you how to design the rest of the workbook. You might want to use a separate worksheet for each generation. Or you might want to do all of the work in one worksheet. Or you might want to have one area of a worksheet where the universe changes over time. In this case you might want to turn off *Automatic Recalculation* in the *Calculation* tab in the *Options...* selection in the *Tools* pull-down menu and have the formulas recalculate the next generation only when you press F9. The design of the workbook is up to you.

Be sure that the rules are applied only to cells in one generation to obtain the configuration of cells in the next generation. The workbook should be easy to use and should accurately portray the progress of life in the universe over at least a dozen generations, and preferably more, for any initial configuration.

(a) Try your workbook with the preceding initial configuration, with the three initial configurations that follow, and with three new initial configurations of your choice. For each of the initial configurations determine the ultimate fate of the inhabitants, for example whether the colony lives and expands forever, is stable, or dies off.

	A	B	C	D	E	F	G	H	I	J	K	L	M	N
1														
2			Generation					1						
3														
4														
5														
6														
7					1		1							
8					1	1	1							
9					1		1							
10														

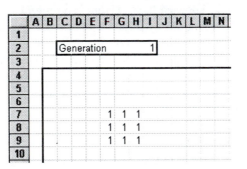

(b) For extra credit, determine the ultimate fate of the following initial configuration. You may need to modify your workbook. (Remember that the universe in the Game of Life is as large as necessary, as is the number of generations.)

(c) For extra credit, find an original initial condition where the colony grows in number and expands forever.

CHAPTER **12**

FUNCTIONS RELATED TO IF

OBJECTIVES

In this chapter you will learn how to:

- Use COUNTIF to count the cells that meet some criteria
- Use SUMIF to add cells meeting some criteria
- Create lookup tables
- Use VLOOKUP for inexact and exact matches
- Use the "IS" functions to check for error conditions

In this chapter we discuss the use of several functions that are related to the IF function in solving problems involving the selection of different values.

THE COUNTIF FUNCTION

The countries of the world are listed in order of Gross National Product per Capita in the worksheet in Figure 12-1. That is, each country is listed, followed by the continent, the Gross National Product for the country, the population of the country in millions of people, and the average Gross National Product per person in the country.

We are interested in calculating various statistics about the countries of the world. For example, suppose we wanted to have a cell that reported the total number of countries in Asia. There are several approaches to solving this problem, but an easy approach involves the use of the **COUNTIF** function. In a cell we could type the formula

=COUNTIF(C7:C189,"=Asia")

	A	B	C	D	E	F	G
2		Countries of the World by Per Capita GNP					
3							
4				GNP in	Population	GNP per	
5		Country	Continent	$ millions	in millions	Capita	
6							
7	1	Switzerland	Europe	254,066	7.0	$36,410	
8	2	Luxembourg	Europe	14,233	0.4	$35,850	
9	3	Japan	Asia	3,926,668	124.9	$31,450	
10	4	Denmark	Europe	137,610	5.2	$26,510	
11	5	Norway	Europe	113,527	4.3	$26,340	
12	6	Sweden	Europe	216,294	8.7	$24,830	
13	7	United States	North America	6,387,686	258.1	$24,750	
14	8	Iceland	Europe	6,236	0.3	$23,620	
185	179	Nepal	Asia	3,174	19.8	$160	
186	180	Sierra Leone	Africa	647	4.6	$140	
187	181	Tanzania	Africa	2,521	25.2	$100	
188	182	Ethiopia	Africa	5,228	52.3	$100	
189	183	Mozambique	Africa	1,375	17.2	$80	
190							

Figure 12-1. GNP and population of the countries of the world.

This formula instructs Excel to count up all of the cells in the range C7:C189 that contain the word "Asia". In fact, we could omit the = sign and just enter the formula

=COUNTIF(C7:C189,"Asia")

The COUNTIF function has two arguments, a range and the criterion. The criterion is written in quotes. The value returned by the function is the number of nonblank cells in the range that meet the criterion.

As another example, suppose we want to have a cell that gives the number of countries that have a GNP above $100 billion. Since in the worksheet GNPs are given in millions of dollars, we could use the formula

=COUNTIF(D7:D189,">100000")

This would return the number of values in D7:D189 that are greater than 100000. We even could use a comma in the number to make it easier to understand. The formula could be

=COUNTIF(D7:D189,">100,000")

THE SUMIF FUNCTION

Now suppose we want to find the total GNP for Asia. To solve this problem we could use the formula

=SUMIF(C7:C189,"Asia",D7:D189)

The **SUMIF** function has three arguments: the range of the cells to be tested, the criterion to be used in the test, and the range that contains the cells to be summed. In this case, for each cell in the range C7:C189 that contains the word "Asia" the number in the corresponding cell in the range D7:D189 will be added into the total that is calculated by the function.

If we want a cell that calculates the total number of people who live in countries that have under $1,000 GNP per capita, we could enter the formula

=SUMIF(F7:F189,"<1,000",E7:E189)

In fact, this worksheet is organized as an Excel list. There are many operations that can be performed with this data, as we will see in Chapter 16.

USING IF FUNCTIONS IN EXTRA COLUMNS

Suppose we would like to have the largest GNP of any country in Africa appear in a cell at the bottom of the worksheet. Well, you might say, let's just use the MAXIF function. Unfortunately, there is no MAXIF function in Excel.

One approach is to use an extra column to pull out the GNP of the countries that are in Africa. (See Figure 12-2.) Here, cell G7 contains the formula

=IF(C7="Africa",D7,"")

which has been filled down column G. Thus the cells in column G contain the GNP for each country in Africa and are blank for each country not in Africa. In cell G191 we place the formula

=MAX(G7:G189)

so that cell G191 contains the highest GNP of any country in Africa.

This technique of using an extra column containing IF functions is useful in solving many different problems.

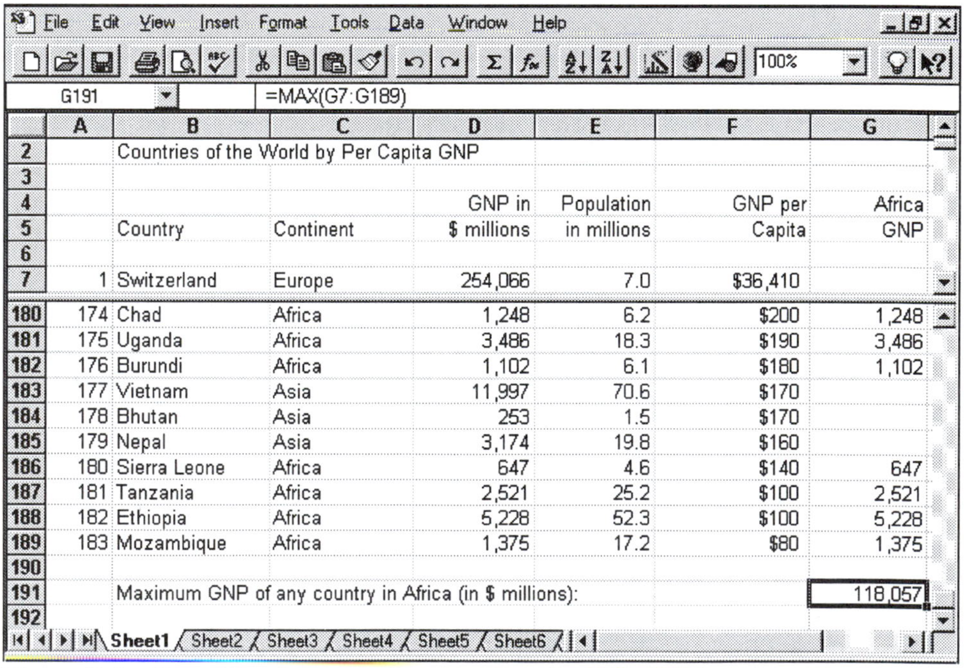

	A	B	C	D	E	F	G
2		Countries of the World by Per Capita GNP					
3							
4				GNP in	Population	GNP per	Africa
5		Country	Continent	$ millions	in millions	Capita	GNP
6							
7	1	Switzerland	Europe	254,066	7.0	$36,410	
180	174	Chad	Africa	1,248	6.2	$200	1,248
181	175	Uganda	Africa	3,486	18.3	$190	3,486
182	176	Burundi	Africa	1,102	6.1	$180	1,102
183	177	Vietnam	Asia	11,997	70.6	$170	
184	178	Bhutan	Asia	253	1.5	$170	
185	179	Nepal	Asia	3,174	19.8	$160	
186	180	Sierra Leone	Africa	647	4.6	$140	647
187	181	Tanzania	Africa	2,521	25.2	$100	2,521
188	182	Ethiopia	Africa	5,228	52.3	$100	5,228
189	183	Mozambique	Africa	1,375	17.2	$80	1,375
190							
191		Maximum GNP of any country in Africa (in $ millions):					118,057
192							

Figure 12-2. Using IF in an extra column to select the GNP of African countries.

THE VLOOKUP FUNCTION

It often is convenient to express a multi-way selection in a table. For example, we might have a tax rate table which indicates that if you earned so much money, then your tax rate is such and such. Or, we might give volume discounts, where the more you purchase, the lower the price. This could be expressed in a volume discount table that indicates how much you must purchase to qualify for the different discounts. Excel provides the special function **VLOOKUP** especially for making selections by looking up values in a table.

The VLOOKUP function has three arguments. The first argument is the number you want to look up. The second argument is the location of the **vertical lookup table**. The third argument indicates which column in the table contains the answer, the value to be returned by the function.

Suppose that the photocopy center charges are based on the number of photocopies ordered, as follows:

PHOTOCOPY PRICES

Number Of Copies	Price Per Page
1 to 19	.06
20 to 99	.05
100 to 499	.04
500 to 999	.035
1000 or more	.03

In cell C15 we have the number of copies. We would like the price per page to appear in cell C17. What formula should go into cell C17?

We could solve this problem using a nested IF function. The cell would contain the formula

=IF(C15<20,.06,IF(C15<100,.05,IF(C15<500,.04,IF(C15<1000,.035,.03))))

This formula works, but it is cumbersome and does not indicate the price table explicitly in the worksheet. If the price changes we would need to find and change the formula. An alternative approach to solving this problem uses a vertical lookup table and VLOOKUP function, as in Figure 12-3. The formula in cell C17 is

=VLOOKUP(C15,E20:F24,2)

This formula instructs the computer to look up the number in cell C15 in the vertical lookup table located in cells E20 through F24. The value of the function

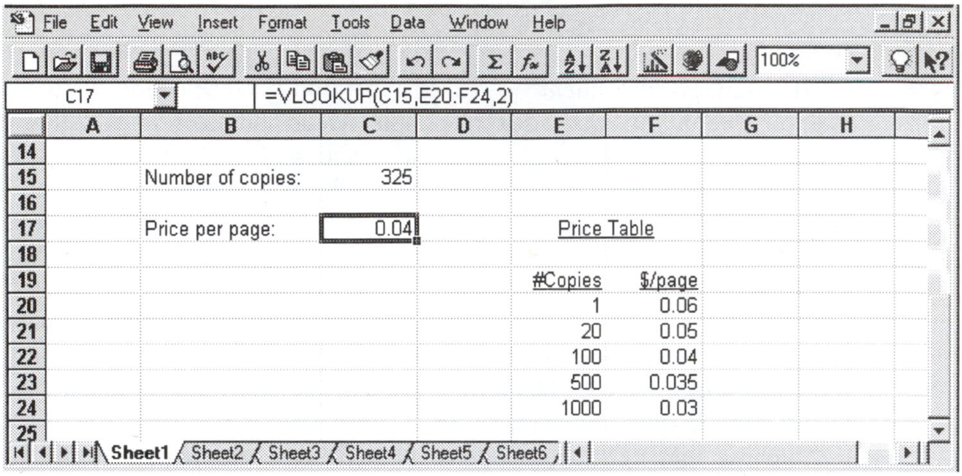

Figure 12-3. Using the lookup table in E20:F24 to find the price per page for the number of copies in C15.

will be the corresponding value in the second column of the vertical lookup table (column F).

A vertical lookup table has a definite organization. The values in the first column normally are in ascending order. The computer takes the number in C15 and compares it to the top left cell in the lookup table. If the number in the cell is less than C15, the computer proceeds to the next cell down. The computer keeps chugging down the left column until it finds a number that is greater than the value in C15. At that point it goes up one cell and over to the column in the vertical lookup table indicated by the third argument. The third argument is called the **column index**. This may sound confusing at first, but it works well.

In the example in Figure 12-3, the number to be looked up in the table is 325. The computer compares 1 with 325. 1 is less than 325 so the computer moves down a cell. 20 is less than 325 so the computer moves down another cell. 100 is less than 325 so the computer moves down a cell. At last, 500 is greater than 325. The computer moves up one cell. This is the row with the answer. Then it moves over to the second column in the vertical lookup table (because the third argument is 2). Finally the computer returns the number 0.04. The number 0.04 is the result of evaluating the VLOOKUP function in cell C17.

Suppose the number in cell C15 was 700. The result of evaluating the VLOOKUP function in C17 would be 0.035.

Suppose the number in cell C15 was 5000. The result of evaluating the VLOOKUP function in C17 would be 0.03. If the number to be looked up is larger than any number in the first column of the table, then the computer stops at the last row in the table.

Suppose the number in cell C15 was -25. The result of evaluating the VLOOKUP function in C17 would be the error message #N/A, which stands for "No value available." If the number to be looked up is less than the first value in the table, then the computer indicates an error.

Suppose the number in cell C15 was 100. The result of evaluating the VLOOKUP function in C17 would be 0.04. In this case the first number in the column that would be larger than the number we are looking up would be 500. The computer would then go up one cell and over to column F.

A major advantage of using a lookup table is that the numbers in the table become an apparent part of the worksheet. The person using the worksheet can see the table rather than having the values hidden inside a nested IF formula. If the pricing policy changes, we can change the numbers in the table rather than trying to edit a complicated formula. For example, if the price per page for 100 to 499 copies is raised to $0.045, the number in cell F22 can be changed to 0.045. In the worksheet in Figure 12-3 the result of evaluating the formula in C17 would become 0.045.

What is the purpose of the third argument, the column index? Suppose we had two classes of customers, regular and preferred, and two sets of rates. The regular customers are "walk-ins", anyone who walks in the door. The preferred customers pay us an annual fee for special service and prices. We could assign regular customers a code of 2 and preferred customers a code of 3. Now we could determine the rate by making the code be the column index, as in the worksheet in Figure 12-4.

File	Edit	View	Insert	Format	Tools	Data	Window	Help		

C17   =VLOOKUP(C15,E20:G24,C12)

	A	B	C	D	E	F	G	H
11								
12		Customer type:	3					
13		(2=regular, 3=prefered)						
14								
15		Number of copies:	700					
16								
17		Price per page:	0.03		Price Table			
18						$/page	$/page	
19					#Copies	regular	preferred	
20					1	0.06	0.05	
21					20	0.05	0.04	
22					100	0.04	0.04	
23					500	0.035	0.03	
24					1000	0.03	0.025	

Sheet1 / Sheet2 / Sheet3 / Sheet4 / Sheet5 / Sheet6

Figure 12-4. The lookup table with two classes of customers.

We entered the Customer Type in C12 and used that entry as the column index in the formula in C17

=VLOOKUP(C15,E20:G24,C12)

Note that we extended the lookup table over to column G in the formula. We could be fancier and have the person type in "regular" or "preferred" and then use an IF function to determine the column index.

This same technique would work for income tax tables where there are different rates for single taxpayers, married taxpayers filing jointly, and so on.

Warning! If a formula containing a VLOOKUP function is to be filled down a column, be sure that the table location is expressed as an absolute address. Otherwise, the address of the table will change as the formula is filled! This is a common but subtle error when using lookup functions.

It often is useful to name a lookup table as well as the other key cells. The formula in C17 could be

=VLOOKUP(COPIES,PRICE_TABLE,CLASS_CODE)

There is an **HLOOKUP** function that is the same as the VLOOKUP function except that it works horizontally, scanning across the top row of a **horizontal lookup table**.

USING VLOOKUP FOR EXACT MATCHES

In the preceding example we wanted to look up a number in a range of values. Sometimes we want only an exact match. Suppose we have a list of the players on a team and their numbers. We would like to create a worksheet that an announcer can use to quickly find the name of a player given his number. We could create the worksheet shown in Figure 12-5.

Here we enter a number into the cell in C4. The computer automatically displays the name of the player in cell C6. The formula in C6 is

=VLOOKUP(C4,B10:C37,2,FALSE)

In this formula we are instructing Excel to look up the value in cell C4 in the first column of the vertical lookup table in B10:C37 and return the corresponding value in the second column, column C, of the table.

The VLOOKUP function call contains a fourth argument, namely FALSE. The VLOOKUP function has an optional fourth argument, which is either TRUE or FALSE. If the fourth argument is omitted, as in the photocopy example in

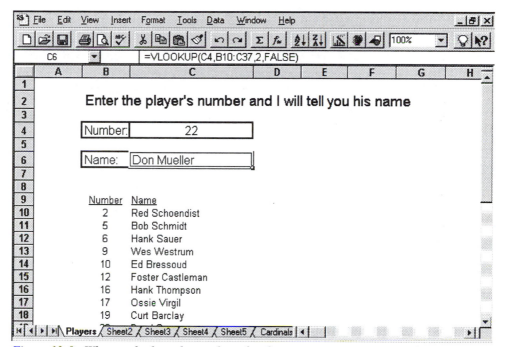

Figure 12-5. When we look up the number of a player we want an exact match.
(Trivia question: What team is this?)

the previous section, the fourth argument is assumed to be TRUE. If the fourth argument is omitted or TRUE, then we are instructing Excel that we want an approximate match and that Excel should find the correct range in the first column of the lookup table in which the value occurs. If the fourth argument is FALSE, as it is in this example, we are instructing Excel that we require an exact match.

For example, if we enter 7 for the player's number, and there is no number 7 in the first column of the lookup table because no player wears the number 7, we don't want the name of the player who wears number 6. We want an indication that we entered an erroneous number. In fact, if we enter the number 7 in cell C4 in the worksheet in Figure 12-5, we get the error message #N/A (no value available) in cell C6.

Note that if we are requiring an exact match in a VLOOKUP function by including FALSE as the fourth argument, then the entries in the left column of the lookup table do not need to be in ascending order. If an exact match is required, as in the worksheet in Figure 12-5, the values can be entered in the lookup table in any order.

THE ISNA FUNCTION

We even could check for the potential error message in the worksheet in Figure 12-5 and insert our own error message by using the Excel function **ISNA**. The function ISNA has a single argument. The function ISNA returns TRUE if the argument evaluates out to #N/A and FALSE otherwise. So, we can embed the VLOOKUP function into the ISNA function and intercept the #N/A error message before it appears, as in Figure 12-6.

The formula in cell C6 now is

=IF(ISNA(VLOOKUP(C4,B10:C37,2,FALSE)), "No such player!",
VLOOKUP(C4,B10:C37,2,FALSE))

This formula instructs Excel that if the value of the VLOOKUP function is #N/A then Excel should display the message "No such player!" in the cell. Otherwise, Excel should display the result of the VLOOKUP function, the name of the player.

Like AND, OR, and NOT, the function ISNA always evaluates to either TRUE or FALSE.

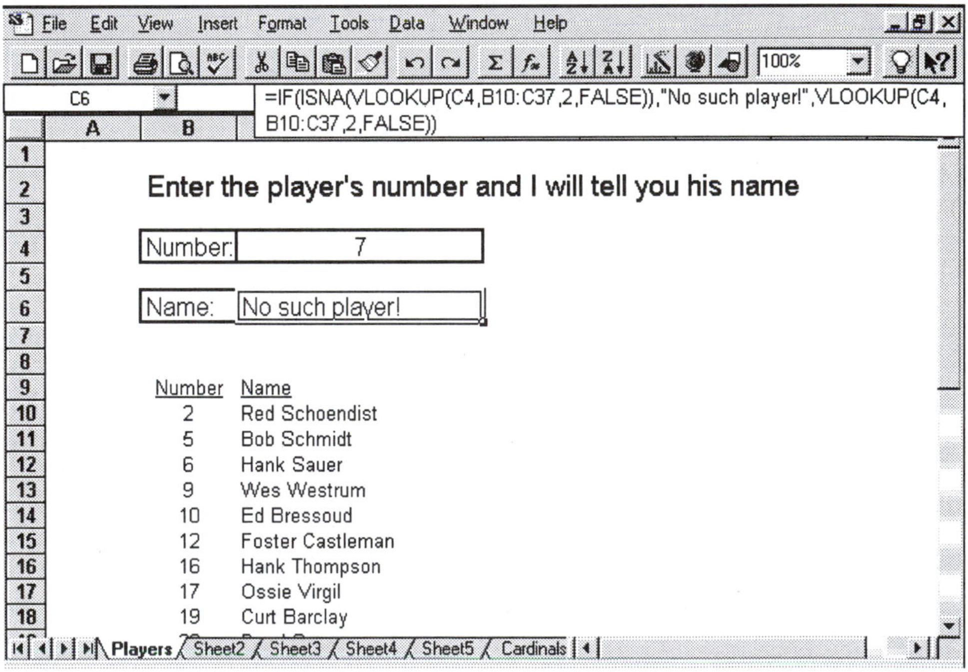

Figure 12-6. "No such player!" is more meaningful to the user than "#N/A".

THE "IS" FUNCTIONS

There are several "IS" functions. Each of these functions has a single argument and returns TRUE or FALSE depending on the evaluation of the argument.

Function	Returns TRUE if
ISBLANK	The argument refers to an empty cell.
ISERR	The argument evaluates to any error value except #N/A.
ISERROR	The argument evaluates to any error value.
ISLOGICAL	The argument evaluates to TRUE or FALSE.
ISNA	The argument evaluates to #N/A.
ISNONTEXT	The argument refers to an item that is not text. (Note that this function returns TRUE if the argument refers to a blank cell.)
ISNUMBER	The argument evaluates to a number.
ISREF	The argument is a reference to a cell or range.
ISTEXT	The argument refers to an item that is text.

LOOKING UP LABELS

It is possible to search for labels in a lookup table as well as values. An example is shown in the phone directory worksheet in Figure 12-7. Enter a name in C6. The computer then looks up the name in the table below and responds with the telephone number. The formula in C8 is

=VLOOKUP(C6,B11:C405,2,FALSE)

Excel looks up the value in C6 in the left column of the lookup table in B11:C405. When it finds an exact match (because the fourth argument is FALSE) in B11:B405, Excel returns the corresponding value in column C, the second column of the lookup table. If it does not find an exact match, Excel will return #N/A, just as with looking up numbers.

Normally with text we want an exact match. If we do not want an exact match, we simply can make the fourth argument TRUE or leave it off altogether. If we are looking up the range within which a cell falls, in other words if the fourth argument is missing or TRUE, then the first column needs to be in ascending order. Ascending order for text is alphabetical order.

Excel is **case insensitive** in looking up text in a lookup table. That is, looking up CAROL is the same as looking up Carol or carol.

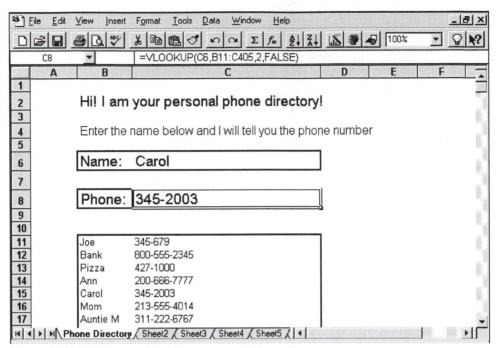

Figure 12-7. Looking up labels in a personal phone directory.

COMPUTER EXERCISES

12-1. The Weather Bureau would like a worksheet to help it keep track of some simple statistics. In column B from B8 through B38 enter the numbers 1 through 31. In column C from C8 through C38 enter the highest temperature recorded for your town for each day during the last month. (You can make up these temperatures.) In column D from D8 through D38 put SUNNY, CLOUDY, RAIN, or SNOW. In the top lines of the worksheet put appropriate titles and column headings. Beginning in cell B40 and continuing down put the following labels:

> AVERAGE TEMPERATURE FOR MONTH
> HIGHEST TEMPERATURE
> NUMBER OF SUNNY DAYS
> NUMBER OF DAYS ABOVE 50 DEGREES
> AVERAGE TEMPERATURE OF RAINY DAYS
> HIGHEST TEMPERATURE OF A RAINY DAY
> DAY OF THE HIGHEST TEMPERATURE OF MONTH
> SECOND HIGHEST TEMPERATURE OF MONTH

Widen column B appropriately. Your task is to enter formulas so that the appropriate statistics are calculated automatically in C40 through C47. The DAY OF THE HIGHEST TEMPERATURE OF MONTH would be 23 if the highest temperature of the entire month occurred on the twenty-third of the month. In case of a tie, select the latest day. Do not use the Sort command. You may use extra columns. Of course, your worksheet should work for any sequence of temperatures and weathers.

12-2. Contributors are classified as follows: under $100 SUPPORTER, $100 to $399 PATRON, $400 to $999 FELLOW, $1,000 or more BLUE CHIP. Create a worksheet that allows you to enter a name and a contribution and then automatically displays the contributor's classification. Use a lookup table.

12-3. (a) Create a worksheet that gives a price quote. You will enter (1) an item name and (2) the quantity of that item purchased. Your worksheet should look up the item name in the Price Table to find the unit price. Then it should calculate the total amount. Look up this amount in the Discount Table to find the quantity discount percent. Then your worksheet should calculate the discount amount, the total, add in 6% sales tax, and give the final amount due for the order.

PRICE QUOTES

| ITEM: | (input) |
| QUANTITY: | (input) |

UNIT PRICE:
TOTAL BEFORE DISCOUNT:
DISCOUNT %:
DISCOUNT AMOUNT:
TOTAL AFTER DISCOUNT:
SALES TAX:

TOTAL:

PRICE TABLE

ITEM	UNIT PRICE $
CONNECTORS	3.98
GROMMITS	15.99
HAPSES	0.35
WIDGETS	8.79

DISCOUNT TABLE

AMOUNT$	DISCOUNT
0	0%
100	5%
500	10%
1000	15%

Try your worksheet on the following three orders: 100 CONNECTORS, 2000 WIDGETS, 300 FARANGES.

(b) Create a new workbook that allows the customer to order some quantity of each of the items at once. The discount should be applied to the total amount ordered. Try your workbook on one order of 30 CONNECTORS, 0 GROMMITS, 50 HAPSES, 5 WIDGETS.

12-4. In your History course there are three hour exams, a paper, and a final exam. Each of these is graded between 0 and 100. In determining the final grade, the professor has decided to drop each student's lowest hour exam grade. The two highest hour exam grades will count 1/6 each, the paper will count 1/3, and the final exam will count 1/3 in determining the overall average for the course. The final letter grade for the course will be based on the overall average, as follows: below 60 is an F, 60 to 65 is a D, 65 to 75 is a C, 75 to 80 is a B-, 80 to 90 is a B, 90 to 95 is an A-, 95 and above is an A.

(a) There are 10 students in the course. Create a worksheet that automatically calculates and displays the overall average and final letter grade for each student. Enter 10 names and sets of grades that fully test the formulas in the worksheet. You should enter a name, three hour exam grades, a paper grade, and a final exam grade for each student. Everything else should be calculated automatically.

(b) In deciding the Grade Point Average, an A is worth 4 points, a B is worth 3 points, a C is worth 2 points, a D is worth 1 point, and an F is worth 0 points. An A- is worth 3.666 points and a B- is worth 2.666 points. Add formulas to your worksheet so that the course Grade Point Average is calculated and displayed. For example, the average grade for the 10 students in the course might be 2.8.

(c) To further encourage students to work hard on their papers, the professor has decided that whoever receives the highest grade on the paper will receive at least an A- in the course whatever the student's grades on the exams. Modify your worksheet so that the student who receives the highest grade on the paper automatically receives at least an A-.

12-5. Form 1040EZ is the simplest form for filing your income taxes. The form is intended for people who are single with no dependents and who had taxable income of less than $50,000 including taxable interest income of $400 or less. Obtain a copy of the form from your bank, post office, or library or over the net. For this exercise you are to replicate this form as a worksheet. The worksheet should allow the user to enter Total wages, Taxable interest, and so on. Excel should calculate all appropriate values, including the tax owed. Try to make the worksheet resemble the form as closely as possible.

CHAPTER 13

DATES AND TIMES

OBJECTIVES

In this chapter you will learn how to:

- Use serial numbers to represent dates and times
- Enter dates and times into a worksheet
- Write formulas to perform calculations on dates and times
- Format cells as dates and times

The calendar we use was developed 2,000 years ago by Julius Caesar and improved slightly by Pope Gregory XIII in 1582. We are so used to the system of 12 months per year and 28, 29, 30, or 31 days per month and leap days almost every fourth year that we don't think twice about it. Still, it is difficult to perform calculations in the calendar system. How many days is it until Christmas? A payment was due on November 27. When will the payment be 60 days overdue? How many days have you been alive? (Not surprisingly, the calculations are difficult in the same way that doing arithmetic with Roman numerals is difficult.)

Similarly, we are used to the division of the day into 24 hours (usually expressed as 12 hours AM and 12 hours PM), the hour into 60 minutes, and the minute into 60 seconds. But calculations using this time notation system are awkward too. How many minutes are there between 9:38 AM and 3:32 PM? A movie that is 2 hours and 27 minutes long begins at 8:46 PM. When will the movie end? How many seconds are there in a day?

The capabilities provided in Excel simplify date and time calculations. The secret lies in the use of serial numbers to represent dates and times.

SERIAL NUMBERS

In Excel, each day between January 1, 1900 and December 31, 2078 is assigned a sequential **serial number**. January 1, 1900 is serial number 1. January 2, 1900 is serial number 2. February 1, 1900 is serial number 32. January 1, 1901 is serial number 367. November 25, 1998 is serial number 36124. December 31, 2078 is serial number 65380.

Time of day is represented by a fraction of a serial number. The serial number 36124.5 is noon on November 25, 1998. The serial number 36124.75 is 6:00 PM on November 25, 1998. The serial number 36124.6650694444 is 3:57:42 PM on November 25, 1998. Strictly speaking, the serial number 36124 is actually 12:00 midnight at the beginning of November 25, 1998.

Can you see how serial numbers make date and time calculations easier? To determine the number of days between two dates just subtract one serial number from the other.

AN ERROR IN EXCEL

As you may have noticed, there is a minor error in assigning serial numbers. The serial number 60 is assigned to February 29, 1900. But that day never existed! There was no leap day in 1900, because 1900 was not a leap year. Years ending in 00 are not leap years unless they are divisible by 400. Thus, all dates after February 29, 1900 are assigned serial numbers one greater than they should be. If you think about it, this error is only rarely consequential. Calculations of the length of time between a date in January or February 1900 and a date in March 1900 or later are off by a day. All other calculations are unaffected. Still, in such a well-designed program any known error is worth noting, if only for some future trivia question. Actually, the developers of Excel are not responsible for the error. This dating system was used in Lotus 1-2-3 and adopted by Excel as is so that Excel would remain compatible with Lotus 1-2-3.

A SECOND DATE SYSTEM

To correct the error, but add to the confusion, there is an optional second date system that sometimes is used in Excel. This date system begins at January 1, 1904 rather than January 1, 1900. In this system, all of the serial numbers correspond to dates four years later. You can determine which date system you are using by selecting *Options...* in the *Tools* pull-down menu and then clicking on the *Calculation* tab. (See Figure 13-1.) If the *1904 Date System* box is checked, you are using the **1904 Date System**. If the box is blank, you are using the **1900 Date System**. Just for consistency, if you are using dates in your workbook I suggest that at the beginning of your session on Excel you look to make sure that the box is not checked and that you are employing the standard 1900 Date System.

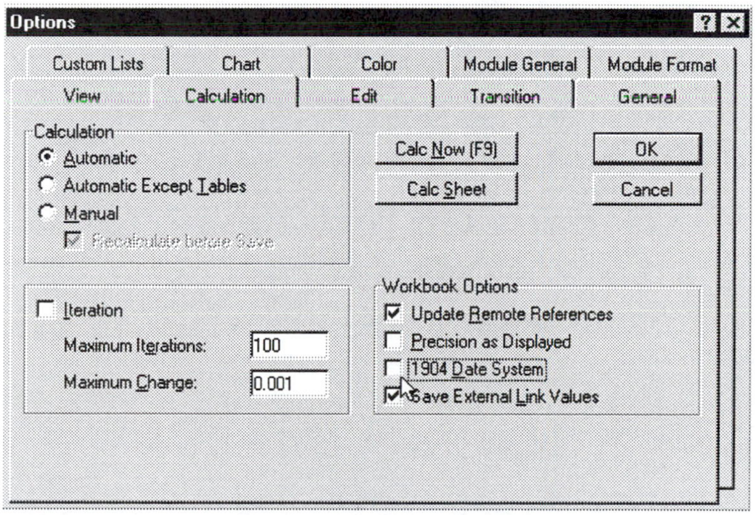

Figure 13-1. How to switch between date systems.

ENTERING DATES INTO THE WORKSHEET

How can we calculate how many days there are between September 23, 1997 and January 14, 1998? The short answer is to subtract the serial number for September 23, 1997 from the serial number for January 14, 1998. But how can we determine the serial numbers for those dates? If we enter a date into a cell in the proper format, the computer recognizes the entry as a date and automatically converts the date into the corresponding serial number, as in Figure 13-2. Here we have typed 9/23/97 into cell D4 and 1/14/98 into cell D6. Excel recognizes these as dates and automatically converts them into serial numbers. Thus, the value of cell D4 actually is 35,696, the serial number for September 23, 1997, as is apparent if we format cell D4 in comma format, as in Figure 13-3.

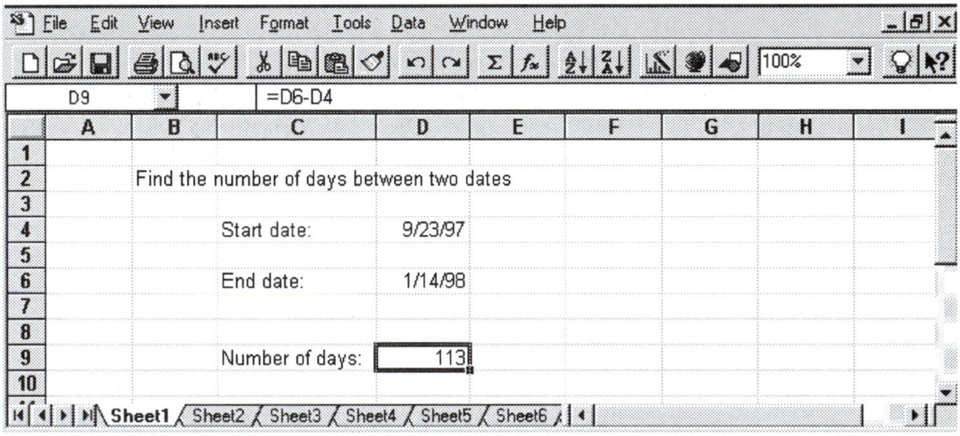

Figure 13-2. To find the number of days between two dates, enter them and subtract.

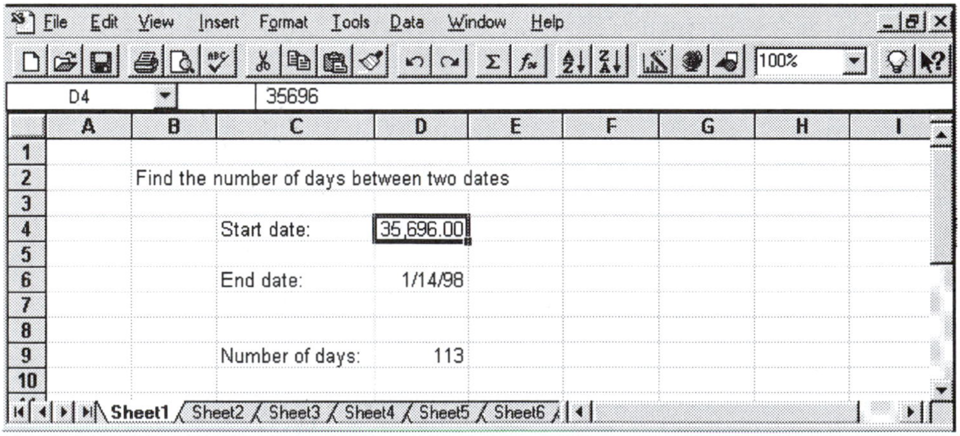

Figure 13-3. Any number can be formatted to appear as a number or as a date.

We have to be very careful here. The date has to be typed in just right. For example, if we type a space before the date, the computer will not recognize the entry as a date. Rather, the entry will be taken as a label, as text, as in Figure 13-4. Here, Excel is trying to subtract a label from a number, which yields the #VALUE! error message. You can tell that cell D4 now contains a label because the entry is aligned to the left of the cell rather than to the right of the cell. Recall that Excel automatically aligns labels on the left of the cell and numbers on the right of the cell, just so you can tell which cells contain labels and which contain numbers.

What are the allowable formats for dates? Excel will recognize each of the following as a date

    September 23, 1997
    23-Sep-97
    9/23/97
    Sept 23, 97
    9/23/1997
    9-23-97

and automatically will convert the entry into the equivalent serial number. If you enter

    9/23
    September 23
    23-Sep

or variants into a cell, the computer will interpret it as September 23 of this year.

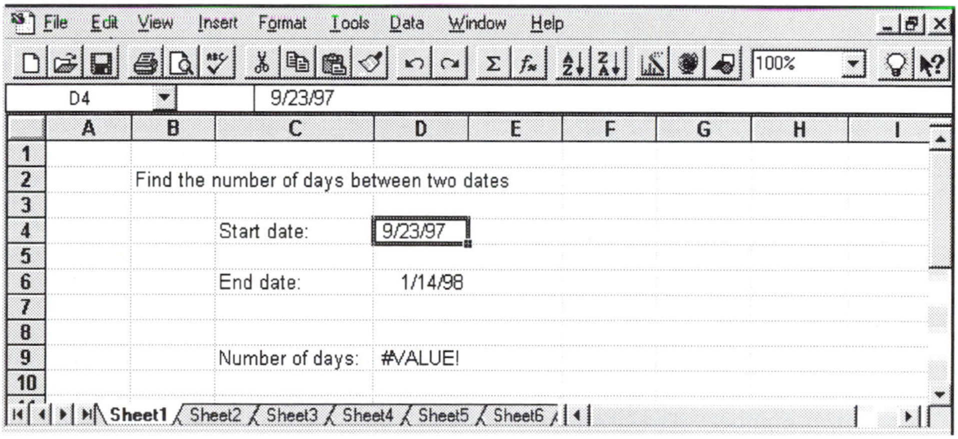

Figure 13-4. If we type a space before the date then the entry is regarded as a label.

USING DATES DIRECTLY IN FORMULAS

In the example in Figure 13-2, we entered the dates into cells and then used the cell addresses in the formula =D6-D4. Suppose we want to do the calculation in a single formula. If we type the formula

$$= 1/14/98 - 9/23/97$$

into a cell, we get the answer -0.00330520246774512. Why? Excel has interpreted the slashes as division operators! So the computer divides 1 by 4 and then that answer by 98, and so on. To do the date arithmetic directly in a formula, we need to place quotes around the dates:

$$= \text{"1/14/98"} - \text{"9/23/97"}$$

Now Excel will interpret the text in the quotes as dates, automatically convert these dates into their equivalent serial numbers, and perform the subtraction, yielding the value 113, the number of days between the two dates.

THE TODAY FUNCTION

The computer has a **system clock** which keeps track of the current date and time. This clock has its own battery so it stays current (excuse the mild pun) even when the computer is shut down. Excel can access the system clock using the **TODAY** function. If we enter the formula

$$=\text{TODAY( )}$$

into a cell, the cell will contain the serial number for today. The computer automatically will format this number as a date, so today's date will appear in the cell. The parentheses following TODAY are necessary to indicate this is a function and not the name of a cell.

THE DATE FUNCTION

The **DATE** function has three arguments: a year, a month number, and a day of the month. The result of evaluating the date function is the corresponding serial number. The formula =DATE(1998,1,14) calculates the serial number for January 14, 1998, which is 35809. Thus the following formula also calculates the number of days between September 23, 1997 and January 14, 1998

$$=DATE(1998,1,14) - DATE(1997,9,23)$$

Entering this formula into a cell in Excel yields an answer of 113.

DATE FORMATS

Excel has several built-in formats for dates. If you specify a date format for a cell that contains a number, Excel takes the number as the serial number of a date, and displays the corresponding date. The different formats are indicated in the *Cells...* selection in the *Format* pull-down menu in the *Number* tab, (see Figure 13-5).

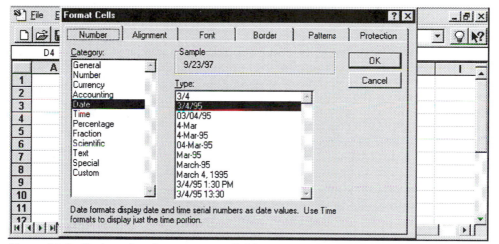

Figure 13-5. Various date formats are available.

DATE FUNCTIONS FOR CONVERTING FROM SERIAL NUMBERS

There are three date functions that convert a serial number into the corresponding year, month, and day of the month.

The **YEAR** function converts a serial number into the corresponding year. For example, =YEAR(35809) is 98 because the serial number falls in 1998.

The **MONTH** function converts a serial number into the corresponding month of the year. For example, =MONTH(35809) is 1 because the serial number falls in January.

The **DAY** function converts a serial number into the corresponding day of month. For example, =DAY(35809) is 14 because the serial number falls on January 14, 1998.

If the argument to any of these three functions is not a valid serial number, that is, if the argument is less than 0 or greater than 65380, then the function will evaluate to #NUM!.

EXAMPLE: HOW MANY DAYS UNTIL JULY 1?

Our organization uses a July 1 budget year. Budgets begin and end at midnight (at the beginning) of July 1. We would like to be able to calculate how many days are left before our current budget expires. If the current budget year ends on July 1, 1998, we could write the formula in one of two ways:

$$="7/1/1998" - TODAY()$$

or

$$=DATE(1998,7,1) - TODAY()$$

The only problem is that each year we would have to adjust the year in the quotes or in the first argument in the DATE function by hand. How could we write the formula so it always works automatically whatever the current year? As a first try we could substitute the current calendar year for the 1998 in the preceding formula, as follows:

$$=DATE(YEAR(TODAY()),7,1) - TODAY()$$

Here, YEAR(TODAY()) evaluates to the current calendar year, to 1998 if this is 1998. This formula works if the current month is January through June, if we are in the same calendar year as the budget end. However, if this were October then the above formula would be incorrect. If the month were July through December, the formula would evaluate to a negative number because =DATE(YEAR(TODAY()),7,1) would yield the serial number of the July 1 in the current calendar year, of the previous July 1 rather than the next July 1. To solve this problem we could use an IF function where the condition is TRUE if today's month is before July and FALSE if today's month is July or after.

$$=IF(MONTH(TODAY())<7,(DATE(YEAR(TODAY()),7,1)-TODAY()),$$
$$(DATE(YEAR(TODAY())+1,7,1)-TODAY()))$$

If the month is before July, the computer calculates the serial number of July 1 of this year minus today's serial number. Otherwise, if the month is July or after, the computer calculates the serial number of July 1 of next year minus today's serial number.

HOURS, MINUTES, AND SECONDS

Serial numbers represent days. The fractions of a serial number represent fractions of a day. For example, 0.5 represents 12 hours. An hour is 0.0416666667, which is 1/24. A minute is 0.0006944444, which is 1/(24*60). A second is 0.0000115741, which is 1/(24*60*60) of a day.

Midnight is 0. 6:00 AM is 0.25. Noon is 0.5. 7:30 PM is 0.8125. 11:58:23 PM is 0.998877314814815.

The same types of built-in functions and display formats are provided for times as are provided for dates.

THE NOW FUNCTION

The **NOW** built-in function evaluates to the serial number for the date and time right now according to the system clock. The value of the formula

$$=NOW( )$$

changes each time the worksheet is evaluated.

TIME FORMATS

There are several formats for displaying times in Excel. The time formats are reached through the *Cells...* selection in the *Format* pull-down menu in the *Number* tab. (See Figure 13-6.) There also are formats that allow you to display both the date and the time.

When a cell is displayed in a strictly time format, the digits to the left of the decimal point in the number in the cell are ignored. Only the fractional part of the number is used to determine what is displayed. Thus a cell with the number 65.59 would appear the same as a cell with the number 42051.59 if the cells have the same time format. Both would be displayed as 2:09:36 PM, the time that is 0.59 through the day.

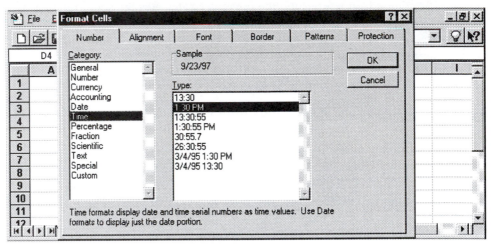

Figure 13-6. Time formats.

ENTERING A TIME INTO A CELL OR FORMULA

As with a date, a time can be entered directly into a cell. If you type 9:52 into a cell, Excel will interpret the entry as a time. The cell will contain the serial number for 9:52 AM, namely 0.4111111111. The cell will be formatted as a time, so 9:52 will appear in the cell, just as you typed it.

The **TIME** function has three arguments: the hour based on a 24-hour clock, the minute, and the second. The result of evaluating the TIME function is the equivalent serial number. For example, =TIME(19,12,0) evaluates to 0.8, as 7:12 PM is 80% through the day.

The movie began at 8:46 PM. The movie is 2 hours and 27 minutes long. When will the movie be over? A formula for determining the answer is

$$= \text{"8:46 PM"} + \text{"2:27"}$$

which yields the value 0.967361111111111 in the cell. Displaying this cell in a time format gives you the answer 11:13 PM.

Another possible formula to use is

$$=\text{TIME}(20,46,0) + \text{TIME}(2,27,0)$$

which also yields 11:13 PM.

EXAMPLE: TESTING THE ENGINES

United Engines performs extensive tests on their products. They would like a worksheet to allow them to enter the starting date and time of a test and the number of hours for the test and then calculate and display the ending date and time for the test.

The worksheet is shown in Figure 13-7. The date at the start of the test is entered into cell C4. The time at the start of the test is entered into cell C5. The number of hours the test is to run is entered into cell C7. Cells C9 and C10 both have the same formula:

$$= C4 + C5 + C7/24$$

This formula adds the serial number for the date of the start plus the serial number of the time of the start plus the number of days that the test is to run. Cell C9 is given a date format. Cell C10 is given a time format. Both C9 and C10 contain the same formula and, hence, the same value, namely 35,622.90625, which is the serial number for 9:45 PM on July 11, 1997.

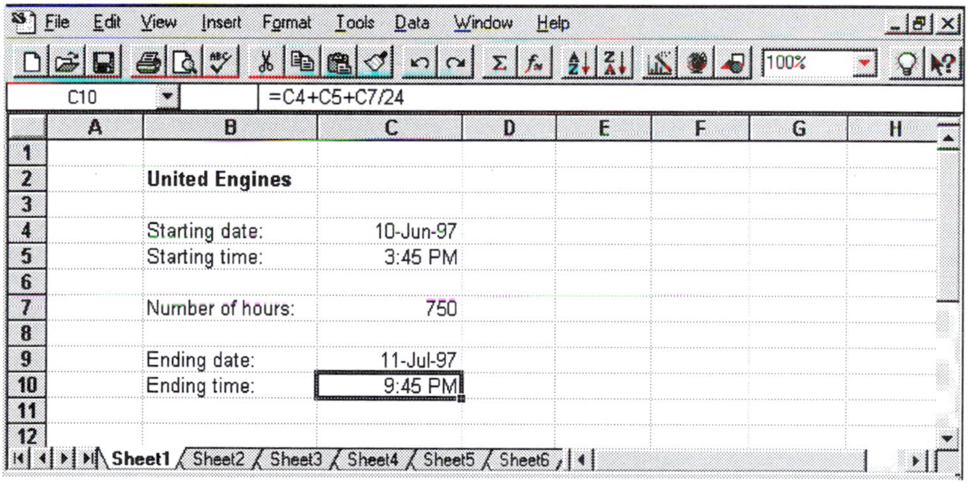

Figure 13-7. Calculating the date and time of the end of the test.

TIME FUNCTIONS FOR CONVERTING FROM SERIAL NUMBERS

There are three time functions that convert a serial number into the corresponding hour, minutes, and seconds.

The **HOUR** function converts a serial number into the corresponding hour of the day. For example, =HOUR(35809.847) is 20 because the serial number falls between 8 PM and 9 PM.

The **MINUTE** function converts a serial number into the corresponding minute of the hour. For example, =MINUTE(35809.847) is 19 because the serial number falls between 8:19 PM and 8:20 PM.

The **SECOND** function converts a serial number into the corresponding second of the minute. For example, =SECOND(35809.847) is 41 because the serial number falls closest to 8:19:41 PM.

The serial number 35809.847 corresponds to 8:19:41 PM on January 14, 1998, to the nearest second.

PENCIL AND PAPER EXERCISE

13-1. Write down the formula that calculates each of the following quantities. Then identify the type of format in which the cell is to be displayed. You may use the computer to check the formulas. (You do not need to write down the result of evaluating each formula. You just need to write down the formula itself and the format in which the answer will be displayed.) I have answered part (a) just to give you the general idea.

(a) The date that is 90 days after December 23, 1998.
        Answer: The formula is ="23-Dec-1998" + 90
                     Format the answer as a date.

(b) The number of days Franklin D. Roosevelt was President. FDR was inaugurated on March 4, 1933. He died in office on April 12, 1945.

(c) The date that is 1000 days from today.

(d) The date that was 1000 hours ago.

(e) The number of days until the year 2010.

(f) The date of serial number 10000.

(g) The serial number for April 3, 2046.

(h) The year for serial number 50000.

(i) The date of the 200th day of 1999.

(j) The number of days you have been alive.

(k) The number of hours between 11:52AM on 05-Nov-98 and 8:07AM on 25-Dec-98.

(l) The time 1000 hours from now.

(m) The hours:minutes:seconds between 6:46:32 AM and 10:23:15 PM.

(n) The number of minutes in the 1990s.

(o) The exact time 60% through the day.

(p) The time and date 100,000 minutes after 4:12 PM on November 12, 1998.

COMPUTER EXERCISES

13-2. Use the TODAY function to create the following worksheet. Your worksheet should work automatically whatever the day.

	A	B	C	D	E	F	G	H	I
1									
2		Today is	21-Feb-98						
3									
4		This is day	52	of the year	1998				
5									
6		There are	314	days remaining in the year.					
7									

Today / Sheet2 / Sheet3 / Sheet4 / Sheet5 / Sheet6 /

13-3. NASA has commissioned you to create a worksheet for Mission Control. The design is given below. The time and date of launch will be entered as shown in C5 and D5. The worksheet should display the current time and date automatically. The elapsed length of the mission so far should be calculated and displayed in two ways: (1) in terms of days in C10 and then hours, minutes, and seconds in E10 and (2) in terms of hours and fractions of hours in C12. To update the display, you will need to press F9, the Recalculation key.

	A	B	C	D	E	F
1						
2		OFFICIAL MISSION CLOCK				
3						
4						
5		Mission Launch:	19:34:10	4-Jul-97		
6						
7		Current Mission Time:	16:12:36	21-Feb-98		
8						
9						
10		Current Mission Length:	231	days	20:38:26	
11						
12		Current Misssion Length in Hours:	5,564.64			
13						

Sheet1 / Sheet2 / Sheet3 / Sheet4 / Sheet5 / Sheet6 /

13-4. The local department store has hired you to create a well-labeled worksheet that displays in four cells the number of days, hours, minutes, and seconds from now until Christmas.

13-5. Create a worksheet that allows you to enter in any date as a label and then in separate cells gives the date 30, 60, 90, and 120 days from the entered date.

13-6. John loves riding on roller coasters. His lifetime dream is to set the world endurance record for riding a roller coaster and have his achievement be recorded in the *Guinness Book of World Records*. Now John has his chance. The local amusement park is excited about supporting John for the publicity his great accomplishment will bring. According to the book, the current record is 503 hours set in Montreal, Canada, in 1983. The amusement park would like John to break the record at 8:00 PM on July 4. Create a worksheet to determine the date and time he should begin.

13-7. You have taken a part-time job as manager of the Happy Hamburger Stand. The Stand is open from 6 AM to 11 PM. Employees work all different odd schedules. Employees are paid at the rate of $6.00 per hour from the moment they check in to the moment they check out. So, for example, an employee who checked in at 6:00 PM and checked out at 9:15 PM would earn $19.50 for the day.

(a) Create a well-labeled worksheet that accepts two entries, the check-in time and the check-out time, as inputs. The worksheet should show the number of hours the employee worked and the amount of money the employee is to be paid for the day. No other inputs are allowed.

(b) The Stand is so popular under your management that you decide to stay open until 3 AM. Create a second worksheet that accepts check-in and check-out times between 6 AM and 3 AM. Again, the worksheet should show the total number of hours the employee worked and the amount of money the employee is to be paid for the day. Still, the only two cells used for input should be the entries for the check-in time and the check-out time.

(c) The Stand is doing a booming business at dinnertime, but you are having a difficult time hiring employees to work then. You decide to pay $8.00 per hour for any time worked between the hours of 5 PM and 8 PM. For example, an employee who checked in at 6:00 PM and checked out at 9:15 PM, now would earn $23.50 for the day. Modify your worksheet accordingly. Your third worksheet should work for any check-in time and check-out time. You may use extra cells to hold partial results, but clearly label the final answer. Still, the only two inputs should be the entries for the check-in time and the check-out time.

13-8. You have been hired by Club 2000 to design and implement a worksheet for the "greeter" at the door to use to determine whether people are old enough to enter. Create a well-labeled worksheet that allows the greeter to enter into a cell the person's birth date as listed on the person's driver's license. In a separate cell should appear either WELCOME if the person is at least 21 years old or SORRY, YOU ARE UNDERAGE otherwise. Use TODAY and IF.

CHAPTER 14

FINANCIAL FUNCTIONS

OBJECTIVES

In this chapter you will learn how to:

- Create worksheets to solve problems involving the time value of money
- Use the PMT function to calculate loan payments
- Use the Function Wizard to assist you in entering functions
- Use the PV, RATE, NPER, and FV functions to analyze financial situations
- Make investment decisions using IRR and NPV

Excel often is used to help analyze financial problems.

A basic concept in finance is the **time value of money**. The value of money changes over time because of the potential of earning interest on the money. Which is more valuable, $1,000 today or $1,001 two years from now? The $1,000 today is more valuable because with almost no risk you could put the $1,000 in the bank, earn interest, and have over $1,080 two years from now.

Furthermore, if you leave the money in the bank, the interest compounds. During the second year you earn interest not just on the amount you deposited in the bank but also on the interest that you earned the first year. Suppose you decide to start saving for a down payment for a house. You open a bank account that pays 5% per year. Every year you put $2,500 into the account. How much money will you have in four years? How long will it be before you have $20,000?

Suppose you have $10,000 that you would like to invest for four years. The bank will guarantee you 6% interest per year. Your cousin has this great idea for starting a business. If you invest the $10,000 with her, she promises to pay you $2,000 after one year, $3,000 after two years, $4,000 after three years, and $5,000 at the end of four years. Which investment would pay the higher rate of interest? In making the decision of what to do with your money you may decide to invest in the bank because it is much less risky or you may decide to invest with your cousin because she is family, but at least you ought to be able to figure out how the options compare in terms of the rate of return on your money.

The calculations in financial analyses can be quite complex. A lot of money can be riding on making the correct calculations. To help in this important application area, several financial functions are provided in Excel. These functions facilitate many calculations involving the time value of money.

CALCULATING LOAN PAYMENTS WITH THE PMT FUNCTION

Wouldn't it be nice to drive around town in a bright red Ferrari F50 with a 513 horsepower V12 engine? Here is a new one advertised in the paper for only $477,500. Not bad. I can scrape up $3,000. My buddy just got an auto loan at 12% annual interest. Maybe I could take out a loan and then pay it back over 5 years. I wonder what the monthly payment would be on a $474,500 loan.

When borrowing money for an automobile loan or for the mortgage for a house or condo, the money usually is paid back in equal monthly payments. Part of these payments cover the interest that is owed. Part of the payments go to pay off the principal. The principal of a loan is the amount of money that was borrowed. After each payment, the amount owed on the principal is decreased. After the final payment the loan is paid off. The formula for calculating the fixed monthly payment is built into the **PMT** function.

The PMT function has five arguments (inputs): the periodic interest rate, the number of periodic payments, the present value, the future value, and the type:

PMT(rate, nper, pv, fv, type)

When using the PMT function, or any financial function, the first step is to decide on the period. All figures must be expressed in terms of a common period of time. If the payments are to be made each month, then the period would be a month. This means that the first argument to the PMT function, the interest rate to be paid, must be stated as the monthly interest rate. The second argument, nper, would be the number of monthly payments to be made, the number of periods of the loan.

How much would the monthly payment be for the Ferrari?

The interest rate is 12% per year. The monthly interest rate would be 12%/12 or 1%. This could be written in the formula either as 1% or as .01.

We would make monthly payments for 5 years, for a total of 60 monthly payments.

The present value of the loan would be the principal, the amount borrowed, which would be 474500. Here, we need to be careful not to include a dollar sign or any commas. If we put in a dollar sign, Excel will think it's the beginning of an absolute address. If we include a comma to mark off the thousands, Excel will think the comma is separating two different arguments.

The future value is the amount of money that will be exchanged at the end of the loan. Here, the future value would be 0 as the loan will be all paid off after 60 months. In some cases there is a "balloon payment", an amount to be paid off at the end of the loan period. This would be included as the future value.

Finally, the type of the loan is either 0 or 1. The type is 0 if the payment is due at the end of each month. The type is 1 if the payment is due at the beginning of each month. Normally the bank would require you to make your first payment at the end of the first month and subsequent payments would be due at the end of each succeeding month, so the type would be 0.

The formula for calculating the monthly payment for the Ferrari would be

=PMT(1%, 60, 474500, 0, 0)

Entering this formula into a cell yields the answer ($10,544.99). The parentheses mean this is a negative number. That is, each month we would need to pay the finance company $10,544.99. Taxes and insurance and gas and tune-ups are extra. You know, I've always wanted an eight year old Chevy.

One of the tricky parts of using financial functions in Excel is the sign of the number. A positive number represents money you are receiving, cash coming into your wallet. A negative number represents money you are paying, cash going out of your wallet. In this example we are receiving $474,500 from the bank at the beginning of the transaction of the loan so the present value would be +474500. Each month we are paying money to the bank out of our wallet so the monthly payment is represented in Excel as a negative number.

The last two arguments in the PMT function call are optional, in the sense that if they are 0, you can leave them off. Thus, we could write the formula

$$=PMT(1\%, 60, 474500)$$

Rather than entering the numbers for the loan directly into the formula, we could put them into separate cells and refer to the cells in the formula, as in the worksheet in Figure 14-1. The advantage of this approach, of course, is that to change the specifics for the loan, we would just need to change the numbers in the cells rather than going in and editing the formula. Also, these numbers show on the worksheet and in a printout of the worksheet. Most lending institutions state the interest rate and the length of the loan in years so the worksheet in Figure 14-1 is designed accordingly. The interest rate and length of the loan are converted to monthly figures in the formula. The actual data in the worksheet in Figure 14-1 show the figures for a $200,000 mortgage at 8% per year over 30 years. Note that a balloon payment would be entered as a positive number in C7. It would be money out of our pocket at the end of the loan period, negative cash flow for us. The balloon payment is converted to a negative number in the formula in C10 by placing a minus sign before the entry for C7 in the fourth argument in the formula.

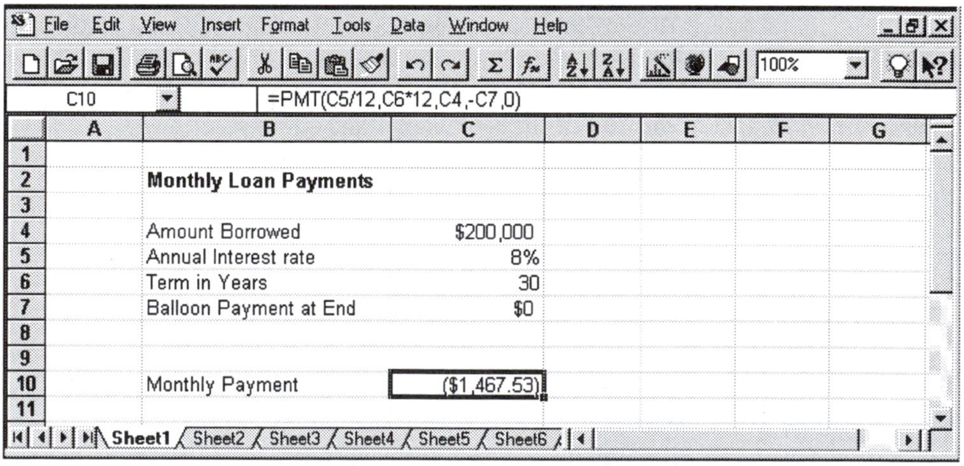

Figure 14-1. A worksheet for calculating the monthly payment for a loan. In this case, the loan is for $200,000 for 30 years.

USING THE FUNCTION WIZARD

Financial functions are a great place to make use of the **Function Wizard**. To call up the Function Wizard, click on the Function Wizard button.

In Step 1 of the Function Wizard you select the function you wish to use, as in Figure 14-2. The list of arguments and a brief description of the function is shown at the bottom of the dialog box. You can ask for *Help* to find out all about the function if you wish. Click on *Next* to move on to Step 2. In Step 2, fill in the arguments as in Figure 14-3.

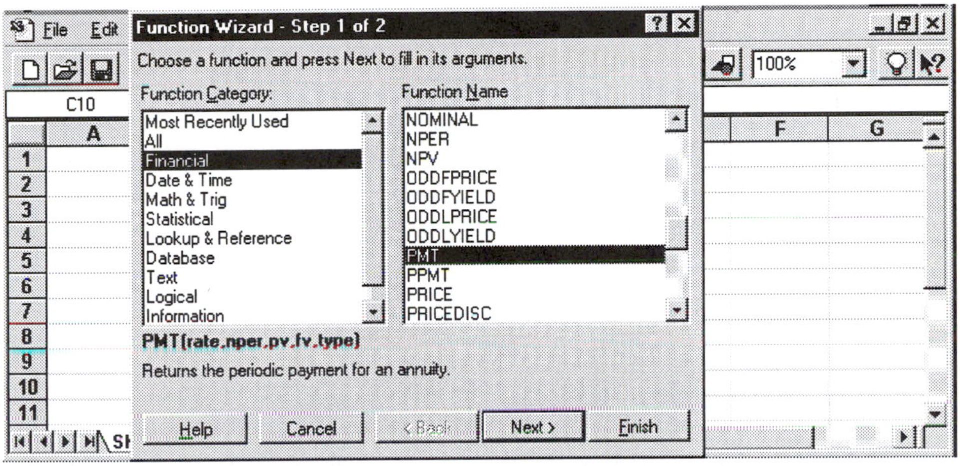

Figure 14-2. Select a function in the first step of the Function Wizard.

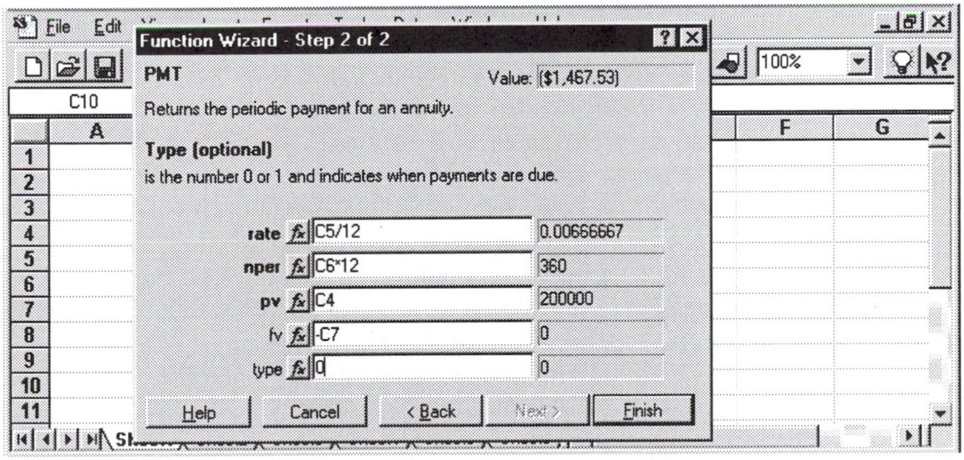

Figure 14-3. Fill in the arguments to the function in the second step of the Function Wizard.

A major advantage of the Function Wizard is that it gives you the order of the arguments, which I never can remember. To enter cell addresses in the arguments in Step 2, you can either type the addresses or click on the cells themselves. If the cells you need to refer to are hidden by the Function Wizard window, you can drag the window to one side and scroll the worksheet. You can see the result of evaluating the function in the top right of the dialog box. Click on *Finish* and you have the formula in Figure 14-1.

CALCULATING FUTURE VALUES USING THE FV FUNCTION

I have $20,000 to invest right now. Each year I plan to invest $5,000 more. I figure I can earn 8% per year on my investment. How much will I have accumulated in 10 years?

To solve this problem we would use the **FV** function. The FV function calculates the future value of an investment assuming constant periodic payments and a constant interest rate throughout the life of the investment. The FV function has five arguments:

FV(rate, nper, pmt, pv, type)

Again, the first step is to determine the time period involved in the investment. Since all of the information is stated in years, we will use a time period of a year. So, the rate and number of periods will be stated in terms of years. The annual rate is 8%. The number of years of the investment is 10. The annual payment is $5,000 out of our wallet, so we'll enter -5000 into the formula for pmt. The present value is -20000, our initial investment. We plan to make our annual investment at the end of each year. That is, the first payment of $5,000 will be made one year from now rather than right now. So the type of the investment is 0 rather than 1.

Using the FV function to solve the problem of the future value of our investment, we get the formula

=FV(8%, 10, -5000, -20000, 0)

Entering this formula into Excel tells us we will have accumulated $115,611.31 after 10 years. We have deposited a total of $70,000 so the remaining $45,611.31 is the amount we have earned in interest.

Suppose we are uncertain about being able to make the $5,000 deposit each year. We just want to see what an initial deposit of $20,000 would earn in 10 years at 8% if we left it alone. Now the formula would be

$$=FV(8\%, 10, 0, -20000, 0)$$

Here there is no periodic payment, so the third argument, pmt, is 0. Excel tells us that at 8% interest in 10 years the $20,000 investment would turn into $43,178.50.

THE BASIC IDEA OF THESE FINANCIAL FUNCTIONS

These investments (or loans) have five basic parameters:

pv   the value or cash flow at the beginning of the investment
rate   the interest rate per time period
nper   the total number of time periods
pmt   the payment that is made each time period
fv   the value or cash flow at the end of the investment

Given any four of these parameters, there is a financial function to calculate the fifth. For the PMT function we know the present value, the interest rate, the number of periods, and the future value. PMT tells us the amount of the periodic payment. For the FV function we know the present value, the interest rate, the number of periods, and the periodic payment. FV tells us the future value of the investment.

THE NPER FUNCTION

My goal is to become a millionaire, to accumulate a million dollars. I have $100,000 saved up in an investment earning 10% per year. If I deposit $25,000 additional each year, how many years until I have the $1,000,000?
The **NPER** function has five arguments:

$$NPER(rate, pmt, pv, fv, type)$$

Filling in the arguments

$$=NPER(10\%, -25000, -100000, 1000000, 0)$$

we find it will take 13.4 years until I am a millionaire!
Suppose by some good fortune I find myself with a million dollars. I decide to put it in an safe investment at 5% per year and retire to a tropical island. I figure

I will need $80,000 per year to live the tropical lifestyle to which I would like to become accustomed. How many years will it be until I run out of money?

This is still a problem for NPER. Entering the formula

=NPER(5%, 80000, -1000000, 0, 1)

yields an answer of 18.5 years before I run out of money. The fifth argument, the type, is 1 because I want that first withdrawal right away and each subsequent withdrawal at the beginning of the year.

Suppose I could earn 10% per year on my money. The formula

=NPER(10%, 80000, -1000000, 0, 1)

yields an answer of #NUM!. This is an error message. In this case it means that there is no such number. If you think about it, at 10% interest per year I will be earning more than I am spending so I can withdraw $80,000 per year forever and my investment will continue to increase in value! NPER has no value; the number of periods the investment will last is infinite.

THE RATE FUNCTION

Suppose we have $20,000 to invest and we would like to grow it into $50,000 in 5 years. What interest rate would we need to receive?

The **RATE** function has six arguments

RATE(nper, pmt, pv, fv, type, guess)

The final argument, the guess, is optional. The guess is the user's guess about what is the correct answer. There is no algebraic formula for calculating the rate, so the computer does it iteratively, by trial and error. The guess is the starting point for the computer's attempts to find the correct answer. If the user leaves off the guess, the computer automatically will begin with a guess of 10%.

To solve this problem we enter

=RATE(5, 0, -20000, 50000, 0)

and the computer informs us we will require an annual interest rate of 20.11%.

If we had wanted to grow the $20,000 into $5,000,000 in 5 years, then we would enter

=RATE(5, 0, -20000, 5000000, 0)

Now the computer evaluates the formula to #NUM!, meaning it couldn't come up with an answer. The problem is that the computer started with a guess of 10% but the required rate is much higher. If we instruct the computer to begin with a guess of 100% per year

=RATE(5, 0, -20000, 5000000, 0, 100%)

then the formula evaluates to 202%, meaning we need to receive more than 200% interest each year. We must triple our money each year to achieve this rather ambitious objective.

We need to enter a number for the guess in the RATE function if the final answer is not close to 10%.

THE PV FUNCTION

Mike is hoping to spend 18 months on a Greek island programming the great new computer game (and tasting a little ouzo). Mike figures he will need $2,000 per month to live and $800 at the end of the period for transportation home. How much money would Mike need to deposit initially in an account paying 6% interest per year to be able to withdraw $2,000 per month for 18 months and have $800 left at the end?

The **PV** function has five arguments:

PV(rate, nper, pmt, fv, type)

The formula would be

=PV(6%/12, 18, 2000, 0, 800, 1)

Here the time period is the month so we divide the annual interest rate by 12. The formula evaluates to ($35,248.57), meaning Mike must now deposit $35,248.57 in the account to be able to make the desired withdrawals.

MAKING INVESTMENT DECISIONS USING IRR

Let's return to the investment decision we posed in the beginning of the chapter. You have $10,000. The bank will pay you 6% interest per year if you deposit your $10,000 there for four years. Your cousin says that if you invest the $10,000 in her new business she promises to pay you $2,000 after one year,

$3,000 after two years, $4,000 after three years, and $5,000 at the end of four years. Which investment would pay the higher rate of interest? Here we have periodic (annual) payments being made, but the payments are not equal. This frequently is the case in proposed investments in business. Thus the set of five functions just discussed (PMT, FV, NPER, RATE, PV) would not pertain here, because they require all of the periodic payments to be the same.

A different set of functions in Excel is designed to help analyze situations where there is an arbitrary stream of cash flows.

The **IRR** function is used to calculate the interest rate returned on an investment involving various positive and negative payments that are made on a regular basis. The IRR function calculates "internal rate of return". The use of the IRR function to calculate the internal rate of return for the investment in your cousin's business is shown in the worksheet in Figure 14-4.

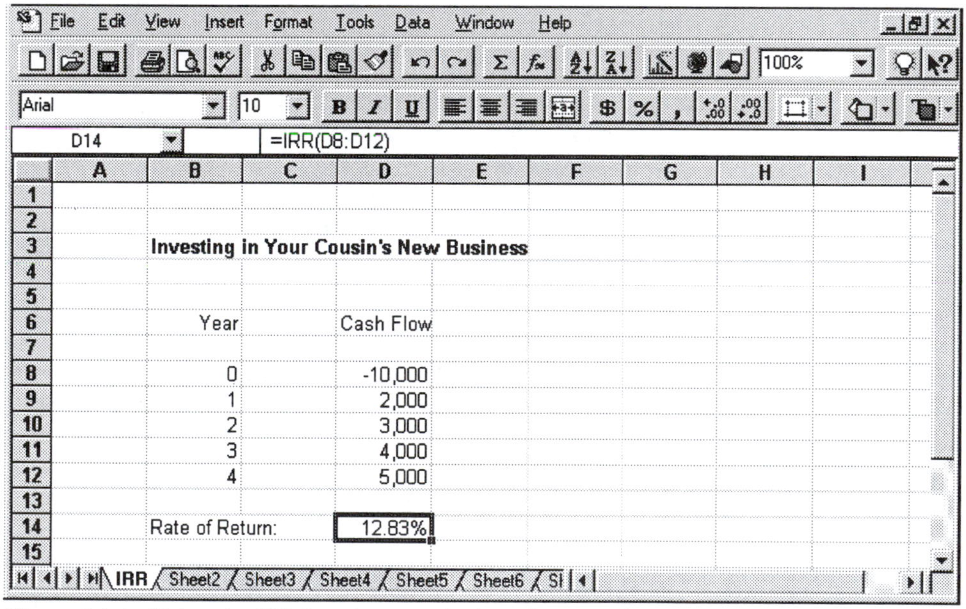

Figure 14-4. Using the IRR function to calculate the rate of return on an investment in your cousin's business, assuming she pays you back as promised.

The cash flows are listed explicitly in column D. As usual in Excel, any investments you make, money you pay out, are entered as negative numbers. Any returns on your investment, money you receive, are entered as positive numbers. Using the IRR function in the worksheet we can see that investing in your cousin's business under the terms proposed would result in a rate of return of 12.83%. The bank is paying only 6% so you would receive a higher rate of return from your cousin.

The IRR function has two arguments

IRR(cash flows, guess)

The first argument to the IRR function is the range of addresses where the series of cash flows is located on the worksheet. The cash flows should be in sequential cells, either down a column or across a row. The period of time from one cash flow to the next must be the same. The resulting rate of return is for that period. That is, if the time between each payment in the cash flows is one year, then the result of evaluating IRR will be an annual rate of return. If the time between each payment in the cash flows is one month, then the result of evaluating IRR will be a monthly rate of return. Note that in the worksheet in Figure 14-4, the year numbers in column B are there just to help make the worksheet understandable by people. The numbers in column B are not used by the computer in the IRR calculations.

The IRR function assumes that the initial cash flow in the range occurs right now and not at the end of the first period. The initial cash flow usually is negative and represents an initial investment.

There must be at least one negative number (representing an amount invested) and one positive number (representing an amount received) within the cash flows. Otherwise you'll get the dreaded #NUM! error message, because there would be no rate of return.

It is possible to list the cash flows explicitly within the function argument by putting them within curly brackets { }. Thus, we could do the entire calculation using the formula

=IRR({-10000,2000,3000,4000,5000})

Of course, the advantage to using the worksheet in Figure 14-4 is that it is easy to play "What if" by changing one of the values in the cells. Suppose your cousin is so successful in her business and so grateful for your investment that she decides to give you $10,000 at the end of year 4 instead of $5,000. Now, what would be the annual rate of return on your investment? To find out we can just change the number in D12 to 10,000, as in Figure 14-5.

The internal rate of return of the series of cash flows -10,000, 2,000, 3,000, 4,000, 10,000 is 23.54%.

If at the end of the second year you would need to invest another $2,000 rather than receiving $3,000, you would change the number in D10 to -2,000.

The second argument is the guess. IRR is basically an extended version of the RATE function that works when the payments throughout the investment are of different amounts. Just as with the RATE function, there is no closed algebraic formula for calculating the IRR. The computer uses trial and error and begins

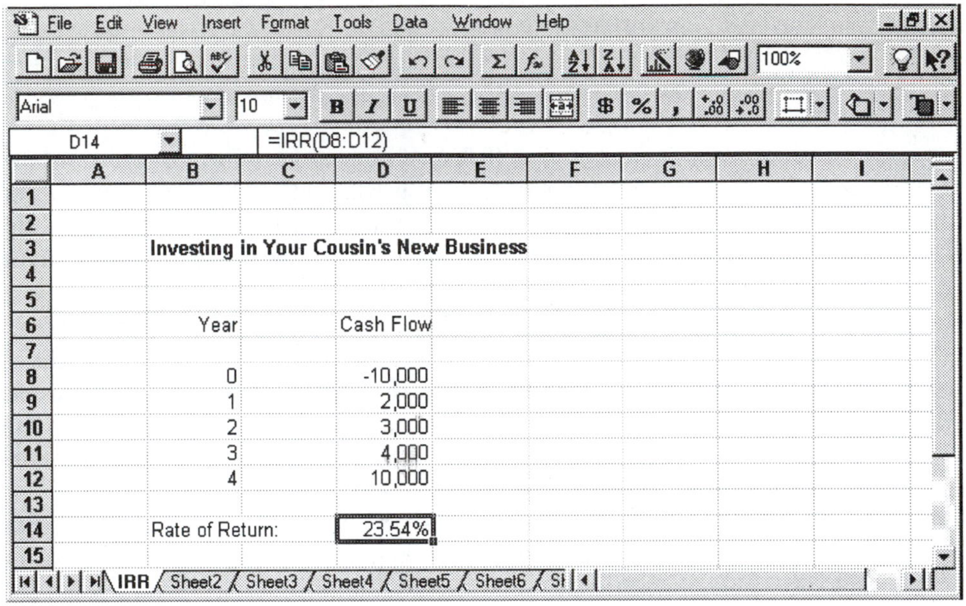

Figure 14-5. Your cousin is so successful and grateful to you for the loan that she pays you back $10,000 in year 4.

with the guess. Entering a guess is optional. If none is included by the user, the computer assumes a guess of 10%.

NET PRESENT VALUE

An alternative approach to analyzing an investment in terms of its internal rate of return is to calculate its **net present value**. In a present value calculation you state future cash flows in terms of their value in today's dollar. If money earns 10% per year, then $500 today would be worth the same as $550 a year from now. So the present value of $550 a year from now using a **discount rate** of 10% would be $500. Similarly, the present value of $605 two years from now using a discount rate of 10% would be $500. (1.10 * 500 is 550. 1.10 * 550 is 605.) The net present value of an investment is the total value of each of the cash flows for the investment stated in terms of today's dollars.

When making a present value calculation, you must use a discount rate. The discount rate is the rate at which money changes in value each year. Roughly speaking, the discount rate is the interest rate the bank will pay or it is the inflation rate in the economy.

If the net present value of an investment is greater than zero, then it is a good investment relative to the discount rate. If the net present value is less than zero, then it is a poor investment relative to the discount rate. Or, alternatively, if you are comparing the merits of two potential investments, you would select the investment with the higher net present value.

A net present value analysis of the investment in your cousin's business is shown in the worksheet in Figure 14-6. The net present value of the investment is calculated by finding the present value of the future cash flows and subtracting the $10,000 initial investment.

The **NPV** function is used to calculate the present value of a stream of possibly varying future cash flows.

NPV(discount rate, cash flows)

The first argument is the discount rate, the rate at which money changes value each period. After the discount rate comes the future cash flows. These arguments can be the addresses of the values in the worksheet, as in the function used in cell E13 of the worksheet in Figure 14-6.

=NPV(E4,E8:E11)

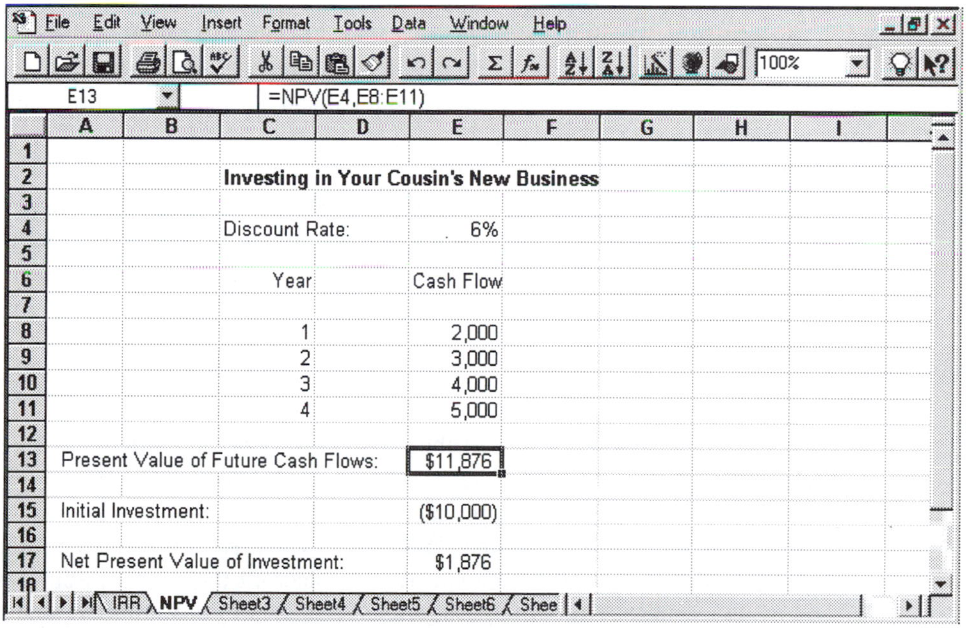

Figure 14-6. A net present value analysis of your cousin's new business shows a positive net present value of $1,876 using a 6% discount rate. The investment would make you $1,876 in today's dollars.

Or, unlike in the IRR function, the cash flows can be listed explicitly as a sequence of arguments in the NPV function (without the curly brackets). So, we also could perform the calculation in one formula

$$=NPV(6\%,2000,3000,4000,-5000) - 10000$$

The NPV function is similar to the PV function discussed earlier. However, where the PV function assumes that the cash flow each period is a constant, the NPV function allows for different amounts each period. If in each year you would receive $4,000, then you could use the PV function. If, as is the case in the current example, the cash flows are not the same from year to year, you would use NPV to calculate the present value.

In the worksheet in Figure 14-6 we used a discount rate of 6% because that is the rate the bank would pay. The net present value for the investment is calculated by taking the present value of the future cash flows and subtracting the initial investment required. In cell E17 we see that the net present value of the investment is $1,876. Investing in your cousin's business would be worth $1,876 more in today's money than investing the money in the bank at 6% interest.

Unlike the IRR function the NPV function assumes that the first of the cash flows occurs at the end of the first period rather than right away. Note that the NPV function is somewhat mis-named. The NPV function does not calculate the net present value of an investment. Rather, the NPV function calculates the present value of a series of possibly different future cash flows that occur at fixed intervals. The net present value is then calculated by subtracting any initial investment that might be made right now.

The IRR function and the NPV function are closely related. The NPV function is used in the series of calculations made for the IRR function. Indeed, if we use the internal rate of return of the investment as the discount rate, then the net present value of the investment will be 0.

WINNING THE LOTTERY

We now have covered seven of the financial functions available in Excel. All of the functions are designed to facilitate analyses involving the time value of money. These calculations take practice so let's do one more example.

Many states have initiated state lotteries. Typically you pay $1 to select the numbers that you think will be drawn. If you select all the numbers correctly you win a fortune! But do you? Suppose you have selected your numbers and the day after the drawing you learn that they have drawn your numbers and you have won $1,000,000! You are the big winner! You head down to the state lottery office to collect your million dollars. But at the office you learn that the lottery commission does not give you the million dollars all at once. Rather they pay the money to you in 20 equal annual payments. You receive $50,000 now and $50,000 per year at the end of each of the next 19 years.

How much have you really won? Clearly that last $50,000 payment 19 years from now is not going to be worth very much if inflation picks up. It is legal to sell your winning ticket. There are companies that will pay you cash now for a winning ticket. Suppose someone offered you $100,000 right now for your ticket (and all the winnings). Would you take it? No, your winnings are worth more than $100,000 even though they are spread out over 20 years. Suppose the person offered you $900,000 right now for your ticket. Yes, $900,000 today is worth more than $1,000,000 paid out in 20 equal annual payments.

How can we figure out how much your lottery winnings would be worth in terms of today's money? What we are asking for is the present value of the winnings. There are two functions that calculate present value, NPV and PV. The NPV function calculates the present value of a series of possibly unequal future cash flows. The PV function calculates the present value of a series of equal cash flows. The lottery winnings are paid in equal amounts so PV is the function to use. A worksheet to calculate the present value of winning the lottery is shown in Figure 14-7.

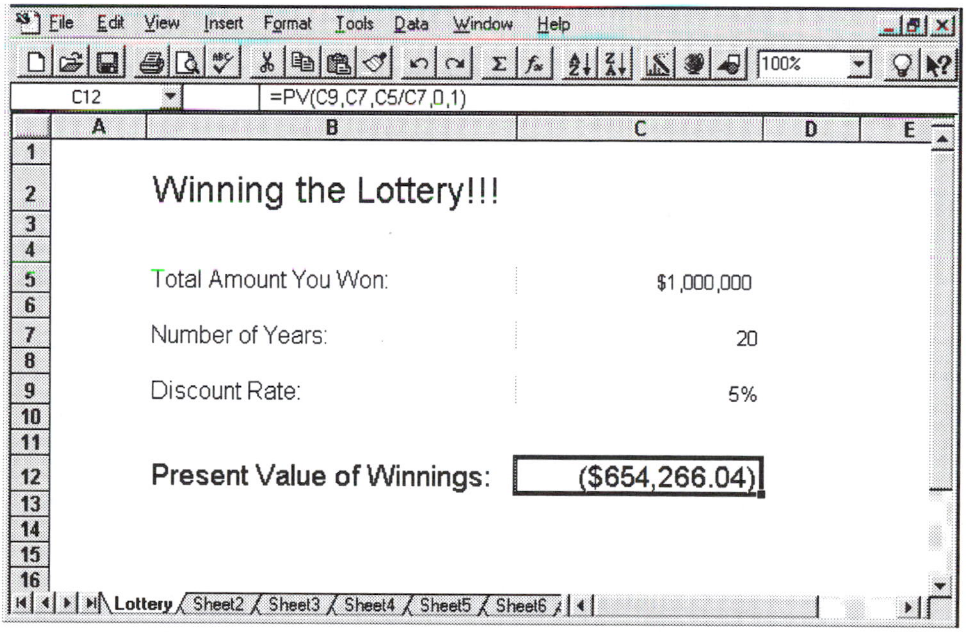

Figure 14-7. The present value of winning $1,000,000 in the lottery paid out in 20 annual payments. This is the amount it would be fair to pay for 20 equal annual payments of $50,000 assuming a discount rate of 5%.

The formula in C12 calculates the present value using the PV function. The final argument of the PV function is the type. In this case the type is 1 because the first payment is made right now, at the beginning of the first period.

Assuming a discount rate (inflation rate) of 5%, the present value of 20 annual payments of $50,000 each is $654,266.04. Another way of looking at the problem is that you would have to deposit $654,266.04 in an account earning 5% per year to be able to withdraw $50,000 today and $50,000 at the end of each of the next 19 years. So if you believe the discount rate to be 5% for the next 20 years, you might want to accept an offer of $700,000 for your winnings and decline an offer of $600,000. Of course, our analysis has not taken into account the income taxes you would have to pay on your winnings.

Look at the situation from the state's point of view. The state can take a million dollars and put it in the bank. If they earn 5% per year, they would make $50,000 per year in interest, which they pay you. At the end of the 20 years the state would still have its $1,000,000 intact.

OTHER FINANCIAL FUNCTIONS

Understanding the time value of money is critical to being able to analyze many financial situations. The financial functions of Excel provide important tools. We have looked at just the basic financial functions. There are dozens of additional financial functions built into Excel and included in the Analysis ToolPak add-in.

PENCIL AND PAPER EXERCISE

14-1. Write down the formula that calculates each of the following quantities. You may use the computer to try your answers. You need only write down the formula. You do not need to calculate the result of evaluating the formula.

(a) The monthly payment on a 30 year mortgage for $4,500,000 at 8% per year.

(b) The value of your Michael Jordan basketball card in 30 years if it is worth $6.50 today and appreciates at 9% per year.

(c) The annual rate of increase in the value of a house that was purchased for $59,000 in 1973 and sells for $232,000 today.

(d) The value of your retirement account in 50 years if you deposit $2,400 each year and receive 6% interest on your money.

(e) The value of your retirement account in 50 years if you deposit $200 per month for 50 years and receive 6% interest on your money.

(f) The annual interest rate you must receive to triple your money in 10 years.

(g) The monthly interest rate you are paying to Joe the Shark if you borrow $10,000 today and pay back $1,000 each month for 11 months and then pay back $10,000 a year from now.

(h) The amount of money you would need to accumulate to be able to retire for the rest of your life on $100,000 per year if your money earns 10% per year.

(i) The number of months a new company could last if it raised $2,000,000 and had a burn rate (spending rate) of $60,000 per month, assuming it kept its cash in an account earning 5% per year.

(j) There are two major companies in the widget market. United Widgets had sales of $20 million last year and is expected to grow at the rate of 4% per year. Widgets International had sales of $14 million last year. Give a formula that will indicate the annual rate at which Widgets International must grow to catch up to United Widgets in 7 years.

(k) The year in which the country of Palavia will reach 10,000,000 people given that it has 3,488,710 people today and its population is increasing by 2.4% per year. For example, your formula might tell us that Palavia will reach 10,000,000 people in the year 2015.

COMPUTER EXERCISES

14-2. The Friendly Mortgage Company offers your choice of 10 year, 20 year, and 30 year home mortgages all at the same interest rate. Create a worksheet that will allow you to enter the amount of the mortgage and the annual interest rate. For each type of loan the worksheet should calculate: (a) the monthly payment, (b) the total amount paid back to the mortgage company, and (c) the total amount of interest paid. That is, your worksheet should have two cells of input and nine cells of output.

14-3. Your broker suggests that you buy a zero coupon bond ("zero") with a face value of $20,000 maturing in 10 years that sells today for $6,237. That is, you pay $6,237 today and receive $20,000 10 years from now. You would like to find out the yield, the effective annual interest rate you would receive, on the zero.

(a) Create a worksheet for analyzing zeros that allows you to enter the face value, the time to maturity, and the current price. The output should be the yield. Of course, your worksheet should work for any inputs.

(b) Create a similar worksheet that allows you to enter the face value, the actual maturity date, and the current price. The output should be the yield. Use the TODAY function.

14-4. You are presented with a proposal for a project. The bottom line is that it is claimed that if you invest $20 million in a project this year, you will receive $5 million, $18 million, and $12 million over the following three years.

(a) Set up a worksheet that will tell you both the net present value of this project assuming a 12% discount rate and the internal rate of return for this project.

(b) You decide that most likely the project will cost $24 million this year and return $4 million, $14 million, and $10 million. What would be the net present value and internal rate of return?

14-5. The "Rule of 72" is a very convenient rule of thumb for performing mental calculations on the effect of compound interest. The rule indicates the approximate doubling time for money at a given interest rate or the approximate interest rate required to double your money in a certain period of time. The Rule of 72 states that to find the time required to double an investment at a given interest rate, divide the interest rate into 72. Equivalently, the Rule of 72 states that to find the interest rate required to double your money in a certain number of years, divide the number of years into 72. For example, the rule states that investments at 6% double in 12 years. Investments at 9% double in 8 years. Investments at 18% double in 4 years.

How is this helpful? What will a $20,000 investment at 14% be worth in 10 years? At 14% the doubling time is approximately 5 years. So in 5 years the investment will double in value to $40,000. In five more years the investment will double again to $80,000. So, $80,000 is the approximate answer.

For this exercise you are to check the validity of the Rule of 72. Create a worksheet with three columns and 72 rows plus column headings and titles. In the first column should be interest rates from 1% through 72%. In the next column should be the actual time for money to double at this interest rate as calculated using the NPER function. In the third column should be the amount of time for money to double at this interest rate predicted using the Rule of 72. Is the Rule of 72 reasonably accurate?

14-6. You are considering purchasing a new car. The price would be $17,239. You would pay $2,000 now and the rest monthly in a four year loan. The automobile dealership is offering a sales promotion where either (a) you will receive a $1,000 rebate check right now and the annual interest rate on the loan will be 11.9% or (b) the annual interest rate on the loan will be 2.9% but there is no rebate. Create a worksheet to compare the two options by calculating the present value of each of the options, assuming an 8% discount rate. Which is the better deal? Write a paragraph to justify your answer.

14-7. NetPower is a start-up company. They are out on the capital market looking for funding. They are willing to sell you 20% of the stock in their company for an investment of $500,000. According to their business plan they expect to lose money for the first two years. Then their big product will kick in and they expect to make money in the third and fourth year. These funds will be plowed back into the company for expansion. They then expect to be acquired by a major company for $10,000,000 in the fifth year. At this point you would cash out and receive 20% of the proceeds. Create a worksheet to analyze this venture in terms of the rate of return and the net present value of your investment. Since this is a very risky venture and you would buy in towards the beginning, you would expect a return of at least 40% per year on your money. Does NetPower seem like a reasonable investment opportunity?

14-8. You have been asked to analyze the proposed Skopi Project.

Initial investment in the project would be $10 million, which would be spent on planning, design, and construction. This phase would take 3 years. It is proposed that in year 0, $1 million be spent. In year 1, $3 million be spent. In year 2, $6 million be spent.

Revenues would be generated beginning in year 3. In year 3, revenues would be $1 million. In year 4, revenues would be $3 million. In years 5 through 13, revenues would be $6 million per year. In year 14, revenues would be $3 million. At the end of year 14, the project would be scrapped. In year 15, the project would return $2 million in the scrap value of the equipment.

Expenses would be as follows. Annual operating expenses for years 3 through 14 are figured at $1.25 million for raw materials, $1 million for maintenance and repairs, $0.5 million for labor, and $0.25 million for other expenses.

(a) Develop a worksheet that figures out the internal rate of return of this project. You should have a separate input area with separate cells for each of the assumptions. You should have columns for each of the years from 0 through 15. You should have separate rows for each of the revenue and expense items and for the total revenues and total expenses. The bottom row should be annual cash flow. You should have a separate well-labeled cell for the rate of return. Sketch the worksheet on paper before entering it into the computer. Have your worksheet calculate the internal rate of return using the preceding assumptions.

(b) Draw a graph in Excel that shows the projected revenues, expenses, and cash flow over the life of the project.

(c) Next try some sensitivity analysis. You might want to put a copy of the full worksheet for each of these scenarios on a different sheet. Suppose revenues for years 5 through 13 are only $4 million. What would be the internal rate of return? Suppose construction costs are $10 million in year 2? Suppose labor costs are double those expected?

(d) Put together a professional report on your analysis of the project. The company expects at least a 14% rate of return on its money. What is your recommendation on this project? Include appropriate copies of worksheets and graphs in your report. To what parameters is the rate of return most susceptible?

(e) Put together a 15 minute presentation on your analysis of the Skopi Project suitable for delivery to the Executive Committee of your company. Use PowerPoint or some other software package to prepare the presentation.

14-9. You have been assigned the task of comparing two sources of energy for a proposed manufacturing plant.

(a) Build a worksheet that determines the more economical of the two choices by comparing the present value of the expenses associated with each choice. A basic design for the worksheet and some projected data are given below. You may fill in whatever intermediate calculations you wish, but be sure to label these cells clearly. The bottom row of the worksheet should use an IF function to indicate whether Electricity or Fuel Oil is a more economical choice.

COMPARISON OF ENERGY SOURCES

	Electricity		Fuel Oil	
Unit Cost	$0.160	per kwh	$1.45	per gallon
Setup Cost	$15,000		$25,000	
Annual Consumption	700,000	kwh	125,000	gallons
Annual Maintenance	$3,000		$2,000	
Number of Years	8		8	
Discount Rate	0.12		0.12	

Present Value:

More Economical Energy Source:

(b) There is some uncertainty in the prices that can be negotiated in a long-term supply contract for the energy sources. Listed below are three possible scenarios. Create a new worksheet for each scenario, having your worksheet determine which choice would be more economical. To do this, you should be able to change just the values in the appropriate cells at the top of your worksheet. All other calculations should then be done automatically by the computer.

THREE UNIT COST SCENARIOS

Scenario	Electricity		Fuel Oil	
1 (original)	$0.160	per kwh	$1.45	per gallon
2	$0.195	per kwh	$1.75	per gallon
3	$0.125	per kwh	$1.15	per gallon

(c) Write a brief but professional report giving your recommendation on the energy source to select. Include appropriate copies of your worksheets.

14-10. A loan amortization table shows the effect of each payment on the amount of principal still owed. A worksheet for constructing loan amortization tables for 48 month loans is shown below. The worksheet has two input cells: (1) the principal of the loan (the original amount borrowed) and (2) the annual interest rate. All other numbers in the worksheet are calculated. Changing either or both of these input numbers will create a new amortization table.

Note that in the table, the amount of interest owed each month is the monthly interest rate times the amount of the principal still owed at the beginning of the month. The amount of the payment that goes to reducing the principal is the amount of the payment that is left over. If all of the calculations are correct, then the principal owed at the end of the forty-eighth month should be 0.

(a) Duplicate the worksheet below. Try it on the loan indicated and then on a $53,000 loan at 12% and on a $4,000 loan at 2.9%.

(b) Construct a similar worksheet for 36 month loans. Try the worksheet on the same three sets of data.

(c) Construct a worksheet that produces an amortization table for any term loan of from 1 to 5 years (60 monthly payments). The worksheet should have three input cells: the principal of the loan, the annual interest rate, and the number of years for the loan. This is a bit tricky. While you might have 60 rows of formulas, the table should only appear to have one row for each month of payment. All rows below the final payment should appear blank.

File Edit View Insert Format Tools Data Window Help						_|8|x|
A	B	C	D	E	F	G
1						
2			Loan Amortization Table for 48 Month Loans			
3						
4		Principal:		$16,353.00		
5		Annual Interest rate:		9.90%		
6						
7	Resulting Monthly Interest Rate:			0.825%		
8	Resulting Monthly Payment:			$413.97		
9						
10		Principal at	Monthly	Interest	Principal	Principal at
11	Month	Beginning	Payment	Payment	Payment	End of Period
12	1	$16,353.00	$413.97	$134.91	$279.06	$16,073.94
13	2	$16,073.94	$413.97	$132.61	$281.36	$15,792.58
14	3	$15,792.58	$413.97	$130.29	$283.68	$15,508.90
15	4	$15,508.90	$413.97	$127.95	$286.02	$15,222.88
57	46	$1,221.70	$413.97	$10.08	$403.89	$817.80
58	47	$817.80	$413.97	$6.75	$407.22	$410.58
59	48	$410.58	$413.97	$3.39	$410.58	$0.00
60						

48 month / Sheet2 / Sheet3 / Sheet4 / Sheet5 / Sheet6

14-11. Mary and John have been married for three years. They both work. Their salaries total $95,000 per year. They currently are paying $1,800 per month rent plus utilities. Between savings and wedding gifts they have managed to accumulate $58,000, which they have in a money market account.

Mary and John are thinking about buying a house. They have done some looking and after much dispute have settled on a suburban house that costs about $220,000. Annual real estate taxes would be about $2,800. They are asking the age-old questions: Can we afford it? Will we be better off financially 10 years from now if we buy the house instead of continuing to rent?

Your task is to design and implement a worksheet that will analyze the financial implication over the next 10 years of buying versus renting.

The issue of home ownership is a complicated one in this society. You can make some assumptions:

- Assume a fixed rate mortgage for 80% of the purchase price of the home. Mary and John will pay 20% of the price as a down payment when they purchase the home. Find out the prevailing mortgage rate by checking in the local newspaper or by calling a bank. John and Mary would use the $58,000 for the down payment, closing costs, and moving expenses.

- Assume that everything (house values, rents, real estate taxes, salaries) goes up with inflation. Have a separate cell for the inflation rate.

Of course, if they buy, Mary and John would no longer get the interest they now receive from the $58,000 in the money market account.

A very important aspect of home ownership in the United States is the income tax advantage. If Mary and John own their own home, then real estate taxes and the interest (but not the principal) they pay on their mortgage are deductible for income tax purposes. You will need to find out what income tax bracket Mary and John are in, assuming no other dependents.

From a financial point of view would Mary and John be better off buying a house or continuing to rent? Write a professional report for Mary and John. Include appropriate parts of the worksheet and a chart or two.

CHAPTER 15

RANDOM NUMBERS AND SIMULATION

OBJECTIVES

In this chapter you will learn how to:

- Use RAND to generate random numbers
- Create worksheets to simulate probabilistic situations
- Simulate situations with multiple possible outcomes using lookup tables
- Model queuing problems
- Generate random integers

One way of dealing with the complexities of the world is to build a model to simulate a situation or environment. The model then can be tested and manipulated. These results can be used to predict what will happen in the world. An airplane company wants to know how a proposed new plane will fly, so it builds a model and places the model in a wind tunnel and runs tests. Or, it creates a computer program that allows engineers to specify the plane on the screen and then mathematically simulate the plane flying under different conditions.

Of course, the effectiveness of using a model to predict what really will happen depends on how well the relevant aspects of the situation are captured in the model. One certainly can imagine an airplane whose design worked great on the computer but that crashes when it is first flown. There is a saying in the computer field, "Garbage In, Garbage Out," or "GIGO". If you put nonsense into the computer, you will get nonsense out. Don't believe everything that comes out of the computer. Just because "The computer says" something doesn't mean it is right.

People have attempted to create computer models for all kinds of situations. There are computer models of the weather. Enter in the temperature, wind velocity, and so on at many different locations on the earth. The computer predicts what the weather will be like tomorrow or next week. There are computer models of the economy. Suppose we raise the income tax rate. What will be the effect on the economy a year from now or five years from now?

We have seen how Excel can be used as a simulation tool. "What if" analysis is computer simulation. To predict the profitability of a new enterprise, create an Excel worksheet to model the projected finances and try it out under different scenarios.

Some situations are best modeled probabilistically. One third of the time this will happen; two thirds of the time something else will happen. These situations can be modeled on the computer with the use of **random numbers**. Simulations that make use of random numbers often are called **Monte Carlo simulations**. Monte Carlo is a city on the Mediterranean Sea that is the site of a well-known gambling casino.

In this chapter we will discuss random numbers in Excel and their use in simulations.

THE RAND FUNCTION

Random numbers are generated in Excel using the **RAND** function. The RAND function has no arguments. The value of the RAND function is a number between 0 and 1 (but not including 1). The user cannot predict what this number will be. An example of a worksheet with 10 random numbers is shown in Figure 15-1.

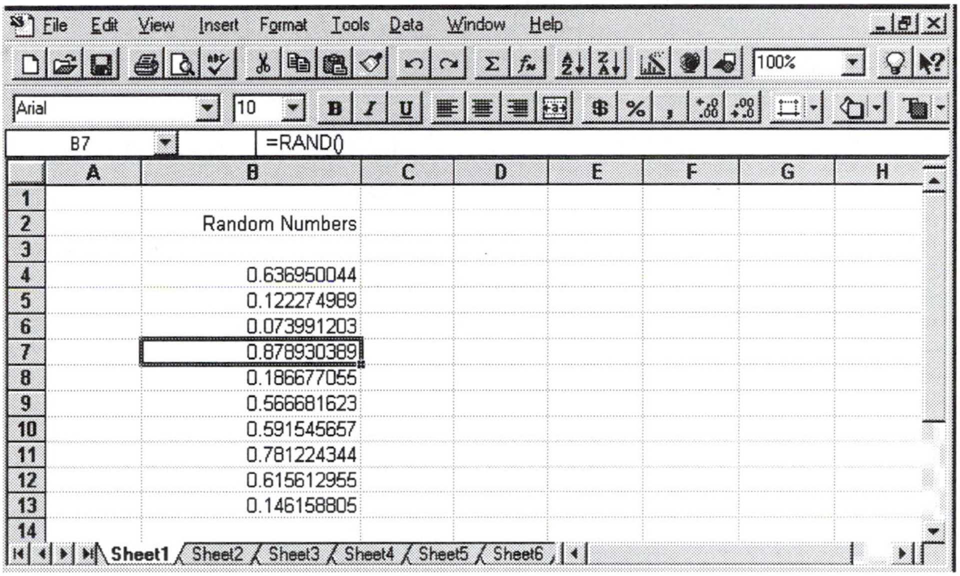

Figure 15-1. Generating ten random numbers.

The value of each call to the RAND function is calculated out to 15 digits to the right of the decimal point. Only nine decimal places of each number are displayed in each random number in Figure 15-1. To see the full numbers, select the cells and click on the Increase Decimal Places button.

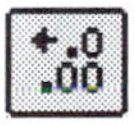

When entering the RAND function into a formula you must include the parentheses

$$=RAND(\ )$$

even though there is nothing placed between them. If you enter =RAND with no parentheses, Excel will expect RAND to be the name of a cell so you will get a #NAME? error message.

The RAND function is a strange beast. Each time the worksheet is recalculated, the value of each RAND changes! You can force a recalculation at any time by pressing function key F9 on the keyboard.

FLIPPING COINS

Suppose we want to simulate flipping a coin in Excel. Each time we recalculate the worksheet (by pressing F9), the computer flips the coin again.

The computer will say HEADS or TAILS, but we won't know in advance which it will be. We would like HEADS and TAILS each to occur 50% of the time.

To accomplish this, we will use random numbers generated by the RAND function. We would like half the possible numbers produced by RAND to be HEADS and the other half of the numbers to be TAILS. Thus, we check the random number against 0.5. If the random number is less than 0.5, we call the result HEADS. Otherwise, we call the result TAILS. The formula is

$$=IF(RAND(\ ) < 0.5, \text{"HEADS"}, \text{"TAILS"})$$

The worksheet is shown in Figure 15-2.

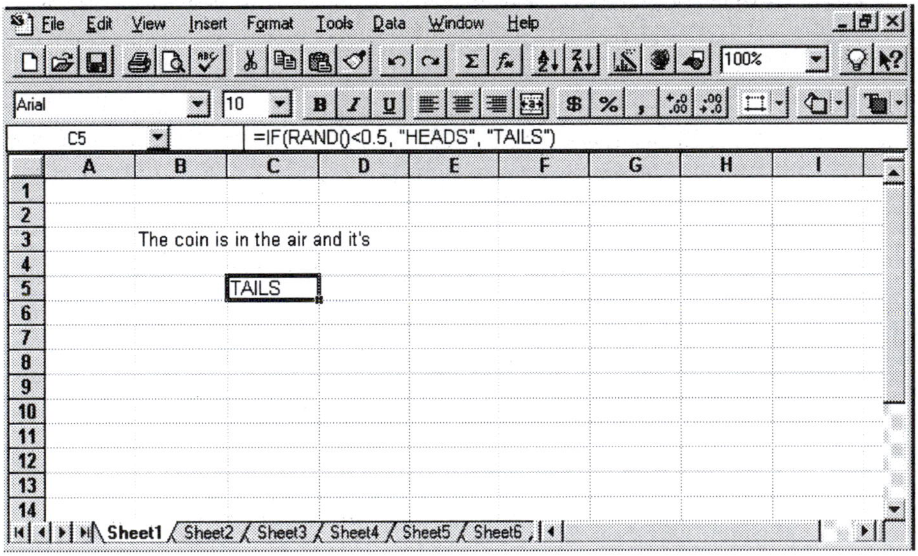

Figure 15-2. Simulating the flip of a fair coin.

Each time we press F9 a new random number between 0 and 1 is produced by RAND and hence a new coin is flipped with equal likelihood of a HEADS or a TAILS. We have no way of knowing before each recalculation whether the computer will say HEADS or TAILS.

Should we check if the random number is less than 0.5 or less than or equal to 0.5? Since 0 is a possible random number but 1 is not, it seems fairer for 0.5 to count as a TAILS. Actually, there are so many possible random numbers that the probability of exactly 0.5 being generated is too small to worry about!

Suppose that we would like to rig the worksheet so that 70% of the time the flip comes out HEADS and only 30% of the time the flip comes out TAILS. We could change the formula, as follows

=IF(RAND() < 0.7, "HEADS", "TAILS")

Now 70% of the random numbers (all the numbers between 0 and 0.7) will result in HEADS and only 30% of the random numbers (all the numbers from 0.7 to 1) will result in TAILS.

Suppose we would like three possible outcomes. We would like HEADS 49% of the time, TAILS 48% of the time, and 3% of the time we would like the outcome to be COIN ROLLS AWAY.

The first step is to divide up the numbers between 0 to 1 into three segments that correspond to the desired outcomes. We assign the numbers from 0 to 0.49 to correspond to HEADS. (This is 49% of the numbers.) The numbers from 0.49 to 0.97 will correspond to TAILS. (This is 48% of the numbers.) The numbers between 0.97 and 1 correspond to COIN ROLLS AWAY. (This is 3% of the numbers.) This is illustrated in Figure 15-3.

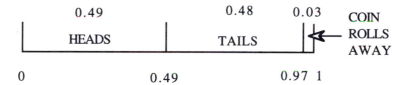

Figure 15-3. Dividing up the number line from 0 to 1 so that 49% of the numbers correspond to HEADS, 48% of the numbers correspond to TAILS, and 3% of the numbers correspond to COIN ROLLS AWAY.

To implement this distribution in the worksheet we might first think of writing a formula like

=IF(RAND()<.49,"HEADS",IF(RAND()<.97,"TAILS","COIN ROLLS AWAY")

This formula is the right idea but it has a subtle error. The problem is that each time the RAND function is called, it returns a different value. Thus the two calls to RAND in the preceding formula will return different random numbers and the desired probabilities will not be obeyed.

The remedy is to place the call to RAND in a different cell, for example G5, and then refer to that cell in the formula, as in

$$=IF(G5<.49,"HEADS",IF(G5<.97,"TAILS","COIN\ ROLLS\ AWAY"))$$

This solution is shown in Figure 15-4. Now the same random number is used in both places in the formula. To flip another coin, press F9 to recalculate the worksheet. This generates another random number in G5 and another result in C5. If you would like, the actual random number can be placed in a cell off the screen or on another sheet so it does not show.

An alternative to using the nested IF function is to use a lookup table. Lookup tables have the advantage of showing the cutoff points for the random numbers explicitly in the worksheet. An equivalent worksheet for flipping coins that uses a lookup table is shown in Figure 15-5. The key formula, in C5, is

$$=VLOOKUP(G5,G11:H13,2)$$

To determine the outcome of the coin flip, the random number in G5 is looked up in the table in G11:H13. Recall from Chapter 12 that the VLOOKUP function takes the value of the first argument (the value in G5) and compares it against the entries in the first column of the lookup table beginning with the first entry (in G11). When it finds a value in the column that is greater than the number it is looking up, it goes up one row and over to the second column of the table and that is the value it returns. For example, if the value in G5 is 0.76, the VLOOKUP function would return TAILS.

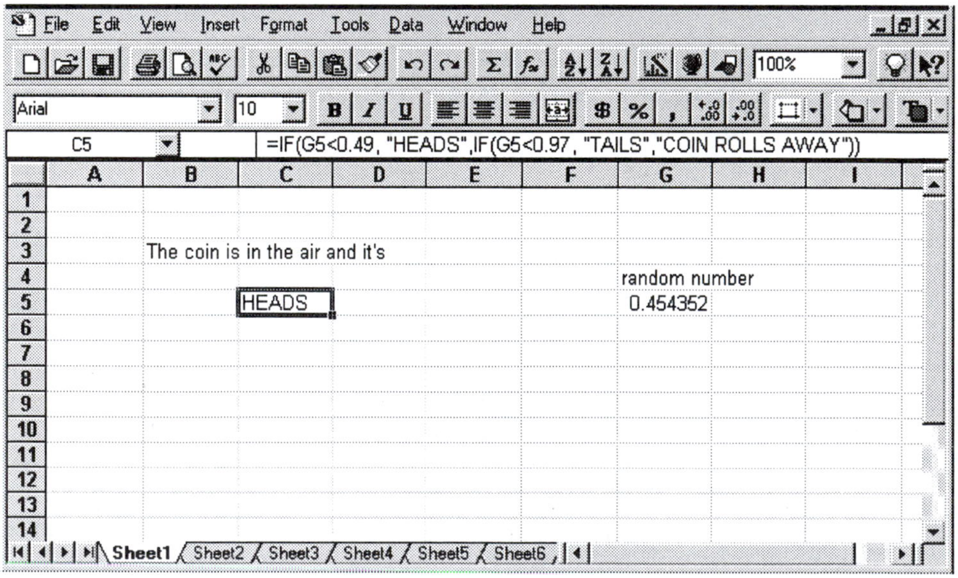

Figure 15-4. Flipping a coin with three possible outcomes.

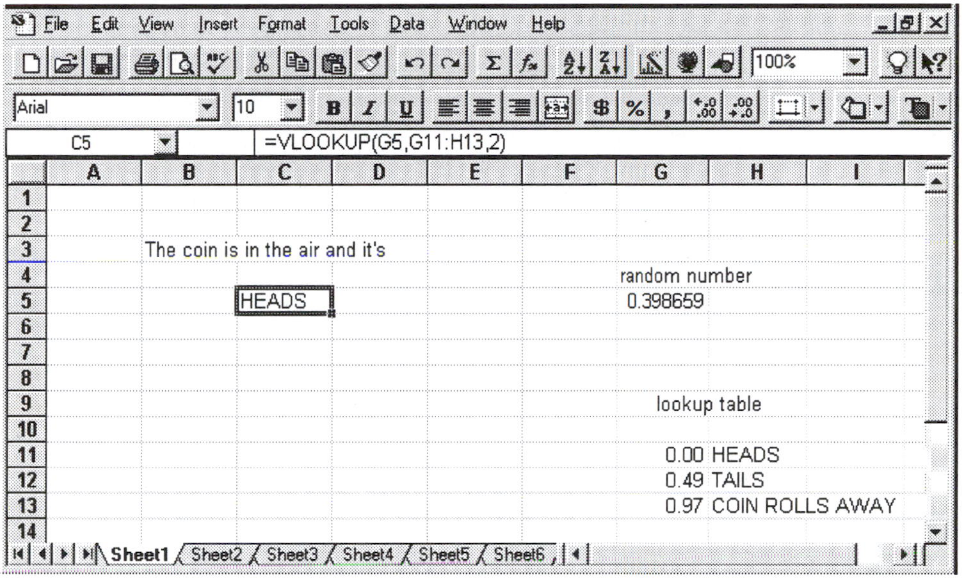

Figure 15-5. Flipping a coin with three possible outcomes using a lookup table.

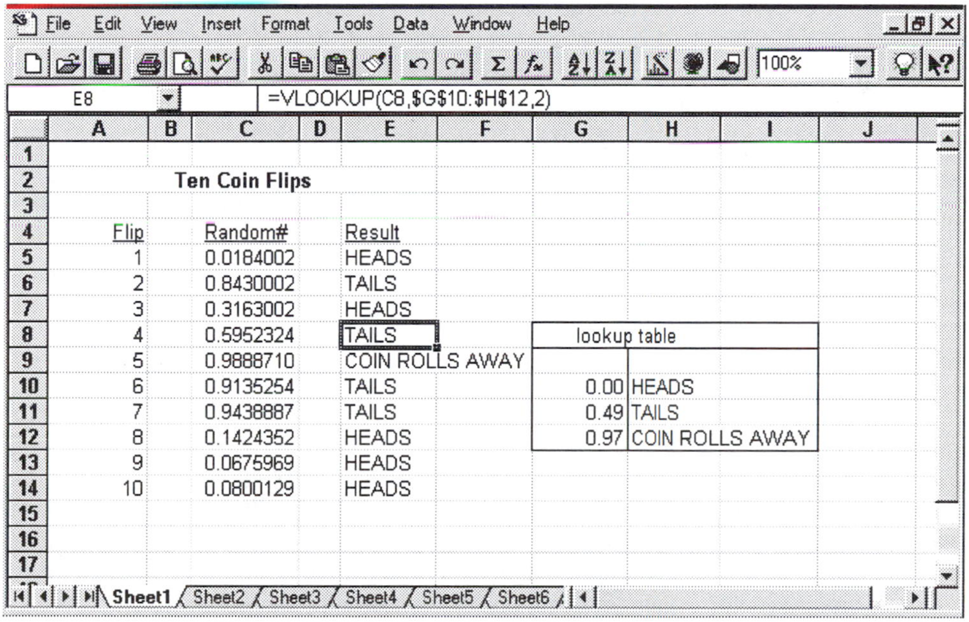

Figure 15-6. Each flip requires a separate random number.

The worksheet in Figure 15-6 simulates ten coin flips. Here we create a new random number for each coin flip. Each cell in column C contains the formula =RAND(). The formulas in the cells in column E look up the corresponding random number in the lookup table. The formula in E8 is

$$=VLOOKUP(C8,\$G\$11:\$H\$13,2)$$

Absolute addressing is used when referring to the lookup table so that the addresses do not change when the formula is filled down column E.

It is important that we use ten different random numbers in this worksheet, one for each coin flip. If we used only one random number and referred to it ten times, then all of the coin flips would come out the same.

Each time we press the recalculation key F9, ten more coin flips are simulated.

QUEUING PROBLEMS

A common application for Monte Carlo simulation is in queuing problems. A **queue** is a waiting line. People form a queue for a bus or when waiting to cash a check in a bank or to pay for their groceries in a supermarket. In particular, a queue is a line where the first people to arrive in the line are the first to be served. That is, a queue is what people think of as a "fair" waiting line. (A **stack** is a line where the first to arrive are the last to be served. This occurs, for example, if people are lined up for the bus and the bus stops so that the door opens at the end of the line. The last person on line would be the first on the bus.) In some situations there is one large master queue (for example, in most banks). In some situations there are multiple queues (for example, in most supermarkets).

People have studied queuing problems for years. How many tollbooths should be built at the entrance to the bridge? If too few are built, the traffic will back up too far. Widening the highway for tollbooths is expensive. If too many tollbooths are built, money will be spent unnecessarily. How many checkout registers should be built in the supermarket? At a busy intersection, for how long should the green light be on in each direction? How should tasks be divided up on an assembly line? All of these are problems involving queues.

One approach to solving queuing problems is to model the process on the computer. Once the basic model is set up, we can change some of the assumptions and see what the results would be in the model. We can do "What if" analysis with queuing models just as we can with financial models. Of course, the usefulness of the results depends on the fidelity with which the relevant portions of the world have been captured in the model.

SANTA CLAUS' AFTERNOON

It is late November and you are working as an intern in a local department store. The rival department store across town has set up Santa Claus in a big chair in their store and has invited parents to bring their children in to meet him. Their promotion seems to be working well. Your store manager has asked you to do the same in your store. To make the idea even more attractive to parents, you plan to hire a photographer to take instant photographs of the children sitting on Santa's lap.

You have limited space in the store. The department next to the area where Santa will sit is Fine Jewelry, and the manager of the department does not want a long line of screaming kids winding through the department. You decide to try a quick computer simulation to see how long the line is likely to become.

Santa Claus will be in the store from 2 PM to 5 PM each afternoon. You figure that with each kid sitting down, pulling Santa's beard, saying he or she has been good, and telling Santa what he or she wants for Christmas and then with the photographer taking a picture, that Santa can serve a child in 30 seconds, or two per minute. How many children will arrive each minute? You decide to visit the rival department store with your watch and a pad and to use their arrivals as an estimate for your store. After observing for a while you decide that in 10% of the minutes no children arrive, in 20% of the minutes 1 child arrives, in 30% of the minutes 2 children arrive, in 30% of the minutes 3 children arrive, and in 10% of the minutes 4 children arrive.

Now we need to translate this into an Excel model. Each row in the model will correspond to a different minute with Santa. We will draw a new random number each minute and use the random number to determine the number of children who arrive using the preceding distribution. For simplicity, we will assume that all children arrive right at the beginning of each minute. The number of children who see Santa each minute will depend on the number of people still waiting from the previous minute and the number of arrivals. If no children are there, then Santa has the minute off. If there is only one child there, then Santa will see the one child. If there are two or more children, then Santa will see two children that minute and any remaining children will wait on line.

The worksheet for the simulation is shown in Figure 15-7.

In column A the times are listed from 2:00 PM through 4:59 PM. This was accomplished by typing 2:00 PM into A6, 2:01 PM into A7, selecting A6 and A7, and then dragging the Fill Handle down to A185. The result was that AutoFill correctly filled in the minute-by-minute sequence of times.

Column B contains the random numbers. Each cell in B6:B185 contains the formula

=RAND( )

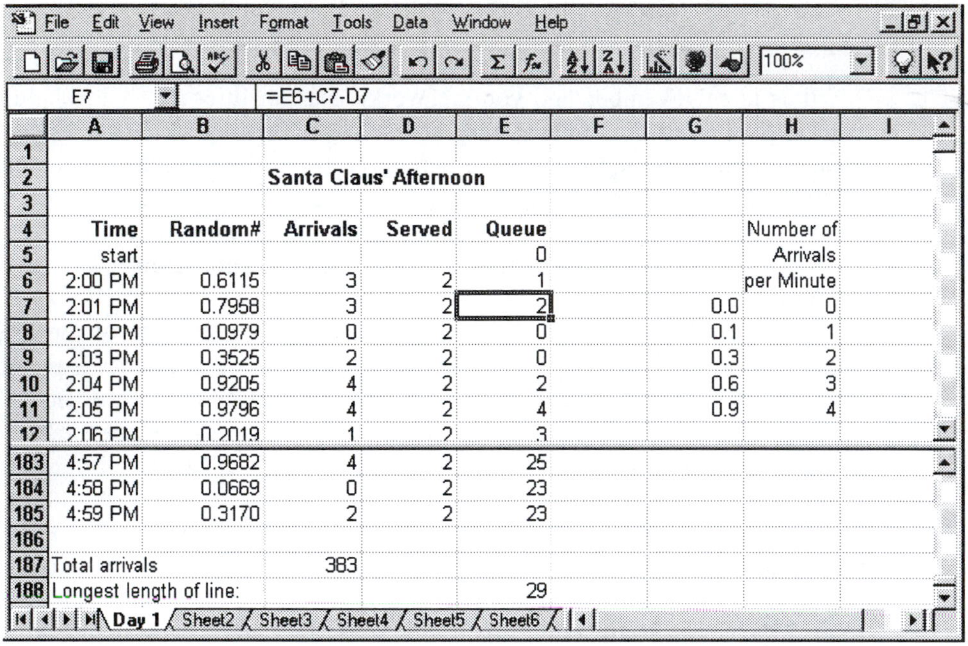

	File Edit View Insert Format Tools Data Window Help								
	E7		=E6+C7-D7						
	A	B	C	D	E	F	G	H	I
1									
2			**Santa Claus' Afternoon**						
3									
4	**Time**	**Random#**	**Arrivals**	**Served**	**Queue**			Number of	
5	start				0			Arrivals	
6	2:00 PM	0.6115	3	2	1			per Minute	
7	2:01 PM	0.7958	3	2	2		0.0	0	
8	2:02 PM	0.0979	0	2	0		0.1	1	
9	2:03 PM	0.3525	2	2	0		0.3	2	
10	2:04 PM	0.9205	4	2	2		0.6	3	
11	2:05 PM	0.9796	4	2	4		0.9	4	
12	2:06 PM	0.2019	1	2	3				
183	4:57 PM	0.9682	4	2	25				
184	4:58 PM	0.0669	0	2	23				
185	4:59 PM	0.3170	2	2	23				
186									
187	Total arrivals		383						
188	Longest length of line:				29				

Day 1 / Sheet2 / Sheet3 / Sheet4 / Sheet5 / Sheet6 /

Figure 15-7. A minute-by-minute simulation of Santa's afternoon.

The number of children who arrive at the beginning of each minute is calculated in column C using the lookup table in G7:H11. The lookup table is set up so that there is a 10% chance that no children arrive, a 20% chance that 1 child arrives, a 30% chance that 2 children arrive, a 30% chance that 3 children arrive, and a 10% chance that 4 children arrive. This is illustrated in Figure 15-8.

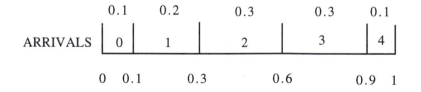

Figure 15-8 Dividing the numbers between 0 and 1 so that 10% correspond to 0 arrivals, 20% correspond to 1 arrival, 30% correspond to 2 arrivals, 30% correspond to 3 arrivals, and 10% correspond to 4 arrivals.

The formula in C6 is

$$=VLOOKUP(B6,\$G\$7:\$H\$11,2)$$

The formula has been filled from C6 down to C185. This generates the number of children who arrive each minute.

Remember that we are estimating that Santa Claus can see at most two children per minute. In any minute the number of children available for Santa to see is the number of children already waiting in line plus the number of children who just have arrived. Thus, the formula in D6 for the number of children served is

$$=MIN(E5+C6,2)$$

This formula is then filled down to D185. This formula might require a little thought. Recall that MIN returns the smallest of its arguments. Suppose there are 4 children waiting in line and 1 child arrives. The number of children Santa can see that minute is $=MIN(4+1,2)$, which is $=MIN(5,2)$, which is 2.

Finally, column E contains the queue, the length of the line each minute. Here we set E5 to 0, assuming that the line would be 0 when Santa begins, though it certainly is possible that people might show up at 1:55 PM to see Santa at 2:00 PM. The length of the line each minute will be the length of the line the previous minute plus the number of arrivals minus the number of children who see Santa. So the formula in E6 is

$$=E5+C6-D6$$

This formula is filled down column E.

At the end of the day in Figure 15-7 we see that there are 23 children waiting in line and that the longest the line has been is 29 children. A total of 383 children have arrived to see Santa during the three hours.

To simulate another day we would press F9 again. A new set of random numbers would appear. For each minute a new set of arrivals would be generated, Santa would see children, the line would grow or shrink. We could determine the total number of children seen that day and the longest length of the line during the day.

We also could copy the worksheet over to a new sheet, as in Figure 15-9, and accumulate a number of different simulations. We then could compute statistics on the simulation of a month's worth of days.

What can we conclude? Under these assumptions the system is saturated. Santa would be worked at full capacity and there would be quite long lines. (Thirty children waiting in line with their parents can cause some disturbance in a

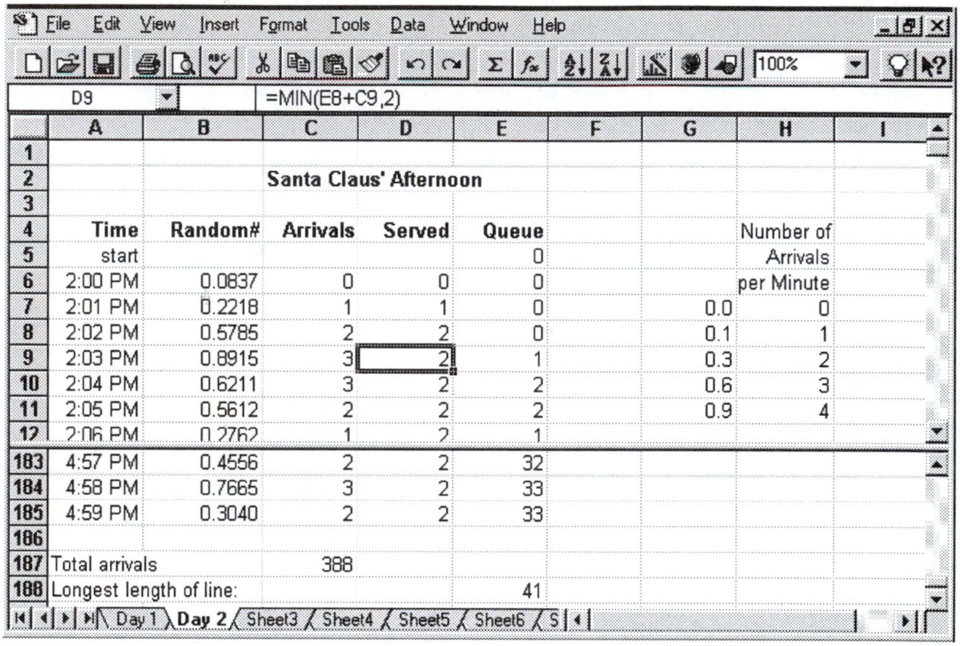

File Edit View Insert Format Tools Data Window Help

D9 =MIN(E8+C9,2)

	A	B	C	D	E	F	G	H
1								
2			Santa Claus' Afternoon					
3								
4	Time	Random#	Arrivals	Served	Queue			Number of
5	start				0			Arrivals
6	2:00 PM	0.0837	0	0	0			per Minute
7	2:01 PM	0.2218	1	1	0		0.0	0
8	2:02 PM	0.5785	2	2	0		0.1	1
9	2:03 PM	0.8915	3	2	1		0.3	2
10	2:04 PM	0.6211	3	2	2		0.6	3
11	2:05 PM	0.5612	2	2	2		0.9	4
12	2:06 PM	0.2762	1	2	1			
183	4:57 PM	0.4556	2	2	32			
184	4:58 PM	0.7665	3	2	33			
185	4:59 PM	0.3040	2	2	33			
186								
187	Total arrivals		388					
188	Longest length of line:				41			

Day 1 | Day 2 | Sheet3 | Sheet4 | Sheet5 | Sheet6 | S

Figure 15-9. Another busy afternoon for Santa.

small area.) The manager of the Fine Jewelry department has reason to be concerned. You should think about ways to improve the situation. Perhaps the visits with Santa could be speeded up a bit or Santa could be hired for more hours to dissipate the demand or a second Santa could be hired or you could go to a reservation system. Forewarned is forearmed.

This exercise was somewhat fanciful and simple-minded, but Monte Carlo simulation has proved useful in understanding a wide variety of queuing problems. In more sophisticated simulations we might model a probabilistic distribution for serving people as well as for arrivals. For example, some children might come with long lists of toys they want and take more time with Santa. Parents who arrive might leave if the line is too long. The probability distribution for arrivals might change as the day progresses. For example, more people might arrive right after school lets out. We might have multiple lines and multiple servers. All of these situations and more could be modeled by expanding the worksheet.

GENERATING RANDOM INTEGERS USING INT

The RAND function generates random numbers between 0 and 0.99999... (to 15 decimal places). In some situations it is useful to be able to generate a random

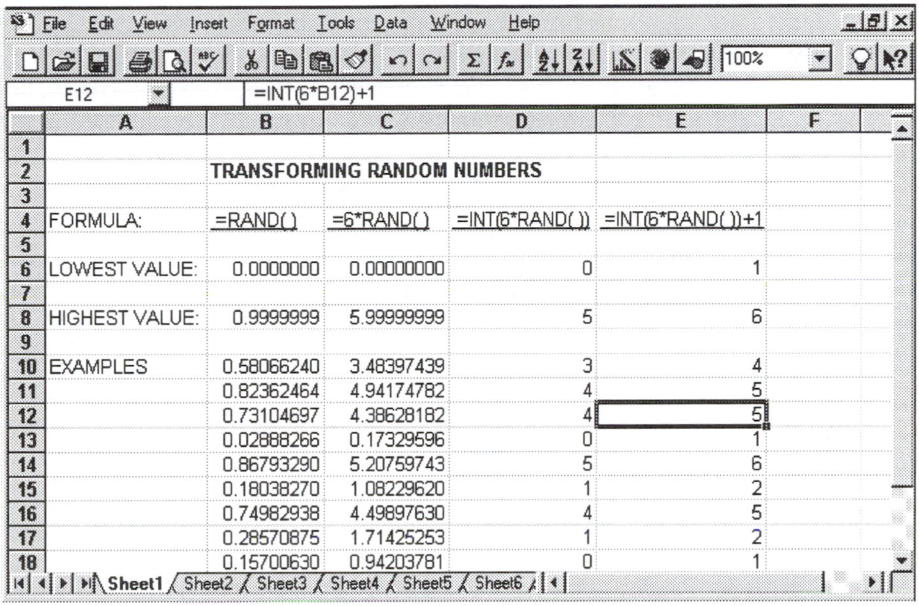

	A	B	C	D	E
1					
2		TRANSFORMING RANDOM NUMBERS			
3					
4	FORMULA:	=RAND()	=6*RAND()	=INT(6*RAND())	=INT(6*RAND())+1
5					
6	LOWEST VALUE:	0.0000000	0.00000000	0	1
7					
8	HIGHEST VALUE:	0.9999999	5.99999999	5	6
9					
10	EXAMPLES	0.58066240	3.48397439	3	4
11		0.82362464	4.94174782	4	5
12		0.73104697	4.38628182	4	5
13		0.02888266	0.17329596	0	1
14		0.86793290	5.20759743	5	6
15		0.18038270	1.08229620	1	2
16		0.74982938	4.49897630	4	5
17		0.28570875	1.71425253	1	2
18		0.15700630	0.94203781	0	1

Figure 15-10. Transforming random numbers. Multiplying a number times RAND() expands the range. Taking the INT transforms the number into an integer. Adding a number shifts the range.

set of integers instead. For example, we might want to simulate the rolling of a die by generating the integers 1, 2, 3, 4, 5, 6, with equal probability. We could set up a nested IF function or a lookup table to accomplish this, but there is a more direct method.

First, we can expand the range of the random numbers by multiplying the RAND function by a number. For example, the formula =6*RAND() would produce random numbers between 0 and 5.9999... . Since the RAND function generates numbers from 0 to 0.99999... , the lowest number generated by =6*RAND() would be 0 and the highest would be 5.9999... . This is demonstrated in column C of Figure 15-10. Similarly, the formula =100*RAND() would generate random numbers from 0 to 99.999... .

Now we can convert these numbers to integers using the **INT** function. The INT function has a single argument. The INT function rounds down the argument to the nearest integer. So =INT(3.8) is 3.

The formula =INT(6*RAND()) will generate the integers 0, 1, 2, 3, 4, 5 randomly with equal likelihood. The INT function converts the value of its argument into an integer by rounding down to the nearest integer. Any number between 0 and 0.99999... is converted to 0. Any number between 1 and 1.99999... is converted to 1, and so on. This is illustrated in column D of Figure 15-10. The random numbers in B10:B18 are multiplied by 6 in C10:C18. These numbers are then transformed into integers in D10:D18 using the INT function.

We have the random integers 0, 1, 2, 3, 4, 5. By adding 1 to the previous formula we can generate the random integers 1, 2, 3, 4, 5, 6. Hence, to simulate a die by generating the random integers 1, 2, 3, 4, 5, 6 we can use the formula

$$=INT(6*RAND())+1$$

This is illustrated in column E of Figure 15-10.

The general formula for generating a random integer from some sequence of integers is given by

$$=INT(N*RAND())+L$$

where N is the number of integers in the sequence and L is the value of the lowest integer in the sequence.

For example, if we would like to generate random integers from the sequence 40, 41, 42, ... 59 we could use the formula

$$=INT(20*RAND())+40$$

because there are 20 integers in the sequence and the lowest integer is 40.

This method works for generating integers from a sequence where we want each integer to be equally likely to occur. If we do not want the outcomes to occur with equal probabilities, then we would use nested IF functions or lookup tables as discussed earlier in the chapter. Or we can use the Random Number Generation tool in the Analysis ToolPak, which is discussed in Chapter 17.

ROLLING A PAIR OF DICE 10,000 TIMES

From playing Monopoly and other board games, and from trips to the casinos, we are interested in the probabilities of different outcomes when we roll a pair of dice. We set up the worksheet in Figure 15-11. In column A we have the number of the roll. In columns B and C we simulate rolling each die. The formula in each of the 20,000 cells in B5:C10004 is

$$=INT(6*RAND())+1$$

The worksheet uses 20,000 different random numbers. In column D we have the total that would result for the roll. In column G we summarize the 10,000 rolls using the COUNTIF function. We see that the most common combination is a 7 and that it occurs over 16%, or about one-sixth, of the time.

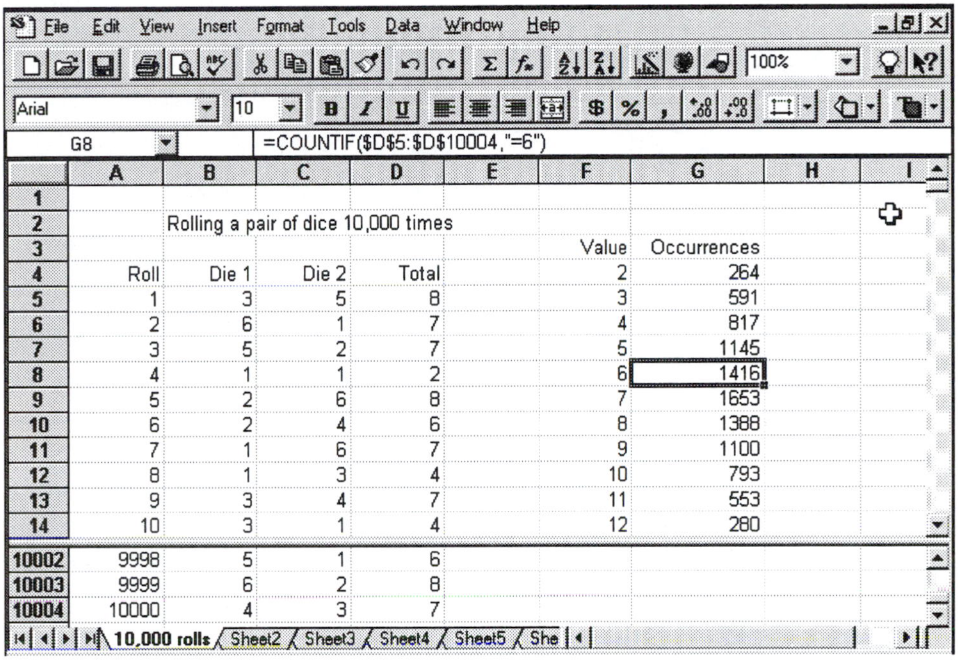

	A	B	C	D	E	F	G
1							
2		Rolling a pair of dice 10,000 times					
3						Value	Occurrences
4	Roll	Die 1	Die 2	Total		2	264
5	1	3	5	8		3	591
6	2	6	1	7		4	817
7	3	5	2	7		5	1145
8	4	1	1	2		6	1416
9	5	2	6	8		7	1653
10	6	2	4	6		8	1388
11	7	1	6	7		9	1100
12	8	1	3	4		10	793
13	9	3	4	7		11	553
14	10	3	1	4		12	280
10002	9998	5	1	6			
10003	9999	6	2	8			
10004	10000	4	3	7			

Figure 15-11. Simulating 10,000 rolls of a pair of dice.

PENCIL AND PAPER EXERCISE

15-1. Write out on paper how to use RAND to generate each of the following distributions. Show all formulas and tables.

(a) 50% I WIN
50% YOU WIN

(b) 80% I WIN
20% YOU WIN

(c) 55% I WIN
30% YOU WIN
15% TIE

(d) 35% I WIN
25% YOU WIN
30% TIE
10% RAINED OUT

(e) 32%   I WIN
    22%   YOU WIN
    25%   WE BOTH WIN
    15%   WE BOTH LOSE
     6%   RAINED OUT

(f) 50%   1
    50%   2

(g) 25%   7
    25%   8
    25%   9
    25%   10

(h) the years (integers) from 1900 through 1999 with equal likelihood

(i) the (integer) temperatures from -37 degrees through 120 degrees with equal likelihood

(j) the integers 2, 4, 6, 8 with equal likelihood

(k) the numbers 3.0, 3.1, 3.2, ... 4.9 with equal likelihood

COMPUTER EXERCISES

15-2. Create an Executive Decision Maker. The user will type in a decision that needs to be made. For example, SHOULD WE LAUNCH A TAKEOVER BID OF IBM? or SHOULD I ASK PAT OUT FOR A DATE? Your worksheet should respond with one of the following answers with the frequencies indicated.

    60%   GO FOR IT !
    30%   NO. THE TIME IS NOT RIGHT.
    10%   PLEASE GATHER MORE INFORMATION.

15-3. For each day in the month of January, the probabilities are

    .19   that it will snow
    .36   that it will be cloudy
    .30   that it will be sunny
    .15   that it will rain

Create a worksheet that uses RAND to "predict" the weather for the month of January. Each time F9 is pressed, the worksheet should show a different prediction. The worksheet should look like:

```
I  PREDICT

JANUARY   1        CLOUDY
JANUARY   2        RAIN
JANUARY   3        CLOUDY
   ...
JANUARY   30       SNOW
JANUARY   31       SUNNY
```

15-4. Create an automated Fortune Teller. The user will type his or her name and the computer will tell the person's fortune. You should have at least eight possible fortunes, for example: "You will become the ruler of your country" or "You will have ten children" or "You will be the first person to land on the sun". Each time a person types in a name one of the fortunes should be displayed. If the cell with the person's name is blank, then the cell that shows the fortune should be blank. As soon as a name is entered, a fortune should appear. The fortunes themselves should not be visible on the worksheet. Put them off to the side or, better, on another worksheet. Print the worksheet five times: with the names of three different friends and their fortunes, once with the name cell blank, and once with the full formulas showing (or handwritten if too long).

15-5. Our soccer team has 12 games scheduled. The coach figures that for each game the probabilities are:

Our Score	Opponent's Score
10% the team scores 0 goals	35% the opponent scores 0 goals
20% the team scores 1 goal	10% the opponent scores 1 goal
40% the team scores 2 goals	10% the opponent scores 2 goals
20% the team scores 3 goals	10% the opponent scores 3 goals
10% the team scores 4 goals	35% the opponent scores 4 goals

Note that the probabilities for the team's goals are independent of the probabilities for the opponent's goals.

Create a worksheet that "predicts" the season. You should have one row in the main body of your worksheet for each game. You should have columns for at least: game number (1 through 12), random number for us, number of goals we score, random number for them, number of goals they score, result of game for us (win, lose, draw). At the bottom of the worksheet show the predicted record for the season: the number of wins, losses, and draws. Print your worksheet three times: twice with different values showing (recalculate in between) and once with all of the formulas showing.

15-6. Your stockbroker suggests you buy 1,000 shares of International Electronics. The stock currently is selling at $38.75 per share. From research in the library you discover that the stock is quite volatile and that, based on recent past data, in

21% of the weeks it goes up $1.00
17% of the weeks it goes up $0.50
10% of the weeks it remains unchanged
35% of the weeks it goes down $0.50
17% of the weeks it goes down $1.00

(a) Create a worksheet to simulate the price of the stock and the value of your portfolio for 100 weeks assuming the preceding distribution. You should have 100 rows in the main part of your worksheet, one for each week. You should have separate columns for the week number, a random number, the price change that week, the closing price of the stock that week, the value of your portfolio. Have separate cells at the top of the worksheet for the resulting High, Low, and Close for the stock price over the 100 weeks, that is the highest price the stock reaches, the lowest price the stock reaches, and the closing price after 100 weeks. Have a separate cell that shows the amount of money you would have made (or lost) on the investment. Finally, have a cell containing either "I made money at the end of 100 weeks" or "I lost money at the end of 100 weeks" or "I was even at the end of 100 weeks". Run your simulation several times. Based on the past history data and your simulations, is this a good investment?

(b) On telling your broker your findings she suggests that you employ the following strategy: Buy the 1,000 shares of stock now. Put in a Sell order for the stock at $43.75 or at 100 weeks, whichever comes first. That way if the stock reaches $43.75 you will sell out and achieve a profit of $5 per share. Otherwise you will sell out at the end of 100 weeks and take whatever profit or loss results. On inquiry your broker tells you that there will be a commission cost to you of $79 for purchasing the stock and another $79 for selling the stock. Create a worksheet like the worksheet in part (a) for simulating your broker's strategy. Run the simulation 10 times and record the consequences of using this investment strategy.

(c) Prepare a brief report on this investment strategy. Include copies of appropriate worksheets and graphs. Would you make money or lose money on average using this strategy? How much on average? Should you invest?

15-7. The game of Rock-Paper-Scissors is played by two people. At the count of three each person puts out either a closed fist (Rock), a flat hand (Paper), or two fingers (Scissors). The winner is decided as follows: Rock breaks Scissors. Paper covers Rock. Scissors cuts Paper. If both players make the same selection, it is a tie.

(a) Create a worksheet so you can play Rock-Paper-Scissors against the computer. There will be a cell for you to enter in your choice (ROCK, PAPER, or SCISSORS). There will be another cell where the computer makes its choice. The computer should choose among the three alternatives randomly using RAND. Each choice should be equally likely. (No fair peeking at the person's choice in this formula!) A third cell should indicate the outcome: YOU WIN, I WIN, or TIE. Test your worksheet until all nine possible combinations are tried.

(b) What happens in your worksheet if the person misspells the entry? Modify your worksheet so it says ILLEGAL ENTRY in this case rather than YOU WIN, I WIN, or TIE.

(c) Create a workbook that allows you to play the computer 25 times. The workbook should automatically keep track of the number of times you win, it wins, and there is a tie. There are a couple of approaches to solving this problem. One approach is to have a single worksheet that automatically accumulates the results. This is a bit tricky as it will involve circular references where the cells refer to themselves in their formulas. A second approach involves having 25 sheets with the Rock-Paper-Scissors worksheet. The twenty-sixth sheet would have the summary statistics on it. You might want to set Excel to manual recalculation.

15-8. Each day during the summer you plan to go downtown, set up a table, and sell pet tarantulas in cages. Your supplier has agreed to make weekly shipments of the tarantulas in their cages. For you to get the best rate your supplier insists that you contract ahead of time for a fixed number of tarantulas to be shipped at the beginning of each week. You would like to know how many tarantulas to agree to purchase each week.

You plan to work downtown every day for ten weeks. You figure that each day you are equally likely to sell 0, 1, 2, ... or 12 tarantulas. One of your selling points will be that you offer a money back guarantee. If the customer (or his or her family) wishes, he or she can bring back the tarantula and cage and you will refund the money with no questions asked. You figure that each day you work there will be 0, 1, 2, or 3 returns with equally likely probability. These tarantulas can then be resold.

(a) Create a worksheet to simulate the summer on a day-by-day basis. At the top of the worksheet have a cell for entering the number of tarantulas and cages to be shipped each week. When this number is changed, the rest of the worksheet should change accordingly. You should have 70 rows in the main part of your worksheet, one for each day. You should have columns at least for the day number, the number of tarantulas received that day (every seven days you will receive a shipment), the number of tarantulas sold that day, the number of returns that day, the number of tarantulas in inventory at the end of the day. Assume that the shipment arrives early in the morning before you leave for the day. You should use different random numbers for determining the amount sold and the amount returned. As you can see, many inventory problems can be modeled as queuing problems.

At the bottom of the worksheet put cells to calculate the maximum and minimum size of the inventory during the summer and the net number of tarantulas sold (sales - returns).

You would like never to have fewer than 10 tarantulas and never to have more than 100 or so tarantulas on hand in inventory. Certainly, you would like never to run out of tarantulas during the summer. Try different numbers for the shipment size. By pressing F9 simulate several summers. How many tarantulas should you agree to purchase each week assuming the accuracy of the assumptions?

(b) In trying the simulations in part (a) you probably were more likely to run short in the beginning of the summer and to be overstocked toward the end of the summer. One solution is to double the standing order of tarantulas for just the first shipment to use as a base inventory. Change the formula in that cell accordingly. How many tarantulas should you agree to purchase each week assuming the accuracy of the assumptions?

15-9. So that people feel they are getting more value for all of the taxes they pay, the United States government has decided to hold a giant national lottery. Everyone in the country automatically is entered. Once a month a Social Security number will be selected at random. Whoever has that Social Security number will be given $10,000,000 tax free.

You have been hired to create the worksheet that will generate the random Social Security number. Social Security numbers have the form 012-34-5678. Each of the billion possible Social Security numbers should be equally likely to be selected in your worksheet.

For you to receive full payment for your work the government contract officer insists that all 0's in the Social Security number selected appear in your worksheet and that the dashes appear in their usual places in the number.

15-10. The game of Chuck-a-Luck is popular at carnivals and fairs and also is played in casinos. Chuck-a-Luck is played with three large dice tumbling over in a cage. You can bet on various outcomes. We will assume here that each bet is for $1. Different bets pay different odds if you win. Here are some of the bets available:

      1. Single Value. You bet on a number from 1 through 6. If the number appears on one die you win $1. If the number appears on two dice you win $2. If the number appears on all three dice you win $3.

      2. Triple. If any number comes up on all three dice you win $30.

      3. High-Low. You bet on either High (total of 11 through 17) or Low (total of 4 through 10). You always lose on a triple. Otherwise you win $1 if you chose right.

(a) Create a worksheet like the one shown on the next page to play Chuck-a-Luck on the computer. In this worksheet you will first enter a number between 1 and 6 to bet for Single Value. Next pick High or LOW. We will assume that you will play for ten rolls with the same bets. On each roll you will bet $1 on Single Value, $1 on Triple, and $1 on High or Low. The worksheet will roll the three dice and tally how well you do.

A picture of columns A through J of the worksheet is shown on the next page. Cell G3 contains the number you selected for Single Value. Cell I3 contains HIGH or LOW. Each time you press F9 the three dice are rolled ten times. The results of your ten sets of bets are tabulated. Try the worksheet several times. Be sure to check your worksheet carefully because the formulas required are tricky. The worksheet below is not typical. As you'll see, it's cheaper to play on the computer than it is at the carnival!

(b) Modify your worksheet so it has 200 rows of dice rolls instead of 10. This will give you an even better idea of the odds of winning and losing.

	A	B	C	D	E	F	G	H	I	J
1				**Chuck-A-Luck**						
2								Bets		
3			Step Right Up and Place Your Bet:				4		HIGH	
4										
5							Single		High/	
6			Roll	Die #1	Die #2	Die #3	Value	Triple	Low	
7			1	5	5	5	($1)	$30	($1)	
8			2	6	6	5	($1)	($1)	$1	
9			3	4	5	4	$2	($1)	$1	
10			4	2	3	3	($1)	($1)	($1)	
11			5	4	5	5	$1	($1)	$1	
12			6	2	2	2	($1)	$30	($1)	
13			7	6	3	3	($1)	($1)	$1	
14			8	5	6	3	($1)	($1)	$1	
15			9	5	5	3	($1)	($1)	$1	
16			10	4	6	4	$2	($1)	$1	
17							($2)	$52	$4	
18			**Grand Total After 10 Rolls:**			**$54**				

CHAPTER 16

DATA MANAGEMENT WITH LISTS

OBJECTIVES

In this chapter you will learn how to:

- Work with large amounts of data organized as lists
- Enter new data using forms
- Find the data that match certain criteria using AutoFilters
- Sort the data into alphabetical or numerical order
- Calculate subtotals of the data
- Summarize the data using pivot tables

One of the major uses of computers is for data management, for keeping track of large amounts of data. Airline reservations, personnel, accounts payable and receivable, inventory, payroll all can involve large amounts of data and all profitably have been automated. A special type of software, called **database management systems**, has been developed for data management. There are database management systems for very large computers and for personal computers and for all types of computers in between. Whereas a wordprocessor can be considered a computerized typewriter and an electronic spreadsheet can be considered a computerized calculator and ledger paper, a database management system can be considered a computerized filing cabinet.

Excel has some powerful and useful data management features. We are going to explore these capabilities in this chapter. But before we begin, it is important to point out that Excel is not considered a database management system itself. One major difference is that in a database management system most of the data is kept on the disk, thus allowing the computer to deal with millions of pieces of data. In Excel the data you are working on are in the worksheets. Excel works well with dozens or hundreds or thousands of pieces of data, but not with millions or billions of pieces of data.

It is possible to access large databases from Excel using MS Query. MS (Microsoft) Query is a separate program that often is included with the Microsoft Office package. MS Query can be accessed directly from Excel using the MS Query add-in. MS Query allows you to access databases of various types, created using various programs, including Btrieve, Paradox, dBase, ORACLE, FoxPro, and SQL. With MS Query various portions of much larger databases can be downloaded into Excel and manipulated using the tools available in Excel. It also is possible to create smaller sets of data within Excel itself. In either case, the data in Excel usually are in the form of a **list**.

WHAT IS A LIST?

A list is a range of data that is organized so that all of the information about a single person, object, or transaction occupies a single row and so that each column contains information of the same type. The top row of the list contains the name of the data in the corresponding column.

As an example, consider the following situation. The owner of the Tri-Valley Auto Dealership decides that he would like to learn more about his customers and about which type of customers are purchasing which types of vehicles so he can segment his advertising better. He decides to keep some simple data on each of his customers and the type of vehicle each has purchased. So far, he has sold 13 vehicles. The data are shown in the worksheet in Figure 16-1.

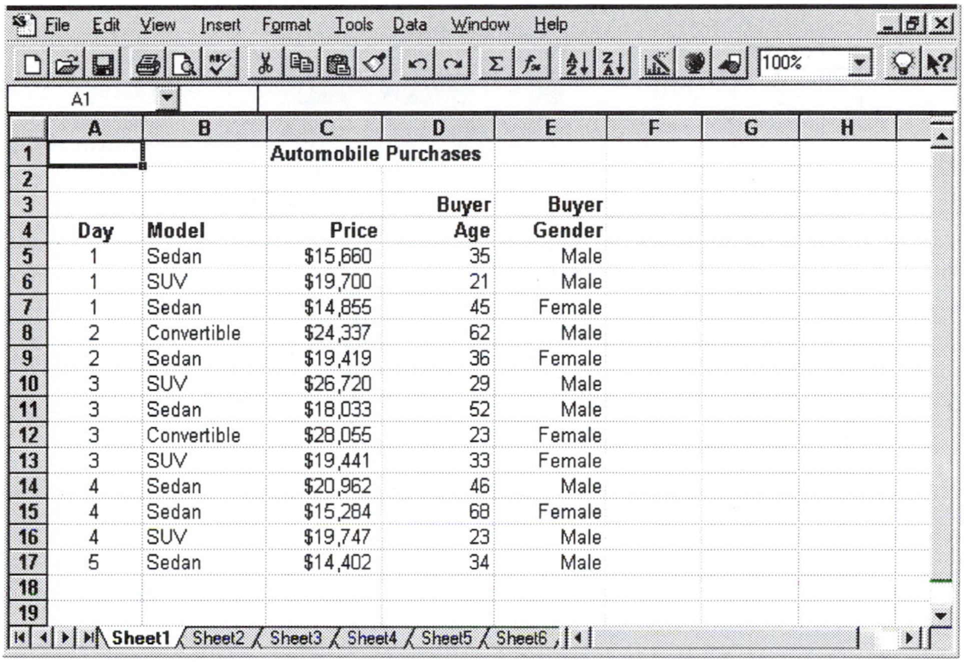

	A	B	C	D	E
1			Automobile Purchases		
2					
3				Buyer	Buyer
4	Day	Model	Price	Age	Gender
5	1	Sedan	$15,660	35	Male
6	1	SUV	$19,700	21	Male
7	1	Sedan	$14,855	45	Female
8	2	Convertible	$24,337	62	Male
9	2	Sedan	$19,419	36	Female
10	3	SUV	$26,720	29	Male
11	3	Sedan	$18,033	52	Male
12	3	Convertible	$28,055	23	Female
13	3	SUV	$19,441	33	Female
14	4	Sedan	$20,962	46	Male
15	4	Sedan	$15,284	68	Female
16	4	SUV	$19,747	23	Male
17	5	Sedan	$14,402	34	Male

Figure 16-1. A database in Excel takes the form of a list.

Here, each row corresponds to the information about a different vehicle that was sold and the customer who purchased it. Column A contains the day of the sale. Column B contains the type of vehicle. The dealership offers three basic models: a family sedan, a sports utility vehicle (SUV), and a convertible. Column C shows the purchase price of the vehicle. And so on.

In database terminology, in a list in Excel, a row corresponds to a **record** and a column corresponds to a **field**. The list itself is contained in A4:E17 of the worksheet. Row 4 contains the names of the columns. Note that a list can have only one row of names at the top, so officially row 3 is not part of the list. Each name in the top row of the list must be unique. None of the cells in the top row of the list should be blank.

Excel provides several capabilities for working with lists. We will explore some of those capabilities now.

USING FORMS TO ENTER NEW RECORDS

The *Data* pull-down menu contains the data management commands. If we place the active cell somewhere within the data and then select *Form...* from the *Data* pull-down menu, the dialog box in Figure 16-2 results.

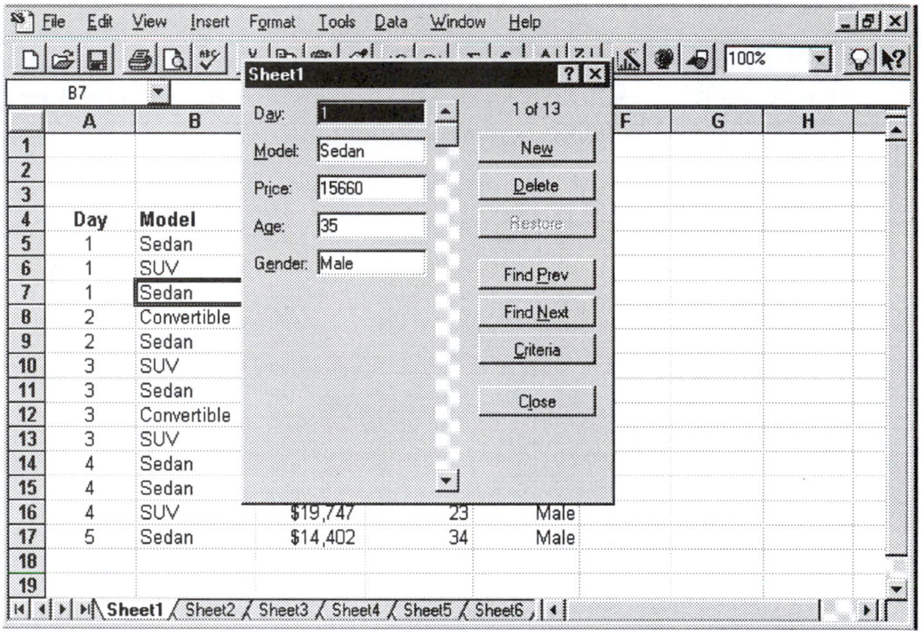

Figure 16-2. This dialog box results from selecting Form... in the Data pull-down menu.

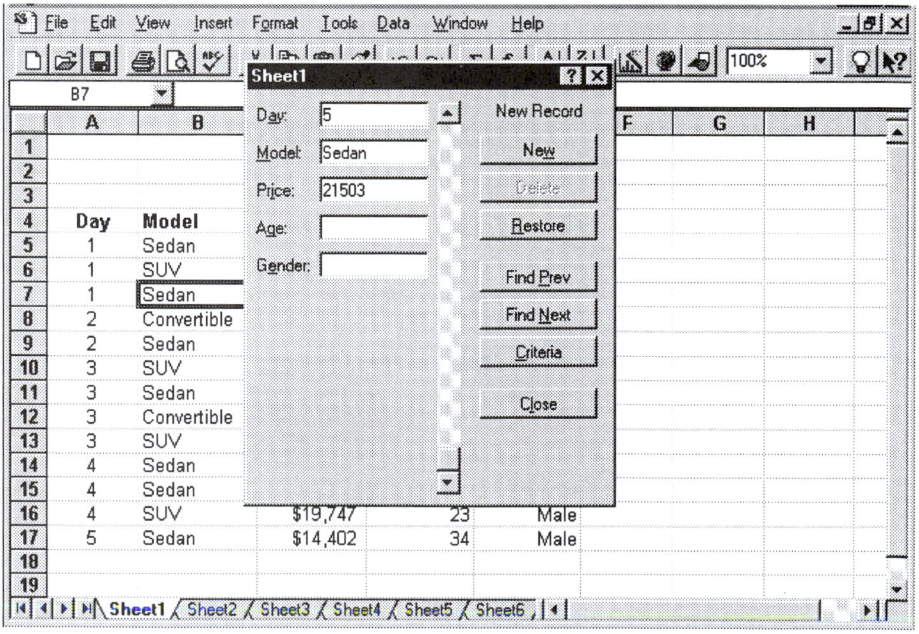

Figure 16-3. Entering the new data values in the form.

To enter a new record into the list, we press the *New* button in the *Form* dialog box. The field items are blanked out and we can enter them one at a time into the form. To move from one box to the next we can either click on the next box or we can press the Tab key. (See Figure 16-3.)

When we are finished with the final data item of a new record, we can press *New* if we have another record to enter or *Close* if we are finished entering records. In either case, the new record automatically will be entered at the bottom of the list in the worksheet. Of course, we could have just entered the information directly in the cells at the bottom of the list, but it wouldn't have been as snazzy or as much fun.

FINDING RECORDS WITH AUTOFILTERS

The list in our worksheet now contains 14 records. It is possible for lists to have up to 16,384 records (the number of rows in a worksheet). We might want to find records that match certain criteria. For example, we might want to find all of the sedans that were purchased by females. Or we might want to find all the vehicles that were purchased for over $20,000 by people under 25. Excel provides a couple of techniques to find records in a list. The easiest approach is through the use of **AutoFilters**.

To activate AutoFilters, place the active cell somewhere within the list and then select *Filter* in the *Data* pull-down menu. Within the submenu in *Filter* select *AutoFilters*. Small boxes with arrows appear next to the column names in the top row of the list. These are pull-down menus! Click on the arrow and you can see the choices. (See Figure 16-4.)

If we want to see only the records of sedans purchased by females, we filter the list in two stages. First we find the vehicles purchased by females. Then we find which of those vehicles were sedans. (We could just as easily filter in the other order.)

First we click on the *Gender* pull-down menu now located in cell E4 and select *Female*. The result is that only the records of the vehicles purchased by females are shown. (See Figure 16-5.) All rows in the list that do not have the word *Female* in column E are hidden. In the worksheet in Figure 16-5 you can see that rows 5, 6, 8, 10, etc. are hidden.

Now to show just the sedans purchased by females, we click on the *Model* pull-down menu in column B4 and select *Sedan*. Only the records for sedans purchased by females will be shown. All other records will be hidden.

To unhide (display) the rows, we can reverse the process. Select *All* in the *Model* pull-down menu and then *All* in the *Gender* pull-down menu. All of the records will be displayed. Or, alternatively, we can select *Filter* in the *Data* pull-down menu and then *Show All* in the submenu.

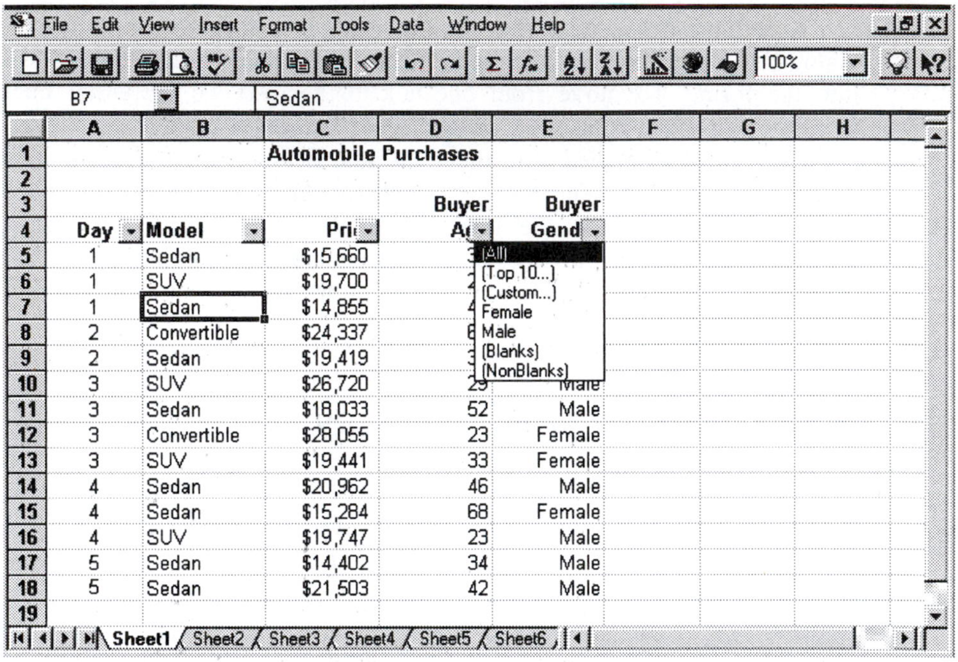

Figure 16-4. AutoFilters appear as pull-down menus.

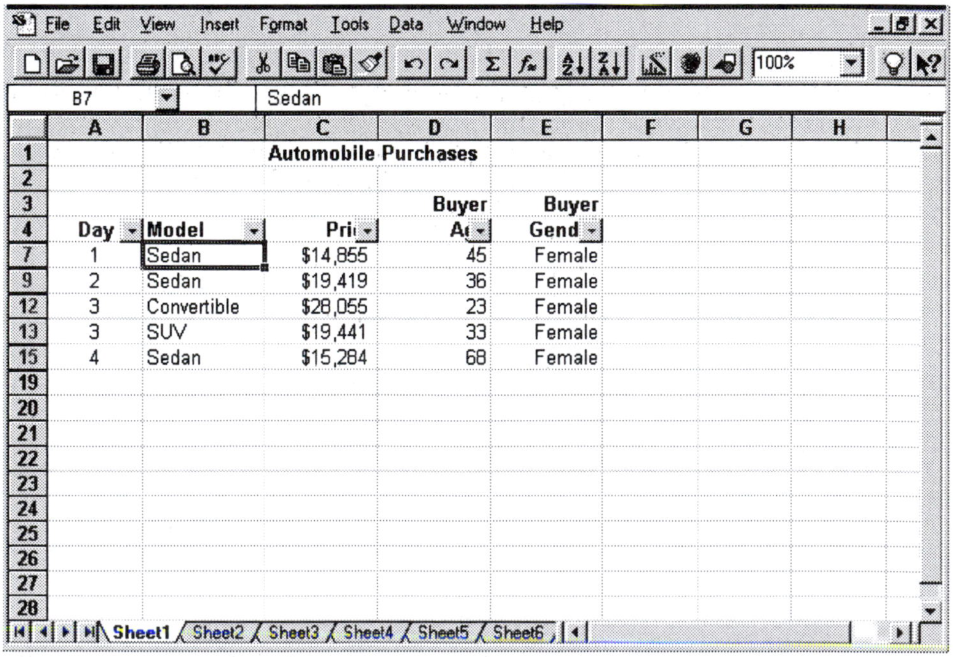

Figure 16-5. After filtering out all vehicles except those purchased by females.

To find the vehicles that were purchased for over $20,000 by people under 25, we first make sure all of the records are displayed. Then we go into the *Price* pull-down menu in cell C4 and select *(Custom...)* in the menu. In the *Custom AutoFilter* dialog box we select > and then type in 20,000, as in Figure 16-6.

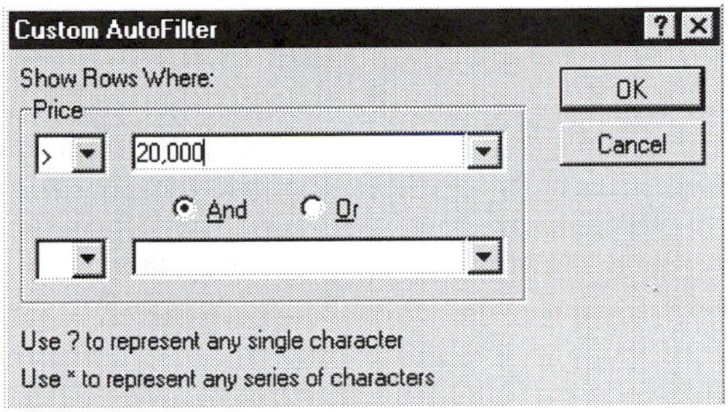

Figure 16-6. Setting a custom AutoFilter.

When we click on *OK* only the records for the vehicles with price greater than $20,000 are displayed. (See Figure 16-7.)

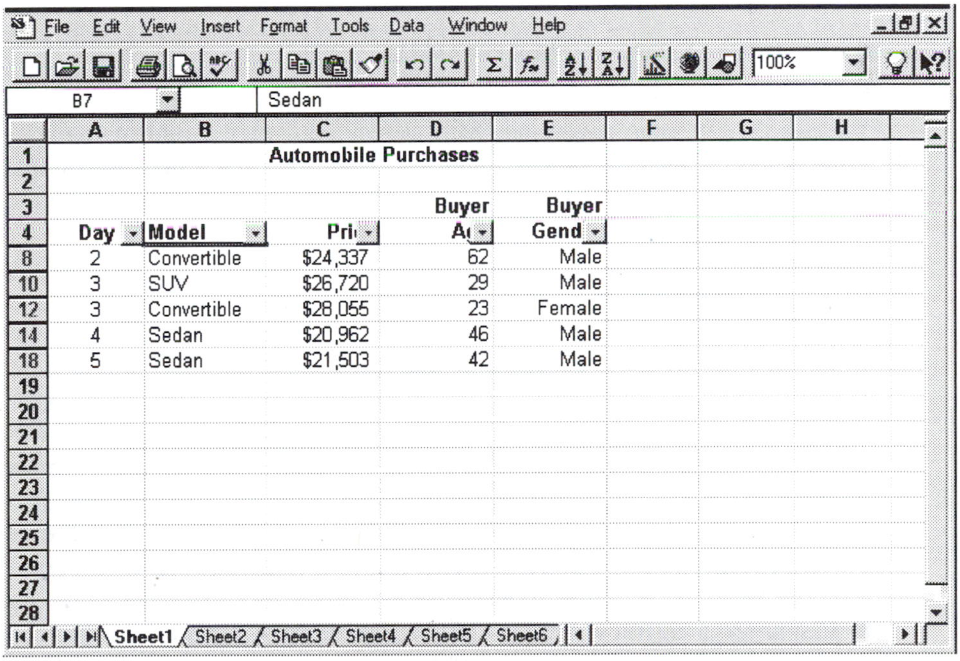

	A	B	C	D	E
1			Automobile Purchases		
2					
3				Buyer	Buyer
4	Day	Model	Pri	A	Gend
8	2	Convertible	$24,337	62	Male
10	3	SUV	$26,720	29	Male
12	3	Convertible	$28,055	23	Female
14	4	Sedan	$20,962	46	Male
18	5	Sedan	$21,503	42	Male

Figure 16-7. The vehicles that sold for over $20,000.

Notice that the *Custom AutoFilter* dialog box has room for two criteria for the field. This allows us to select the vehicles priced >20,000 and <40,000. Or, we could select the vehicles with Model ="Sedan" or ="Convertible".

To display just the records of the vehicles that were purchased for over $20,000 by people under 25, we could now select *(Custom...)* in the *Age* pull-down menu in E4 and then select < and type in 25. The record for that nice convertible in row 12 will be the only record in the list displayed.

A special feature of Excel for Windows 95 is the **Top 10** AutoFilter. This AutoFilter allows you to select, for example, the records of the 5 vehicles with the highest prices or the records of the 3 vehicles sold to the youngest people.

AutoFilters hide rows, but the rows still are there in the worksheet. If you do calculations on a column, the hidden values will be included in the calculation. For example, if in cell C20 we put the formula =SUM(C5:C18), all vehicle prices will be included in the calculation, not just the vehicle prices of the records that are showing. To calculate, for example, the average price of the sedans that were sold, we need to use another technique.

To erase the AutoFilter pull-down menus from the worksheet select *Filter* in the *Data* pull-down menu and then select *AutoFilter* in the submenu. The AutoFilter pull-down menus will be erased and the worksheet will return to its original appearance.

SORTING

When we **sort** objects we alphabetize them or put them in numerical order. For example, if your bank sends back your checks at the end of the month, you might sort the checks to put them in numerical order, or you might sort the playing cards in your hand when you are playing gin or Go Fish.

The records in the automobile list already are sorted by day. We could sort them many other ways. To sort a list, click on a cell in the list and then select *Sort...* in the *Data* pull-down menu. The *Sort* dialog box allows us to enter the name of the column that is to serve as the main basis for the sort. This field is known as the **primary key** for the sort. In Figure 16-8 we have selected *Model* as the primary key and indicated to Excel that we would like the models listed in ascending order (A to Z). The box below in the dialog box allows us to enter a **secondary key**. The secondary key is the field that is to serve as a "tie-breaker". The question is, in what order should we put all of the vehicles of the same model type? In the dialog box in Figure 16-8 we specify that the secondary key should be *Price* and that we want all of the vehicles of each model sorted by price in descending order. (Notice that the *Sort* dialog box also has a box available for a **tertiary key**, a field to use to sort records that have the same values for both the primary key and the secondary key.)

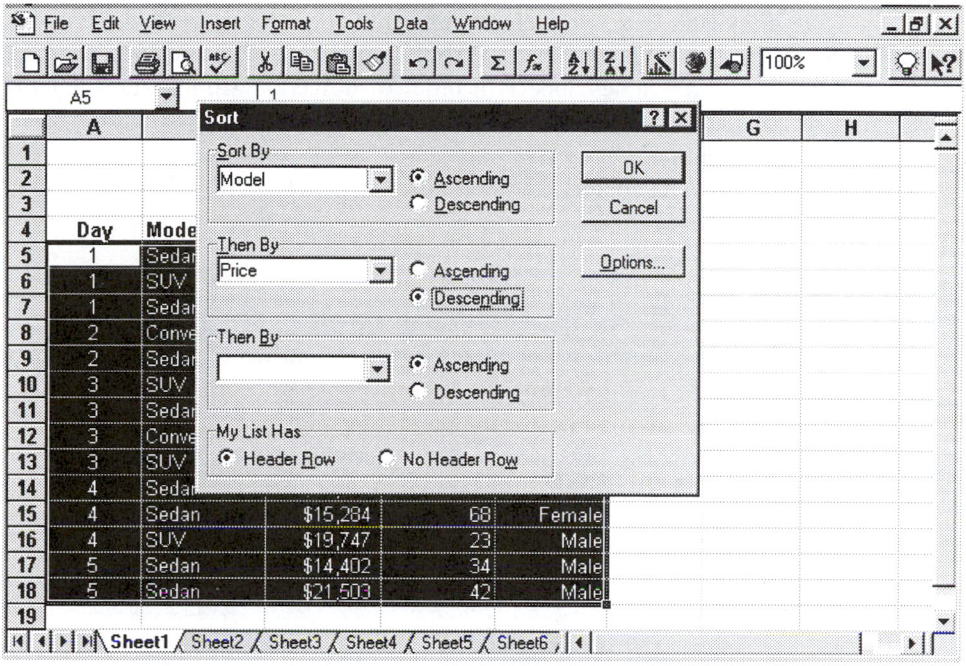

Figure 16-8. Specifying the columns to use for sorting.

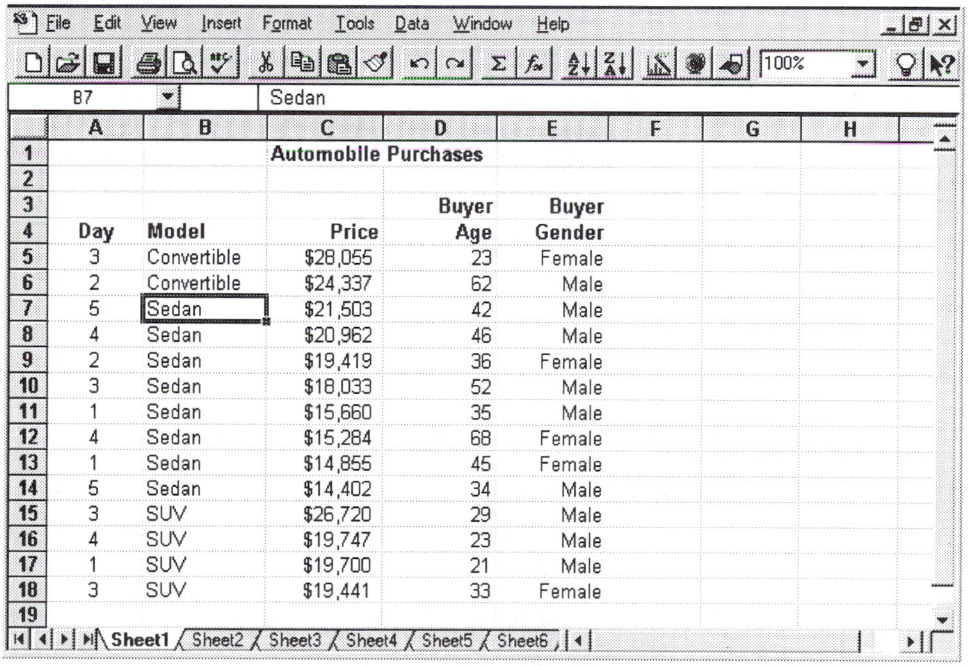

Figure 16-9. The rows sorted by Model and within Model by Price.

We click on *OK* and Excel automatically sorts the records, as shown in Figure 16-9. First come all of the convertibles, then all of the sedans, then all of the SUVs. The convertibles appear in order of descending price and then the sedans appear in order of descending price and then the SUVs appear in order of descending price.

Excel allows us to sort on any fields.

SUBTOTALS

Once a list is sorted, we can have Excel add **subtotals** or similar calculations. For example, we might want to find the average price of each model of car that was sold and the average age of the purchaser. To accomplish this, we first click somewhere within the list of data so the active cell is within the list. We select *Subtotals...* in the *Data* pull-down menu. Excel displays the *Subtotal* dialog box, as in Figure 16-10.

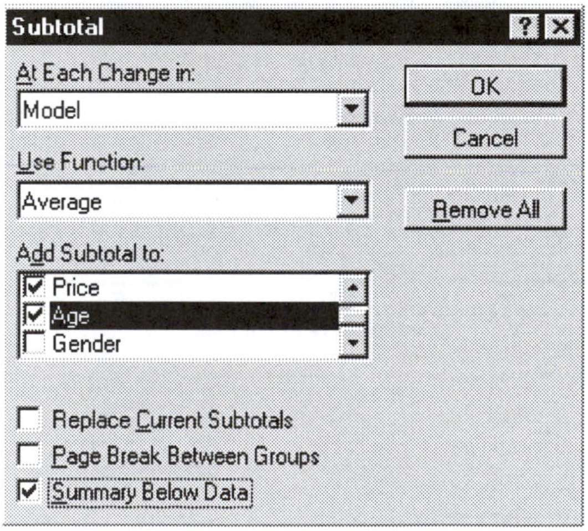

Figure 16-10. Specifying Subtotal calculations

In the *Subtotal* dialog box we first select *Model* as the data are sorted on Model and we want to insert a calculation for each different value of Model. Next we indicate that the function we want to calculate for the records of each type of Model is *Average*. We check off *Price* and *Age* because these are the fields for which we want to calculate the Average. We check off *Summary Below Data* because we want the calculations to appear below each set of data (rather than above). Finally we click on *OK*. Excel inserts the calculations in the worksheet, as shown in Figure 16-11.

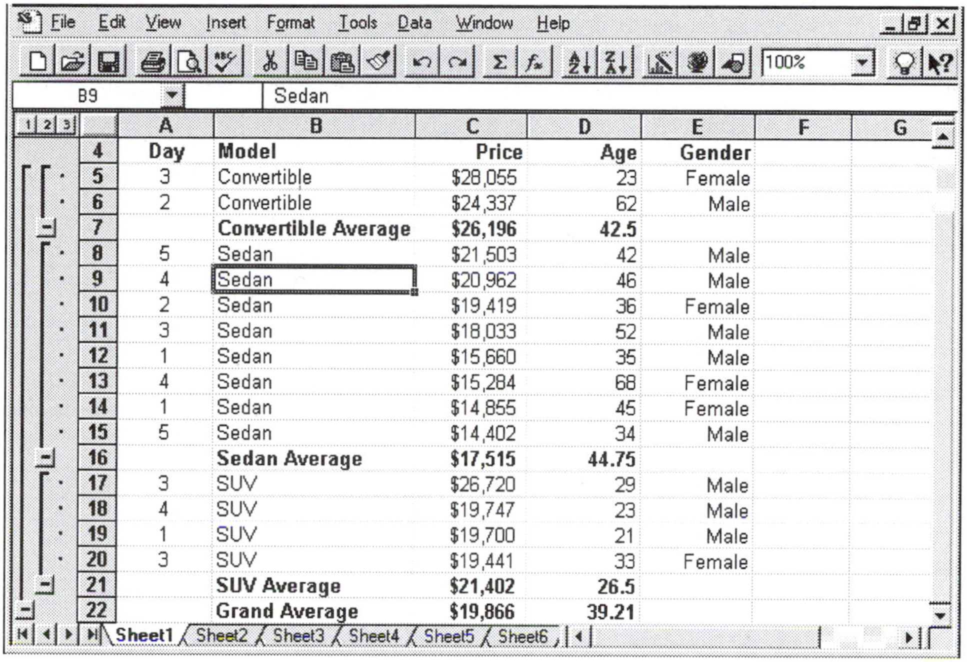

	A	B	C	D	E
4	Day	Model	Price	Age	Gender
5	3	Convertible	$28,055	23	Female
6	2	Convertible	$24,337	62	Male
7		**Convertible Average**	**$26,196**	**42.5**	
8	5	Sedan	$21,503	42	Male
9	4	Sedan	$20,962	46	Male
10	2	Sedan	$19,419	36	Female
11	3	Sedan	$18,033	52	Male
12	1	Sedan	$15,660	35	Male
13	4	Sedan	$15,284	68	Female
14	1	Sedan	$14,855	45	Female
15	5	Sedan	$14,402	34	Male
16		**Sedan Average**	**$17,515**	**44.75**	
17	3	SUV	$26,720	29	Male
18	4	SUV	$19,747	23	Male
19	1	SUV	$19,700	21	Male
20	3	SUV	$19,441	33	Female
21		**SUV Average**	**$21,402**	**26.5**	
22		**Grand Average**	**$19,866**	**39.21**	

Figure 16-11. The average purchase price and age of purchaser for each model.

The new row 7 shows us the average price of convertibles and the average age of purchasers of convertibles. These actually are "sub-average" calculations. In the new row 22 we see the Grand Average price of all vehicles and the Grand Average age of all purchasers. The range of each of the calculations is indicated at the left of the worksheet.

To remove the subtotal calculations we again select *Subtotals...* in the *Data* pull-down menu and click on the *Remove All* button (see Figure 16-10 again.). The worksheet is returned to its prior form.

PIVOT TABLES

An Excel list can have thousands of rows of data. Often it is difficult to see patterns with all of that data. What we need is a summary of the data. **A pivot table** is a summary of a list of data.

We begin again with the list of data on the vehicles sold and their purchasers. With the active cell somewhere in the list we select *Pivot Table...* in the *Data* pull-down menu. This calls up the **PivotTable Wizard.** The first screen of the PivotTable Wizard is shown in Figure 16-12.

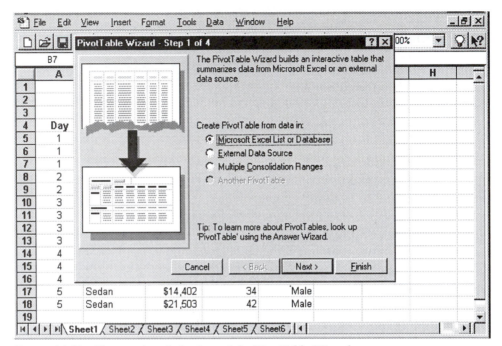

Figure 16-12. The opening dialog box of the PivotTable Wizard.

In the first step, the PivotTable Wizard asks us the source of the data for the pivot table. We click that it is a *Microsoft Excel List or Database*. Here, we are informing Excel that the data is internal to the current workbook and that it is all located in one list on one worksheet. As you can see in the dialog box in Figure 16-12, there are several other possible sources of data for the pivot table.

In the second step (Figure 16-13) the PivotTable Wizard correctly figures out the location of the list of data. If necessary, we could correct the guessed location of the list by dragging across it in the worksheet or by simply typing in the correct cell addresses for the range. It is important that the top row of the list, which contains the headings, be included in the range.

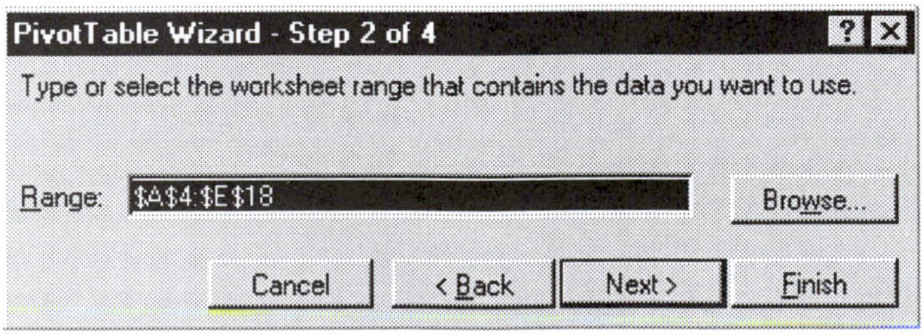

Figure 16-13. The Wizard correctly guesses the range of the list.

The third step of the PivotTable Wizard is where the work gets done. This is where we actually specify how we want the data to be summarized in the pivot table we are creating. The initial version of the dialog box for Step 3 is shown in Figure 16-14.

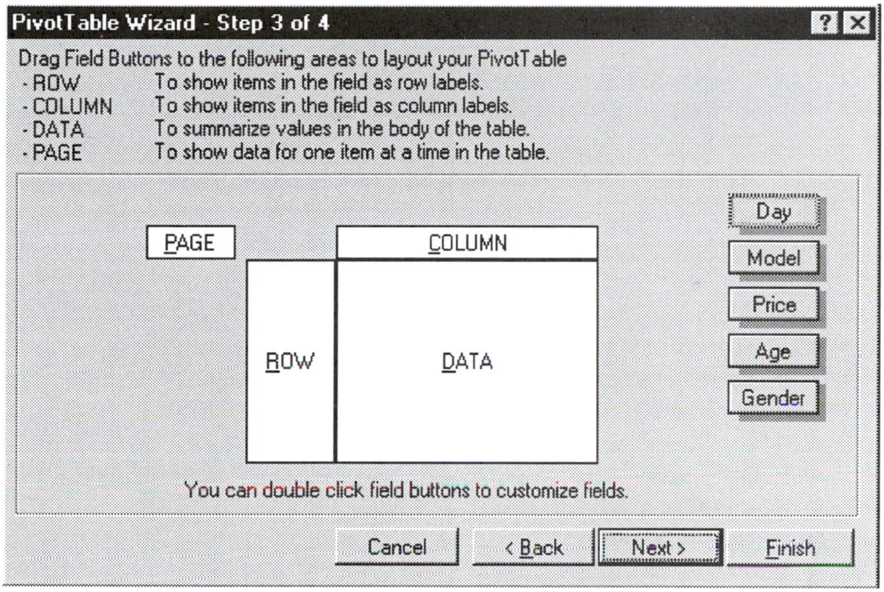

Figure 16-14. The key dialog box for setting up the pivot table.

The different fields or variables in our data list are shown on the right side of the dialog box in Step 3. The idea is to drag those variables over to the proper locations for the pivot table. For example, suppose we are interested in learning the average ages of the females who purchased convertibles, the females who purchased sedans, the females who purchased SUVs, the males who purchased convertibles, the males who purchased sedans, and the males who purchased SUVs. That is, we want the data summarized in a Model by Gender pivot table that shows Average age. In terms of the pivot table, we want Model to be the Rows, Gender to be the Columns, and average Age to be the Data. To specify this in the dialog box, we drag the *Model* box on the right over to the *ROW* box and release the mouse button. Then we drag the *Gender* box over to the *COLUMN* box and the *Age* box over to the *DATA* box. The result is the dialog box in Figure 16-15.

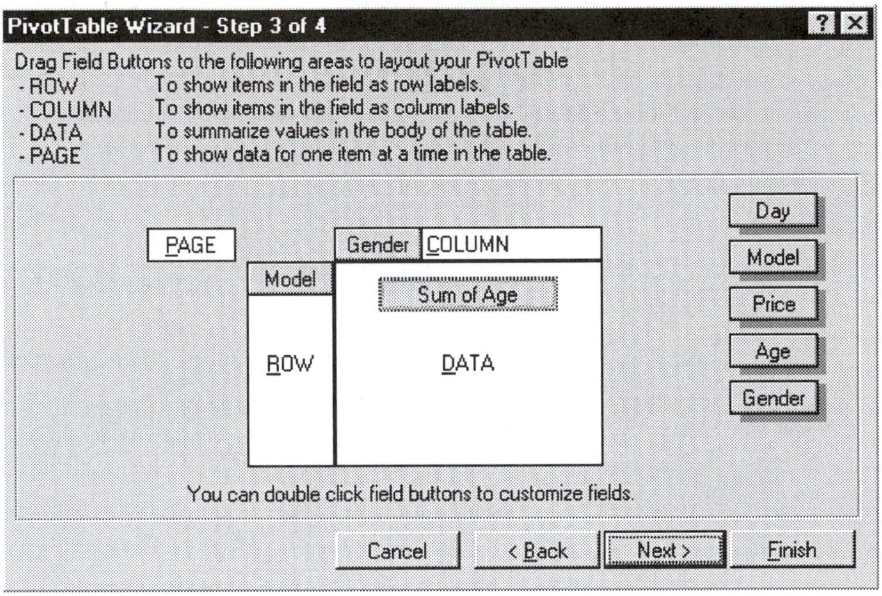

Figure 16-15. Informing the Wizard how we want the data summarized.

We are almost there. The PivotTable Wizard has guessed that we want to display *Sum of Age*. We really want to know the average age. We double-click on the *Sum of Age* box in the middle of the dialog box to modify it. The PivotTable Wizard now displays the *PivotTable Field* dialog box. We click on *Average* instead of *Sum* in the *Summarize by:* box, as in Figure 16-16.

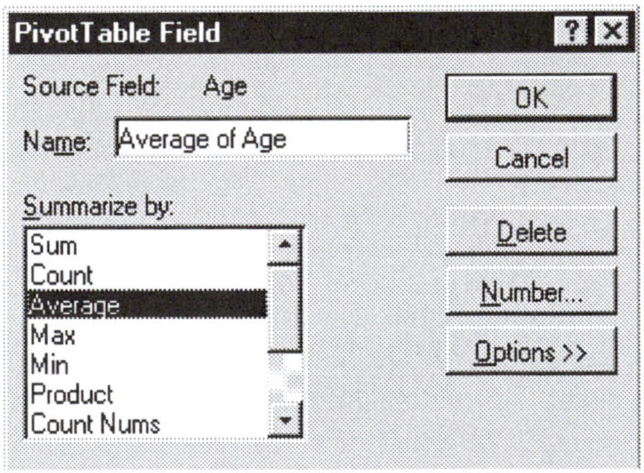

Figure 16-16. We want Average of Age.

Now when we click on *OK* the PivotTable Wizard knows we want to display the average age of the purchasers. We click on *OK* and the PivotTable Wizard moves on to the fourth and final step. In Figure 16-17 we enter the desired location of the pivot table in the worksheet.

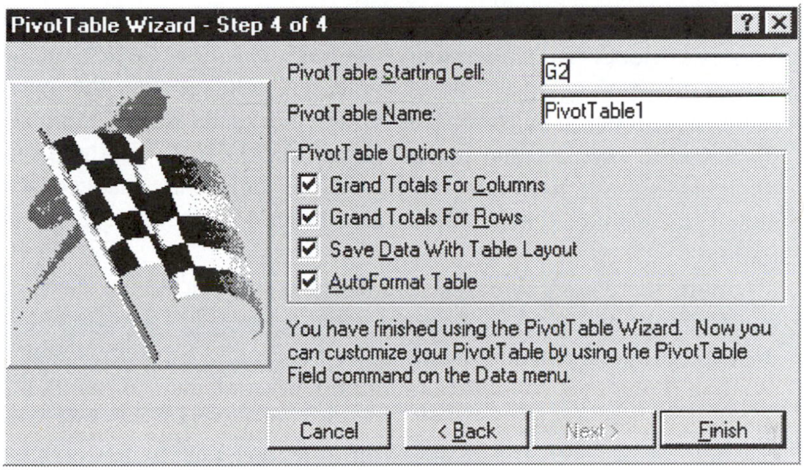

Figure 16-17. The final step is specifying the location of the pivot table.

The checkered flag indicates that this is the final step. Click on *Finish* and the PivotTable Wizard produces the pivot table in Figure 16-18 for us.

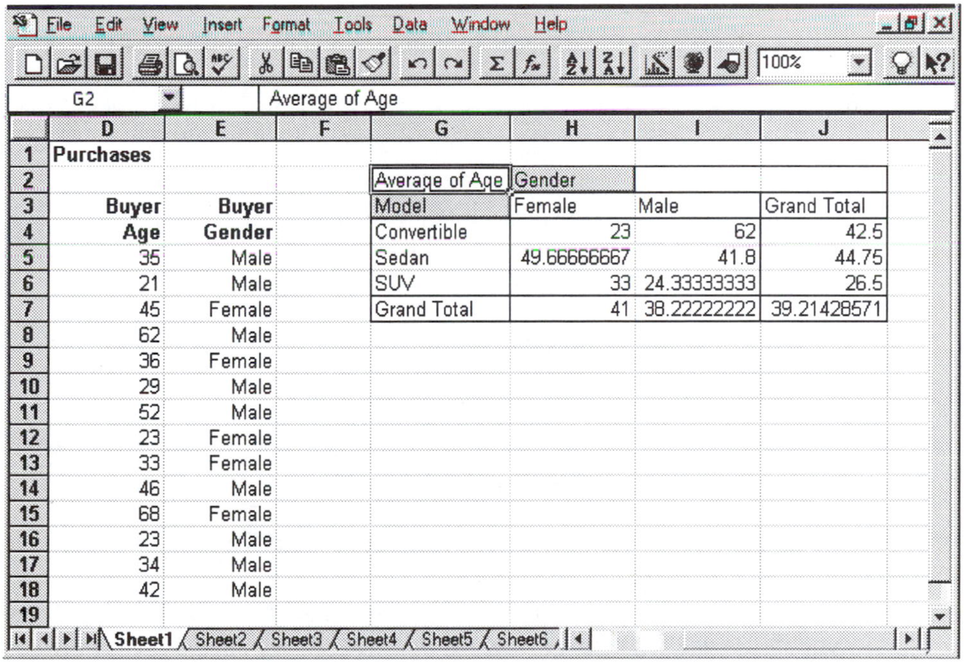

Figure 16-18. The pivot table provides a very useful summary of the data.

In the pivot table we see the data summarized for us just as we requested. This is a Model by Gender analysis. Each cell in the table indicates the average age of the purchasers. For example, H5 tells us that the average age of the females who purchased sedans is 49.67. We could format the numbers so they are displayed to one decimal place. Note that the cells in the pivot table contain numbers and not formulas. If any of the values are changed or if new rows are added, we must call up the PivotTable Wizard again to generate an updated pivot table.

With the PivotTable Wizard we could summarize the data in many different ways simply by dragging different variables over to the different locations in step 3 of the process. In this example we have only 5 columns and 14 rows of data. We could have 50 columns and 14,000 rows of data to summarize. In this case we might want a more detailed analysis. For example, we might want to separate out the analysis of the males from the analysis of the females, so that the analysis of the males appeared in one area and the analysis of the females appeared in another. In step 3 we would drag the *Gender* box over to the *PAGE* box. We would be adding a third dimension to the pivot table.

COMPUTER EXERCISES

16-1. Enter the real estate worksheet in Figure 1-3 (in Chapter 1).

(a) Use Form to enter in a new home: 18 Elm Street, 4 bedrooms, 2 baths, 0.5 acres, Oil heat, 17 years old, on the market for $229,900.

(b) Use AutoFilters to display all of the homes with 4 or more bedrooms.

(c) Use AutoFilters to display all of the homes that heat with gas.

(d) Use AutoFilters to display all of the homes that cost between $100,000 and $200,000.

(e) Use AutoFilters to display all of the homes that are on a lot of at least 0.75 acres, heat with oil, and cost under $300,000.

(f) Sort all of the homes in descending order by price.

(g) Sort all of the homes in ascending order by heat type and within each heat type in descending order by number of bedrooms.

(h) Use Subtotals to find the average number of bedrooms, lot size, age, and price of homes of each of the different heat types.

(i) Use the PivotTable Wizard to find the total value of the homes for sale of each heat type and number of bedrooms.

(j) Use the PivotTable Wizard to find the average value of the homes for sale of each heat type and number of bedrooms.

(k) Use the PivotTable Wizard to find the average age of the homes for sale of each heat type and number of baths.

16-2. Susan is a consultant with three different clients: Allied Electronics (AE), Dynamic Solutions (DS), and International Networks (IN). She bills her clients by the hour. She is very busy and tends to switch her attention from one client to another throughout the day. Her principal activities are talking on the phone, having meetings, and working on her computer. In order to be sure that each client is billed fairly, she constantly keeps Excel open on her computer and quickly makes an entry for each period of time she spends:

Client	Minutes	Activity
DS	10	phone
IN	27	computer
DS	8	phone
DS	42	meeting
AE	12	phone
...		

(a) Enter the preceding information into a worksheet.

(b) Use a Form to make 20 more entries into the worksheet.

(c) Use AutoFilters to display only the meetings.

(d) Use AutoFilters to display all the phone calls for AE that exceeded 5 minutes.

(e) Display all of the entries sorted by activity and within each activity sorted by time.

(f) Display all of the entries sorted by client and within each client by activity and within each activity by time.

(g) Use Subtotals to display the total amount of time for each client.

(h) Find the average amount of time of a telephone call.

(i) Use the PivotTable Wizard to display a summary of the total amount of time spent on each activity for each client.

CHAPTER 17

ANALYZING DATA USING THE ANALYSIS TOOLPAK

OBJECTIVES

In this chapter you will learn how to:

- Use add-ins
- Access the Analysis ToolPak
- Obtain descriptive statistics on data
- Create histograms of data
- Calculate correlations
- Perform t-tests on data
- Calculate linear regressions

People use Excel to solve a wide variety of problems. One of the most popular applications of Excel is to analyze data. The **Analysis ToolPak** provides additional capabilities for analyzing data.

The Analysis ToolPak is an **add-in** program. An add-in program is a program you can add to Excel to increase its capabilities. The Analysis ToolPak is a third-party add-in, meaning it was developed by an independent company. (Microsoft is the first party; you are the second party.) Microsoft includes the Analysis ToolPak with your purchase of Excel.

GETTING ACCESS TO THE ANALYSIS TOOLPAK

If today is your lucky day then the Analysis ToolPak already will have been added into the Excel on the computer you are using. To determine if this is the case, look in the *Tools* pull-down menu and see if there is an entry toward the bottom of the menu for *Data Analysis...*, as in Figure 17-1. If you see *Data Analysis...* you can skip the rest of this section.

If *Data Analysis...* is not present in the *Tools* pull-down menu, then the Analysis ToolPak needs to be added in to Excel. In the *Tools* pull-down menu select *Add-Ins...* . You will see a list of the add-ins available on your disk. If you see *Analysis ToolPak* listed, this still is your lucky day. Click on the box next to *Analysis ToolPak*, as in Figure 17-2, and click on *OK*. The Analysis ToolPak will be added ("attached") to Excel. (Note: Be sure to use the version titled *Analysis ToolPak* rather than *Analysis ToolPak - VBA*. This latter version adds capabilities to Visual Basic in Excel.)

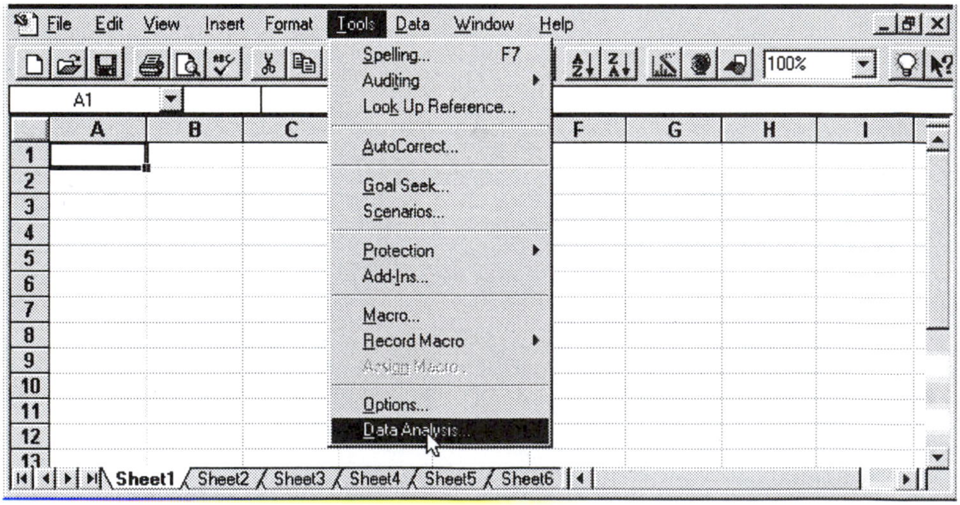

Figure 17-1. Selecting the Analysis ToolPak.

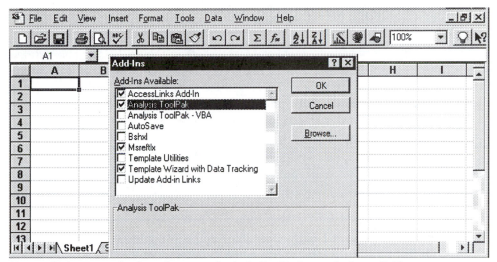

Figure 17-2. Put a check mark next to Analysis ToolPak to make it available to use.

If you do not see *Analysis ToolPak* listed in the add-ins available, then you have a bit more work to do. You need to go back to your original disks or CD-ROM for Excel (or Microsoft Office) and run the Setup program again. Select the *Custom* option and instruct the Setup program to install the Analysis ToolPak. The reason the Analysis ToolPak might not have been included in the original installation was to save space. Once you have installed the Analysis ToolPak using the Setup program, you can reenter Excel, run the *Add-Ins* selection in the *Tools* pull-down menu as described in the previous paragraph, and you should be ready to make use of the Analysis ToolPak.

WHAT IS IN THE ANALYSIS TOOLPAK?

The Analysis ToolPak adds two types of capabilities to Excel: functions and tools.

Once you attach the Analysis ToolPak you will find some 93 new functions in Excel. These functions now will appear in the Function Wizard integrated with the original built-in functions. These functions are of five types: Date and Time, Engineering, Financial, Information, and Math and Trig. These functions can be very useful for solving engineering and financial analysis problems.

The second type of capability added by the Analysis ToolPak is 19 statistics tools. These are not traditional built-in functions, but rather tools that analyze data in a worksheet and produce a table of output based on the analysis. It is these tools that are so useful in solving statistical problems.

THE DESCRIPTIVE STATISTICS TOOL

Consider again the real estate worksheet in Figure 17-3. This worksheet lists the homes for sale in a certain town. We are interested in calculating various statistics about the ages and prices of the homes. What is the average age? The standard deviation of the prices? We could calculate each of the statistics in a separate cell by including the appropriate formula. Or, we can use the **Descriptive Statistics tool** in the Analysis ToolPak. We select *Data Analysis...* from the *Tools* pull-down menu. Then we select *Descriptive Statistics*, as in Figure 17-4.

Excel displays the *Descriptive Statistics* dialog box (Figure 17-5). We click in the *Input Range* box and drag across F4:G22 to specify the location of the variables for which we wish to calculate descriptive statistics. We select *Columns* because the data are organized one variable per column. We notify Excel that the first row in the input range contains descriptive labels that can be used as the names of the variables. We inform Excel that we would like the output of the Descriptive Statistics tool to be placed in a new ply (worksheet). Alternatively we could have the output placed somewhere in this worksheet or in a new workbook. It is very important to check off the bottom box of the *Descriptive Statistics* dialog box so that Excel will calculate the full set of statistics.

	A	B	C	D	E	F	G	H
				CURRENT LISTINGS				
4	ADDRESS	BDRMS	BATHS	LOT	HEAT	AGE	PRICE	
5	12 Elm Street	5	3	0.4	Gas	48	$290,000	
6	46 Hearthstone Road	5	2	1.2	Oil	3	$345,000	
7	690 Rice Avenue	3	1	0.6	Oil	25	$109,500	
8	90 Bay Road	2	1	0.25	Oil	33	$78,400	
9	455 Nathan Street	2	1	0.3	Elec	16	$51,300	
10	18 Garden Street	2	1	0.4	Elec	12	$62,700	
11	203 Somerset Avenue	4	2	0.3	Gas	98	$159,500	
12	34 Farley Place	7	4	2.3	Oil	52	$560,000	
13	26 Lantern Lane	3	1	0.3	Solar	9	$104,300	
14	11 Panama Street	3	1	0.5	Gas	38	$87,900	
15	155 Auburn Blvd.	5	2	1.0	Oil	5	$269,600	
16	132 Jamaica Way	4	2	0.3	Gas	67	$149,500	
17	315 Fremont Avenue	3	1	0.4	Nuclear	8	$432,800	
18	1322 Bellevue Road	6	3	0.3	Elec	56	$233,500	
19	5 Pond Street	4	3	1.5	Oil	2	$275,400	
20	349 Hill Road	2	1	1.2	Oil	34	$155,600	
21	702 Main Street	6	2	0.3	Gas	85	$179,900	
22	24 Golan Place	4	2	0.8	Oil	15	$189,900	

Figure 17-3. The real estate worksheet.

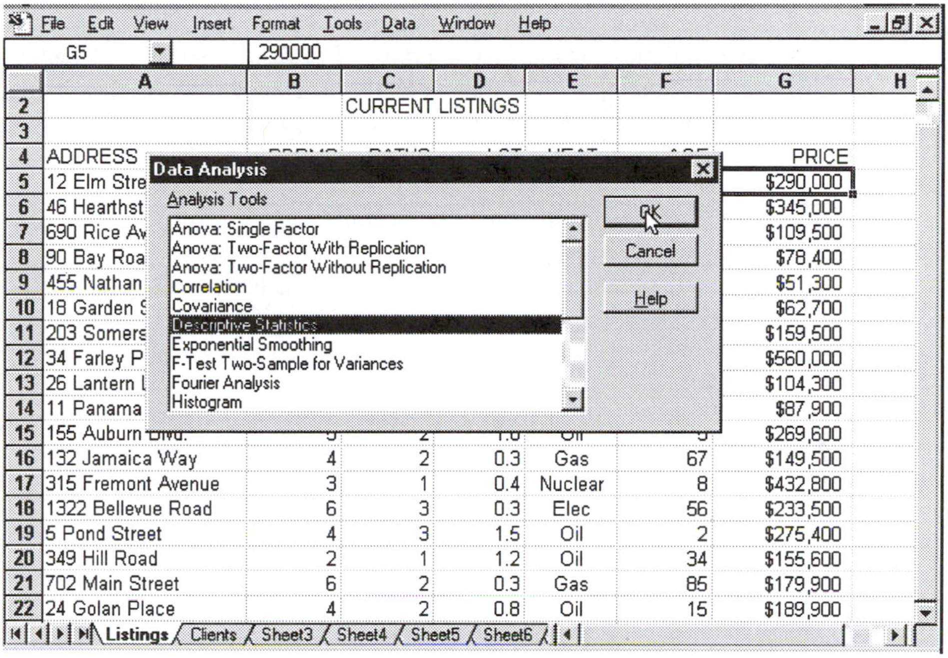

Figure 17-4. Select Descriptive Statistics in the Data Analysis dialog box.

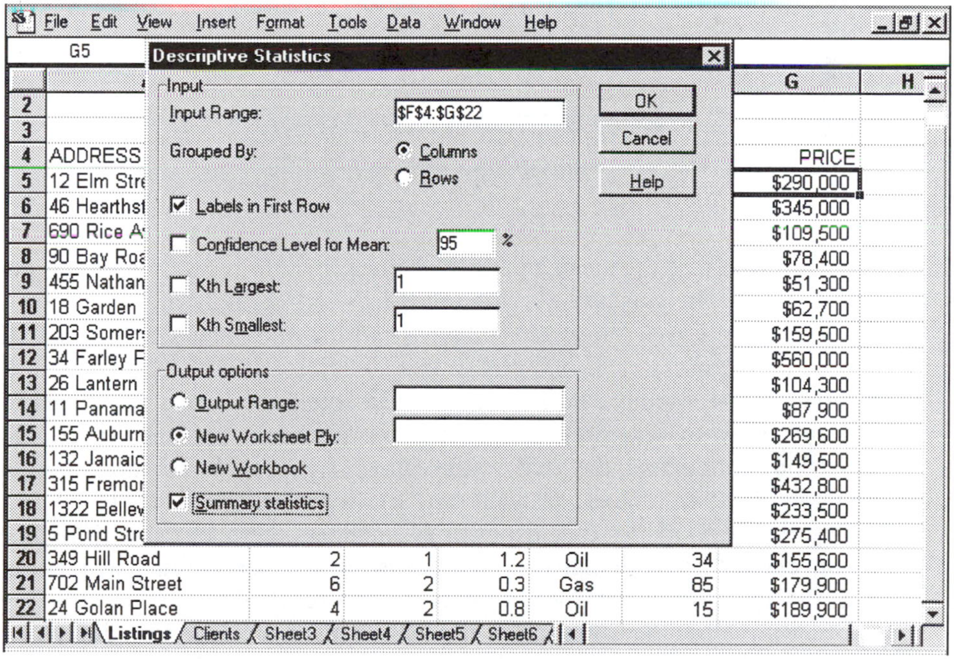

Figure 17-5. The Descriptive Statistics dialog box.

When we click on *OK*, the computer goes to work and calculates the descriptive statistics for the two columns. The results are placed beginning in A1 in a new worksheet, which automatically is placed before the worksheet that contains the data. We widen the columns. The result is shown in Figure 17-6.

	A	B	C	D	E	F
			D7 ▼ 136316.128642595			
1	AGE		PRICE			
2						
3	Mean	33.66666667	Mean	207488.8889		
4	Standard Error	6.807819418	Standard Error	32130.01965		
5	Median	29	Median	169700		
6	Mode	#N/A	Mode	#N/A		
7	Standard Deviation	28.88313165	Standard Deviation	136316.1286		
8	Sample Variance	834.2352941	Sample Variance	18582086928		
9	Kurtosis	-0.05617702	Kurtosis	1.292732276		
10	Skewness	0.878819995	Skewness	1.195404817		
11	Range	96	Range	508700		
12	Minimum	2	Minimum	51300		
13	Maximum	98	Maximum	560000		
14	Sum	606	Sum	3734800		
15	Count	18	Count	18		
16	Confidence Level(95.0%)	14.36326352	Confidence Level(95.0%)	67788.51064		
17						
18						
19						
20						
21						

File   Edit   View   Insert   Format   Tools   Data   Window   Help

Sheet1 / Listings / Clients / Sheet3 / Sheet4 / Sheet5 /

Figure 17-6. Descriptive statistics for Age and Price.

We see that the mean age of the homes for sale is 33.67 and that the median age is 29. The standard deviation of the price is $136,316.

There are two important points. First, the computer doesn't care whether or not the statistics are meaningful in this situation. It just follows its program and produces the output. It is up to you, the intelligent and knowledgeable user, to decide how to interpret the calculations and whether they make any sense. Second, notice that the cells in the output area do not contain formulas. They simply contain values, as you can see with cell D7 in Figure 17-6. The Descriptive Statistics tool deposits the numbers there once, when it is called. If you change the original data, the statistics are not recalculated automatically. Each time you want the statistics to be recalculated you must invoke the Descriptive Statistics tool all over again. This is an important difference between using tools and using formulas in cells.

USING THE HISTOGRAM TOOL

The **Histogram tool** allows you to see the distribution of values in a variable. Suppose we would like to examine the distribution of the prices of the homes. First we enter in **bin ranges** in the worksheet. That is, we inform Excel of the break points for the ranges for the histogram. We would like to see how many houses cost under $100,000, how many cost between $100,000 and $200,000 and so on. We enter $0, $100,000, $200,000, ... into cells I6:I11. We select *Data Analysis...* from the *Tools* pull-down menu. Then we select *Histogram* in the *Data Analysis* dialog box. (See Figure 17-4 again.) Excel displays the *Histogram* dialog box. We fill in G4:G22 for the *Input Range* for the Histogram tool and I6:I11 for the *Bin Range*, as in Figure 17-7. (Excel automatically converts these to absolute addresses.) We click on *Labels* because the top cell of the Input Range contains a label. We click on *Chart Output* at the bottom of the dialog box to request that the Histogram tool automatically chart the results.

Clicking on *OK* after filling in the entries as shown in Figure 17-7 automatically produces a new worksheet with the histogram and a chart. We make the chart larger by dragging on the handle in the bottom right corner. The result is shown in Figure 17-8.

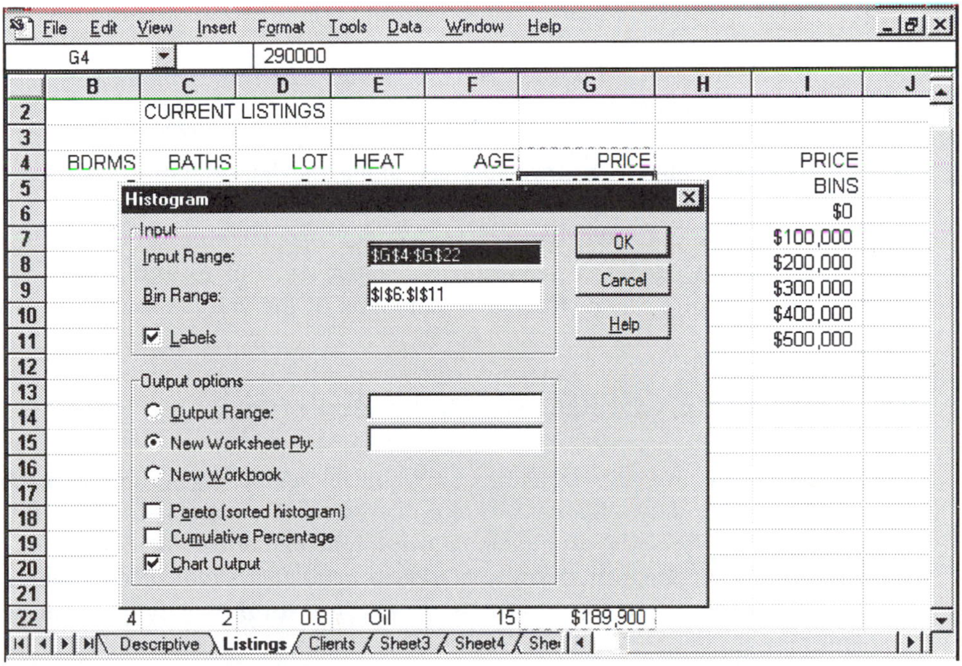

Figure 17-7. Filling in the Histogram tool dialog box.

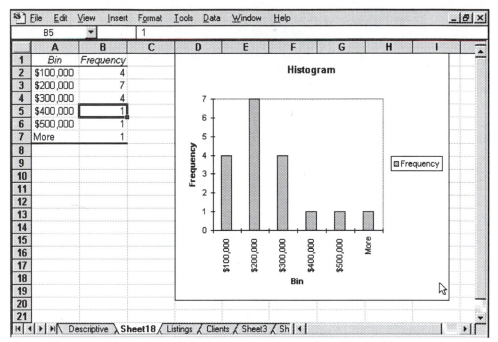

Figure 17-8. The histogram and chart of home prices produced by the Histogram tool.

The histogram in Figure 17-8 is to be understood as saying there are 4 homes with prices under $100,000, 7 homes with prices between $100,000 and $200,000, 4 homes with prices between $200,000 and $300,000, and so on. The numbers in column A of the table and along the horizontal axis of the chart are the highest values of the bins. The chart is a regular Excel chart that is embedded in the worksheet. We can select the chart by clicking on it and then make changes in the chart, as discussed in Chapter 10. For example, we could change the wording of a title or the maximum value of the vertical axis.

USING THE CORRELATION TOOL

The tools we have examined so far have treated each variable, each column of data, separately. Suppose we are interested in understanding the interactions between the variables. For example, we might be curious as to how the variables correlate. Do homes with many bedrooms tend to be old? Do expensive homes tend to have large lots? The **Correlation tool** will help us answer these questions.

The Correlation tool, like most of the tools in the Analysis ToolPak, works only on numeric values. With the Correlation tool all of the data must be contiguous. The Heat data in column E of the Real Estate worksheet consist of text rather than numbers. (See Figure 17-3, again.) Before we can use the Correlation tool we need to get the Heat data out of the way. So we select E4:E22 and then move it over to the blank column H by grabbing it at the top of the selected area and dragging it over. Now column E is blank. We select F4:H22 and drag it over to the left one column. The heating column now is in G4:G22 on the right of the data; all of the numeric values are contiguous (next to each other) in the range B4:F22.

In the Correlation tool dialog box in Figure 17-9 we specify that we want to correlate the five variables in columns B, C, D, E, and F. We request a new worksheet with the correlation outputs.

From the output of the Correlation tool in Figure 17-10 we can see that the number of bathrooms correlates very highly (0.86) with the number of bedrooms. The price of the home correlates highly with bedrooms, baths, and lot size but not at all with the age of the home.

Notice, again, that the cells in the correlation matrix contain numbers rather than formulas. Changing the original data will not cause the correlation matrix values to be changed automatically. Rather, we would need to run the Correlation tool each time we change the data.

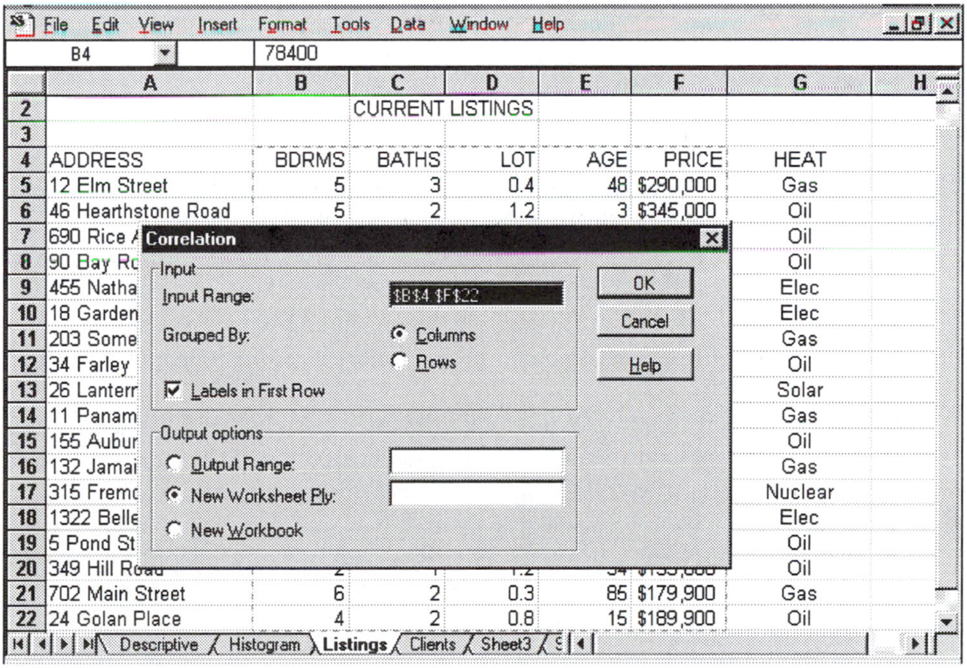

Figure 17-9. Specifying the correlations.

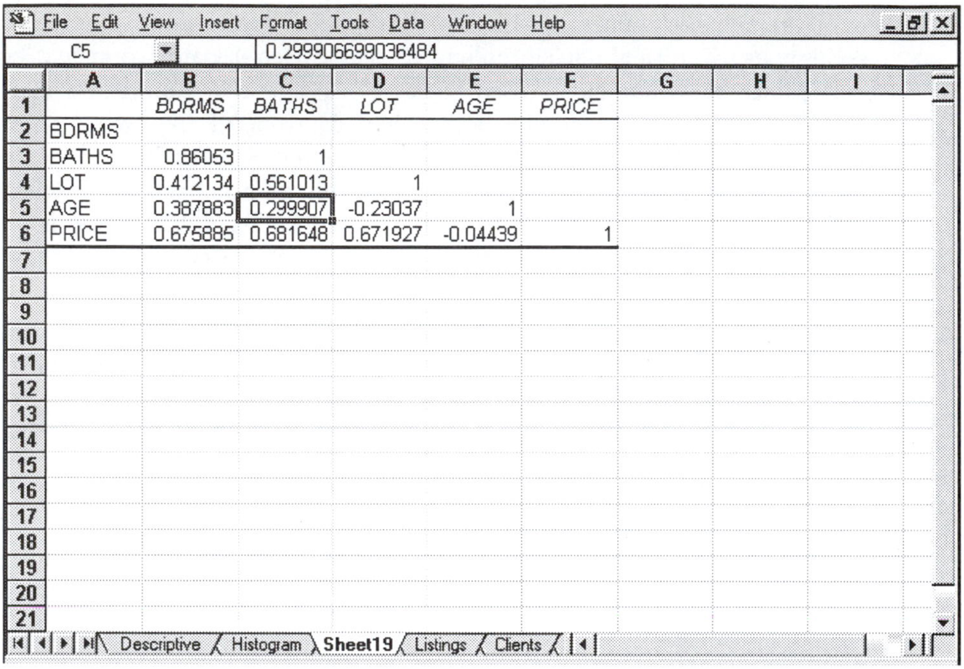

File Edit View Insert Format Tools Data Window Help

C5 | 0.299906699036484

	A	B	C	D	E	F
1		*BDRMS*	*BATHS*	*LOT*	*AGE*	*PRICE*
2	BDRMS	1				
3	BATHS	0.86053	1			
4	LOT	0.412134	0.561013	1		
5	AGE	0.387883	0.299907	-0.23037	1	
6	PRICE	0.675885	0.681648	0.671927	-0.04439	1

Descriptive / Histogram / Sheet19 / Listings / Clients

Figure 17-10. The correlations between the variables.

USING A t-TEST TOOL

Elite athletic shoes sell for $19.99 at discount stores. The manufacturer would like to know how the Elite shoes compare with the $99 well-known brand available at upscale stores at the mall. The manufacturer decides to perform a simple test. He recruits a dozen students and gives them a pair of Elite shoes and a pair of the well-known shoes in their size. The students examine and then try out each pair of shoes. He then asks each student to rate the shoes between 1 and 5, with 5 being the best score. These scores are recorded in a worksheet (see Figure 17-11).

We would like to test the hypothesis that people rate the shoes the same. To do this we test to see if there is no difference between the means of the scores.

A **t-test** is used to determine whether the means of two sets of samples are equal. In this case we would use a paired two-sample t-test, because one person is responsible for each pair of scores. If we had a dozen people rating one type of athletic shoe and a completely different group of people rating the other brand of shoe, we would not use a paired test.

In the *Tools* pull-down menu we select *Data Analysis...* and then *t-Test: Paired Two Sample for Means*. We fill in the entries, as in Figure 17-12.

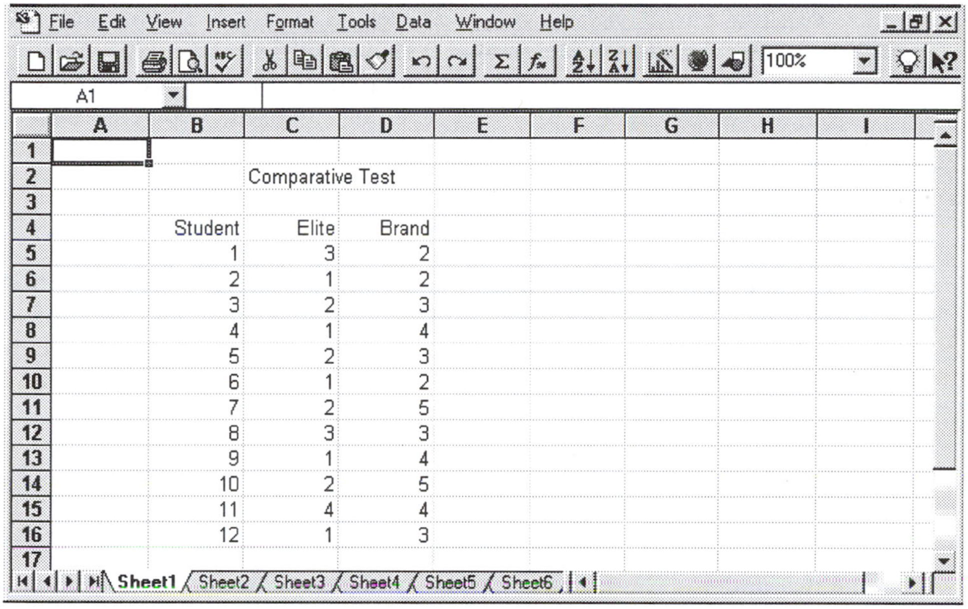

Figure 17-11. The raw data for the comparison of two brands of athletic shoes.

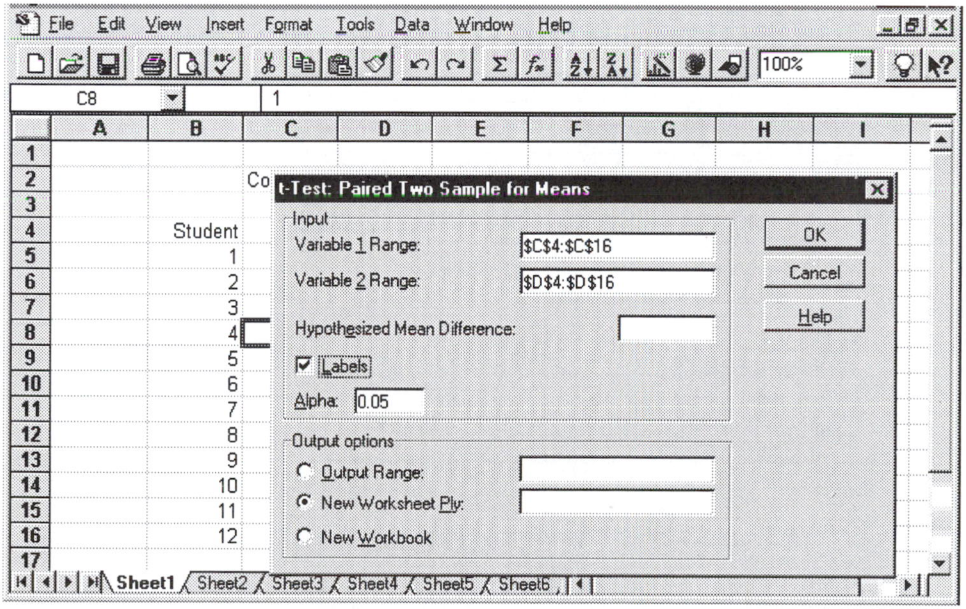

Figure 17-12. Specifying the ranges of the two variables for the t-test.

Clicking on *OK* yields a new worksheet with output produced by the t-Test: Paired Two Sample for Means tool, as shown in Figure 17-13. Examining this output we see that the mean score for the Elite shoes is 1.9 whereas the mean for the well-known brand is 3.33. We asked only a dozen people. Is this difference in the mean statistically significant?

Because we had no hypothesis before the study that one brand would score better than the other, it is appropriate to use a "two-tail" test. We see in cell B14 that the critical value of t for a two-tail test with this number of degrees of freedom is 2.20. The value of t calculated for these scores is 3.56, which is greater than 2.20. Thus, the difference between the two sets of scores is significant at the 5% level. If these scores were drawn randomly from populations having the same means, means as different as these would occur less than 5% of the time by chance. Looking at cell B13 we see that, indeed, if these scores were drawn randomly from populations having the same means, means as different as these would occur less than 0.45% of the time by chance or less than one out of 200 times. We reject the hypothesis that the Elite athletic shoes will score the same as the well-known brand. The students do not give equal scores to the two brands. This is bad news for the manufacturer of Elite.

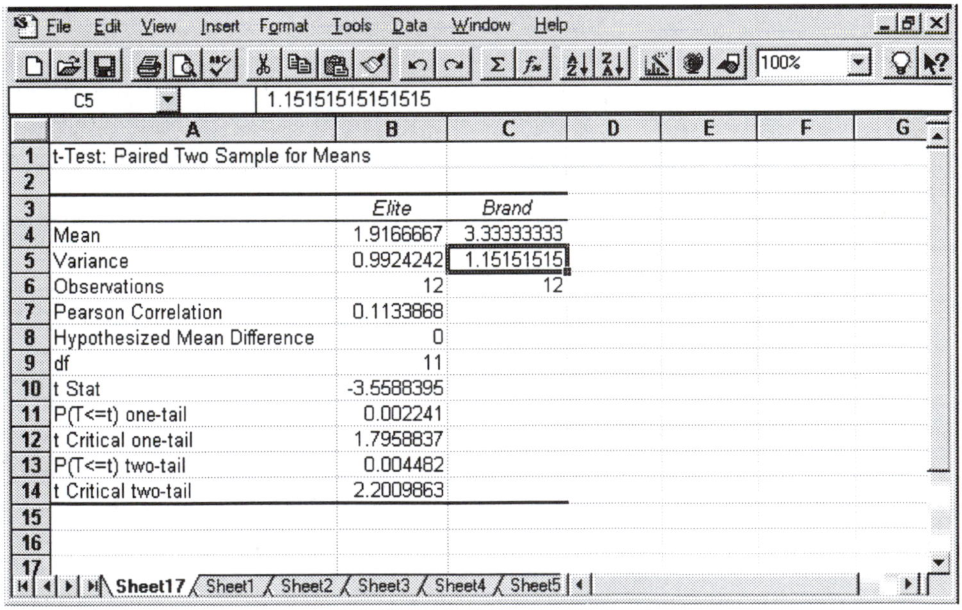

	A	B	C
1	t-Test: Paired Two Sample for Means		
2			
3		*Elite*	*Brand*
4	Mean	1.9166667	3.33333333
5	Variance	0.9924242	1.15151515
6	Observations	12	12
7	Pearson Correlation	0.1133868	
8	Hypothesized Mean Difference	0	
9	df	11	
10	t Stat	-3.5588395	
11	P(T<=t) one-tail	0.002241	
12	t Critical one-tail	1.7958837	
13	P(T<=t) two-tail	0.004482	
14	t Critical two-tail	2.2009863	
15			
16			
17			

Figure 17-13. The t-test result.

USING THE REGRESSION TOOL

International Financial hires recent college graduates to work on commission selling financial securities to the general public. Hiring has been a hit-and-miss affair. Some of the people hired have done very well; some have fizzled in the first year. Bringing new people on board is expensive. The VP of Sales and the Director of Hiring would like to get a handle on who succeeds and who does not. They would like to find out what factors, if any, they could use in predicting how well a person would do as a new hire. They brainstorm. They decide they like to hire athletes and students who are go-getters and report making a lot of money during the previous summer. They come up with four measures that might predict how well a person would do in the sales position: grade point average (GPA) in college, the number of sports teams a person played on in college, the amount of money the person earned in the previous summer, and how well the person did in the job interview (a number between 1 and 10, where 10 is the best, that is given by the interviewer). Last year they hired a dozen new people. They decide to list each of these measures for each person as well as the person's total sales in the first year. These data are given in the worksheet in Figure 17-14.

		GPA	Sports	Summer	Interview		First Year Sales
	1	2.7	3	$0	2		$100,000
	2	3.6	0	$1,500	5		$30,000
	3	2.4	5	$8,500	7		$9,800,000
	4	3.6	1	$2,000	3		$200,000
	5	2.6	7	$6,300	9		$7,450,000
	6	3.2	0	$3,100	6		$1,300,000
	7	3.7	0	$0	5		$65,000
	8	2.9	0	$1,000	7		$300,000
	9	3.0	1	$4,000	2		$2,604,000
	10	3.3	0	$2,900	6		$80,000

Figure 17-14. Recent hires at International Financial.

The **Regression tool** performs linear regression analysis. That is, it fits a line through a set of measures using the least squares method. Regression calculates an equation for predicting the sales performance of an employee based on the four measures given. We call up the Regression tool by selecting *Data Analysis...* from the *Tools* pull-down menu and then selecting *Regression* from the list of Tools available. In the *Regression* dialog box we fill in the location of the Sales data for the Input Y Range and the four measures for the Input X Range. (See Figure 17-15.)

Clicking on *OK* yields the output in Figure 17-16. There is a lot of information here. Starting at the top, in cell B4 we see that the multiple correlation coefficient R is 0.976, which is quite high. The value of R Square is 0.953 so the four factors account for more than 95% of the variance. The Y values are sales that are in the hundreds of thousands or millions, so the sums of squares in the analysis of variance table in C12:D14 are large numbers. Because the columns are narrow and the values are large, the numbers are displayed rounded off in **E format**. The "E" stands for "exponent" or power of 10. The number 2.67E+13 in D12 is 2.67 * 10^13 or 2.67 * 10000000000000. The exact value in D12 is displayed in the formula bar in Figure 17-16.

In the bottom part of the worksheet we see the effect of each of the four measures. We see from the coefficients in B17:B21 that the optimal linear formula for predicting the amount of sales that a first-year hire will make is

= -522052*GPA + 460333*Sports + 825*Summer - 84704*Interview + 168836

Notice that the GPA and Interview have negative coefficients. GPA and Interview are associated negatively with sales. That is, the lower the GPA, the higher the sales! And so much for the interview! The lower the interview score, the higher the sales.

When we go back and plug the linear equation into column J, we can see what the predictions would be for the existing hires. (See Figure 17-17.) Even though according to our calculations we have done extremely well in predicting the first-year sales, there is plenty of error made in the predictions. Still, the formula comes close on the big winners among the salespeople, which probably is what we are most concerned about. We'd like more $5,000,000 sellers. According to the formula, some of the recent hires are predicted to have negative sales. Those are the folks who would do better in other jobs.

Once we have the equation, we use it in Figure 17-17 to predict the sales of new candidates. Candidate A has very low grades, played lots of sports, earned a lot of money last summer, and did terrible on the interview. Candidate A is predicted to be a great salesperson. Candidate B was a straight A student, played no sports, made no money last summer, and did fabulously well in the interview. According to our regression model, all four factors are the kiss of death.

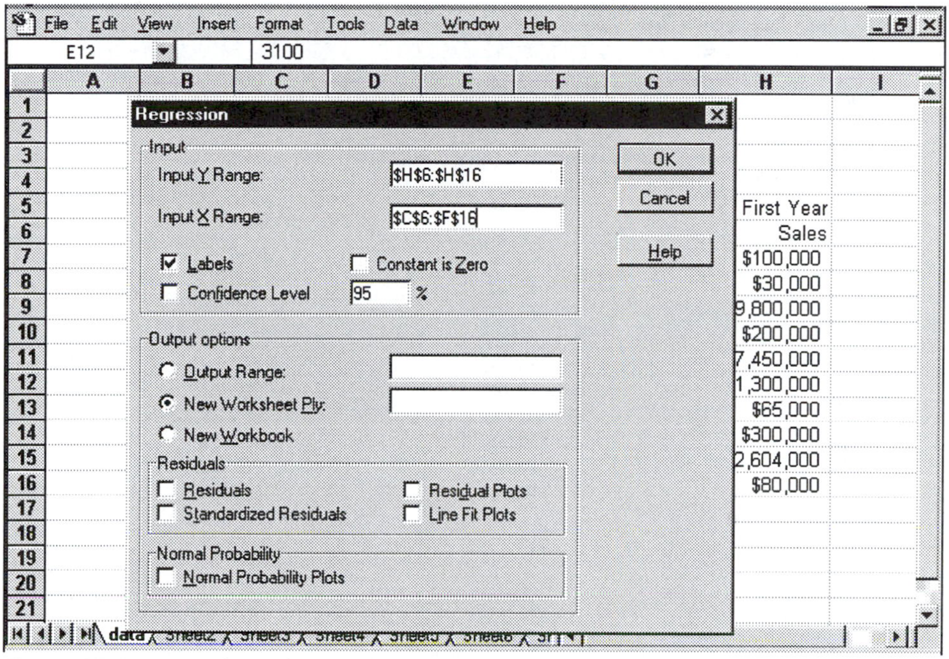

Figure 17-15. Specifying the variables for regression analysis.

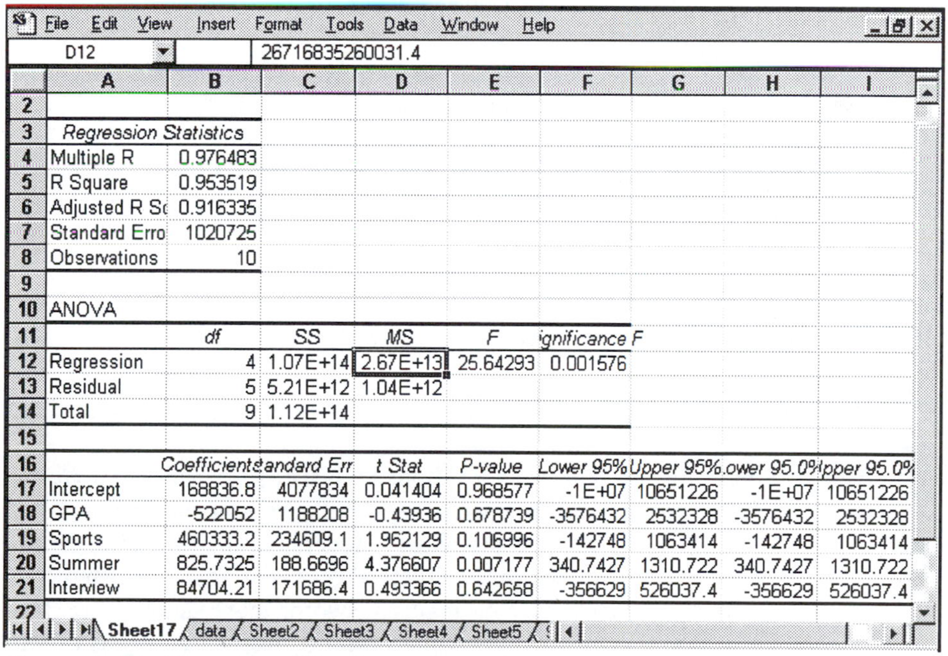

Figure 17-16. The output of the Regression tool.

	B	C	D	E	F	G	H	I	J	K
									J12 = -522052*C12 + 460333*D12 + 825*E12 - 84704*F12 + 168836	

The formula bar shows: `= -522052*C12 + 460333*D12 + 825*E12 - 84704*F12 + 168836` with cell reference J12.

	B	C	D	E	F	H	J
1							
2							
3		Tracking New Hires at International Financial					
4							
5						First Year	Predicted
6		GPA	Sports	Summer	Interview	Sales	Sales
7	1	2.7	3	$0	2	$100,000	($29,113)
8	2	3.6	0	$1,500	5	$30,000	($896,571)
9	3	2.4	5	$8,500	7	$9,800,000	$7,637,148
10	4	3.6	1	$2,000	3	$200,000	$145,670
11	5	2.6	7	$6,300	9	$7,450,000	$6,468,996
12	6	3.2	0	$3,100	6	$1,300,000	$547,546
13	7	3.7	0	$0	5	$65,000	($2,186,276)
14	8	2.9	0	$1,000	7	$300,000	($1,113,043)
15	9	3.0	1	$4,000	2	$2,604,000	$2,193,605
16	10	3.3	0	$2,900	6	$80,000	$330,340
17							
18	A	1.8	6	$11,200	3		$10,977,028
19	B	4.0	0	$0	10		($2,766,412)
20	C	3	2	$3,600	5		$2,069,826
21	null	0.0	0	$0	0		$168,836

Tabs: Regression \ data / Sheet2 / Sheet3 / Sheet4 / Sheet5

Figure 17-17. Using the regression equation to predict the sales of three new candidates.

Also listed is "null". Notice from cell B17 in Figure 17-16 and from the prediction formula that the intercept is 168836. That is, if all of the four measures are 0, the candidate is predicted to have first-year sales of $168,836. If you wish, you can force the intercept to 0 by clicking on the *Constant is 0* box in the *Regression* dialog box. Of course, this would result in different values for the four variable coefficients.

THE TOOLS IN THE ANALYSIS TOOLPAK

Here is a brief summary of the tools in the Analysis ToolPak:

Anova: Single-Factor   Performs a simple analysis of variance. An analysis of variance tests the hypothesis that the means from several samples are equal. Generally, analysis of variance (or anova), is a statistical procedure used to determine whether means from two or more samples are drawn from populations with the same means. Analysis of variance expands on the tests for two means, such as the t-test.

Anova: Two-Factor With Replication	Performs an extension of the single-factor anova that includes more than one sample for each group of data.
Anova: Two-Factor Without Replication	Performs two-factor anova that does not include more than one sampling per group.
Correlation	Measures the relationship between two sets of data. Correlation tells you whether the data sets move together; that is, whether large values of one set are associated with large values of the other (positive correlation), whether large values of one set are associated with small values in the other (negative correlation), or whether the values in the two sets are unrelated.
Covariance	Measures the relationship between two sets of data. Covariance is sensitive to the unit of measure of the two data sets, whereas correlation is independent of the units of measurement.
Descriptive Statistics	Generates a table showing various statistics (such as mean, median, standard deviation) for a set of data. The statistics in the table are a common starting point for further analysis.
Exponential Smoothing	Predicts a value based on the forecast for the prior period, adjusted for the error in that prior forecast. You can use exponential smoothing to forecast sales, inventory, or other trends.
f-Test Two-Sample for Variance	Compares two population variances. Returns the probability that the variances in the two sets are not significantly different.
Fourier Analysis	Performs a Fast Fourier Transform or its inverse. Fourier analysis helps you understand the periodic nature of an ordered set of data.
Histogram	Calculates individual and cumulative frequencies for a set of data. Will calculate a set of data bins or will allow you to specify the data bins to use.

Moving Average	Projects values in the forecast period, based on the average value of the data over a specific number of preceding periods. You can use this procedure to forecast sales, inventory, or other trends.
Random Number Generation	Fills a range with independent random numbers drawn from one of several distributions. This tool provides more options than the RAND function, but the tool must be manually invoked each time you want a new set of random numbers.
Rank and Percentile	Produce a table that contains the ordinal and percentage rank of each value in a data set. Use this procedure to see the relative standings of values in the data.
Regression	Performs a linear regression analysis, fitting a line through a set of data using the least-squares method. Helps analyze how a single dependent variable is affected by one or more independent variable. The results can be used to predict a new value of the independent variable given values of the dependent variables.
Sampling	Creates a sample from a population by treating the input range as a population. Usually used when the input range is too large to process or chart or when you want to extract, say, every fourth piece of data.
t-Test: Paired Two-Sample for Means	Performs a two-sample paired student's t-test. t-tests are used to determine whether the means of two sets of samples are equal. Use this t-test tool when the data in the two sets are paired.
t-Test: Two-Sample Assuming Equal Variances	Performs a two-sample student's t-test. Use this t-test tool when the data are not paired and when the variances of the two sets are assumed to be equal. This is referred to as a homoscedastic t-test.
t-Test: Two-Sample Assuming Unequal Variances	Performs a two-sample student's t-test. Use this t-test tool when the data are not paired and when the variances of the two sets are assumed to be unequal. This is referred to as a heteroscedastic t-test.

z-Test: Two-Sample Means	Performs a two-sample z-test for means with known variances. This test is commonly used to test hypotheses about the difference between two population means.

PAPER AND PENCIL EXERCISE

17-1 How might you go about investigating each of the following situations? For each situation you should: (1) describe your general approach, (2) describe the exact data collection method you would use, (3) design an Excel workbook (on paper) for analyzing the data, (4) tell exactly which tool(s) or functions you would use in your workbook, (5) specify exactly which results, which cells, you would look at and exactly how they would help you in your analysis of the situation.

(a) An automobile manufacturer would like to know which of five different shades of red paint prospective customers would prefer on next year's model XLT convertible.

(b) A psychologist would like to know whether there is any difference in the mathematical ability of people who are left handed and people who are right handed.

(c) A golf magazine would like to investigate the claim of a small manufacturer that its golf ball goes 25 yards farther than does a certain well-known golf ball.

(d) A producer of a popular TV series would like to know whether the viewers want a newly introduced character to be continued on the show or discontinued.

(e) A college admissions office would like to know whether it can use a computer to predict a student's future success in its college given the information provided by each applicant.

(f) The Orange Growers' Association would like to know whether regularly drinking orange juice helps prevent people from getting colds.

(g) A finance company would like to automate the process of deciding which automobile loan applications it should approve. The finance company has access to all applications to the company for automobile loans over the past 10 years and the performance record of the loans it approved.

COMPUTER EXERCISES

17-2. A basketball coach has heard about visualization and decides it might be just what the team needs to improve its foul shooting. The idea is that in the moment before you take a foul shot you picture in your mind your successfully taking the shot and then the ball going through the hoop. Swish. Visualize success and it will be yours. To test out the idea he has the eleven members of his team shoot 20 foul shots each. Then he spends an hour describing visualization and having his team members try it. The next day at the beginning of practice he reminds them about the visualization technique and has each team member take 20 foul shots. Here are the results.

Player:	A	B	C	D	E	F	G	H	I	J	K
Day 1:	15	12	18	8	9	15	9	15	12	10	16
Day 2:	15	14	17	10	10	15	12	14	15	13	17

Summarize the data. Compare the performances without visualizing on day 1 and with visualizing on day 2. Was there an improvement? Was the improvement statistically significant? What do you conclude?

17-3. The Cranston Apperception Test was administered to 24 students majoring in Computers and 24 students majoring in English. The results were as follows:

Computer Majors
25 27 20 17 17 33 27 23 29 23 26 20 29 14 32 30 26 21 20 26 24 26 32 12

English Majors
21 29 16 7 26 23 21 18 28 18 17 29 31 25 20 32 14 32 26 24 27 23 23 17

(a) Generate descriptive statistics for both sets of data.

(b) Determine if there is any statistically significant difference in the means of the scores of the two groups at the 5% level.

17-4. A beverage company is considering a new fruit drink. To learn whether people like the drink they set up a booth at the mall. If you are willing to tell them your age and annual income, they will give you a free 12 ounce cup of the drink, which you are then asked to rate on a scale from 1 (awful) to 10 (nectar of the gods, best stuff I ever drank). You must be at least 18 years old to participate. Here are the data they collect. The annual income is in thousands of dollars.

Person	A	B	C	D	E	F	G	H	I	J	K
Age	19	84	23	31	21	52	18	20	28	25	44
Gender	M	M	F	M	F	M	F	F	M	M	F
Income	17	12	22	27	15	34	22	6	30	18	95
Rating	3	5	6	4	7	2	5	5	5	3	7

Person	L	M	N	O	P	Q	R	S	T	U	V
Age	33	20	73	18	25	19	22	24	32	36	68
Gender	F	M	F	F	F	M	M	M	M	F	F
Income	57	19	31	15	32	13	23	26	30	55	28
Rating	9	6	5	6	6	4	5	3	4	8	5

Your task is to enter the data into a worksheet (think about the best organization of the data). Apply the appropriate tools. What can you conclude about the new drink and to whom it appeals? Write up a professional report. Include appropriate worksheets and charts.

17-5. Consider again the real estate database in Figure 17-3. We are interested in learning if we can construct an equation to predict the price of a home based on the number of bedrooms, number of bathrooms, lot size, and age. Enter the worksheet into the computer or obtain a copy. Use the Regression tool to compute the coefficients of the equation. How good a fit is the equation? Enter the formula into the original worksheet and give the predicted prices for the existing homes. Now use the formula to set the prices of the following homes that are about to come on the market:

15 Foxhall Road: 4 bedrooms, 2 baths, 0.6 acres, 15 years old
395 Washington Street: 3 bedrooms, 2 baths, 0.25 acres, 60 years old
24 Columbia Blvd.: 5 bedrooms, 3 baths, 2.1 acres, 2 years old

Write up a report on the exercise. Be sure to include the formula, its predictions, and how good a job it does. Indicate how you might include the heating type in the prediction.

17-6. This problem is a little more open-ended. Many people are interested in being able to predict the price of a stock a month from now given data that are publicly available today. Examples of information that might be used include revenues, profits, price per earnings ratios, stock prices, stock volume, industry trends, market trends, and so on. For this assignment you are to come up with a formula that predicts the price of a given stock a month from now using your choice of any data available today. Try your formula by predicting historical results. Write up a report on your findings. If your formula is successful, please email your report, with your formula, to james.gips@bc.edu.

CHAPTER 18

GOAL SEEKING AND THE SOLVER

OBJECTIVES

In this chapter you will learn how to:

- Solve problems using Goal Seeking
- Do Goal Seeking directly from graphs
- Use the Solver to solve profit maximization problems
- Enter constraints into the Solver
- Solve linear programming problems with the Solver
- Solve transportation problems with the Solver

In this final chapter we will be looking at two very powerful tools in Excel, Goal Seeking and the Solver.

GOAL SEEKING

Goal Seeking basically allows us to work backward in a worksheet. Suppose in our Computers course the final grade is determined 40% by homeworks and computer exercises, 15% by each of two exams, and 30% by the final exam. Our scores so far are shown in Figure 18-1.

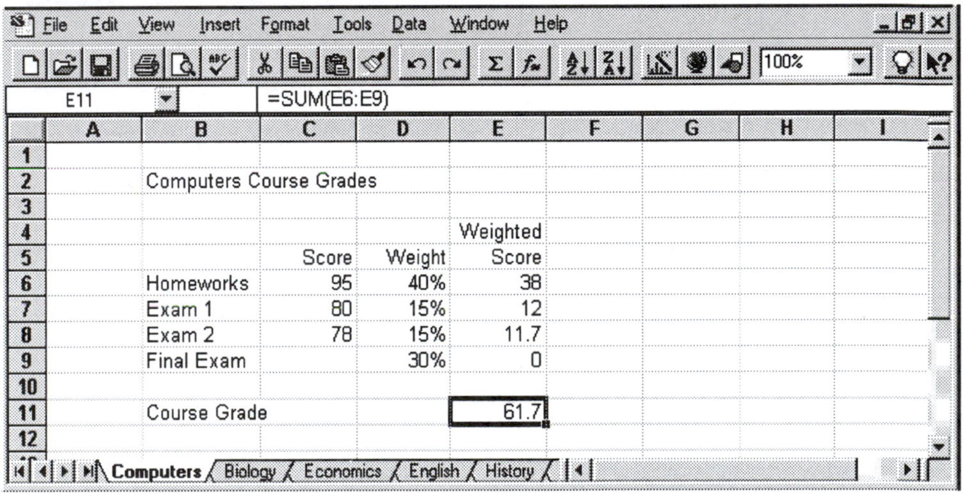

Figure 18-1. Our scores before taking the Final Exam.

With only the Final Exam to go, we would like to know what score we need to get on the Final Exam to have a final Course Grade of 90.

We could solve this problem by trial and error. That is, we could enter an initial value of, say, 90 as our score for the Final Exam. If the resulting Course Grade was below 90, we could try 100 for the Final Exam. If the resulting Course Grade was above 90, we could try 95 for the Final Exam, and so on. We could continue making closer and closer estimates of the score we need on the Final Exam for our Course Grade to be 90.

Excel automates this trial-and-error process for us. From the worksheet in Figure 18-1 we select *Goal Seek...* in the *Tools* pull-down menu. We fill in the *Goal Seek* dialog box as in Figure 18-2.

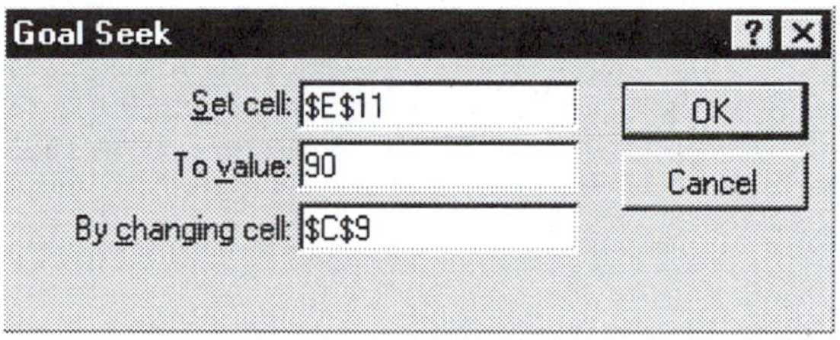

Figure 18-2. We wish to set E11 to 90 by adjusting C9.

We tell Excel we would like cell E11 set to 90 by changing cell C9. (Excel automatically changes all addresses to absolute references in these dialog boxes.) When we click on *OK* Excel goes through several iterations of trial and error and then displays the results of its efforts, as shown in Figure 18-3.

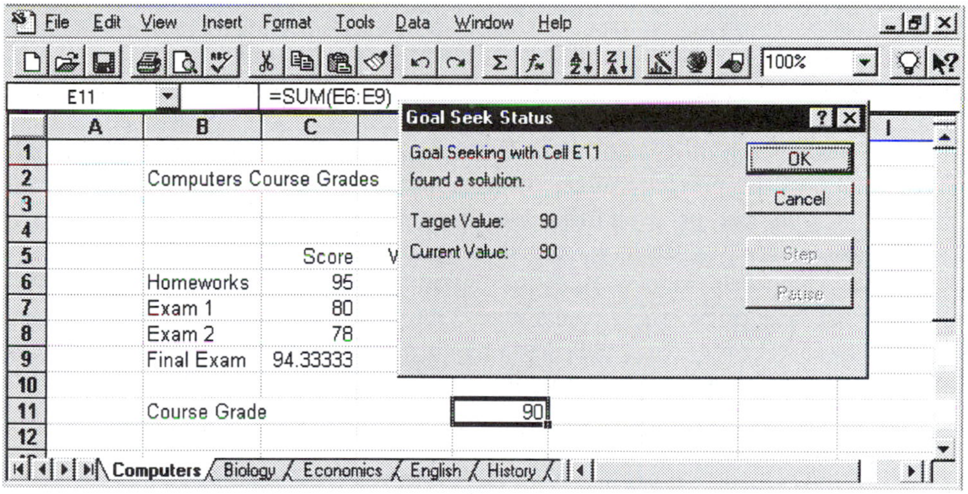

Figure 18-3. The result of the Goal Seeking. We need a 94.33 on the Final Exam.

Excel has found a solution. If we receive a score of 94.333333 on the Final Exam, then our Course Grade will be 90. No problem.

Let's do another example. We would like to purchase a car. The automobile dealer requires 10% of the purchase price as a down payment. The dealer will arrange a loan for the remainder at 9% per year interest to be paid monthly over 4 years. We decide that the highest loan payment we can afford is $300 per month. We would like to buy this spiffy car that the dealer will let us have for a purchase price of only $17,699. We create a worksheet to help us, as shown in Figure 18-4.

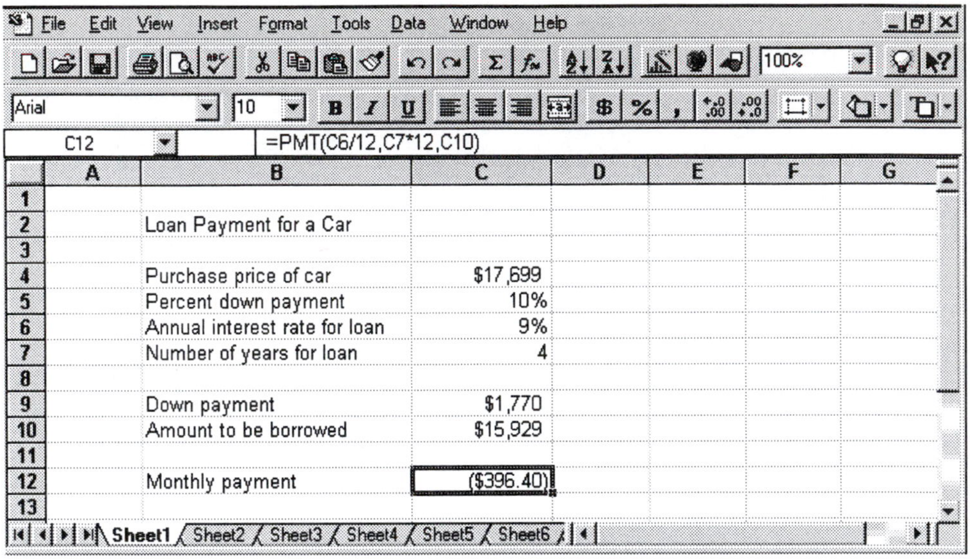

Figure 18-4. Calculating the monthly loan payment for a car.

The top four cells in the worksheet are input cells. The down payment is 10% of the purchase price. The amount to be borrowed is the difference between the purchase price and the down payment. The monthly payment is calculated using the PMT function, as discussed in Chapter 14.

The bad news is that the monthly payment would be $396.40. What purchase price would result in a $300 per month payment? We select *Goal Seek...* in the *Tools* pull-down menu. We fill in the *Goal Seek* dialog box to inform Excel that we would like to set cell C12 to a value of -300 by changing cell C4, as in Figure 18-5.

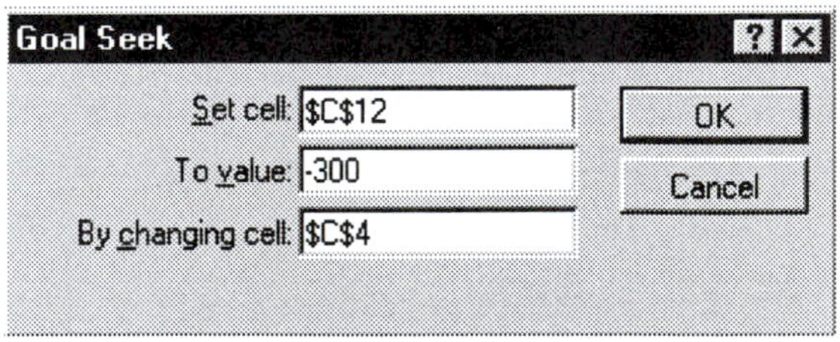

Figure 18-5. We can afford to pay $300 per month.

We click on *OK* and Excel gives us the bad news that the most we can afford is a purchase price of $13,395. (That's why people lease—so they can get a more expensive car for the monthly payment even though they will have to return the car at the end of the lease period.)

GRAPHIC GOAL SEEKING

A nice feature of Excel is the ability to do Goal Seeking graphically. Suppose we decide to open a savings account. We vow that every year, no matter what, we are going to deposit $3,000 into the account. We would like to know how much money we are going to accumulate over each of the next 10 years. We set up the worksheet in Figure 18-6.

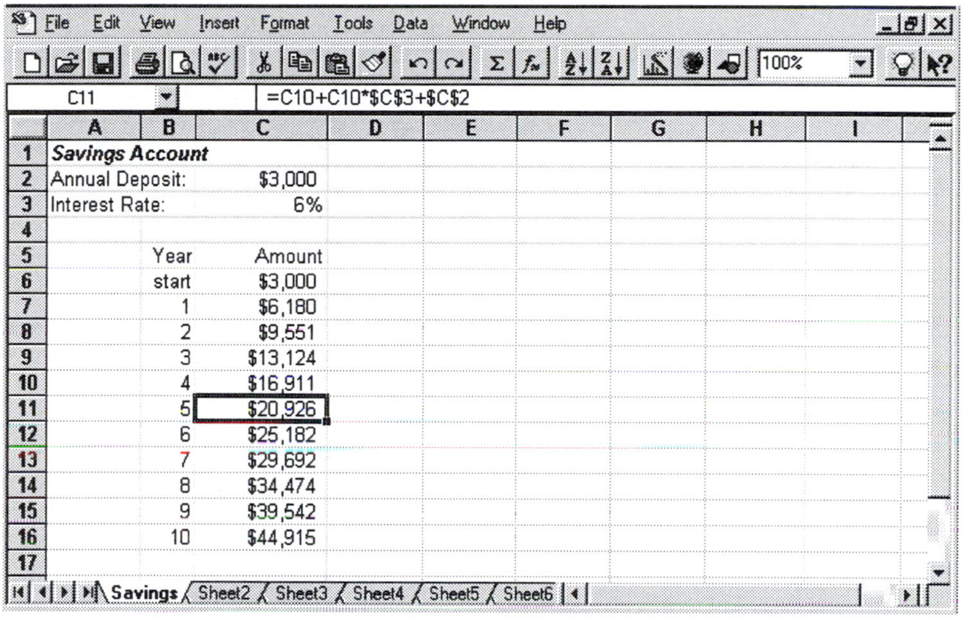

File	Edit	View	Insert	Format	Tools	Data	Window	Help				_|8|x|

C11   =C10+C10*$C$3+$C$2

	A	B	C	D	E	F	G	H	I	
1	Savings Account									
2	Annual Deposit:		$3,000							
3	Interest Rate:		6%							
4										
5		Year	Amount							
6		start	$3,000							
7		1	$6,180							
8		2	$9,551							
9		3	$13,124							
10		4	$16,911							
11		5	$20,926							
12		6	$25,182							
13		7	$29,692							
14		8	$34,474							
15		9	$39,542							
16		10	$44,915							
17										

Savings / Sheet2 / Sheet3 / Sheet4 / Sheet5 / Sheet6

Figure 18-6. An account where we deposit the same amount each year.

Each year the amount in the account is the amount in the account at the end of the previous year plus the interest earned for the year plus the amount deposited at the end of the year. This is implemented in the formula displayed in Figure 18-6 for cell C11

$$=C10 + C10*\$C\$3 + \$C\$2$$

We can graph the progress of our account using the ChartWizard. We select B5:C16 and click on the ChartWizard icon (see Chapter 10). The mouse pointer changes and we select an area to the right of the entries in the current worksheet. We go through the ChartWizard, reset the vertical axis so the maximum value is $100,000, and end up with the chart displayed in Figure 18-7.

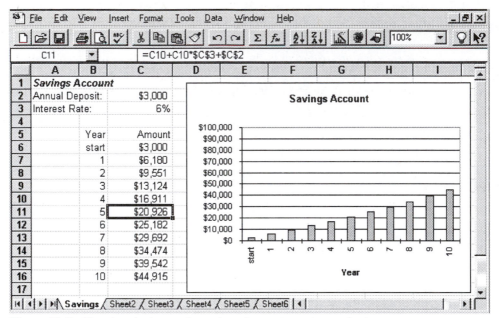

Figure 18-7. Showing the increasing value of our account as a chart.

Now we decide that we would like to have $100,000 at the end of 10 years and not a measly $44,915. We double-click on the chart to select it and then click on the rightmost bar to select the data series and then click again on the rightmost bar to select just that last data point. Small black squares appear around the bar to indicate it is selected. We drag the top of the rightmost bar, as indicated in Figure 18-8, upward to $100,000 where it belongs.

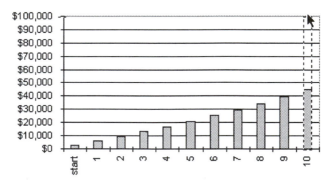

Figure 18-8. Select the rightmost bar and drag it up to $100,000.

Excel automatically displays the familiar *Goal Seek* dialog box.

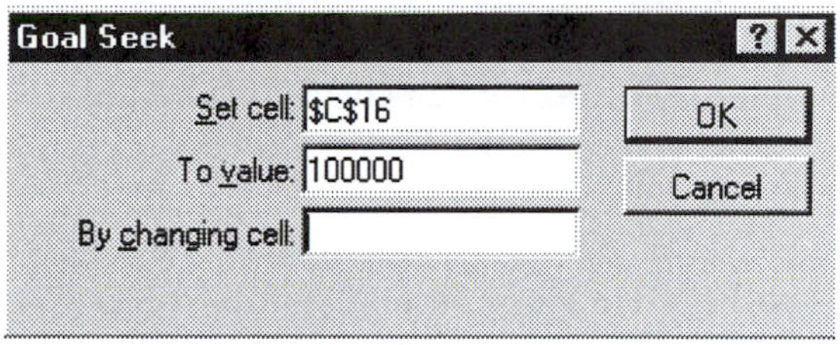

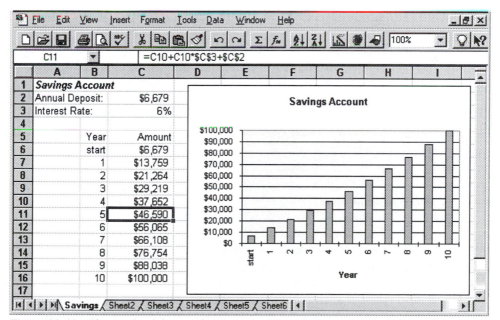

Figure 18-9. *Reaching for $100,000.*

We have two choices for the cell we want to change to fulfill our investment objective. Either we can change the amount we deposit or we can change the interest rate we receive. Unfortunately, the interest rate is somewhat out of our control so we enter C2, the amount deposited each year, as the cell to change. When we click *OK*, Excel goes through its iterative goal seeking and informs us that we will need to deposit $6,679 each year in order to reach our goal of $100,000 in 10 years. (See Figure 18-10.)

Figure 18-10. *The result of the graphical Goal Seeking is that cell C2 has been changed to the amount we need to deposit each year to meet our goal of $100,000 in ten years.*

THE SOLVER

The **Solver** is even more powerful and flexible than Goal Seeking. The Solver can maximize or minimize the value of a cell in addition to setting a cell to a target value. The Solver can change the values of several cells, not just one, to accomplish its goal. The Solver can do its work subject to various constraints, or conditions, that we specify.

The Solver is an add-in. As discussed at the beginning of Chapter 17 for the Analysis ToolPak, an add-in is a specialized feature of Excel that, because not everyone might want to use it and it takes up valuable space, is not automatically included when you run Excel on your computer. To see whether you have the Solver ready to use, look in the *Tools* pull-down menu. About half way down in the *Tools* pull-down menu you should see *Solver...* If the Solver is not present, select *Add-Ins...* in the *Tools* pull-down menu. Scroll down through the add-ins until you see *Solver Add-In*. Click on the box to the left of *Solver Add-In* so the box is selected. The Solver will be added into Excel. If you do not see *Solver* in the list of add-ins, then you will have to go to the trouble of finding your original Excel or Microsoft Office CD-ROM or disks and custom installing the Solver from there into the Excel on your computer. It's worth it.

USING THE SOLVER TO MAXIMIZE PROFITS

As a first example, let's do a simple maximization problem. We decide to publish an "Uncensored Guide to Courses and Faculty" where students give their honest opinions about specific courses and faculty, their recommendations (or warnings) to other students who are thinking about what courses to register for. We believe that if we gave the Guide away for free, we could give away 10,000 copies. For every $1.00 we charge for the Guide, we estimate that 1,000 fewer people will purchase it. So that if we charge $3.00 per copy, we figure we will sell 7,000 copies. If we charge $4.00 per copy, we figure we will sell 6,000 copies. We expect to have fixed expenses of $5,000 for manuscript preparation, delivery, promotion, and distribution. Each Guide will cost us $2.25 to print and bind. We would like to know the best price to charge for the Guide so we can make the most profit. We set up the worksheet in Figure 18-11 to help us.

Just for convenience, the formulas in the worksheet are included in text boxes to the right of the cells. We see that if we set the price at $4.00, we will sell 6,000 copies and end up with a profit of $5,500. Not bad. But we would like to find the price that will yield the maximum profits under these assumptions. We can't use Goal Seeking because we don't have a particular profit we want to achieve. We just want to find the price that results in the highest profit.

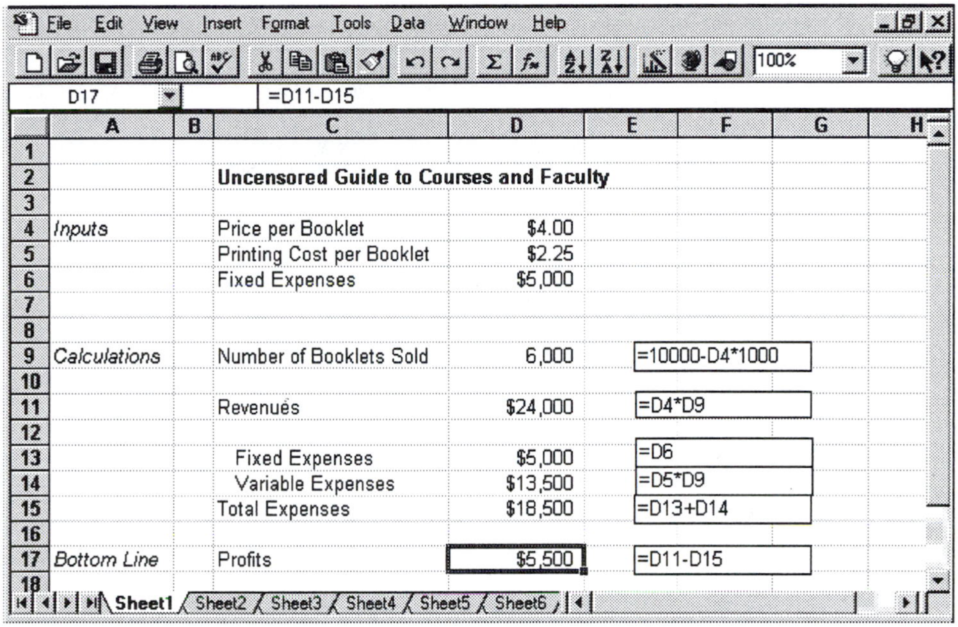

Figure 18-11. Calculating the profits for our Uncensored Guide.

We select *Solver...* from the *Tools* pull-down menu. The *Solver Parameters* dialog box in Figure 18-12 is displayed. In the dialog box we specify that D17 is the Target cell and, on the next line, that we want to maximize the value in D17. We will allow the Solver to change only D4.

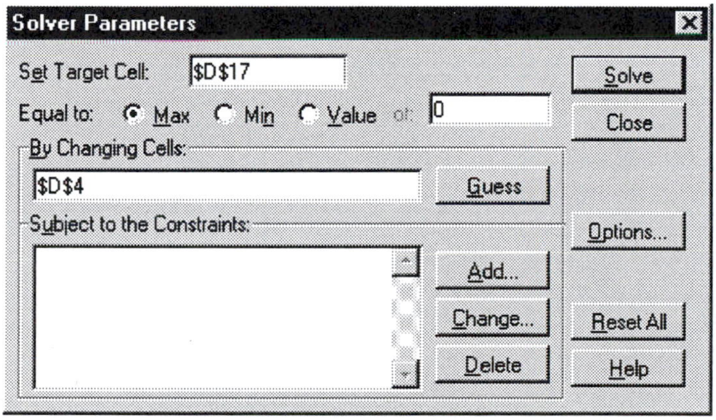

Figure 18-12. Giving specifics to the Solver.

When we click on the *Solve* button, the Solver goes to work and in short order reports back its success.

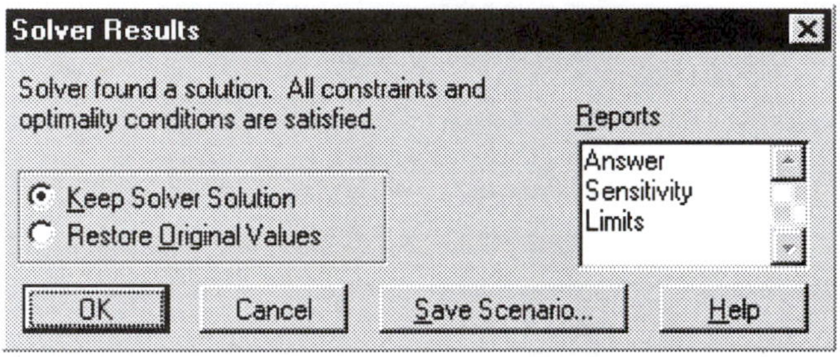

Figure 18-13. The results of using the Solver.

Click on *OK* and we are returned to the original worksheet, but now cell D4 is changed so that the value in D17 is maximized. From the Solver we learn that under these assumptions we should charge $6.13 per Guide and print up 3,875 copies. This will result in profits of $10,016. (See Figure 18-14.)

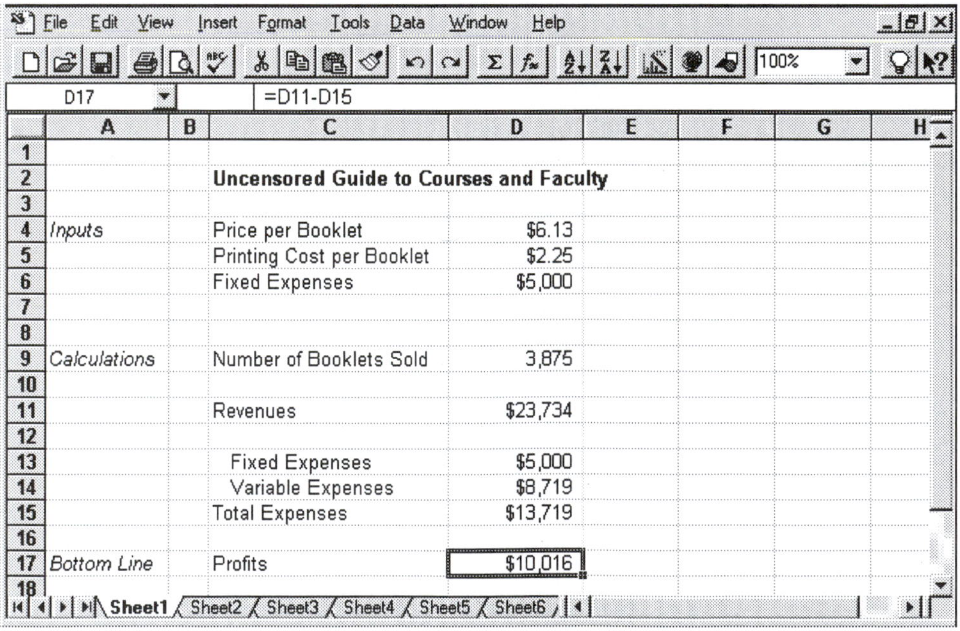

Figure 18-14. Using the Solver to adjust the Price per Booklet to maximize Profits.

USING THE SOLVER FOR A LINEAR PROGRAMMING PROBLEM

In our small manufacturing company we make grommits and widgets. Each grommit requires 4 hours of metal work and 2 hours of electrical work. Each widget requires 3 hours of metal work and 1 hour of electrical work. For each grommit we make we earn $70 of profit. For each widget we make we earn $50 of profit. This week, given our employees and equipment, we will have 240 hours of metal work available and 100 hours of electrical work. The question is, how many grommits and how many widgets should we make in order to maximize our profit?

This problem is an example of a **linear programming** problem. We have a quantity we want to maximize, in this case profits. We have **constraints**, or restrictions, on the solution. In this case we have limits on the number of hours of metal work and electrical work available. We have a range of possible solutions to the problem. The objective and constraints can all be expressed in linear equations or inequalities. There are no exponents in any of the formulas.

Linear programming has been studied for over 50 years. Linear programming techniques are applicable in many different types of problems. The Solver provides a powerful and easy to use tool for solving many linear programming problems.

To solve this production problem we set up a worksheet that contains all of the calculations. (See Figure 18-15.)

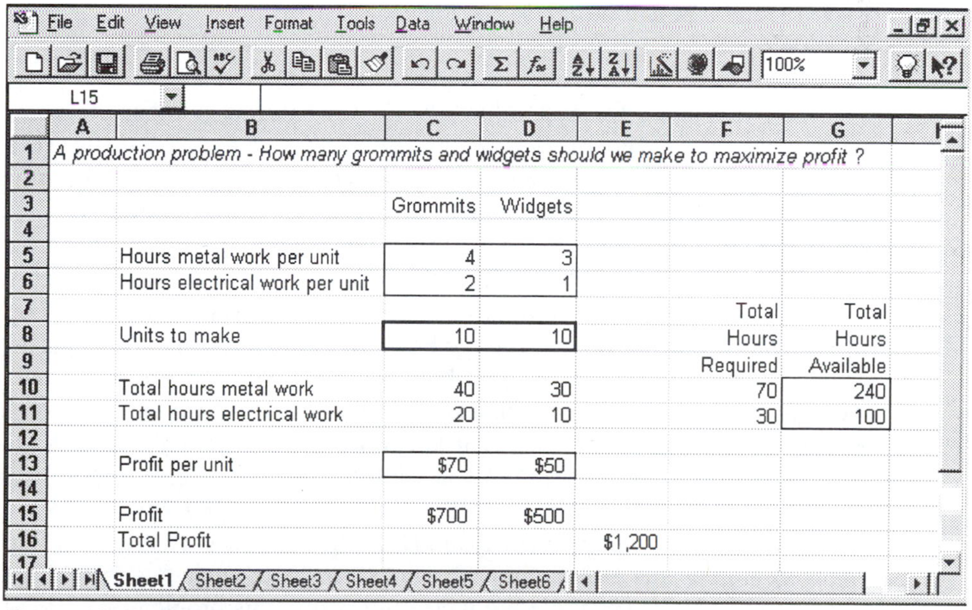

Figure 18-15. Setting up a production problem for the Solver.

In the worksheet, cells with data values that have been entered (C5:D6, G10:G11, and C13:D13) have a thin border. Cells with values that are to be determined by the Solver (C8:D8) have a thick border. Cells with values that are calculated by formulas have no border, as shown in Figure 18-16.

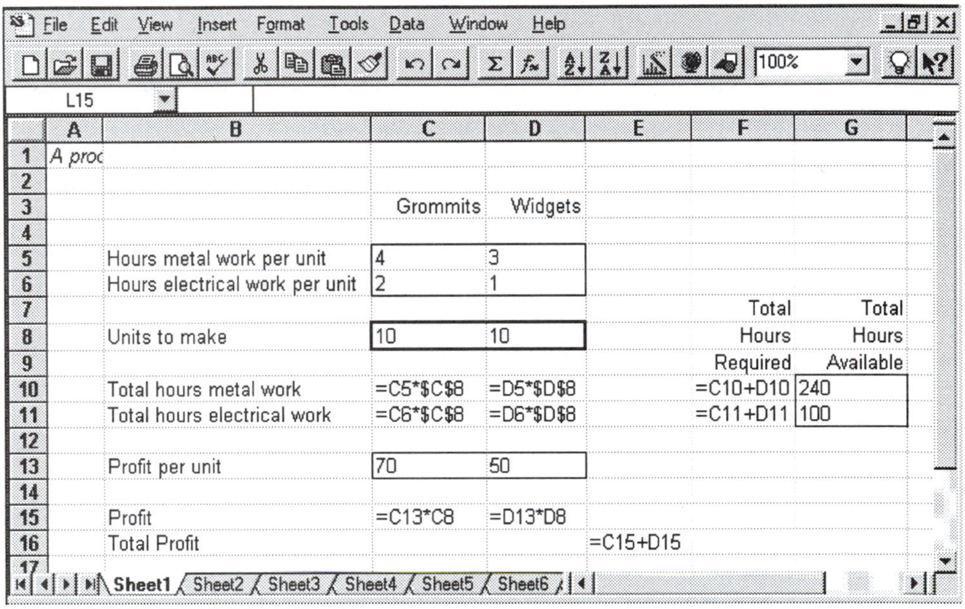

Figure 18-16. The formulas in the production worksheet.

We want to find the best values for C8 and D8, the number of grommits and widgets to manufacture so that we maximize the value in E16, the Total Profit for the week. However, we have the added constraints that the value in F10, the hours of metal work required, must not exceed G10, the number of metal work hours available, and that the value in F11, the hours of electrical work required, must not exceed the number in G11, the hours of electrical work available.

We currently show 10 grommits and 10 widgets being made, yielding a profit of $1,200. However, we have many hours of metal work and electrical work that are not being utilized. We should increase the number of grommits and widgets we plan to make. But by how much? We could enter different numbers by hand and try to maximize the profit by trial and error. Instead, let's use the Solver.

We select *Solver...* from the *Tools* pull-down menu. Excel displays the *Solver Parameters* dialog box, as before. (See Figure 18-17.) We fill in E16 as the cell to maximize by changing cells C8 and D8. The addresses of the cells that can be changed are separated by commas. There can be as many as 200 cells for the Solver to be able to change! We have only two in this problem.

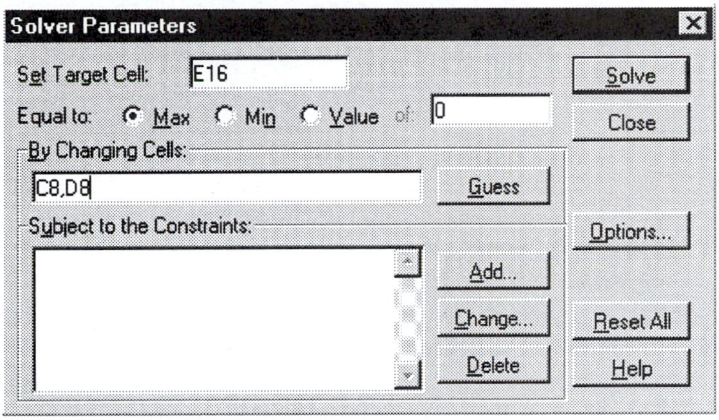

Figure 18-17. Beginning to fill in the Solver parameters.

Now we have some constraints to add. We click on *Add...* in the Constraints portion of the dialog box. We are confronted with the *Add Constraint* dialog box. We enter the constraint F10 <= G10, as shown in Figure 18-18.

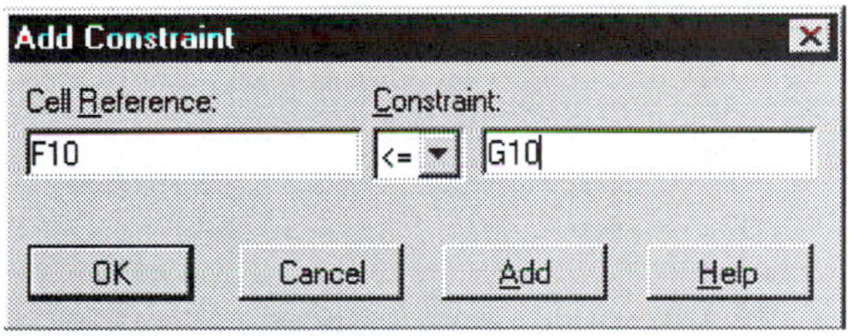

Figure 18-18. The dialog box for adding constraints.

We click on *Add*. The constraint automatically is entered into the *Constraints* field of the *Solver Parameters* dialog box. We fill in the constraint F11 <= G11 and click on *Add*, entering the second constraint. It may not be obvious, but we have more constraints to add. The values in C8 and D8 must be greater than or equal to 0. That is, we cannot make a negative number of grommits or widgets even if it would help maximize profits. So we add the constraints C8 >= 0 and D8 >= 0. We might also want to require that C8 and D8 be integers, that is, that we do not make 3.25 grommits in a week. We could do this by entering C8 into the first field of the *Add Constraint* dialog box and then using the arrow in the operator pull-down menu in the middle of the dialog box to select "int", as shown in Figure 18-19. We are allowed to specify up to 100 different constraints for the Solver.

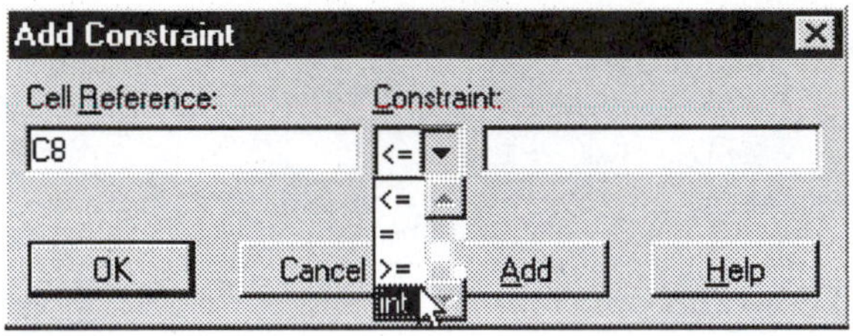

Figure 18-19. Specifying the constraint that C8 must be an integer.

After a constraint is specified in the *Add Constraint* dialog box, a click on *Add* will enter the constraint and keep you in the *Add Constraint* dialog box to enter another constraint. A click on *OK* will enter the constraint and bring you back to the *Solver Parameter* dialog box, as in Figure 18-20.

Note again that Excel automatically adds $ signs so that all of the addresses are absolute references.

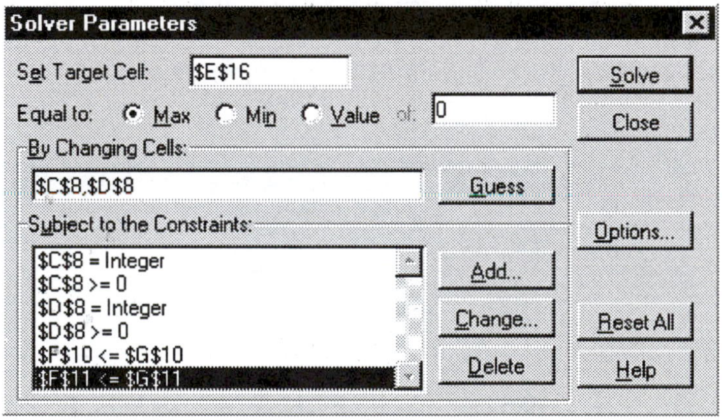

Figure 18-20. The final set of parameters for the production problem.

We click on *Solve* and the Solver goes to work. In short order the Solver reports back its success.

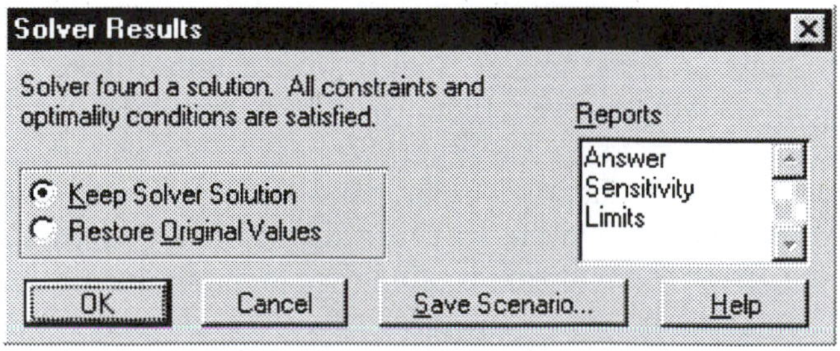

Figure 18-21. The Solver has found an optimal solution.

If we would like, the Solver will give us three reports on its work: an Answer report, a Sensitivity report, and a Limits report. We can select the reports we want to see by clicking on the report names in the field in the right side of the dialog box in Figure 18-21. If we want more than one report, hold down the Ctrl or Control key while clicking. The reports will be inserted into new sheets immediately before the worksheet that contains the data. We select the Answer report and click on *OK*. The original worksheet is displayed with the Solver's solutions entered into C8 and D8. (See Figure 18-22.)

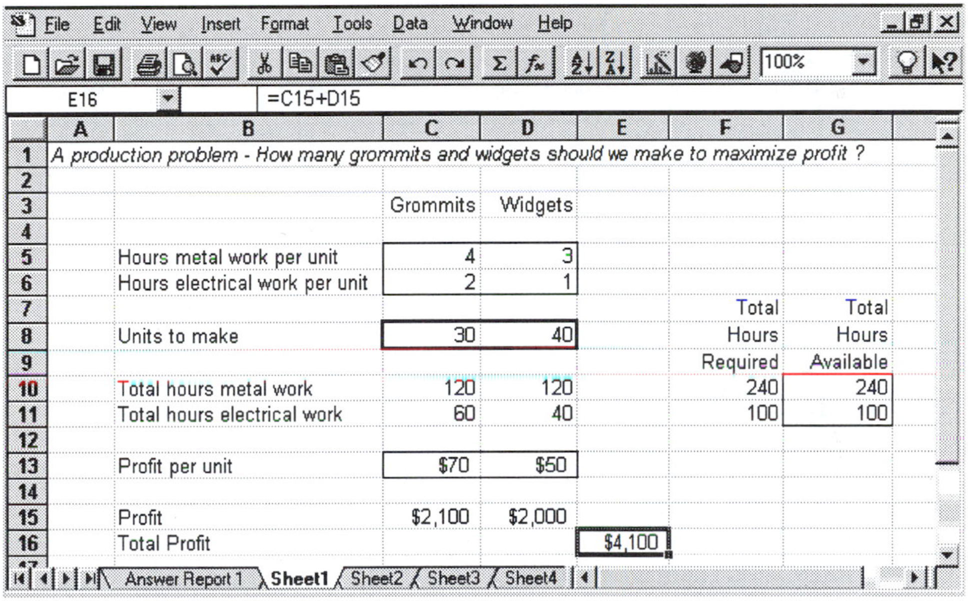

Figure 18-22. The Solver's solution..

The Solver has found that if we make 30 Grommits and 40 Widgets this week, we will produce a maximal Total Profit of $4,100. With this solution, we will utilize all of the metal work and electrical work capacity available, namely 240 hours of metal work and 100 hours of electrical work.

Clicking on the sheet tab for *Answer Report 1* shows the worksheet in Figure 18-23. This worksheet summarizes the results of solving the linear programming problem. As you can see in Figure 18-23, cell E8 contains the final optimal Total Profit found. The cell contains a number, 4100, rather than a formula. If we want to change some of the data values in the original worksheet in Figure 18-16, we would need to run the Solver again to produce a new optimal solution.

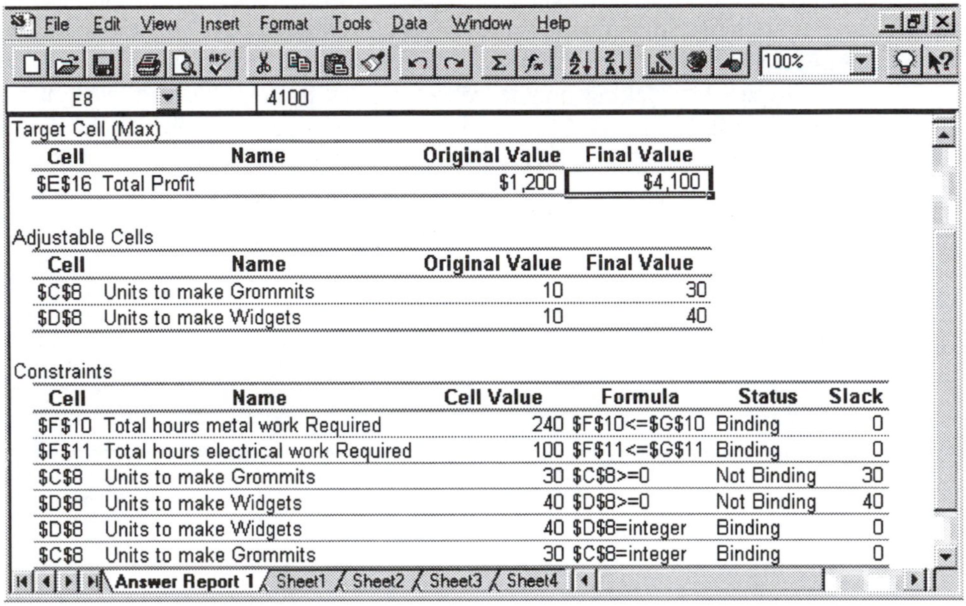

E8 4100

Target Cell (Max)

Cell	Name	Original Value	Final Value
$E$16	Total Profit	$1,200	$4,100

Adjustable Cells

Cell	Name	Original Value	Final Value
$C$8	Units to make Grommits	10	30
$D$8	Units to make Widgets	10	40

Constraints

Cell	Name	Cell Value	Formula	Status	Slack
$F$10	Total hours metal work Required	240	$F$10<=$G$10	Binding	0
$F$11	Total hours electrical work Required	100	$F$11<=$G$11	Binding	0
$C$8	Units to make Grommits	30	$C$8>=0	Not Binding	30
$D$8	Units to make Widgets	40	$D$8>=0	Not Binding	40
$D$8	Units to make Widgets	40	$D$8=integer	Binding	0
$C$8	Units to make Grommits	30	$C$8=integer	Binding	0

Figure 18-23. The Answer report from the Solver.

USING THE SOLVER ON A TRANSPORTATION PROBLEM

We have three warehouses: in San Diego, Riyadh, and Dublin. We have orders from customers in London, Delhi, Lagos, Seoul, and Auckland that need to be filled. Which customers should we ship to from which warehouse? The situation is summarized in the worksheet in Figure 18-24.

In the top half of the worksheet we see the cost of shipping from each warehouse to each customer. For example, it costs $50 per unit to ship from our warehouse in Riyadh to the customer in Delhi.

In the bottom half of the worksheet we have quantity information. At the very bottom, in row 16, is the total number of units needed by each customer. We can see that the customer in Delhi ordered 400 units. On the right, in H11:H14 we see the number of units in each warehouse. We currently have 1400 units in Dublin. The cells in B11:F13 currently contain 1's. These are the values we need to fill in, or rather that the Solver will be filling in. These are the values that dictate how many units will be shipped from each warehouse to each customer.

The key cell is H4. This cell contains the formula that calculates the total cost of all the shipping. This is the value we want to minimize.

H16 =SUM(B16:F16)

	A	B	C	D	E	F	G	H
1		Cost of shipping one unit from warehouse to customer						
2		Customers						Total Cost of Shipping
3	Warehouses	London	Delhi	Lagos	Seoul	Auckland		
4	San Diego	$100	$80	$60	$60	$40		$840
5	Riyadh	$60	$50	$40	$30	$60		
6	Dublin	$30	$40	$50	$50	$90		
7								
8		Number of units to ship from warehouse to customer						
9		Customers					Total to	Total in
10	Warehouses	London	Delhi	Lagos	Seoul	Auckland	Ship	Warehouse
11	San Diego	1	1	1	1	1	5	1550
12	Riyadh	1	1	1	1	1	5	1300
13	Dublin	1	1	1	1	1	5	1400
14	Total to ship	3	3	3	3	3	15	4250
15								
16	Total ordered	900	400	1000	800	1100		4200

Sheet1 / Sheet2 / Sheet3 / Sheet4 / Sheet5 / Sheet6

Figure 18-24. A transportation problem. How many units should be shipped from each warehouse to each destination?

The formula in H4 could be

= B11*B4 + C11*C4 + D11*D4 + E11*E4 + F11*F4 + B12*B5 + C12*C5 + D12*D5 + E12*E5 + F12*F5 + B13*B6 + C13*C6 + D13*D6 + E13*E6 + F13*F6

Alternatively, the formula in H14 can make use of the **SUMPRODUCT** function

=SUMPRODUCT(B11:F13,B4:F6)

This formula calculates the sum of B11*B4 plus C11*C4 and so on, just as in the preceding formula.

There are 15 cells to be filled in (B11:F13) so that the value in H4 is minimized. Plus there are various constraints that must be satisfied. This is a problem for the Solver.

The key in setting up any worksheet for the Solver is to be sure all of the input values are included in separate cells and that all of the formulas needed are included, especially the formula for calculating the value that is to be minimized or maximized.

We select *Solver...* in the *Tools* pull-down menu. In the *Solver Parameters* dialog box, we indicate that the target cell is H4 and that we want the value in the cell to be minimized by changing the cells in B11:F13. Excel allows us to use ranges in both the *By Changing Cells:* entry and also in the constraints. The first constraint is

$$\$B\$11:\$F\$13 = \text{Integer}$$

All the values set from B11 through F13 must be integers. We can't ship fractions of units. The second constraint is

$$\$B\$11:\$F\$13 >= 0$$

We can only ship positive numbers of units. The third constraint is

$$\$B\$14:\$F\$14 = \$B\$16:\$F16$$

This constraint specifies that B14 must equal B16, C14 must equal C16, and so on. That is, that the number of units shipped to each customer must be the same as the number ordered by the customer. The final constraint is

$$\$G\$11:\$G\$13 <= \$H\$11:\$H\$13$$

That is, from each warehouse we can ship at most the number of units in the warehouse. The final Solver Parameters dialog box is shown in Figure 18-25.

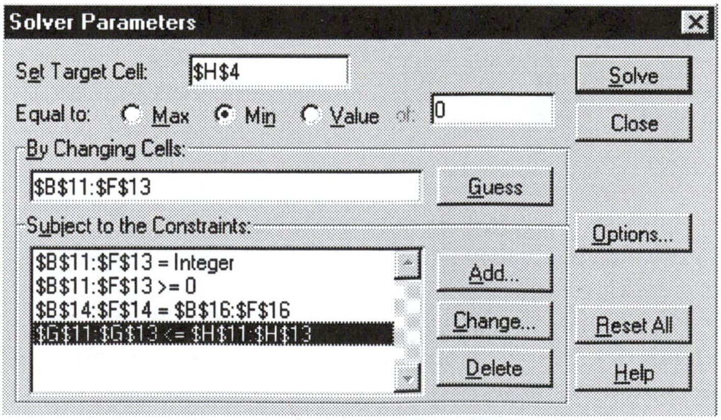

Figure 18-25. The Solver Parameters dialog box for the transportation problem.

We click on *Solve* and in a short time we get the solution shown in Figure 18-26.

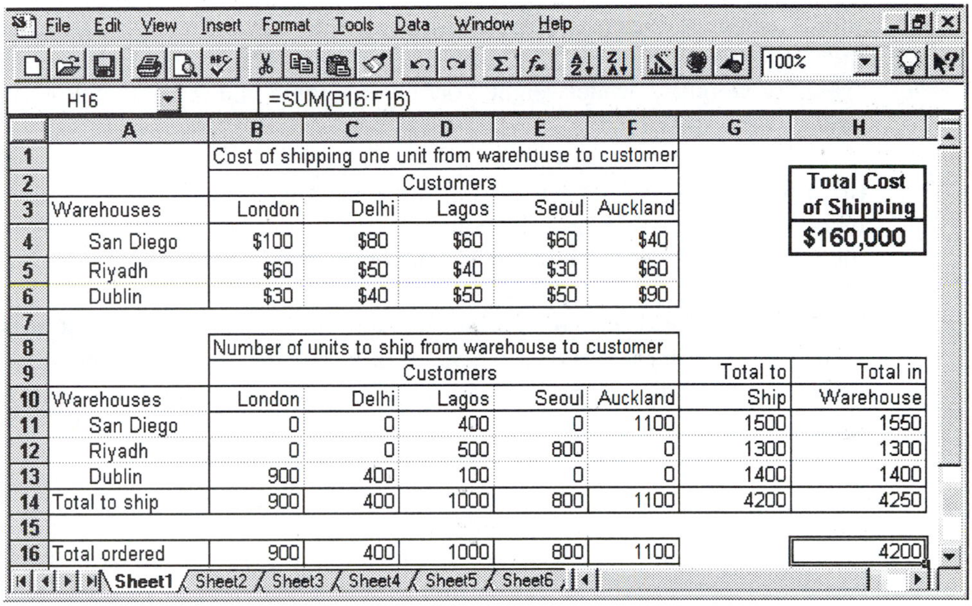

	A	B	C	D	E	F	G	H
1		Cost of shipping one unit from warehouse to customer						
2		Customers						Total Cost
3	Warehouses	London	Delhi	Lagos	Seoul	Auckland		of Shipping
4	San Diego	$100	$80	$60	$60	$40		$160,000
5	Riyadh	$60	$50	$40	$30	$60		
6	Dublin	$30	$40	$50	$50	$90		
7								
8		Number of units to ship from warehouse to customer						
9		Customers					Total to	Total in
10	Warehouses	London	Delhi	Lagos	Seoul	Auckland	Ship	Warehouse
11	San Diego	0	0	400	0	1100	1500	1550
12	Riyadh	0	0	500	800	0	1300	1300
13	Dublin	900	400	100	0	0	1400	1400
14	Total to ship	900	400	1000	800	1100	4200	4250
15								
16	Total ordered	900	400	1000	800	1100		4200

Figure 18-26. The optimal solution found by the Solver.

Note that Lagos is to receive units from all three warehouses.

Excel contains many powerful features. The key is to use them wisely.

COMPUTER EXERCISES

18-1. (From Exercise 2-11) The Body Mass Index (BMI) often is used by scientists and physicians to determine whether a person is underweight or overweight. The BMI is calculated as follows:

Step 1. Multiply your body weight in pounds by 0.45.
Step 2. Multiply your height in inches by 0.025.
Step 3. Square the answer from Step 2.
Step 4. Divide the answer from Step 1 by the answer from Step 3.

A healthy BMI is between 19 and 25. The BMI is said to work equally well for both men and women. Create a worksheet to calculate a person's BMI. There should be four values entered into the worksheet: the person's name, the person's weight in pounds, and the person's height in feet and inches. The worksheet should calculate the total height in inches, the values for each of the steps, and then prominently show the resulting BMI. The worksheet should display "Healthy weight", "Underweight", or "Overweight" in a separate cell based on the value of the BMI.

(a) Try your worksheet on the following people: (i) Jan, 115 pounds, 5 feet 8 inches; (ii) Fran, 325 pounds, 5 feet 1 inch; (iii) Dana, 240 pounds, 6 feet 4 inches; and (iv) Slim, 104 pounds, 5 feet 6 inches.

(b) Use Goal Seeking to determine (i) the weight that would result in a person who is 6 feet 4 inches having a BMI of 22, (ii) the lowest healthy weight for a person who is 5 feet 8 inches (BMI of 19), and (iii) the highest healthy weight for a person who is 5 feet 8 inches (BMI of 25).

18-2. United Manufacturing is planning on spending up to $4,000,000 on new automated assembly machinery. They have decided to purchase two different models of equipment and are trying to decide how many of each model they should purchase. The F300 model costs $350,000 each. The S250 model costs $220,000 each. The F300 has some extra features so at least one third of the models purchased should be the F300. The annual maintenance budget for the new equipment is set at $120,000. The annual maintenance cost of each F300 is $12,000. The annual maintenance cost of each S250 is $7,500. Each F300 will produce 125 units per day. Each S250 will produce 81 units per day. Set up a worksheet and then use the Solver to determine how many of each model to purchase so that the daily production is maximized as long as the other constraints are met.

18-3. Seven new projects are being proposed for our division. Each would require investments over the next three years, but each ultimately would result in a positive return on our investment.

Project	Expenditures in $ Millions			Return in $ Millions
	Year 1	Year 2	Year 3	
A	5	1	8	20
B	4	7	9	36
C	3	8	4	28
D	3	9	2	20
E	7	4	1	18
F	3	2	3	12
G	6	8	9	40

The CEO has decided that we have a maximum of $25 million each year to invest. Just on the basis of the numbers, which combination of projects should we invest in so that the sum of the returns is maximized? Set up a worksheet and use the Solver to come up with a solution. You should set up the worksheet so there is a cell for each project that contains either a 1 (meaning we invest in the project) or a 0 (meaning we do not invest in the project). The Solver should find the combination of 1's and 0's that maximizes the sum of the returns subject to the constraints.

18-4. The Always Open Restaurant is, as the name implies, open 24 hours a day. It is always reasonably busy, but it is busier at some times than at others. Waiters work 8-hour shifts beginning at midnight, 4 AM, 8 AM, Noon, 4 PM, or 8 PM. Management has decided that the minimal number of waiters required for each 4-hour period during the day is as follows:

Midnight to 4 AM	3
4 AM to 8 AM	10
8 AM to Noon	8
Noon to 4 PM	16
4 PM to 8 PM	14
8 PM to Midnight	8

Management would like to know how many waiters should begin their 8-hour shifts at each of the possible times, so that there is at least the minimum required waiters for each shift yet the fewest waiters possible hired.

18-5. The Greentree Financial Management Group manages funds for institutional clients. A pension fund has placed $100,000,000 with the Group. The Research Department at the Group identifies eight types of investments and rates them as follows:

	Expected Annual Yield	Risk Factor
Common stocks - aggressive	12%	2
Common stocks - growth	9%	1.5
Common stocks - conservative	7%	1
Corporate bonds	6%	0.5
Commodities	15%	3
Government bonds	4%	0
Real estate	15%	2.5
Venture capital	40%	5

The pension fund management would like the risk factor for the portfolio as a whole to be less than or equal to 1. Of course given that constraint, they would like to maximize the yield for the entire portfolio.

Use the Solver to find the best allocation of funds among the eight types of investments assuming the validity of the analyses supplied by Research. What is the expected annual yield of the entire portfolio?

18-6. We have three factories (A, B, C) and five distributors (P, Q, R, S, T) of our products. The products are shipped by truck from factory to distributor. At most 180 units of our product fit in a truck. The shipping cost is $1 per unit to load the truck and $1 per unit to unload the truck plus the mileage cost. The mileage cost is based on the mileage the truck must travel between the factory and the distributor. The mileage cost is independent of how many units are in the truck. The mileage cost is the same whether there are 5 units in the truck or 180 units, namely $15 per mile. The maximum monthly productions of the factories are: A 4000 units, B 2000 units, and C 1500 units. The monthly demands by the distributors are: P 1000 units, Q 1600 units, R 1500 units, S 2000 units, and T 1400 units. The mileage chart of the distances between factories and distributors is:

	Distributors				
	P	Q	R	S	T
Factories					
A	100	140	200	150	35
B	50	65	60	70	80
C	40	150	100	90	130

Use the Solver to determine the number of units to send each month from each factory to each distributor so as to minimize the total shipping costs. Your worksheet also should show the number of trucks to send from each factory to each distributor and the total shipping cost.

INDEX